A CLASS BY HERSELF

POLITICS AND SOCIETY IN TWENTIETH-CENTURY AMERICA

William Chafe, Gary Gerstle, Linda Gordon, and Julian Zelizer, editors

For a complete list of books in this series see:
http://press.princeton.edu/catalogs/series/pstcaa.html

Recent titles in the series

A CLASS BY HERSELF

Protective Laws for Women Workers,
1890s–1990s

Nancy Woloch

Princeton University Press
Princeton and Oxford

Cover photograph: Lewis W. Hine (1874–1940), photograph of workers in a paper box
factory during Hine's investigations of factory labor between 1909 and 1917. Courtesy of the
George Eastman House, International Museum of Photography and Film.

First paperback printing, 2017

Paper ISBN: 978-0-691-17616-1

The Library of Congress has cataloged the cloth edition as follows:
Woloch, Nancy, 1940– author
  A class by herself : protective laws for women workers, 1890s–1990s / Nancy Woloch.
    pages cm. — (Politics and society in twentieth-century America)
  Includes bibliographical references and index.
  ISBN 978-0-691-00259-0 (hardback)
  1. Women—Employment—Law and legislation—United States—History—20th
century.   2. Sex discrimination in employment—Law and legislation—United States.—
History—20th century.   I. Title.
  KF3555.W65 2015
  344.7301'4133—dc23   2014032483

British Library Cataloging-in-Publication Data is available
This book has been composed in Sabon Next Pro and Helvetica Neue
Printed on acid-free paper. ∞
Printed in the United States of America

Contents

■ ■ ■

resolutions to protect women and children; their agenda included mothers' pensions, maximum hours laws, women factory inspectors, and later minimum wage laws. By 1910 the GFWC had almost a million members, at least some involved in "committees on industry" that opposed child labor and overlong workdays. "Get information as to the truth of conditions and spread abroad the knowledge you have gained," urged the head of the GFWC industrial committee in 1910. When "weighty women's groups advocated new measures on behalf of children, and for the sake of women as actual or potential mothers," scholar Theda Skocpol contends, "their demands were hard for legislators to ignore." Among protectionists, clubwomen were numerous and influential; they exerted pressure on civic leaders and public opinion; and their interest intensified over time. With its huge membership rolls, the GFWC provided an arena where proponents of single-sex protective laws could recruit support.[10]

The National Women's Trade Union League (NWTUL), founded in 1903, won public attention in New York's Shirtwaist Strike of 1909–10, when its well-off activists ("allies") joined picketing strikers ("members") to protest employer abuses and demand factory safety laws. The NWTUL sought unionization of women workers *and* protective laws, ideally as a complement to unions. "The two combined can abolish every industrial evil," the league president declared in 1911. But union formation among women proved difficult, and NWTUL leaders by 1915 shifted toward legislation. Protective laws, they argued, reached more women than would ever join unions and spurred unionization of trades that seemed unorganizable; legislation and organization, the NWTUL claimed, were symbiotic. "If we organized even a handful of girls," declared spokeswoman Rose Schneiderman, "and then managed to put through legislation which made into law the advantages they had gained, other girls would be more likely to join a union and reap further benefits for themselves." The shift to legislation also reflected NWTUL failure to secure recognition from the AFL, whose leaders spoke warmly of unionization of women but rarely advanced it. NWTUL leaders such as Schneiderman and labor organizer Pauline Newman, historian Annelise Orleck observes, "found that it was easier for working-class women to articulate and win entitlements from an expanding state than from male colleagues in their own unions." With initial reluctance—and with dissent among activists—NWTUL leaders turned from organizing to lobbying in state legislatures.[11]

Most pivotal in the protectionist campaign was the National Consumers' League founded in 1898, which held a special place in the world of reform. A counterpart to the AALL, the NCL sought to improve women's working conditions in stores and factories. Its mission, wrote Maud Nathan, the longtime head of the New York City branch, was "Investigate, agitate, legislate." In 1899, Florence Kelley accepted an appointment as general secretary of the NCL, a position she held for three decades. Demanding, commanding, and charismatic, Kelley attracted a devoted following. She pursued protectionist goals with tenacious zeal, galvanized support among networks of women constituents, and lifted the NCL into the front ranks of progressive reform. Building on the achievements of local leagues that formed the NCL, Kelley turned them into a power base.[12]

FLORENCE KELLEY AND THE NCL

The indulged daughter of a prosperous family, Florence Kelley turned naturally to politics. Her father, William Darrah "Pig Iron" Kelley, a fifteen-term Republican congressman from Philadelphia, backed radical Reconstruction policy, helped draft the Fifteenth Amendment (which enfranchised black men), and supported the eight-hour day. Kelley attended Cornell, class of 1882, where she wrote her senior thesis on the legal status of the child. She then studied law and government in Switzerland. When she arrived in Zurich, she later wrote, "the content of my mind was tinder awaiting a match." The "match" was Socialism, an affiliation that shaped her lifelong outlook and tactics. While in Zurich, among émigré East European and German radicals, Kelley married a fellow Socialist, a Polish-Jewish medical student, Lazare Wischnewetzky, with whom she eventually had three children, born in 1885, 1886, and 1888. She also translated the works of Friedrich Engels, for whom she hoped to gain American readers. After Kelley and her family returned to the United States—they moved to New York in 1886—the couple was active in socialist circles. The Socialist Labor Party, which they joined, proved an inhospitable base; the party expelled the Wischnewetskys in the summer of 1887. In 1891 Kelley's husband abused her, her marriage ended, and she fled to Chicago with her children, of whom she won custody in 1892. A divorce followed in 1900. Perhaps Kelley envisioned herself when she wrote in a letter of 1894 about "the woman who asserts her claim to motherhood without the slavery of marriage."[13]

When Florence Kelley moved west, she carried her ideological baggage. As a Socialist of the 1880s, in Europe and New York, Kelley had confronted "the woman question." Should working-class women place their allegiance with their class, and therefore with Socialism, or with their sex, and therefore with feminism? Gender versus class—which mattered more? For Kelley, class trumped gender. Socialism, though not theoretically inconsistent with women's rights, was more important. Kelley explained her position in a salient letter of 1885 to Nebraska suffragist Clara Berwick Colby (1846–1916), founding editor of the *Woman's Tribune* (1883), a journal that Susan B. Anthony saw as closely attuned to the National Woman Suffrage Association. Kelley began her letter to Colby with some basic socialist algebra. "The inequality between the millionaire capitalist and his employe[e] on the verge of pauperism, on the verge of starvation, is greater than the difference between the millionaire and his wife, and the employe[e] and his wife," she told Colby.

> The mere demand for equality of the sexes is fine as far as it goes, but to make the working woman the mere equal of the working man in these days of wage reductions, lock-outs, short-time . . . and the rest of the workingman's hardships, is a task which will not arouse much enthusiasm among thinking people. Our demand must be more comprehensive, it must prove that we represent the working woman. . . . I wonder whether I have made my idea clear. In the absence of a program, the first principle of suffragists that occurs to one's mind is always equality of the sexes. But, at present, the inequality of men among themselves is so frightful that to make each woman (rich or poor) merely equal to the men of her family, or her class, is to leave the sum total of inequality now cursing society almost unchanged.

To Kelley, sex equality without economic equality was pointless. Or, as she declared to Clara Colby, a campaign devoted to "mere equality of the sexes" would be "a laughing stock." Kelley's socialist convictions erupted again two years later in a passionate speech to the New York Association of Collegiate Alumnae in May 1887, just before her (impending) expulsion from the Socialist Labor Party. "To cast our lot with the workers," she told her sister graduates, "this is the true work for the elevation of the race, the true philanthropy."[14] Kelley's socialist priorities traveled with her thereafter and, even when muted, help to explain aspects of her protectionist stance.

In Chicago, Kelley became a resident at Hull House, Chicago's pioneer social settlement, founded in 1889 by Jane Addams and Ellen Gates Starr. Like Kelley, Addams and several other residents were daughters of politicians; settlement work nurtured their political skills. While at Hull House, Kelley studied law at night at Northwestern, where she earned a degree in 1894. She also drafted the Illinois maximum hours law of 1893, led the campaign to enact it, and, as chief factory inspector, headed the team that enforced it. When an Illinois employer challenged the law, Kelley and her colleagues wrote a brief to defend it, which put forth, among other contentions, the damage caused by overlong workdays to women's reproductive systems, a contention that would dominate future defenses of women-only protective law. The *Ritchie v. People* decision of 1895, which upset parts of the law, foiled Kelley's achievement. But her NCL appointment in 1899 more than compensated for the *Ritchie* setback. Here was a crucial turning point: the following that Kelley had never won among Socialists now became available among middle-class women. Women's support enabled Kelley to promote nationally the cause of worker protection that had floundered in Illinois. Harnessing the energy of consumers' leagues, she bound them to her own agenda.[15]

Consumers' leagues arose in cities in the 1890s. The pioneer league appeared in New York (1890), founded by Josephine Shaw Lowell, leader in social welfare, a founder of the Charity Organization Society (1882), as well as of the first branch of the US Sanitary Commission (1861). Lowell challenged the long hours, low wages, and threats to morality faced by young women store clerks, who labored overtime in rush seasons without extra pay. To end exploitation of store clerks, the New York league, the Consumers' League of the City of New York, compiled a "white list" of department stores that dealt fairly with their employees and sought legislation to limit clerks' hours. (New York State law made blacklists illegal). Consumers' leagues soon arose in other cities—Brooklyn, Boston, Philadelphia, Chicago. Each league compiled a "white list" of local merchants and, like the New York City league, with its retinue of honorary vice presidents (Choate, Lowell, Schiff, Vanderbilt, Van Rensselaer), sought to involve women of prominent families in its activities. Among their members, exceptionally, consumers' leagues welcomed Jews and Catholics. Black members of consumers' leagues, if any, are unrecorded; in at least one instance (Ohio), a state league maintained ties with black civic groups. In most instances, local leagues gradually extended their concerns from store clerks to factory workers; goods, they insisted, must be made and sold under proper working conditions. Through NCL activism, explained leader Maud Nathan, longtime head of the New York City league (1896–1917), "women who spend" could help "women who work."[16]

The label of "consumer," around the turn of the century, was a code word for the middle-class woman. It set apart the purchaser of goods from the goods' producers. The definition permeated NCL rhetoric. "[I]f all the women who spend would demand that their garments, their household furnishings and their food supplies be made under wholesome conditions," Maud Nathan wrote in 1906, then merchants and manufacturers "would be forced to comply in order to find a market for their wares." "[Y]ou women of the Consumers' League," declared Leonora O'Reilly, reformer and former shirt maker, in a 1907 address to the New York City league, "if you will but fill your responsibility as consumers, you will know that you cannot buy a pin, a scarf, a button, a hat, a flower, without putting your weight forever on the side of justice against injustice, or long hours against short hours, or poor wages against better wages, or child labor against adult labor." The nineteenth-century middle class had seen consumption "as the feminine counterpart to productivity, a valued ideal associated with masculinity," historian Nan Enstad notes. NCL activists used women's roles as household buyers to change the economic system. "When there are no more indifferent purchasers," declared the NCL in 1901, "the work of the League will be a perfect work."[17]

With Kelley in charge, the NCL reached its full potential. In 1901 there were thirty local leagues in eleven states, and by 1904, fifty-eight leagues in twenty-one states. Local leagues extended their focus by 1899 from "white lists" of compliant retailers to "white labels," a campaign to regulate conditions in which goods were produced, centered on the muslin underwear industry. In 1906 the focus shifted again, this time to promoting protective laws. The NCL sent representatives, often Kelley, to address state legislators. Capitalizing on women's networks, Kelley steadily expanded NCL influence. Local consumers' leagues colonized preparatory schools and founded collegiate leagues, which Kelley often visited. Noting students' "modern attitudes" toward social science and "minds ... unjaded by philanthropy," she praised their enthusiasm ("At Wellesley the interest never wanes"). "Sometimes a single girl on returning home becomes the nucleus of a whole state," Kelley's colleague Josephine Goldmark recalled. NCL leaders also recruited a well-off constituency through women's clubs. To this end, starting in 1900, Kelley promoted NCL goals at the GFWC's biennial meetings; chaired the GFWC's standing committee on industry, followed by Maud Nathan; and pressed state federations to support protective laws. She also led child labor committees at the National Congress of Mothers (the future PTA) and the National American Woman Suffrage Association. Within a few years, Kelley had eclipsed Nathan, previously the major figure of the consumer league movement, though the two often worked together. By 1916 the NCL claimed sixteen thousand members in forty-three states. It also spawned European affiliates in France, Belgium, Germany, and Switzerland.[18]

Among outreach efforts, Kelley preferred dealing with college students to clubwomen, but the latter were crucial. As chair of the GFWC committee on industry from 1900 to 1902, Kelley pursued a "campaign of education." In progressive spirit, she sent clubwomen home with research questions ("What is the legal age for employing women in your state? Have you a woman factory inspector? Is there a license law for manufactures in homes? What is the legal working day?"). Maud Nathan spoke on "Educating the Purchaser: How Shall It Be Done?" When Kelley's committee bifurcated in 1902–4, Jane Addams took over the child labor cause and Maud Nathan led the committee on industry; Addams and Kelley made return appearances thereafter. Women's clubs undeniably differed in temper and tactics from the NCL. The GFWC favored child labor laws over women's laws (and southern women's clubs ignored the issue of child labor, on which southern textile mills relied). Wary of controversy, clubwomen mingled their concern for women workers with a host of competing causes (home economics, juvenile courts, civil service reform, traveling libraries, and other competitors). Women's clubs' main mode of action was the passage of resolutions, adopted unanimously. Moreover, club members were—as a woman factory inspector from Ohio told the GFWC biennial in 1910—"the wives, mothers, or sisters of . . . manufacturers." Kelley sometimes distanced herself from clubwomen, whose support she needed but whose response to protection, she felt, rested on "sentimental appeals." Still, the NCL program of consciousness raising succeeded. Women's clubs, with their wide geographic reach, held sway in towns untouched by the NCL. Most important, clubwomen's support for protective laws, reiterated year after year, served to legitimize the NCL agenda.[19]

After Kelley's appointment, the NCL enhanced its publicity, activism, and influence. From its headquarters on East Twenty-Second Street in the United Charities Building, where two reform-minded periodicals, *The Survey* and *The Outlook*, were published, it promoted its agenda in these and other progressive journals. Like AALL leaders, who sought to disseminate their expertise among AALL members, Florence Kelley used NCL networks to deploy her own policies. Unlike the AALL, the NCL energetically involved its participants. Kelley urged member leagues to investigate locally "the hours and the wages and cost of living of working women and girls." Local investigators became data collectors and activists. Unlike the huge GFWC, the NWTUL, or other national women's organizations, the NCL secured men's patronage and nominal male leadership. Its president, always a man, from 1899 to 1915 was John Graham Brooks, a Cambridge, Massachusetts, writer and reformer who was part of the committee that appointed Kelley. AALL founder John R. Commons served from 1925 to 1934, and other economics professors became honorary officers; their affiliation underscored the NCL's attachment to social science. Most important, lawyers who worked gratis on the NCL's behalf to defend state protective laws—Louis D. Brandeis and later his protégé, Felix Frankfurter, and then Benjamin V. Cohen—brought the NCL into the judicial process. Alone among Progressive Era women's associations, the

NCL, as of 1908, seized a legal role. Although the NCL at the start comprised a relatively small group—a few thousand well-off women plus the collegiate members, supportive professors, and soon the crucial legal advisers—Florence Kelley's skill and power to inspire vastly increased its impact.[20]

Rage fueled Kelley's dynamism. Admirer Josephine Goldmark, who found Kelley "unsparing in attack" and "implacable against her opponents," noted her "high temper, her impatience, and her tendency never to forgive or forget opposition." To a critic, Crystal Eastman, Kelley was "an exceedingly forceful, almost violent personality, a born fighter." With the magnetic force of her personality, Kelley secured the devotion of loyal disciples whose commitment to legislation kept NCL goals alive for decades to come. Early converts—all college graduates and enthusiasts of social science—included, beside Josephine Goldmark, Molly (Mary W.) Dewson, Mary Van Kleeck, Clara Mortenson Beyer, and Frances Perkins. Goldmark and Perkins were dominant.[21]

Josephine Goldmark (1877–1950), an 1895 Bryn Mawr graduate, had been a graduate student in English and tutor at Barnard in 1903, the year she met Kelley through her older sister, Pauline, an officer of the New York City league. (Another older sister, Alice, married Boston lawyer Louis D. Brandeis in 1891; the oldest Goldmark sister, Helen, married Felix Adler, founder of the Society for Ethical Culture). Goldmark served as the NCL's publications secretary and chair of the committee on the legal defense of labor laws. Joining Brandeis to write the brief for Oregon in *Muller v. Oregon* (1908) and subsequent briefs, Goldmark became a leading protectionist. Frances Perkins (1880–1965) first heard Kelley speak in 1902 as a student at Mount Holyoke, where the NCL had formed a collegiate chapter and where Kelley's speech "first opened my mind to . . . the work which became my vocation." Perkins then worked for New York's Charity Organization Society, studied social science at the University of Pennsylvania and Columbia, taught Sociology at Adelphi, followed Pauline Goldmark as secretary of the NYCL, and worked for New York State's Factory Investigating Commission. In the 1920s Perkins became industrial commissioner of New York State and later FDR's labor secretary in the New Deal. The NCL's most prominent alumna, Perkins remained loyal to NCL principles. "Legislation is the most important thing," she declared. "I'd much rather get a law than organize a union."[22]

Kelley promoted the cause of protective laws in *Some Ethical Gains in Legislation* (1905). The book appeared as the Supreme Court issued its decision in *Lochner v. New York*, which upset a state ten-hour law for bakers, who were men. The New York law violated the right of freedom to contract, guaranteed under the Fourteenth Amendment, said the Court. In *Ethical*

Gains, Kelley offered her own "rights" manifesto. Attacking freedom of contract, she posited a countervailing right, the "right to leisure," a right to which all workers were entitled, she claimed: "To be deprived of leisure is to be deprived of those things which make life worth living." The right to leisure did not appear in the US Constitution, Kelley conceded; rather, she said, it was "a human right, in process of recognition as a statutory right." Its most "virile" form was the campaign to limit employees' hours. Wage earners, Kelley argued, deserved "a part of their share of the universal gain" that arose from improved machinery and higher productivity. Skilled workers, she observed, had already attained a shorter workday through trade unionism and collective bargaining. Kelley sought the same right to leisure for "the weakest and most defenseless of workers": children, young girls, and "the mass of unskilled workingwomen as unorganized and defenseless as the children themselves."[23]

Defenseless and unorganized, women workers could attain the right to leisure only through legislation, Kelley argued. But protective laws were always preferable to labor protest or collective bargaining, she contended. Without protective laws, workers would resort to agitation; they would strive "to attain by strikes what they had failed to achieve by statute." Strikes, Kelley claimed, were "never final" and were limited to well-organized trades; they served only "those most able to make favorable terms for themselves," a group that excluded women, children, and unskilled or feeble men. Kelley classified women workers not only with children, as was commonplace, but in a larger context of the weak, less able, and unempowered. Moreover, she asserted, protective laws would help employers by reducing the struggle between labor and management. Had the 1893 law in Illinois been upheld, Kelley contended, strikes could have been precluded. Finally, if all of the protective laws already enacted (by 1905) had been enforced, "the multitude of men, women, and children affected by them would be so far reaching, that relatively little would be left to the trade agreement," that is, to unions and collective bargaining. Here, then, was a legal strategy: to incrementally achieve a blanket of protection for all workers by passage and enforcement of state laws that protected discrete groups, such as children, women, and whatever categories of men the courts might accept.[24]

By asserting the "right to leisure," Kelley targeted freedom of contract and what she saw as the probusiness bias of courts, as in *Lochner*. "The judicial mind has not kept pace with the strides of industrial development," she charged.[25] She also attacked the methods of the AFL (collective bargaining) and its weapon (strikes). With "rights" theory, that is, the positing of a positive right, Kelley assumed a modern stance. Winning a female constituency for protection, however, demanded less rights-oriented types of argument.

RATIONALES: THE PERILS OF PRAGMATISM

"Women are a shifting body of workers, first because they give up their industrial work at marriage, and second, because of their consequent lack of ambition," wrote social science researcher Elizabeth Beardsley Butler for a study of 1909, the first book in the multivolume Pittsburgh Survey.

> This lack of ambition can have no other effect than to limit efficiency and restrict them to subsidiary, uninteresting, and monotonous occupation. The very nature of their work in turn lessens their interest in it. . . . They do not care to learn; opportunity to learn is not given them; both are causes and both are effects. . . . wages are low, again both causes and effect of their dependence in part on others for their support. They shift about on lower levels of industry from packing room to metal work, from metal work to laundry work: a very few . . . break through the circle and rise.[26]

Butler's disheartening view of women workers—uninterested, unambitious, and inefficient, as well as ill paid—spoke to the Progressive Era middle class. By 1900, five million women earned wages; one-quarter worked in manufacturing, where they were 17 percent of employees. Women flowed into fields that hired them, mainly clothing, cloth, and food production; they dominated the workforce in cotton mills, garment shops, canneries, and commercial laundries. Women workers in industry, typically white, were mainly, though not exclusively, young, single, and either immigrants or daughters of immigrants. Unskilled or semiskilled and transient (most expected to spend limited time in the labor force), they earned about half the pay of men in industry. Numerous, crowded at industry's bottom rungs, and often irregularly employed, women workers lacked the leverage to bargain with their employers. Worker protests, even if successful, rarely led to permanent labor organizations.[27] Women's precarious status in industry played a role in reformers' defense of protective laws.

Protective legislation rarely reached Progressive Era black women: industry rejected them. Some black women found jobs in tobacco processing, south and north, as leaf strippers. Black women also worked as janitors in textile mills, where other workers struck repeatedly in the 1880s and 1890s to prevent the hiring of black labor to work on machines. Far larger numbers of black women labored in agriculture, as tenant farmers and sharecroppers, either for pay or as family members. Black women convicts in southern states worked alongside men to pave roads and tend fields. Overwhelmingly, black women found work as household labor—scrubwomen, laundresses, cooks, maids, and sometimes seamstresses. Married or single, only domestic work beckoned. "Factory and store are closed to her, and rarely can she take a place among other working girls," wrote reformer Mary White Ovington in 1911 of the young New York black worker. "Her hours are the long, irregular hours of domestic service." Household labor and black women's long workdays fell outside the realm of consumers' leagues or protective laws: black women (involuntarily) eluded the protectionist gaze. World War I migration patterns and employment changes would increase black women's presence in industry.[28]

Following Florence Kelley's lead, NCL leaders embraced two defenses of single-sex protective laws. One was strategic: Laws to protect women workers, the type of laws that reformers expected legislators to approve, would serve as an "entering wedge" for protective laws for all workers, that is, for laws that affected men. They would set legal precedents on which reformers could build. Single-sex laws, reformers contended, might even have an immediate impact on men if they worked in the same industries as women, as in Massachusetts textile mills; the Illinois law of 1893, though only briefly in effect, had shortened hours for all workers in Chicago stockyards, Florence Kelley claimed. Men who "wished reduced hours of work for themselves," she argued in 1905, might gain them "indirectly" if they worked in a trade with a large female labor force. Single-sex protective laws would thus serve as a means to achieve (sooner or later) a larger goal: to protect all workers. In the words of Kelley's biographer, Kathryn Sklar, "Gendered policies acted as a surrogate for class policies."[29]

The long-term "entering wedge" strategy reflected reformers' inability to achieve their major goal directly. Kelley stated the reformers' predicament most explicitly in a German social science journal in 1897, before she assumed the NCL mantle:

> It is much easier to find approval by appealing to the sympathy of the masses for the welfare of helpless working women and children than to find it by suggesting absolutely necessary measures to protect the lives, bodies, and hearts of men, who are the fathers, husbands, and breadwinners of the same women and children. It is not easy to gain the sympathy of the whole population for these male workers, because it is assumed that they can protect themselves and that they can achieve what they need by virtue of their right to vote, without appealing to the support of public opinion.[30]

The "entering wedge" strategy found voice occasionally among activists. Ellen Henrotin urged a Chicago rally in 1894 "to agitate for shorter hours for women because it means in the end shorter hours for all workers." A friend of Frances Perkins defined the strategy decades later as "take what you can get now and try for more later." At bottom, the "entering wedge" was a legal strategy: If courts upheld a single-sex protective policy, the same courts might later use that precedent to extend the policy to men. "The important thing is to get the camel's head under the constitutional tent," NCL lawyer Benjamin V. Cohen wrote to his colleague Felix Frankfurter in 1932, "and when that has been done it is time to begin to curry and groom the camel."[31]

British factory laws provided a model of sorts for the "entering wedge" strategy. Since the early nineteenth century, Parliament had passed laws to limit workers' hours in mills and factories, first those of young apprentices, then all child workers, and then women workers. Factory laws became increasingly rigorous. They included maximum hours laws, night work laws, exclusionary laws (to keep children and women out of dangerous jobs, as in mines), and eventually minimum-wage laws. By midcentury, factory laws curbed hours for all employees of textile mills, where men, women, and children worked together. As in the United States, a mix of women activists—unionists, reformers, and factory inspectors—endorsed protection; American reformers often quoted British socialist Beatrice Webb, an influential proponent. "In the life of the wage-earning class," wrote Webb in the 1890s, "absence of regulation does not mean personal freedom." But the two nations differed. America's federal system precluded enactment of a national protective policy; each state acted independently. Unlike British acts of Parliament, American laws were subject to judicial review. Still, in England, with its century of factory acts, effort to protect children and women led to extensive state regulation of industry. Britain's experience—and until World War I, middle-class Americans closely watched Europe—suggested that single-sex laws provided a viable "entering wedge" for further gains.[32]

To what extent was Kelley's constituency of middle-class women aware of the "entering wedge" strategy? In some ways, at least in the Progressive Era, the "entering wedge" was a strategy of stealth; among women backers of protective laws, only members of Kelley's inner circle or other in-the-know social feminists mentioned it. Kelley did not discuss the strategy among clubwomen or in the NCL's long "Annual Reports." Similarly, historians suggest, even NCL members had little notion of Kelley's formative affiliation with Socialism, which she had no need to mention. "Kelley's friends knew that she considered herself a socialist most of her life," writes Kathryn

Sklar, "but many of her associates in the Consumers' League may not have realized it." NCL leaders deftly underexposed their long-term goal; caution prevailed. The "entering wedge" strategy was more explicit in retrospect than during the NCL's formative years.[33]

More often, reformers stressed a second rationale for gendered laws: the difference between men and women in the labor force. Laws based on difference were compensatory, reformers claimed. They would help women workers overcome disadvantages in the workplace and society. Some disadvantages rested on circumstance. To reformers, women were (next to children) an especially needy class of workers: young, temporary, and crowded into low-level, low-paid jobs. If they were overburdened mothers, they combined factory work with household obligations. In either case, as they were unorganized (not members of labor unions), they were easy prey for exploitative employers; as an NWTUL argument claimed, protective laws were needed "because women's wages as a rule are lower than men's, women's economic need is greater than men's." Another facet of the "difference" rationale involved innate and immutable attributes: women were physically weaker than men and were potential—if not actual—mothers. Innate difference and potential motherhood gained potency after the *Muller v. Oregon* decision of 1908. "Difference" arguments, especially any reference to helplessness, proved useful to raise support for protection among middle-class women, such as clubwomen. "Women of larger opportunities should stand for the toilers who cannot help themselves," a GFWC resolution of 1897 declared, and the theme persisted. Women workers, declared the head of the GFWC industrial committee in 1910, were "frequently almost as helpless as the children in obtaining redress from oppression."[34]

The "entering wedge" strategy and the "sexual difference" rationale clashed. To embrace both called for bifocality. "Entering wedge" drew on women workers' commonality with male workers; "difference," in contrast, referred to special needs. If protective laws compensated for gender-linked disabilities or disadvantages, circumstantial or innate, as reformers argued, their extension to men (logically) was unnecessary if not counterproductive. This contradiction emerged in the 1920s. Progressive Era reformers found it irrelevant. They saw protective laws for women workers—like child labor laws or laws curbing workdays for miners, railway workers, and state employees—as part of a growing body of precedents for "general" laws. They also agreed that women's need for protection exceeded that of men; women were more vulnerable. Their "physical endowments and special functions make the protection of their health even more necessary than the protection of men's health," wrote Josephine Goldmark in 1912. "Shortening the workday is something that legislation can effect for women and children today, for men doubtless in the future."[35]

Once involved with "difference," reformers were saddled with it, but at the outset, "difference" seemed an opportunity not a liability. In the courts, since the late nineteenth century, gender difference often worked to women's advantage, as in child custody claims or lawsuits involving physical injury. Reformers' commitment to difference intensified over time, spurred by courts' acceptance of single-sex laws, and hardened in the 1920s, when debate arose among activist women. Historian Annelise Orleck explains, in reformers' defense (discussing NWTUL leaders), "They were not thinking about long-term implications for women's rights" but about immediate improvements in wages, hours, and safety, or "basic economic rights." Florence Kelley welcomed "difference" as an asset in argument. In 1922, defending "the right to differ," she voiced a hope to secure for women wage earners "their right to express by statute the differences that they desire for themselves," in order "to cast off the yoke of uniformity with men."[36]

For Progressive Era reformers, "difference" served many purposes. It appealed to policy makers, to a women's constituency, and to the public, all troubled (in the words of economist Elizabeth Brandeis) by "the exploited working girl who toiled excessive hours for a niggardly wage." It catered to what historian Alice Kessler-Harris calls the "gendered imagination," the prevailing mindset in which men were breadwinners and women family members. "The prime function of woman in society is not 'speeding up' on a machine," declared Chicago reformer Annie Marion MacLean in 1910. "The woman is worth more to society as the mother of healthy children than as the swiftest labeler of cans." To what extent was "difference" a fundamental part of NCL leaders' beliefs? Florence Kelley's stance sometimes wavered. Ready to promote "general" laws, she pragmatically fell back on the safer goal of single-sex laws. She analyzed women's vulnerable position in the workforce; at the same time she endorsed the family wage (the belief that men should support families) and voiced doubt that women belonged in the labor force at all. "Her comments resound with tension between an economic analysis and a case grounded in gender difference," historian Vivien Hart observes. This moment of vibration between two approaches undergirds social feminism. Kelley may have "supported gendered legislation with misgivings," as Hart contends, but she often viewed women's role as workers with equal misgivings. A major misgiving involved working mothers. In two salient instances, Kelley opposed the presence of married women in industry and paid maternity care for women workers.[37]

"[T]he industrial employment of married women today does harm and only harm," Kelley declared in 1910. It depressed the birth rate, demoralized husbands, reduced men's wages, injured children, encouraged industrial homework, increased urban congestion, hurt employers, damaged public health, and harmed the whole community. "However disposed to hard work the men may be, the presence in the market of a throng of unorganized and irregular workers (and married women are both more unorganized and more irregular than others) presses upon the wage rate of men," Kelley wrote. "[S]he presses upon the wage scale of her competitors as the subsidized or presumably subsidized worker must always do." Kelley recommended measures to decrease the numbers of wage-earning wives, among them a family wage: "a minimum wage sufficient to enable fathers to support their families without help from wage-earning wives." Objection to working wives, a tenet shared by transatlantic social feminists, locked Kelley into the Progressive Era male breadwinner ideology—the "gendered imagination"—and put her at odds with future trends in labor history.[38]

Kelley also opposed paid maternity benefits for women workers. In 1912 the New York legislature passed a law barring women from employment for four weeks after childbirth, the "childbirth protection" law. Massachusetts had passed such a law the year before and four more states would follow. As this forced maternity leave was unpaid, the AALL included a provision for maternity compensation in its model bill for compulsory health insurance in 1915. Such a benefit would "mitigate poverty" while the mother was "obliged to be absent from remunerative work," the AALL claimed, and reduce infant mortality. Kelley, in contrast, charged that maternity insurance would encourage shiftless immigrant men to send pregnant wives to work, unfairly burden unmarried working women, and serve as "an actual bribe to increased immigration of the kind of men who make their wives and children work." Again, Kelley took aim at employed mothers: "In families where the mother works for wages, the children suffer, if they do not die outright." A revised bill of 1916 dropped coverage of maternity benefits, but the issue stirred controversy among women reformers. Trade unionist Pauline Newman, among others, challenged Kelley's stance and her rationale; foes of maternity benefits "seem to have little conception of the psychology of the workingmen or women," Newman charged. British women reformers contacted by AALL leaders similarly dismissed Kelley's position. Legislation reintroduced in 1917 restored maternity benefits but ultimately failed. Kelley's opposition had undercut the innovative AALL health insurance initiative at the only moment when it had a chance.[39]

Commitment to difference, though effective, proved a risky maneuver long term; the reformers' rationale had liabilities not immediately visible, though clear in retrospect. Protective laws deprived women workers of agency; they empowered the state to make decisions on women's behalf; they treated women workers ("uninterested" "unambitious" and "inefficient") as unwilling or unable to speak for themselves, or irrational. Difference rationales reinforced gender disparities in the labor market and in law. When Progressive Era reformers defended single-sex protective laws, they often subsumed women's interests in some greater and more important ultimate purpose—whether future achievement of "general" laws or community welfare or the well-being of the unborn.

But these liabilities emerged only gradually. Others arose more immediately: hours limits might mean loss of income for women workers (depending on how they were paid.) When Progressive Era women criticized maximum hours laws, they pointed to lowered wages. "It is not proposed that any additional compensation be given for the loss of time thus sustained," wrote Iowa suffragist Louisa Dana Harding. "[T]his practically amounts to confiscation of whatever amount would have been earned during the forbidden hours."[40] Women textile workers in Lawrence, Massachusetts, voiced alarm in 1911 when state law reduced their workweek from fifty-six to fifty-four hours without a compensatory minimum wage.[41] Dissident labor activist Helen Marot, who had helped NCL officers prepare the Brandeis brief in 1907, resigned from the NWTUL in 1915 as it shifted its focus to protective laws; when hours were reduced, Marot told New York's Factory Investigating Commission, "the wages are reduced or efficiency methods are introduced or new machinery is introduced or some change is made in the management of the shop or speeding up is introduced to make up for this decrease in hours."[42] The pay gap spurred reformers to fight for the minimum wage. Significantly, the most innovative maximum hours laws that applied to Progressive Era men (in contrast to women's maximum hours laws) provided for time-and-a-half pay for overtime. These were an Oregon ten-hour "general" law of 1913 and a federal eight-hour law of 1916 affecting railroad workers, the Adamson Act; the Supreme Court upheld both in 1917. "Workmen, of course, prefer twelve hours when they can make more money than they can in eight hours," AALL founder John R. Commons declared in 1917. "No matter how high the wages, there are always men who are willing to work overtime for more money." This consideration did not apply to women. Protectionism inched forward on uneven legs.[43]

A wary observation came from lawyer and social scientist Sophonisba Breckinridge, the first woman to pass the Kentucky bar, who moved to Chicago in 1895, graduated from the University of Chicago's Law School in 1904, and taught social work at Chicago's School of Civics and Philanthropy, later part of the University of Chicago. "[T]he state sometimes takes cognizance of the peculiarly close relationship which exists between the health of its women citizens and the physical vigor of future generations," Breckinridge wrote in 1906.

> Such legislation is usually called "protective legislation" and the women workers are characterized as a "protected class." But it is obviously not the women who are protected. For some of them this legislation may be a distinct limitation. . . . But no one should lose sight of the fact that such legislation is not enacted exclusively, or even primarily, for the benefit of women themselves. . . .
>
> While this legislation may "protect" women workers against certain forms of brutality and greed on the part of employers, and while it may "protect" some women against the competition of others of lower standards and seemingly greater need, it is still to be borne in mind that the object of such control is the protection of the physical well-being of the community by setting a limit to the exploitation of the improvident, unworkmanlike, unorganized women, who are yet the mothers, actual or prospective, of the coming generation.[44]

Sophonisba Breckinridge, it should be noted, was not protection's foe but an advocate; her reference to the "well-being of the community" is a clue to her social feminism. A factory inspector in 1906, a founding member of the Chicago branch of the NWTUL, and an active member of the Illinois Consumers' League, Breckinridge helped to draft protective laws for women workers and endorsed a version of the "entering wedge" strategy. "Judging from the experience of other communities industrially more advanced [that meant Europe]," she wrote in 1910, "the work days of both men and women may be limited in [trades] in which the long day means special peril to the health."[45]

NCL leaders, too, saw some of the potential liabilities of single-sex maximum hours laws, but they lacked other options. Protection "in general" faced roadblocks set by business, the labor movement, and the courts.

ROADBLOCKS: BUSINESS AND LABOR

The business community endorsed laissez-faire. It opposed the federal income tax, antitrust laws, and state regulation. Protective labor laws intruded on the entrepreneur's prerogatives. They violated property rights, imposed paternalism, and paved a path to socialism; each incursion on employers' rights set the stage for the next. Protective laws were "a dangerous step in the wrong direction," declared a business association in 1905. "If the state is to invade the freedom of contract in one particular, such a step becomes a justification for further acts of paternalistic meddling." Business owners pursued a strategy to preclude an "entering wedge": they sought to cut worker protection off at inception.[46]

Business owners who hired women—such as garment manufacturers, laundry owners, and retailers—opposed protective laws most vigorously and mobilized swiftly. After Illinois passed its pioneer eight-hour law in 1893, Chicago manufacturers attacked it. "About one hundred of the richest manufacturers of this rich state have . . . gotten together to challenge the law," Florence Kelley wrote in 1894. "The Manufacturers' Association does not simply disapprove of the law but ignores and violates it and openly defies the inspectors in every respect." The Illinois Manufacturers' Association spurred similar groups, which in 1895 formed the National Association of Manufacturers (NAM), from then onward a staunch foe of protective laws. NAM members belonged as well to local chambers of commerce and specialized business associations.[47]

Employers of women claimed that maximum hours laws increased expense and disrupted hiring practices. Some enterprises depended on "rush" seasons. Canneries depended on when products were ripe; the income of retailers often rested on holiday sales; laundries, too, experienced seasonal ups and downs. Need for long workdays alternated with slack seasons, when employers counted on letting workers go. "[E]ven if we desired to benefit the health of our employees every way we possibly can," declared a New York mill owner, "we are limited by the necessity of doing business under present conditions, at all events, you have to do it at least at cost. . . . Now, the lowering of [women's] working hours . . . flatly increases the cost and it increases it out of all proportion." Hours regulation, employers claimed, also inflicted disadvantage on those who faced competitors from unregulated states: "If Georgia and South Carolina are working one-ninth more time it handicaps us further," the New York mill owner declared. Businesses believed they faced forces beyond their control. "We are controlled solely by fashion," a New York State button manufacturer claimed. "If fashions ordain that the ladies' garments are to be covered with buttons, large or small, then we all reap a harvest for a season or so. If things go to the contrary we are all flat on our backs."[48]

Canneries, citing the special problems imposed by perishable products, usually eluded maximum hours laws, as did (sometimes) restaurants, stores, and hotels. Employers who faced regulation evaded it, defied it, and then challenged laws in court. Box makers, garment manufacturers, laundries, hospitals, and restaurants—all challenged state laws that limited employees' hours. The prospect of a minimum wage evoked yet more consternation. Business lawyers, who spoke of the "repugnance to the Constitution" of the minimum wage, claimed that "any artificial raising of the cost of production interferes with natural competition." Legislators hesitated to defy business demands, in reformers' view, or did so only cautiously. To attain "labor and social legislation" was "as easy as getting the moon to play with," wrote labor activist Pauline Newman in 1921. "As long as Chambers of Commerce and Manufacturers' Associations direct our government it is nothing but a farce to try to get something done."[49]

The Progressive Era labor movement shared some elements of business aversion to regulation of hours or (especially) wages. "Labor does not depend on legislation," AFL president Samuel Gompers declared in 1901. "It asks ... no favors from the State. It wants to be let alone and to be allowed to exercise its rights." The rights of labor, under Gompers and the AFL, meant collective bargaining, or "pure and simple unionism." To labor, state regulation was unreliable, laden with loopholes, hard to enforce, and easy to overturn; ultimately, it empowered bureaucrats, not labor, and, most grievously, hindered efforts to organize. Labor's opposition to legislation was slow to develop. Until the 1890s, trade unions strongly supported the eight-hour day, achieved through legislation. After 1890 this priority waned. Expansion of judicial power and courts' use of the labor injunction played a role. So did the rise of the AFL (1886), composed of skilled workers, such as cigar makers, printers, and members of the construction trades. Craft unions of the AFL favored collective bargaining, which, in their view, made skilled workers' unions an "equal partner" with employers.[50]

Labor never completely discarded its older goals or hours laws, nor was AFL resistance to protective laws monolithic. Weaker unions might support protection. State federations enjoyed autonomy; state leaders often acted independently. West Coast labor federations strongly supported maximum hours laws in the crucial years of 1911–14. Labor spokesmen frequently endorsed maximum hours laws for women workers, for a range of reasons. Some, as in the Massachusetts textile industry, believed that women's hours laws brought shorter hours for men as well; others saw women (as did some courts) as a dependent class, as well as a threat. Some types of single-sex protective laws—maximum hours laws and exclusionary laws—weakened women's competitiveness in the workforce. "The AFL is in favor of fixing the maximum number of hours of work for children, minors, and women," Gompers testified before a federal commission in 1914. "It does not favor a legal limit of the workday for adult men workers. The unions have very largely established the shorter workday by their own initiative." Only in 1914 did a majority of delegates at an AFL convention adopt a resolution opposing an eight-hour law for all workers. In 1915, delegates resoundingly repeated this vote. Thereafter the AFL withdrew support for all maximum hours laws (save public works laws). They would undercut labor's efforts to win better hours through contracts (though state leaders might still ignore AFL policy). The minimum wage portended even more dire consequences. "If the minimum is fixed by law it will become the maximum," an officer of the carpenters' union ("an old trade unionist") told New York's Factory Investigating Commission in 1915. As the AFL hardened its stance against protective laws, NWTUL interest in protection rose. By the start of the 1920s, Florence Kelley voiced exhaustion with labor recalcitrance. Labor leaders, she claimed, were "slow and reactionary." Women workers could not "wait from decade to decade until these belated leaders catch up."[51]

The labor movement faced its own obstacles: the American federal system and judges' antilabor bias. "High regard for their institutional prerogatives combined with genuine dismay at what they saw as the faction-driven, class-bound character of labor law reforms," argues legal historian William E. Forbath, "led them to see much of the era's important labor legislation as ill-considered, illegitimate tinkering with the common law." Between 1885 and 1900, state and federal courts invalidated about sixty labor laws; cases involved such issues as payment of wages, company stores, maximum hours, and labor injunctions. Judges, mainly Republicans, feared "a treacherous class-based politics" and invidious class legislation. Labor laws, in judges' view, sought not equality but group advantage. Judicial policy, Forbath shows, fostered the AFL's antistatist strategy, though the path of influence led both ways: "Law reshaped labor's language and outlook in conservative directions, but labor also eventually reshaped the law."[52] Similarly, protectionists and the courts entered a two-way relationship.

LAW: CONSTRAINT AND OPPORTUNITY

The legal profession in the late nineteenth century sought to raise standards, limit entry, and secure avenues to profit. Lawyers, writes historian Lawrence M. Friedman, were "exceedingly nimble in finding new kinds of work and new ways to do it." Corporate law, a major new opportunity, in no way replaced other types of law practice, but "superimposed another layer on the profession." Law firms expanded to become businesses. Before the Civil War, few firms had more than three partners; by 1900, big firms of up to ten partners, concentrated in New York and Chicago, hired associates (salaried lawyers), file clerks, and stenographers. Large corporations, notably railroads, established their own law divisions, with general counsels and subordinates. Corporate lawyers sometimes became corporate managers. "Able lawyers have, to a large extent, allowed themselves to become adjuncts of large corporations," Boston lawyer Louis D. Brandeis declared in 1905.[53]

Lawyers' links to business emerged at meetings of state and local bar associations, whose members denounced incursions on property rights and defended employers' rights to conduct business unimpeded by regulations. Speakers at meetings declared that "the right to contract and to be contracted with is sacred," and that "today, more than ever, the bar is the great conservative force in American politics." Most judges agreed. The duty of government, stated Justice David J. Brewer in an 1892 dissent, was to provide "the utmost liberty to the individual, and the fullest possible protection to him and his property." "Judicial Conservatism," writes historian Melvin I. Urofsky, "erected precedents to block future legislative reform and to protect laissez-faire."[54]

The conservative swing of the judiciary derived authority from formalism, a legal philosophy connected with conservative thought. To formalists, the law was logical, coherent, and harmonious. Judges discovered law, based on preexistent law; they did not create law. Formalism was based on deduction from general principles and analogies, or comparisons, among cases. Formalists expected law to play a neutral role in disputes, to sever the legal and political; cases could be decided apart from the political and social context in which they arose. Formalists followed the advice of conservative legal authorities such as Michigan Judge Thomas M. Cooley, whose treatise on *Constitutional Limitations* (1868) advised against tampering with the economic system, and Christopher G. Tiedeman, whose *Treatise on the Limitation of the Police Power* (1886) recommended severe limits. Formalism suited those who resisted state interference with employers' prerogatives.[55]

But a counteractive trend emerged that better suited reformers. The law should not rely solely on abstract concepts, argued advocates of sociological jurisprudence. Rather, judges should consider the social context and potential impact of a statute. Interpreters of law should consider "the social facts upon which law must proceed and to which it is to be applied," wrote Harvard Law School dean Roscoe Pound (an honorary vice president of the NCL) in 1912. They should study "the actual social effects of legal institutions and doctrines," and "look more to the working of the law than to its abstract concept." Sociological jurists "regard law as a social institution which may be improved by intelligent human effort," said Pound, and they responded to social need: "They regard legal precepts as guides to results which are socially just." While formalists saw legislation as intrusive—in NCL counsel Felix Frankfurter's words, as "a kind of interloper in the harmonic system of the common law"—practitioners of sociological jurisprudence applauded legislators' work and deplored courts' aversion to it. Judges began to listen. "Law is, or ought to be, a progressive science," a Washington State court declared in 1902 (upholding a women's ten-hour law). "While the principles of justice are immutable, changing conditions of society and evolution of employment . . . make a change in the application of principles absolutely necessary to an intelligent administration of government."[56]

Competing legal approaches emerged in cases that involved protective laws. The law imposed constraints and demands on protectionists. It required reformers (and their foes) to adopt constitutional ideas and terms. It molded conflicts into forms that courts might resolve. The law shaped reformers' strategies: The "entering wedge" was a tactic to bypass constitutional barriers and capitalize on legal precedents. The law also shaped reformers' concepts; it bound them to "difference" in ways that they may not have at first expected. Paths of interaction arose between reformers and the courts. NCL leaders—starting with Florence Kelley and Josephine Goldmark—drafted laws, compiled data for briefs, and kept track of legal developments. Reformers not only responded to the law but also influenced its development. NCL leaders' interaction with the courts made their relationships with their lawyers crucial; the interests of the two groups, however, historians suggest, may have not been identical. Finally, for reformers, the law presented opportunity. Judicial doubt about state regulation for men in industry impeded the search for "general" laws but offered a few narrow paths through which protective laws might be steered. Gender difference was one such path. Multiplication of women-only laws provided opportunities for women reformers who sought a foothold in public life and could mobilize support among networks of organized women.[57]

A closing word on women and law: the nineteenth-century bar, explains historian Michael Grossberg, was "a man's profession, masculinity a baseline of professional consciousness and community membership." Law was a national fraternity; judges were "a secular replacement for ministers"; and everything that defined law defined men. Corporate law's new dominance hardened boundaries; by 1910, women constituted only 1.1 percent of the bar (as opposed to 6 percent of doctors). Pushed to the margins of the legal profession, women lawyers of the Progressive Era rarely practiced law for paying clients; typically, they held jobs with voluntary organizations, educational institutions, or government agencies. An irony: Florence Kelley, who shaped law far more than most of her lawyer-contemporaries, never practiced it in the traditional way. But exclusion from the legal fraternity did not bar women from legal activism. "Women reformers, situated outside the legal academy and the elite bar, found their professional bases of power within the growing administrative state," legal historian Felice Batlan points out; within the state they could "create positions for themselves and forge their professional identities." Incremental change in women's roles as lawyers would also shape the long-term narrative of single-sex protective laws.[58]

· · · · ·

Among progressive groups that backed protective laws, the NCL was primed to excel. Unlike the AALL, whose leaders handed down policy directives (though Florence Kelley did this, too), the NCL had a national network of engaged local leagues; it commanded grassroots support. Unlike clubwomen, who endorsed a diffuse range of civic causes and steered clear of conflict, NCL activists had a single focus: they challenged unregulated capitalism. Unlike the NWTUL, formed to spur unions, involve working-class women, and break class barriers, and whose leaders turned to protection by default, the NCL had an enduring commitment to an activist state. Like the NWTUL and AALL, the NCL would have appreciated labor movement endorsement, but when such endorsement failed to materialize, it was better fortified to press on without it. Alone among progressive voluntary organizations, the NCL engaged in the judicial process: its lawyers defended protective laws in court. By seizing a role in the legal arena, the NCL carved out its own unique piece of public space, free from domination by either labor or other progressives (save its own lawyers). Just as important, the NCL had Florence Kelley—or vice versa; her mission and that of the organization fused. Persuasive, impatient, unyielding, and formidable, Kelley was an outsize talent whose relentless drive made a difference.

The NCL also benefited from circumstance. Resistance to protective laws "in general" provided a sphere of influence for activist women, who in turn appealed to a women's constituency. The forces arrayed against protection for all workers—the opposition of business, antagonism of labor, reluctance of legislators, hostility of judges, and public indifference—gave women reformers an opportunity, one that Kelley and her colleagues grasped. The courts both narrowed options and provided them. To navigate around constitutional obstacles, reformers adopted a strategy, the "entering wedge," and developed a commitment to "difference" that hardened over time. Just as judicial bias shaped labor policy, so did it mold protective policy. But women activists affected the law as well. As cases that involved protective laws accumulated, judicial preference and reformers' strategy interacted. The first stage of court contests over protective laws, from the 1890s to 1907, set the ground rules.

Gender, Protection, and the Courts, 1895–1907

ON JANUARY 18, 1872, SENATOR MATTHEW HALE CARPENTER of Wisconsin, a well-known constitutional lawyer, argued before the US Supreme Court the case of a family friend, Myra Bradwell, editor of a Chicago law journal. In 1869, at age thirty-eight, Bradwell had applied for a license to practice law. Rejected by the Illinois Supreme Court, at first, because she was a married woman (under common law wives could not own property or enter contracts on their own) and, subsequently, solely on the basis of her sex, Bradwell appealed to the US Supreme Court. Carpenter argued that the recently adopted Fourteenth Amendment, which spoke of the "privileges and immunities" of US citizens, insured Bradwell's right to a law license. Myra Bradwell's appeal might have led to the first Supreme Court decision involving the Fourteenth Amendment. But the justices pushed the Bradwell case aside temporarily to deal with (what no doubt seemed) a more significant Fourteenth

■ ■ ■

The Lochner Bakeshop. Immigrant Joseph Lochner worked alongside his employees in the small bakery that he opened in 1894 in Utica, New York. The photo of the cellar bakeshop is from around the time of *Lochner v. New York* (1905), when the Supreme Court upset New York's ten-hour law for bakery workers. From the Collection of Joseph Lochner, Jr., photographer: Dante Tranquille, image courtesy of Mr. John Brady and Mrs. Joanne Brady.

Amendment contest. The *Slaughterhouse Cases* concerned a Louisiana law that regulated the slaughter of livestock in and around New Orleans. The law required all butchery to be carried out in a single slaughterhouse, run by a private corporation, and required that corporation to provide space for all butchers at prices fixed by the legislature; independent butchers argued that the law would put them out of work, thereby abridging their Fourteenth Amendment "privileges and immunities." Once again, Matthew Hale Carpenter took the case, though *this* time on behalf of the state. The Louisiana law was a health measure, he contended, guaranteed by the police power of the state.[1]

The US Supreme Court delivered the two decisions in reverse order of their argument. First, on April 14, 1873, in the 5–4 *Slaughterhouse* decision, the Court upheld the state. "The Banned Butchers Are Busted," a triumphant Carpenter telegraphed his clients in New Orleans. The next day, in *Bradwell v. Illinois*, the Court rejected (8–1) Carpenter's argument. The practice of law, to which Myra Bradwell wished access, was not among the "privileges and immunities" the Fourteenth Amendment guaranteed; states could bar women from practicing law. Indeed, as *Slaughterhouse* controlled *Bradwell*, lawyer Carpenter's victory in the first case led to his defeat in the second. Both decisions rested on narrow interpretations of the Fourteenth Amendment. In each, the majority held that the "privileges and immunities" clause of the Fourteenth Amendment did not limit a state's power to control and regulate activities that they had traditionally controlled, such as licensing. To the *Slaughterhouse* dissenters, legislatures, not courts, threatened individual liberties—though, inconsistently, three of those dissenters supported Illinois in *Bradwell*. In both cases, the decisions left major issues—corporate regulation and women's rights—in the hands of the states. Finally, and perhaps exceptionally, as each case made its way to the Supreme Court, new developments changed the circumstances in which the cases had begun. The banned butchers and their foes reached an agreement in 1871, and Illinois legislators, in 1872, passed a law to guarantee women freedom to enter professions of their choice. Myra Bradwell eventually became a member of the Illinois bar.[2]

But the landmark decisions of 1873, with all their peculiarities and inconsistencies, opened up contested areas of law. What impact would the new Fourteenth Amendment have on the rights of individuals (or corporations, which were legal individuals)? What powers might state legislatures assume? "No questions have ever given me more trouble in making up my own mind," Justice Samuel Miller, author of the *Slaughterhouse* majority opinion, wrote in 1873.[3] By raising these questions, the two 1873 decisions set the stage for conflict over protective labor laws. This chapter considers the early cases on maximum hours laws, the first type of protective labor law that courts considered. It also explores the unexpected clash of two goals: the goal of worker protection and that of women's rights. In what circumstances did foes of protective laws challenge maximum hours laws in court? How did states defend the acts of their legislatures? On what bases did courts give women equal status or special status? What constitutional principles were at stake? Overall, how did the courts shape protective policy?

FREEDOM OF CONTRACT VERSUS THE POLICE POWER

Passed in 1866 and ratified in 1868, the Fourteenth Amendment was designed to protect the civil rights of newly freed slaves against infringement by the ex-Confederate states. A stunning achievement, the amendment was one of Reconstruction's crucial legacies. But the Fourteenth Amendment failed to further its intended purpose for decades to come. Instead, it "slumbered in the Constitution for more than half a century without beginning to bear out the hopes of its framers," writes historian Garrett Epps. The Supreme Court in the 1870s and 1880s joined a relentless retreat from Reconstruction goals—from the obligation to protect the rights of African Americans. Instead of securing black rights, the Fourteenth Amendment served the need of business to ward off regulation by state legislatures.[4]

Businesses that sought to revoke state regulations of hours and wages shaped a consistent line of argument. They turned to the doctrine of "freedom of contract." The due process clause of the Fourteenth Amendment, they claimed, guaranteed the right of employers and workers to negotiate wages, hours, and working conditions. The clause states that no state shall "deprive any person of life, liberty, or property without due process of law." Due process had a long history. The Fifth Amendment, ratified in 1791, uses the same language. Post–Civil War employers cared most about the "liberty" and "property" that the due process clause guaranteed. The Illinois Supreme Court set forth the employers' stance in the 1895 decision that toppled that state's maximum hours law. "The privilege of contracting is both a liberty and a property right," the court stated. "Liberty includes the right to acquire property, and that means and includes the right to make and enforce contracts." Labor, moreover, *was* a type of property, the court explained; an employee was entitled to sell his labor (or property) to an employer. Similarly, challengers of protective laws often presented their arguments as if in defense of workers' rights. Laws that regulated labor, they claimed, tampered with property rights and defied the Constitution.[5]

The "freedom of contract" on which employers relied was not the long-heralded right to which they referred but a recently established right. A prominent source was Justice Stephen J. Field's dissent in the 1873 *Slaughterhouse Cases*. Field asserted the judiciary's obligation under the Fourteenth Amendment's due process clause to protect citizens' rights against hostile state action. "[E]quality of right . . . in the lawful pursuits of life . . . is the distinguishing privilege of citizens," Field wrote. Field referred to the banned butchers; thereafter, corporate lawyers relied on the Fourteenth Amendment to urge courts to protect private property from regulations state legislatures made. The employer's defense of private property reflected an innovative interpretation of the due process clause. Formerly a "procedural" safeguard that encompassed a citizen's right to obtain a lawyer or to call witnesses, the due process clause of the late nineteenth century became "substantive," a guarantee of rights against legislative intrusion. The conservative judicial revolution of the 1890s, writes legal historian Arnold M. Paul, "vastly expanded the scope of judicial supremacy."[6] It also offered advantage for business.

Contention over substantive due process arose in the states, where legislatures sought to regulate workplaces or labor practices. New York provided the first instance. In *In re Jacobs* (1885), which upset a state law of 1884 that banned tenement cigar making, the state's highest court, the Court of Appeals, cited the cigar maker's due process right "to live and work where he will." According to *Jacobs*, the "unjust law" deprived the worker of his property, which comprised "the disposition of his labor and skills," as well of his "personal liberty." The law was a "paternalistic insult to free labor." *In re Jacobs* also asserted the power of courts to "determine what is reasonable." Claims about freedom of contract recurred in two 1886 cases in Pennsylvania and Illinois that involved payment of wages in scrip, or certificates for the purchase of goods in company stores. In both instances, state legislatures had abolished this method of payment. State courts overturned the laws, which, they declared, sought to subvert workers' rights and bar employees from freely contracting with their employers. The Pennsylvania court left no doubt that gender and a worker's freedom to contract were linked: "[I]t is an insulting attempt to put the laborer under legislative tutelage, which is not only degrading to his manhood, but subversive of his rights," the court declared in *Godcharles v. Wigeman*. "He may sell his labor for what he thinks best . . . just as his employer may sell his iron or coal, and any and every law that proposes to prevent him from so doing is an infringement of his constitutional privilege, and consequently vicious and void." With this opinion, historian Arnold Paul observes, "freedom of contract had arrived." In *Allgeyer v. Louisiana* (1897), a case that involved a law to regulate insurance contracts, the Supreme Court affirmed the right of freedom to contract. Employers used freedom of contract continually thereafter to attack state protective labor laws.[7]

Defenders of protective laws challenged the doctrine of freedom of contract; it was hardly inviolate or even long established, they claimed, but rather a newly minted right. Legislatures and courts had traditionally modified contract rights, protectionists pointed out, for instance, to protect the weaker party to the contract. Defenders of protective laws also charged that freedom of contract was a "legal fiction." Employers and workers did not bargain from positions of equal strength; in real life, defenders of protective laws explained, workers lacked the leverage to shape their conditions of employment. "The worker in fact obeys the compulsion of circumstance," wrote Josephine Goldmark of the NCL in 1912. "The alternative is to work or to starve. To refuse means to be dismissed." The Supreme Court in 1898 made an important concession that validated the protectionist stance; employers and workers, the Court noted, "do not stand upon an equality." Finally, critics charged, freedom of contract could deprive legislatures of *their* freedom to represent constituents. The word "liberty" was "perverted," charged Justice Oliver Wendell Holmes in a dissent of 1905, when used to "prevent the natural outcome of a dominant opinion."[8]

But courts conceded that freedom of contract might be modified, as did the Supreme Court in 1897 in *Allgeyer*. To carve out exceptions to freedom of contract, lawyers relied on the "police power" of the state: any sovereign power can overrule individual rights or property rights to preserve the health, safety, and welfare of its people. Defenders and opponents of protective laws agreed that the state might exert such a power; they differed only as to its extent, which was vague. "This power is, and must be from its very nature, incapable of any very exact definition or limitation," observed Justice Miller in the *Slaughterhouse* decision of 1873. In each case, therefore, a court had to determine how far the police power might stretch; it had to assess the validity of an alleged threat to the public welfare and whether the law to mitigate the threat was reasonable. "Reasonable" was the crucial concept. Did legislators have reasonable grounds to believe a law would remedy a particular hazard to health or welfare? What was reasonable? As historian Melvin I. Urofsky points out, "The police power at any time was essentially what the courts declared it to be."[9]

Yet another issue arose in challenges to protective laws. Employers objected to such laws not only as violations of freedom of contract but also as "class legislation" that arbitrarily chose a category of people for benefit or disfavor. Class legislation, they claimed, violated the Fourteenth Amendment's equal protection clause (no state shall "deny to any person within its jurisdiction the equal protection of the law"). Courts considered whether the law in question was a reasonable "health and welfare" law or an illegitimate "labor law," a law enacted solely to advance the interests of a favored group. When defending protective laws, states' attorneys sought to convince judges that the classification in question was "reasonable" and not "arbitrary."[10]

From the 1890s onward, courts dealt with a series of conflicts between employers who attacked protective laws and states' attorneys who defended them. To employers and their lawyers, freedom of contract was an imperiled right and the police power had to be narrowly defined. To the states, freedom of contract was a tactic to secure or enhance employers' prerogatives; industrial conditions justified a broad interpretation of the police power. To employers, protective laws arbitrarily treated one group of people differently than another; to the states, such classification was reasonable. To employers, any question about the rationale of a protective law "must be answered by the court"; states preferred the authority of legislatures, whose members "know from experience what laws are necessary to be enacted for the welfare of the communities in which they reside."[11] As cases multiplied, each side sought to strengthen the arguments offered in previous cases; to reinforce precedents on which future decisions could rely; and to accuse the other side of self-serving motives, for which lofty legal principles were just camouflage. At the start maximum hours laws were the major issue. The first case came soon after *Slaughterhouse* and *Bradwell*.

A LOWELL MILL: *COMMONWEALTH V. HAMILTON MANUFACTURING CO.* (1876)

The first protective law challenged in state court was the Massachusetts law of 1874 that provided a ten-hour day and a sixty-hour week for women and children in manufacturing. State legislators passed the law after many tries; a preponderance of women and children in the textile industry, wrote reformer Clara Beyer, "made the work of organization hopeless." The law, said Beyer, was intended "to compensate the workers for their weak bargaining position" and "to bring the textile industry up to the standard already established in other trades." The state's governor, a supporter of the law, regarded it as "experimental." At first it was unenforceable, too; employers could be prosecuted only for "willfully" violating it. State legislators erased this loophole in 1879.[12]

Mary Shirley, an employee of a textile mill in Lowell, Massachusetts, challenged the law. She wanted to work more hours and boost her income. In *Commonwealth v. Hamilton Manufacturing* (1876), the state's highest court upheld the law, citing the police power, without further explanation. The court denied that the law infringed on a woman's "right to labor as many hours per day or per week as she desired." Rather, it provided that she could not work continuously for more than the maximum hours in a factory. Presumably Mary Shirley might work yet additional hours if she did so in another workplace. The decision did not address the issue of gender, though women constituted the majority of workers affected. Nor did the Massachusetts case provide much of a rationale for future cases. But the next maximum hours case did.[13]

A CHICAGO BOX FACTORY: *RITCHIE V. PEOPLE* (1895)

The bill passed by Illinois in 1893 to outlaw sweatshops and regulate working conditions in the garment trade contained two controversial provisions: section 5 provided an eight-hour day for women workers in factories or workshops and section 9 provided for a dozen factory inspectors, five of them women. Florence Kelley, appointed chief factory inspector, promoted and defended the law. In Kelley's view, the Illinois law was not merely a precedent on which to build but it immediately reduced hours not just for women but for men as well.[14]

Chicago employers reached a similar conclusion: the clause affecting women not only raised the specter of an eight-hour day for men in manufacturing but also brought it about: workplaces forced to limit women's hours curbed those of male employees as well. Employers organized the Illinois Manufacturers' Association (1893), which two years later became the National Association of Manufacturers, and prepared to defy the law. Employers pressed nine cases—those of a box maker, candy maker, shoemaker, and three garment manufacturers, each of whom employed one or more women workers over eight hours a day. The lead challenger, William C. Ritchie & Co. of Chicago, a manufacturer of paper boxes, ran a factory with over 350 employees, three-quarters women. (Ritchie had recently tangled with Florence Kelley's office; he had won five child labor cases.) Among Ritchie's employees were Mollie Fach and Lizzie Furlong, each twenty-seven, whom the company had employed for over nine and three-quarter hours a day; at Ritchie's original trial, each woman testified against the law. Lizzie Furlong stated that she wanted to work the longer number of hours and that "if she worked only eight hours she could not earn sufficient to support herself so well." Other women witnesses, similarly, testified that they wanted to work longer hours and earn more money. Mary Breen, who had worked nine hours in a candy factory, stated that her wages had fallen from $5.50 to $3.60 a week under the eight-hour law and that "she needed all the money she could get for the support of her family." Lower state courts upheld the law, and manufacturer Ritchie appealed to the Illinois Supreme Court.[15]

Ritchie's lawyer, Levy Mayer, founding partner of his Chicago law firm and counsel to the Illinois Manufacturers' Association, argued that the 1893 law violated the due process clause of the Fourteenth Amendment. The brief for Ritchie, uniquely (and hedging its bets) posited that women were at once special ("peculiarly adapted" to the garment trades and other "lighter trades") and equal. The Illinois law, said Ritchie's lawyers, "deprives women of the right to work for more than eight hours in one day at those particular callings for which she is best fitted by nature." At the same time, the brief for Ritchie rejected "disqualification on account of sex." "It can no longer be doubted," said Ritchie's lawyers, that women have equal rights as men to the protection of the Constitution," including the right "to work as they choose." In addition, the Illinois law was "class legislation of the most odious kind," as it affected just some types of women workers (garment workers) and not others, such as stenographers and bookkeepers. A chart with some statistics claimed that long hours did not cause women's health to degenerate. The brief concluded that restrictions on hours would curtail productivity, increase competition, reduce wages (for men as well as women), "pauperize the poor," encroach on rights of both employer and worker, and injure the nation. The Illinois law, said Ritchie's lawyers, "springs from the seeds of paternalism and socialism, which have no place in our government."[16]

Two reform-minded lawyers who worked with Florence Kelley's office, John W. Ela and Andrew Alexander Bruce, defended the law. Ela and Bruce argued in their brief that long hours deprived women of work by harming their health. They also drew a connection between public welfare and women's reproductive capacity. The "distinction between the physical strength and power of endurance of men and women has always been observed," stated Illinois's lawyers. "The natural and invariable distinction between the sexes, have become a part, not only of our laws but of our civilization." Eight states beyond Illinois recognized the distinction, and the reports of state labor bureaus, said the brief for Illinois, strongly supported the shorter workday:

These reports are almost all founded upon medical investigations and will show conclusively that the injury to a girl or woman in her sexual function, the breaking down not only of her own health and the shortening of her own life and productive power, but the injury to society in the form of a physically and often mentally degenerate offspring, for whom society must afterward care, resulting from such employment, are dangers which the state in the exercise of its police powers should carefully guard against.... The law does not deprive women of an opportunity to labor, in any true sense. All the scientific evidence is one way, viz.—that labor in factories more than eight hours a day deprives the average woman (to say nothing of girls and delicate women) of their health. They break down in a few years; they are deprived of the power to bear children, at least healthy children; their lives are shortened; so that in the end they are in fact *deprived* of labor by a long day.

Like the brief for Ritchie, the brief for Illinois presented a small amount of "social science" data—quotes from the studies of state researchers. Defenders of the Illinois law, significantly, offered the first version of what would become the "mothers-of-the-race" argument, an argument similar to its later incarnation in *Muller v. Oregon* (1908). Indeed, *Ritchie* in several ways provided a rehearsal for *Muller*, save with opposite results.[17]

The Illinois Supreme Court rejected the eight-hour provision for women in the law of 1893 because, the court said, it violated the Fourteenth Amendment. According to Justice Benjamin Magruder, in *Ritchie v. People* (1895), the provision was class legislation: "it discriminates against one class of employers and employees in favor of all others." That is, the law affected only women in factories and their employers; it did not reach women who worked as domestic servants, for instance, or in other workplaces, such as stores or offices, or the employers of those women. Next, the law violated freedom of contract, deprived women of that freedom, and lacked a direct connection to public health or safety. The state's claim that the law promoted public health, said Justice Magruder, was based not on "the nature of things done, but on the sex of the persons doing them." A restriction based solely on sex was arbitrary and unreasonable. Moreover, the police power of the state could be used only "to promote the health, comfort, welfare of society or the public," said Magruder. "[I]t is questionable whether it can be exercised to prevent injury to the individual engaged in a particular calling." In addition, there was "no reasonable ground ... for fixing upon eight hours in one day as the limit with which woman can work without injury to her physique." But the Court's main objection: the law was "a purely arbitrary restriction upon the fundamental right of the citizen to control his or her own time and faculties." Justice Magruder then pointed to the expansion of women's right to contract in Illinois: the state had passed an 1867 law that guaranteed a woman's right to work overtime, an 1872 law that precluded barring a person from an occupation because of sex, and an 1874 law that entitled married women to sue and be sued. Citing the increase in women's rights, "the tendency of legislation in this State," he contended that "the mere fact of sex will not justify the legislature in putting forth the police power of the state for the purpose of limiting her rights."[18]

Ritchie offered a model of how judges might reject single-sex protective laws (just as *Muller* later offered a model of what judges needed to accept them). The first decision to apply the due process clause to women workers, the *Ritchie* decision posited freedom of contract against sex discrimination. Florence Kelley, who had worked tirelessly to retain the eight-hour law in Illinois, voiced anger that the Fourteenth Amendment could be used in this manner. "The measure to guarantee the Negro freedom from oppression has become an insuperable obstacle to the protection of women and children," she declared. Kelley's anger persisted. Her reports to NCL members after 1899 referred to the *Ritchie* decision as "cruel and anti-social" and "reactionary and injurious." To reverse *Ritchie* remained her paramount goal. Progressive supporters of the Illinois law, meanwhile, noted the state's losing argument. "[T]he incessant jar and rumble of machinery" could injure a woman's ability to reproduce, noted the *Yale Law Journal* in 1895, "and it cannot be doubted that it is the duty of the state to protect posterity."[19]

The *Ritchie* decision also included a special twist on women's rights. Two decades earlier, when Chicago lawyer Myra Bradwell challenged her exclusion from the state bar, the courts had issued pronouncements about female difference. In 1869 the Illinois Supreme Court rejected Bradwell's application: "God designed the sexes to occupy different spheres of action," it stated. When the US Supreme Court upheld the state's action in *Bradwell v. Illinois* (1873), Justice Joseph P. Bradley, in a concurring opinion, stated: "The paramount mission and destiny of woman are to fulfill the noble and benign office of wife and mother." After losing her state case, Myra Bradwell had promoted a state law of 1872, mentioned by Justice Magruder in *Ritchie*, that enabled women to enter all occupations. Magruder used the 1872 law, which advanced women's rights, to derail the 1893 protective law. The *Bradwell* decision, scholar Frances E. Olsen contends, exemplified "false paternalism" because it injured Myra Bradwell; the *Ritchie* case exemplified "false equality" because women workers did not enjoy equality, and the decision would not improve their condition. "Antipaternalism may pretend an equality between people that does not exist," Olsen writes. "The pretense of equality may facilitate the continuation of actual inequality." Depending on the context, Olsen shows, both special treatment and equal treatment held potential for harm.[20]

Finally, the *Ritchie* decision is important for Illinois's *losing* argument, the "mothers-of-the-race" argument, one that emerged from Florence Kelley's office in the 1890s. The argument advanced what reformer Sophonisba Breckinridge called "the peculiarly close relationship which exists between the health of . . . women citizens and the physical vigor of future generations." It rested on Darwinian ideas about the evolution of species, on Social Darwinist hopes that human effort could change society for the better, on eugenic campaigns to prevent "race degeneration," and on the widespread belief that women were a biological link to the future. To turn-of-the-century Americans, the "mothers-of-the-race" argument justified state regulation of women's lives in the interest of the children they would one day have. The argument also gave precedence to concerns about the "race," the "community," or society-at-large over the individual—the woman worker. The "mothers-of-the-race" argument reappeared in state cases in 1900 and 1902 and remained in the courts for decades to come.[21]

Illinois could not appeal the *Ritchie* decision to the Supreme Court. The Judiciary Act of 1789, which remained in effect until replaced by a new Judiciary Act in 1914, permitted appeals to the Supreme Court only when a state's highest court had upheld the denial of a right arising under the US Constitution or federal law. This had not occurred. As the *Ritchie* decision was not a federal decision, it did not prevent states other than Illinois from passing maximum hours laws for women workers or state courts from upholding them. By 1895 twelve states had passed such laws, though most were weak or unenforced; between 1895 and 1908, nine states passed stronger laws. More immediately, in 1898, the Supreme Court entered the battle over protective laws. It decided a major case in reformers' favor.

A UTAH MINE: *HOLDEN V. HARDY* (1898)

Reluctant to accept maximum hours laws that affected men, courts in the 1880s and 1890s upset such laws in several states (Nebraska, California, Ohio). In Utah, distinctively, the state constitution of 1896 required the legislature to enact laws "to provide for the health and safety of the employees in factories, smelters, and mines." On March 30, 1896, legislators passed an eight-hour law for workers in mines and smelters (concentrating mills or places that melt ores to separate the metal contained in them). Within three months, on June 20, 1896, complaints arose against the owner of the Old Jordan Mine in Salt Lake County for requiring a miner to work ten hours a day underground and another employee to work in a smelter for twelve hours a day. Two Utah courts upheld the law. A business such as mining introduced particular problems of health and safety, the courts concluded; workers in smelters were exposed to noxious fumes.[22]

In *Holden v. Hardy* (1898), the Supreme Court upheld the Utah decisions by 7–2. The majority opinion, written by Justice Henry B. Brown, a strong supporter of freedom to contract, declared that special and dangerous conditions justified state intervention; it supported the legislature's view "that a limitation is necessary for the preservation of the health of the employees." Reasonable grounds existed "for believing that such determination is supported by the facts," wrote Justice Brown. The facts included the history of the mining industry, the dangers of mining (deprivation of fresh air and sunlight, foul atmosphere, high temperatures) and of smelting (influence of noxious gases), and the passage of similar protective laws in other states. *Holden* extended the reach of the police power in significant ways. First, the Utah law was not "class legislation"; it justifiably distinguished mining from "ordinary employments" because miners' work was more dangerous. Thus *Holden* brought the hazards of industry into play. Second, the decision considered the health of individual workers as part of "public welfare." The police power could be used not only to promote the well-being of the community at large but also that of specific individuals. (This point had troubled Justice Magruder in the *Ritchie* case.) Third, the Utah law did not violate freedom of contract; the legislature had grasped that employers and workers "do not stand upon an equality, and that their interests are, to a certain extent, conflicting." Here was *Holden*'s crucial point: Unequal bargaining power could justify use of the police power.[23]

But only under specific conditions: if health and safety were involved. Justice Brown linked the two points—unequal bargaining power and health and safety concerns—in a final statement on state intervention. Fearing discharge, workers might be "constrained" to work under unhealthy conditions, Brown wrote. The state might interfere in such instances, instances in which the parties were unequal (when they "do not stand upon an equality") *and* in which "the public health demands that one party to the contract might be protected against himself." Even if a worker chose to work under unhealthy conditions, "the State still retains an interest in his welfare, however reckless he may be," stated *Holden*. "The whole is no greater than the sum of its parts, and when the individual health, safety, and welfare are sacrificed or neglected, the state must suffer." Brown's complex (and paternalistic) statement at the decision's end both merged the interests of the individual and the state (injury to the first injured the second) and separated them (the state might act on behalf of the individual even if the latter wished otherwise). The end of the decision, political scientist Howard Gillman suggests, reflects Justice Brown's contention that class legislation remained illegitimate, save under specific conditions. Thus this crucial opinion, by a conservative judge, was also a guarded and limited opinion.[24]

Holden v. Hardy legitimized maximum hours laws for miners and other employees who worked in dangerous conditions or with dangerous machinery. By 1916, fourteen states limited miners' hours. Scores of laws curbed workdays in smelters, glassworks, sawmills, cording work, and many other trades that employed men. Significantly, the Utah law of 1896 quickly became one that affected only men. On June 4, 1896, a few months after legislators enacted it, again following directions embedded in the state constitution, they passed a law barring women from work in mines or smelters. Meanwhile, state courts upheld laws to limit women's hours in industry.[25]

WOMEN'S HOURS LAWS: PENNSYLVANIA, WASHINGTON, NEBRASKA

The *Ritchie* decision of 1895 affected only Illinois; unhampered by it, many states passed maximum hours laws for women workers. At the turn of the century, state courts in Pennsylvania, Nebraska, and Washington upheld such laws. Just as the *Ritchie* decision tied freedom of contract to assertions about sexual equality, the new decisions—like the brief for Illinois in 1895—linked the use of the police power to protect health and welfare to sexual difference. Women, like children, declared decisions in the three states, constituted a special class that needed state protection, as men did not. "Adult females are a class as distinct as minors," declared a Pennsylvania judge in 1900, "separated by natural conditions from all other laborers."[26]

Pennsylvania, one of the first states to pass a (weak) ten-hour law for all workers (1848) enacted in 1897 a law that limited women's workdays to twelve hours (and sixty hours a week). The law covered women workers not only in factories but also in other enterprises, such as laundries, stores, workshops, and offices; in 1901 the state added bakeries and in 1905 "any establishment" (this excluded domestic labor in homes, work on farms, and jobs in coal mines, from which Pennsylvania had barred women since 1885). A state court upheld the law in *Commonwealth v. Beatty* (1900). Employers argued that the law tried "unjustly to deprive an adult woman of her liberty and property," discriminated against women, and violated the state constitution. The court disagreed. The decision built on recent precedents: decisions that upheld limits for public employees, railroad workers, and miners. It cited *Holden v. Hardy* to the effect that injury to the individual hurt the public at large ("When the individual health, safety and welfare are sacrificed, the state must suffer") and added that "the object of such legislation is the good of the public as well as of the individual." It also set forth the distinctive nature of women workers: their weaker physiques and (as in the losing brief for Illinois in 1895) their roles as potential mothers. "Surely an act which prevents the mothers of our race from being tempted to endanger their life and health by exhaustive employment can be condemned by none save those who expect to profit from it," the Pennsylvania court declared. "If such legislation savors of paternalism it is in its least objectionable form." Overlong hours of work constituted "unreasonable and dangerous employment," the court concluded. Such hours injured women's health "and hence the interest of the state itself." In an afterthought, the decision noted: "The adult female or even the employer may think otherwise, but self-interest from a financial standpoint is often an unsafe guide."[27]

Two years later, state supreme courts in Washington and Nebraska upheld ten-hour laws for women workers in manufacturing, stores, hotels, and restaurants. The Washington decision, *State v. Buchanan*, like that in Pennsylvania, spoke of women's physical condition and roles as future mothers to invoke the police power:

> It is a matter of universal knowledge with all reasonably intelligent people of the present age that continuous standing on the feet by women for a great many hours is deleterious to their health. It must logically follow that that which would deleteriously affect any great number of women who are the mothers of succeeding generations must necessarily affect the public welfare and public morals. While the principles of justice are immutable, changing conditions of society and the evolution of employment make a change in the application of principles absolutely necessary to an intelligent administration of government.

Reference to "a matter of universal knowledge" laid the groundwork for the expression "facts of common knowledge" that Louis D. Brandeis would use in the brief for *Muller v. Oregon* (1908). Scholar Nancy Erickson points out that neither brief in *State v. Buchanan* brought up the mothers-of-the-race argument.[28] The judges did this on their own.

In the Nebraska decision, *Wenham v. State*, two months earlier, the Nebraska Supreme Court, similarly, justified the police power on the grounds of "physical limitations." At issue was an 1899 ten-hour law, identical to that in Washington, challenged by an employer. William Wenham, owner of the Nonpareil Steam Laundry in Omaha, had employed Lizzie Falkoner for over ten hours a day and sixty a week (indeed for fourteen-hour days and an eighty-four-hour week). The Nebraska Supreme Court stated:

> Certain kinds of work, which may be performed by men without injury to their health, would wreck the constitutions and destroy the health of women, and render them incapable of bearing their share of the family and the home. The state must be accorded the right to guard and protect women as a class, against such a condition; and the law in question, to that extent, conserves the public health and welfare.

The Nebraska court, however, also stressed women's distinctive situation in the workforce due to political and economic circumstances. Women had always "to a certain extent been wards of the state" the court declared. In recent years, they had been "partly emancipated from their disabilities. But they have no voice in the enactment of the laws by which they are governed, and can take no part in municipal affairs." Women had economic disabilities, too. The employer and male employee were "practically on an equal footing," but not so the employer and female employee. Few occupations were open to her, her "field of remunerative labor" was restricted, and she faced competition for the work available to her. Under such circumstances, "[t]he employer who seeks to obtain the most hours of labor for the least wages has such an advantage over them that the wisdom of the law, for their protection, cannot well be questioned." The Nebraska court in *Wenham* set forth an array of reasons beyond innate nature that women workers held a distinctive position.[29]

Approval of women's maximum hours laws, the range of factors that made women different, and the way state judges latched onto the mothers-of-race argument were significant. Mention of factors that distinguished women's status, innate or circumstantial, implied that similar laws were inappropriate for men. Although the Nebraska Supreme Court accepted maximum hours for women workers, it had recently rejected a maximum hours law for men. In 1891, Nebraska had passed a "general" eight-hour law for all workers—"mechanics, servants, and laborers." The state supreme court in 1894 struck down the law because it treated different types of workers differently, thus violating the equal protection clause; it also denied the constitutional right to contract. Even after *Holden*, in 1899, a Colorado court had refused to follow the *Holden* precedent. It upset the state's eight-hour law for miners (identical to Utah's law of 1896) as class legislation that violated freedom of contract. The pretext: Colorado lacked the constitutional provision mentioned in the Utah decision, an irrelevant point.[30] Six years later, a maximum hours law for men reached the Supreme Court.

A UTICA BAKERY: *LOCHNER V. NEW YORK* (1905)

Joseph Lochner, an immigrant from Bavaria in 1882, worked in a bakery for eight years before buying one, in Utica, New York. Lochner's nonunion bakery was small. "His shop was probably located in the cellar of a tenement house, employed just a few helpers, and operated on a shoestring," writes historian Paul Kens. But Lochner's case looms large. In 1901 Lochner broke an 1895 state law that curbed hours of work in bakeries and confectionaries to ten a day and sixty a week. Convicted and fined for keeping an employee, Aman Schmitter, at work overtime, Lochner lost two appeals in New York courts (3–2 and 4–3). State courts upheld the bakery law as a health measure under the police power; baking, said the state's highest court, the Court of Appeals, was an unhealthy trade and led to respiratory diseases. Lochner's next appeal did not seem hopeful, even to his supporters.[31]

But in a close decision (5–4), the Supreme Court in *Lochner v. New York* (1905) upset the New York law. According to Justice Rufus W. Peckham's majority opinion, New York had not proved its case that overlong hours endangered either bakers or the public. The New York law thus arbitrarily violated freedom of contract. "Clean and wholesome bread does not depend upon whether the baker works but ten hours per day or only sixty hours per week," Peckham wrote.

> The act is not, within any fair meaning of the term, a health law, but it is an illegal interference with the rights of individuals, both employers and employe[e]s, to make contracts regarding labor upon such terms as they may think best, or which they may agree upon with the other parties to such contracts. Statutes of the nature under review, limiting the hours in which grown and intelligent men may labor to earn their living, are mere meddlesome interferences with the rights of the individuals.

Baking was no more unhealthful than other occupations, Peckham argued, for "almost all occupations more or less affect the health." If the state could regulate baking, then "[n]o trade, no occupation, no mode or earning one's living, could escape this all-pervading power." Moreover, according to the *Lochner* opinion, the New York law was class legislation that treated bakers, who were "equal in intelligence and capacity to men in other trades," as if they were different. Finally, the law represented an unwelcome trend. Legislative interference with "the ordinary trades and occupations … seems to be an the increase," Peckham noted, and "many of the laws of this character, while passed under what is claimed to be the police power for the purpose of protecting the public health or welfare, are in reality passed from other motives."[32]

In sum, the Constitution guaranteed workers the right to labor as long as they chose, and the state could not abridge that right without proving that intervention was necessary for public welfare. In this case, the state had failed to present a convincing argument. To the *Lochner* majority, the New York law was not a health and safety law but rather an illegitimate "labor law" (enacted by those with "other motives.") The *Lochner* decision thus drew a firm line between Utah miners and New York bakers. Two strong dissents vied for preeminence. Justice John Marshall Harlan, joined by two other justices, contended that "employers and employees in such establishments were not upon an equal footing" and that the Court lacked the power to challenge the state legislature. Harlan also cited various extralegal authorities that he located on his own (unmentioned in any brief) to show that long hours in bakeries damaged workers' health. Justice Oliver Wendell Holmes Jr. found a conservative bias: "This case is decided upon an economic theory which a large part of the country does not entertain." The Constitution, declared Holmes, was not intended "to embody a particular economic theory, whether paternalism . . . or *laissez faire*," nor should the Court stop a state from experimenting with a new "truth."[33]

Several factors make the *Lochner* case distinctive—out of step with both the cases that preceded it and those that followed. First, it had exceptionally tangled roots. New York State bakers' unions, which had organized some firms but not others, promoted the 1895 law to affect nonunion bakeries, secure uniform industry-wide standards, and thereby promote their own interests. To the *Lochner* majority, the case concerned union power, not public welfare. Second, through a happy accident of timing, the law had swept through both houses of the New York State legislature, unopposed, and passed unanimously. The law's good fortune continued in the state courts. Reformers must have been elated in 1904 at the concurrent opinion of Court of Appeals judge Irving G. Vann, who endorsed an "entering wedge" strategy. As statutes were valid that limited the hours of women and children, Vann declared, "no person, regardless of age or sex," should labor in a trade "which is, in fact, to some extent, detrimental to health." Vann's exquisitely vague use of words ("to some extent") welcomed protective laws for men. Judge Vann also offered in his opinion his own research on the hazards of baking bread: a compilation of data from medical publications and statistical sources. Four years before *Muller v. Oregon* (1908), legal historian Felice Batlan points out, Judge Vann had begun "looking outside the law to scientific facts to determine a case." A third distinctive factor in *Lochner*: the negative (though divided) Supreme Court decision was not just a surprise but also a close call. Some scholars suggest that Justice Peckham's majority opinion was originally intended to be a dissent and that Justice Harlan's dissent had been intended as the court's opinion—which means that one justice in the majority switched his vote at the last minute.[34]

Most important, the distinctive status of the *Lochner* case reflects the efforts of the lawyers who argued it. In his minimal brief for New York, the state's attorney general, Columbia-trained Julius M. Mayer, preoccupied with another case that he found (mistakenly) more important, tried half-heartedly to link bakers' hours to public welfare. Bakers with skin diseases might spread them to the public, Mayer stated, and night work deprived bakers of sunlight, which harmed their health. Lochner's ambitious lawyer, Henry Weismann, in contrast, was far more involved in the case. In the 1890s, Weismann had played a role in the bakers' union and in the campaign for the 1895 law, but he had suddenly switched positions, joined the bar, and bought a bakeshop. "When I was young . . . I thought labor was right in all things," Weismann told the press after his victory. "Later I became a master baker [employer], and, undergoing an intellectual revolution, saw where the law was unjust to employers." In a much stronger brief than Mayer's, Weismann (valedictorian of his class at Brooklyn Law School in 1903) claimed that bakers were no less healthy than other workers. Weismann's brief included in its appendix some statistical tables on the mortality rates of occupations and excerpts from English medical journals, such as the *Lancet*, on health standards in bakeries. Ironically, considering reformers' subsequent attachment to social science, a lawyer for business submitted relatively up-to-date social science data to the Supreme Court; his goal was not to defend a protective law but to upset it. (Both sides in *Ritchie* had included forerunners of such data in their briefs in 1895.)[35]

Why had New York State's attorney general done so little to win the *Lochner* case? Legal historians Paul Kens and David E. Bernstein each consider this question. Elected in 1904 and in office only a few months, Julius M. Mayer may have either lacked interest in New York's bakery law or opposed the law, or perhaps he expected an easy victory. The other New York State appeal that vied for his attention, the *Franchise Tax Cases*, which he won, enriched the state. The franchise issue involved taxes on over $400 million of state property (streetcar lines, gasworks, and other public utilities). No doubt Mayer saw the bakery case as minor in comparison. What Mayer failed to do and should have done, Paul Kens points out, was to offer scientific evidence showing that bakery work was unhealthy for men. The justices expected such evidence. Had Mayer been up to the job, the history of protective laws—and in consequence, much of women's history—might have been far different. But he was not.[36]

At a banquet in his honor after his stunning victory, an exultant Henry Weismann called the decision "a warning to the Radicals and Socialists, who would subvert individual liberties to the paternal sway of the State."[37] Some foes of the decision disagreed. "People of conservative tendencies who welcome this decision as blow to Socialism . . . will be disappointed," declared *The Outlook*, a reform journal, the same week.[38] More often, reformers saw *Lochner* as a grievous setback. Progressives in the legal community decried formalism. Law professor Roscoe Pound wrote: "Legal monks who pass their lives in an atmosphere of pure law, from which every worldly and human element is excluded, cannot shape principles to be applied to a restless world of flesh and blood."[39] Debate over *Lochner* persists among historians.[40] Still, the upshot of the case in 1905 was clear: For the first time, the Supreme Court had upset a state protective law. Dismayed reformers found two years later that their spurt of bad luck had not ended.

A NEW YORK BOOKBINDERY: *PEOPLE V. WILLIAMS* (1907)

In 1903, New York passed a ten-hour law for women workers that also barred women from work at night between 9:00 p.m. and 6:00 a.m. A factory inspector found Katie Mead, an adult woman of twenty-one, at work at 10:20 p.m., in violation of the law, in a New York City bookbinding establishment. Although convicted in a lower court, the proprietor of the bookbindery, David L. Williams, won in two state appellate courts for the same reason Lochner had won in 1905: The state had not proved a connection between the law and the goal of protecting health. Relying on the recent *Lochner* decision, New York's highest court, the Court of Appeals, decisively invalidated the night-work provision in *People v. Williams* (1907).

State judge John Clinton Gray, who wrote the majority opinion, had chosen in 1904, when the Court of Appeals voted on Joseph Lochner's case, to support the state law that curbed bakers' hours. Although concerned about paternalism, Gray had stated that courts "must presume" that the New York legislature intended "to promote the public welfare."[41] In the *Williams* case Gray changed his tune. He now concluded that the legislature had "overstepped the limits" set by the state constitution not to interfere with citizens' rights. The night-work provision in the 1903 law did not explicitly promote health. Judge Gray found "nothing in the language of the section which suggests the purpose of promoting health." Thus the law was not a proper exercise of the police power. Moreover, it discriminated against female citizens. "An adult female should not be treated as a ward of the state," said the court. "She is no more a ward of the state than is the man. She is entitled to enjoy unmolested her liberty of person and her freedom to work for whom she pleases ... and as long as she pleases.... She is not to be made the special object of the paternal power of the state.... Women's rights legislation has advanced to the point where she has come to possess all of the responsibilities of the man and she is entitled to be placed upon an equality of rights with the man." Like the *Ritchie* decision, which spoke of "the tendency of [women's rights] legislation in this State," the *Williams* decision voiced an assumption that women's rights law was moving toward equality. Like *Lochner*, *Williams* impeded protectionist progress and left a hurdle over which reformers would have to leap.[42]

By the end of 1907, the courts had reached a workable method of determining which types of protective laws to uphold and which to reject. There had to be a close fit between the ends of the law—health and safety—and the means that the law provided to reach those ends. In laws that passed muster, such as the Utah law affecting miners, or the turn-of-the-century women's hours laws, judges were convinced that legislatures had legitimate reason to act as they did. In the first instance, legislators had reason to conclude that mining endangered miners, and, in the second, that women workers suffered from special disabilities. When laws failed to pass muster, in contrast, judges concluded that those laws were "arbitrary" or that proponents had failed to connect the dots between means and ends—they had neglected to present courts with convincing arguments about the reasonable nature of the law. In *Lochner*, the Supreme Court summed up standards for future use: "[T]here must be ground, reasonable in and of itself, to say that there is a material danger to the public health or the health of the employees, if the hours of labor are not curtailed."

· · · · ·

Between 1895 and 1907 state and federal courts began a legal conversation about state protective laws. Maximum hours laws held center stage. Challengers were often small or modest-sized enterprises—or coalitions of such businesses—that tested laws by courting arrest and disputing the charges against them. In court, challengers relied on the due process clause of the Fourteenth Amendment; they embraced freedom of contract, a concept that rose to prominence in the 1890s, and also cited the amendment's equal protection clause. Defenders gave wide latitude to the police power, the state's power to protect the health and welfare of its citizens. Courts decided in each instance how far the police power extended. Most protective laws went unchallenged, and among those challenged, courts upset only a fraction. Still, challenges by foes of protection shaped the campaign to achieve it. Reformers and reform-minded legislators suspected that laws affecting only women would fare better in the courts. Thus single-sex laws moved to the head of reformers' agendas.

As the sequence of decisions unfolded from 1895 to 1907, the police power contracted and expanded. Contests were close; many courts were divided; and, as the pendulum swung back and forth, each case reshaped the ground rules for future cases. *Ritchie*, with its narrow view of the police power, set a model for rejecting protective laws. It also linked freedom of contract with women's rights. *Holden* tilted the balance back in the other direction, though cautiously. This crucial decision brought the hazards of industry under scrutiny, linked harm to individuals to harm to the state, and gave the interests of the state priority over those of individuals. State decisions on women's maximum hours laws (Pennsylvania, Washington, and Nebraska) declared that injury to women workers endangered future offspring and thus hurt society at large. *Lochner*, which cast a long shadow over future cases, derailed reformers' hopes of protection for men, and *Williams*, relying on *Lochner*, imperiled night work laws for women.

Throughout the era, the legal system imposed a discussion of gender. In cases that involved women workers, decisions that upset protective laws, such as *Ritchie* and *Williams*, defended equal status for women—even if that status represented, in scholar Frances E. Olsen's words, a "false equality." Decisions that upheld single-sex laws, in contrast, explored the role of sexual difference, mentioned women's reproductive capacity, and linked hours limits to the good of posterity and the welfare of society—a line of argument that had first emerged from Florence Kelley's office in the early 1890s in the brief for Illinois in *Ritchie*. Thereafter, judicial opinion steered states' attorneys—and the reformers who backed protective labor laws—into gender-based strategies. Such was the situation in the fall of 1907, after *Williams*, when an appeal from an Oregon businessman reached the Supreme Court. At this crucial juncture, the National Consumers' League vaulted into the judicial process.

A Class by Herself: *Muller v. Oregon* (1908)

"ON NOVEMBER 14, 1907, FLORENCE KELLEY and I were actors in a little scene which, though of course we did not know it then, marked a turning point in American social and legal history," recalled reformer Josephine Goldmark decades later. The two women had gone to visit Goldmark's brother-in-law, Louis D. Brandeis, a successful Boston lawyer, at his home in Back Bay overlooking the Charles River. Their goal: "to ask Mr. Brandeis to appear in the Supreme Court of the United States to defend the Oregon ten-hour law for women." The case, "soon to become famous," was *Muller v. Oregon*. "Mr. Brandeis looked out over the river. 'Yes,' he said, thoughtfully, 'I will take part in the defense.'" Goldmark wrote: "Thus began that collaboration between

■ ■ ■

Curt Muller in front of the Lace House Laundry. Portland laundry owner Curt Muller (arms folded) challenged his state's ten-hour law for women workers in *Muller v. Oregon* (1908). In 1906 Muller sold his first laundry, the Grand Laundry, which figured in the *Muller* case, and bought the Lace House Laundry, above, in another part of town.

Mr. Brandeis and the Consumers' League which gave a revolutionary direction to judicial thinking, indeed to the judicial process itself."[1]

Two months later, the US Supreme Court reviewed the case of Curt Muller, the owner of a Portland laundry that had kept a woman at work overtime. Convicted of violating Oregon's law of 1903 that barred the employment of women in factories and laundries for more than ten hours a day, Muller challenged the constitutionality of the law, which, he claimed, violated his right of freedom to contract under the due process clause of the Fourteenth Amendment. Representing Oregon, lawyer Brandeis argued that the state could curb freedom of contract to protect the health and welfare of its people. In a long brief, he sought to show how long hours affected worker health and public welfare. Overwork, the "Brandeis brief" contended, "is more disastrous to the health of women than of men, and entails upon them more lasting injury." Moreover, "the deterioration is handed down to succeeding generations" and "the overwork of mothers thus directly attacks the welfare of the nation." On February 24, 1908, the Supreme Court unanimously upheld the Oregon law. "As healthy mothers are essential to vigorous offspring," declared Justice David J. Brewer, "the physical well-being of woman becomes an object of public interest and care in order to preserve the strength and vigor of the race."[2]

The *Muller v. Oregon* decision marked a momentous triumph for progressive reformers, as Goldmark's comments suggest, and a turning point in the movement for protective laws. At the same time, by declaring woman "in a class by herself," the Supreme Court embedded in constitutional law an axiom of female difference. The *Muller* decision thus pushed public policy forward toward modern labor standards and simultaneously distanced it from sexual equality. This chapter considers questions that have arisen over the *Muller* case and the two legal issues it involves: state regulation of private enterprise and the status of women under law. It also examines the statute in question, Oregon's ten-hour law of 1903 and the circumstances in which it arose. The story starts in Portland, Oregon, around the turn of the century. Charges against Curt Muller emerged from a conflict over hours limits that had been brewing in Portland for several years—a clash that involved employers, workers, unions, lawyers, pressure groups, and not least of all, a lively local economy.

LOCAL ROOTS OF THE *MULLER* CASE

In 1900, Oregon was a rural state with booming population growth. The number of Oregonians leaped by almost 80 percent from 1880 to 1890 and again from 1900 to 1910. Many newcomers—including Curt Muller (1877–1950), an immigrant from Germany and more recently a migrant from Saint Louis—settled in Portland, a center of manufacturing and trade, and the third fastest-growing city in the nation between 1890 and 1910. The state economy rested on farming, timber, mining, railroad building, canning, and woolen textile mills. The biggest employers—agriculture, lumber, railroads—hired only men. Women who worked for wages, most of them in Portland, found jobs in homes, factories, laundries, restaurants, canning plants, and as telephone operators. In 1900, almost one-fourth of Portland's female population was employed, mainly in domestic work but also in manufacturing. Among industrial workers, garment workers were most numerous, followed by those who worked in commercial laundries, an expanding sector. At the turn of the century, 542 women worked in Oregon laundries and by 1910 almost three times as many.[3]

Commercial laundry workers, mainly though not always women, ran power-driven machinery. They worked at mangles, large machines with revolving, heated iron cylinders; with ironing machines, which resembled mangles; and at many processes that demanded hand work, including starching, ironing, sorting, shaking, stacking, and wrapping. Steam arose from boiling vats; ammonia and other chemicals used in the bleaching process filled the air. "The work is not the light and often pleasant occupation of sewing or folding," a British authority (quoted in the "Brandeis brief") explained in 1902. "It is not done sitting down." Typically, laundry workers labored long hours, especially in rush seasons, but their main complaint (at least among Portland laundry workers) was irregular work and lack of overtime pay. Some protested their situation. In the first week of May, 1902, Portland's laundry workers—members of Local 90 of the Shirt, Waist, and Laundry Workers' Union—waged a successful strike that involved, at the outset, 252 out of 325 laundry employees, with more joining in later.[4]

Local 90 was part of Oregon's growing labor movement. AFL leader Samuel Gompers had visited Portland in the 1880s, and his visits inspired AFL affiliates. The state's major labor organization, the Oregon State Federation of Labor, formed in 1902, supported strikes. Four of seventeen strikes that year, including the strike of the Portland laundry workers, involved women workers. At its first convention, in May 1902, the same month as the laundry workers' strike, the Oregon State Federation of Labor endorsed a package of labor laws, including an eight-hour day for all workers; no resolutions called for limits on the hours of women alone. But in a last-minute decision, labor leaders shifted from the demand for an eight-hour day for all workers to a more modest proposal, one for a ten-hour day for women workers. What motivated the last-minute switch? Labor leaders surely knew of the women's ten-hour laws in Nebraska and in neighboring Washington, upheld in 1902 by those states' supreme courts.[5] A ten-hour women's bill, labor leaders undoubtedly reasoned, compared to the more ambitious and far-reaching eight-hour demand, had better prospects; it was more likely to win legislative support and judicial approval.[6]

On January 3, 1903, representatives of labor proposed the ten-hour women's law to the state legislature, along with other progressive measures (such as those to regulate child labor and to create a state bureau of labor statistics). The original bill covered women workers not only in factories and laundries, but also in stores, hotels, and restaurants (as did the laws upheld in 1902 in Nebraska and Washington), as well as in homes. However, employers pressed the Senate Judiciary Committee to exempt these latter categories, which fell by the wayside. The final measure, passed by both houses on February 19, 1903, applied only to women who worked in a "mechanical establishment, or factory, or laundry." Beyond curbing hours, the law forced employers to provide suitable seating. It became effective on May 31, 1903. Like women's hours' laws elsewhere, the Oregon law affected a small minority of workers. Only 11 percent of Oregon workers in 1903 were women; of these 3,592 women wage earners, the law covered fewer than 20 percent. Similarly, the law affected only a small minority of enterprises; it targeted only businesses that hired women, which were typically small businesses, not the state's biggest industries. Agriculture, lumber, and railroads were unaffected. Not so laundries.[7]

Portland laundry owners did not at once attack the new ten-hour law but rather confronted a more immediate threat, the laundry workers' union—the Shirt, Waist, and Laundry Workers' Union, Local 90—that had so recently challenged their authority in the 1902 strike. First, laundry owners united in a Laundrymen's Association. Next, in the spring of 1903 (just before the new law went into effect), they locked out their employees, two-thirds of them women; by May, five hundred employees were locked out. At the same moment, a new pressure group, the Citizens' Alliance, emerged. Catalyzed by the recently formed National Association of Manufacturers (1895), the new group supported the laundry owners. The issue at stake, in the view of employers and their allies, was control of their own enterprises. As a laundry owner declared, "We don't want the union to tell us how to run our business."[8]

On July 17, 1903, the laundry owners won the lockout. Some workers returned to laundry work, at whatever jobs they could find; others found no jobs. The lockout virtually destroyed the union; Local 90 had four hundred members in 1902 but only thirty-nine two years later. The Oregon labor movement, however, tried to help those workers who had lost their jobs. In May 1903, the Federated Trades Assembly began the Federated Trades Cooperative Laundry to employ the locked-out workers under union conditions. The cooperative laundry, located at Seventeenth and Quimby Streets in northwest Portland, lasted only briefly. When the cooperative proved unable to sustain itself financially, the Federated Trades Assembly sold it in January 1904 to the Stein brothers, who renamed it the Columbia Laundry. The enterprise was still a union shop. Then, on April 29, 1905, the Stein brothers sold the business to two businessmen who had just arrived from Saint Louis, Curt Muller, a German immigrant of 1903, and his partner, Alexander Orth. The new owners renamed the enterprise the Grand Laundry. Muller's partner faded from the record, but the Grand Laundry, formerly the Federated Trades Cooperative Laundry, soon became a locus of conflict.[9]

By the spring of 1905, then, the clash between laundry owners and laundry workers had entered a new phase. Since 1902, the two groups had vied for control. The laundry workers' union, Local 90, was by 1905 almost dead, but a group of current or former union members, veterans of the 1902 strike and the 1903 lockout, still labored at the Grand Laundry. With the union powerless, Portland's laundry owners, united since 1903 in the Laundrymen's Association, turned their attention toward the recently enacted ten-hour law of 1903. The former cooperative laundry, now owned by Curt Muller (and still staffed by one-time union members), was a tempting site for their efforts. In the spring and summer of 1905, laundryman Muller, with the backing of his fellow laundry owners, tested the new ten-hour law by violating it. Oregon's labor commissioner, O. P. Hoff, who enforced the law, gave Muller at least one warning for violations. Muller finally goaded the commissioner into arresting him. The day of his final violation was Labor Day, a holiday that the Oregon legislature had made official in 1904. Most employers gave their workers a day off, but this was not the case at the Grand Laundry.[10]

MULLER GOES TO COURT

On September 4, 1905, Labor Day, an overseer at the Grand Laundry in Portland, Oregon, Joe Haselbock, required an employee and labor activist named Emma Gotcher to work overtime in violation of the Oregon ten-hour law of 1903. Two weeks later, in the Circuit Court of Multnomah

County, the state of Oregon pressed criminal charges against the laundry's owner, Curt Muller. Muller, as we have seen, had owned his laundry only for a few months. The union whose members labored at the Grand Laundry was the effectively defunct Shirt, Waist, and Laundry Workers' Union, Local 90, of which worker Emma Gotcher was a member. Indeed, she had been elected a trustee of the union in 1902, when it was at the peak of its power. Like most of her fellow workers, she was a veteran of the 1902 strike and the 1903 lockout.[11]

For his defense in the circuit court, Curt Muller hired two local lawyers. One was E.S.J. (Edward Stonewall Jackson) McAllister (1869–1926), a young single-taxer from Virginia who had recently finished his studies in that state and then moved west. Admitted to the Oregon bar in 1904, McAllister had just started to practice law. Muller's other lawyer, William D. Fenton (1853–1925), a well-known corporate counsel, was a far more prominent figure in Portland; his clients included major businesses such as the American Steel and Wire Company and Standard Oil. Fenton also served as general counsel for the local lines of the Southern Pacific Railroad. An employers' advocate, he had recently feuded with Oregon's labor commissioner over a proposed law to limit railroad workers' hours. Consistently, lawyer Fenton shared with his corporate clients a hostile attitude toward organized labor. There never was, he declared, "a more unfeeling hand planted upon the bowed neck of honest toil than that of the labor unionist."[12]

Laundryman's Muller's case moved swiftly through the Oregon courts. Arraigned on September 18, 1905, Muller pleaded not guilty. Brought to trial on October 16, he withdrew his not guilty plea and filed a demurrer, in which he claimed that no crime had been committed. The circuit court then heard arguments from Fenton, representing Muller, and from deputy district attorney Bert E. Haney on behalf of the state. Fenton's argument rested on the *Lochner* decision. The Oregon law, he contended, violated Muller's right to contract freely with his workers and was thus an unconstitutional use of the police power. It was also class legislation that did not apply equally to other workers. Representing Oregon, Haney defended the law, which, he said, was a reasonable exercise of the police power; it was not unconstitutional. Nor was it class legislation, as it applied equally "to all women similarly situated," that is, all women employed in factories and laundries. The circuit court also heard the testimony of seven witnesses subpoenaed by the district attorney, all women, one of them Emma Gotcher. The others—Bertha Gerhke, Helen Peterson, Esther Brooks, Eunice McLeod, a Mrs. Reeves, and Maude Reeves—were no doubt workers at the Grand Laundry who supported Emma Gotcher's account of the events of September 4. These women—Emma Gotcher and her coworkers—were the first and last Portland laundry workers visible in the *Muller* case.[13]

Circuit court judge Alfred F. Sears sympathized with Muller. As recent expansion of women's rights had "almost annihilated any distinction between the sexes," he doubted that "any real distinction exists between a law requiring the hours of a baker in the state of New York and those of a laundress in Oregon." Judge Sears felt, indeed, "that in this instance the legislature has pushed its exercise of the police power to the verge" and perhaps beyond. But he hesitated to upset the work of the state legislature and decided "to resolve my own doubts in favor of the law." On January 23, 1906, the Circuit Court of Multnomah County sustained the ten-hour law of 1903, found Curt Muller guilty of a misdemeanor, and fined him $10 (the minimum fine permitted under the 1903 law) plus court costs. The local laundry-owners' association, which had supported Muller in his attack on the 1903 law, continued to offer support. Two fellow laundry owners, L. T. Gilliland and John Tait, paid his court costs and guaranteed his bond for appeal. According to a local labor publication, the *Portland Labor Press*, the Citizens' Alliance threw its support toward the employers.[14]

When fined, Muller immediately appealed to the Oregon Supreme Court, to which the opposing teams of lawyers submitted briefs; these briefs rehearsed the arguments that would shortly reach the United States Supreme Court. In each, the lawyers raised the issue of gender. "It is time we had ceased to classify women, in general, with children, criminals, and idiots," claimed Fenton and McAllister, on behalf of Muller. "They are citizens, and their privileges and immunities may not thus be abridged by legislative majority."[15] Deputy District Attorney Haney, joined by the district attorney and Oregon's attorney general, conceded that the loss of freedom to contract might injure *some* women workers, but that the "welfare of the state at large" took precedence. Continuous standing on the feet for long hours "would deleteriously affect great numbers of women who are the mothers of succeeding generations" and "will necessarily affect the public welfare and public morals."[16] Oregon's lawyers, in short, put forth in 1906 the "mothers of the race" argument that had first emerged in the brief for Illinois in *Ritchie v. People* in 1895 and that would soon reappear in the Brandeis brief.

On June 26, 1906, Muller lost in court for the second time. Chief Justice Robert Bean upheld the 1903 law on the basis of *Holden v. Hardy* plus the recent decisions on laws that curbed women's working hours in Nebraska and Washington. The Oregon law, he declared, was not "an arbitrary and unwarranted limitation of the right of contract" but "within the police power of the state."[17] Rejected by the Oregon courts and backed by his fellow laundrymen, Muller then appealed to the United States Supreme Court. At this point the National Consumers' League began to take an active role in the Oregon case.

THE NCL STEPS IN

By 1906, the NCL had extended its influence to Oregon. An Oregon Consumers' League (OCL) had begun in 1903, the year of the passage of the ten-hour law. The year before, Florence Kelley and Maud Nathan, vice president of the NCL and president of the New York City consumers' league, had visited the Pacific coast for a meeting of the General Federation of Women's Clubs in Los Angeles; their trip west left in its wake consumers' leagues in Los Angeles, San Francisco, San Jose, and Portland. The OCL involved members of Oregon's leading entrepreneurial families. By November 1906, the league claimed 140 members. The OCL urged sanitary working conditions in factories, endorsed the state labor commissioner's efforts to enforce the state's child labor law, and strove to extend the 1903 ten-hour law to saleswomen. Between January 1906, when Muller brought his case to the Oregon Supreme Court, and June, when the court upheld the law, the OCL had contacted the NCL. "The Consumers' League of Oregon sounded the note of warning that the ten-hour law of that state was in danger of annulment and with it the legislation of many states embodying the same principle," Florence Kelley told NCL members in an annual report. In October 1907, when the OCL informed the NCL of Muller's intent to appeal to the Supreme Court, NCL leaders sprang into action. To Kelley, the OCL's alerts illustrated the NCL role as a "clearing house for information and center for effective cooperative effort." With NCL involvement, historian Robert D. Johnston shows, the *Muller* case became a clash between two contingents of the middle class: the upper-middle-class reformers of the NCL and OCL who supported the law and the lower-middle-class businessmen like Muller who challenged it.[18]

Kelley was now at a crucial juncture in her life's work. Since 1899, when she had been hired as its general secretary, the NCL had expanded at a breathtaking pace. Denouncing child labor, tenement sweatshops, long hours, and low wages, Kelley became, in Josephine Goldmark's words, "a guerilla warrior . . . in the wilderness of industrial wrongs." With Kelley in charge, the NCL's distinctive agenda emerged. As Kelley explained in *Some Ethical Gains in Legislation* (1905), published just as the Supreme Court issued the

Lochner decision, the NCL believed in the state rather than unions as the best means to insure working people's rights and in the superiority of protective statutes to collective bargaining, to "the trade agreement with its precarious renewal and threat of strikes to secure enforcement." The main barriers to worker protection, Kelley argued, were the objections of judges, as exemplified in the *Ritchie* and *Lochner* decisions. How could the courts be "enlightened and instructed concerning conditions as they exist?" Curt Muller's appeal in 1906 presented an opportunity to "enlighten" the courts, to win influence for the NCL, and to exact redress for the despised *Ritchie* decision of 1895, for which Kelley had always nurtured special loathing.[19]

In 1907 Florence Kelley and Josephine Goldmark began to seek a lawyer to argue Oregon's case. That the two NCL leaders embarked on such a search was exceptional; voluntary organizations did not customarily choose attorneys to represent states. In *Holden v. Hardy* (1895), the AFL had hired a lawyer to defend Utah's eight-hour law for miners, but only because the Utah state's attorney had refused to do so; such was not the case in Oregon. In this instance, Kelley simply seized the initiative. "[W]e are trying to *add* a very powerful attorney . . . to the Atty. Gen'l of Oregon for the oral argument," she wrote to her son Nicholas Kelley in November 1907. At first Kelley and Goldmark met failure. Leading New York lawyer Joseph H. Choate, who had argued many cases before the Supreme Court, who had recently had served as US ambassador to Great Britain (1899–1905), and whose wife was an honorary vice president of the New York Consumers' League, either rejected the two women or vice versa, as in Goldmark's account: "'A law *prohibiting* more than ten hours a day in laundry work,' he boomed. 'Big strong laundry women. Why shouldn't they work longer?'" At this point, wrote Goldmark, Florence Kelley "swept out of the room." Kelley recalled the occasion slightly differently. In her account, the former ambassador had confused commercial laundry work with domestic labor ("If Mrs. Choate hires a big, strong Irish woman to wash her clothes . . ."). According to Kelley, "We found ourselves on the sidewalk before we had a chance to explain that the law applied only to women in laundries, not to home workers." Future NCL lawyer Felix Frankfurter had yet another version of the search for a lawyer: Kelley, he said, endured multiple rejections. "[N]o eminent lawyer cared to argue such a case," he recalled. "There was no money in it." But on November 14, 1907, Goldmark's brother-in-law, Louis D. Brandeis, agreed to act as unpaid counsel to the NCL and also to represent Oregon, though only on two conditions: if invited to do so by the state's attorney and if given control over how the case should be litigated. Oregon agreed to his terms. Suddenly, both Brandeis and the NCL were major players in the Oregon case.[20]

In 1907 Louis D. Brandeis had only begun to win a national reputation. According to his biographer, Melvin I. Urofsky, "few knew of him outside Massachusetts." A graduate of Harvard Law School in 1877, Brandeis had first worked for a year in Saint Louis and then opened a law practice in Boston with a law school friend. By the 1890s, he had earned professional acclaim; his business clients, mainly small and medium-sized enterprises (manufacturers, wholesalers, and retailers), appreciated what historian Thomas C. McCraw calls his "almost extrasensory instinct for the winning ground." Progressive and idealistic, Brandeis also defended the public interest; he fought for lower utility costs, took on insurance companies, proposed a plan for savings bank life insurance, and battled to prevent monopoly control of Boston's transportation system. Finally, Brandeis was among those dissenting lawyers who challenged the philosophy of "formalism" that prevailed in late nineteenth-century courts and supported "sociological jurisprudence." Laws should not be judged by logic alone, the dissidents argued, but on the basis of the conditions from which they arose. They turned to experience—the concrete, the details, the "facts." "Far more likely to impress clients by knowledge of facts than by knowledge of law," Brandeis wrote early in his career in a memorandum to himself.[21]

Deploring the roles of Progressive Era lawyers as "adjuncts of large corporations," Brandeis envisioned alternative roles. In a 1905 speech to the Harvard Ethical Society, he proposed that the lawyer assume the role of mediator—that he "take a position of independence, between the wealthy and the people, prepared to curb the excesses of either." Lawyers neglected the public interest, Brandeis charged. "We hear much of the 'corporate lawyer,' and far too little of the 'people's lawyer.'" Brandeis became the latter; he worked without fee in the public interest, as he would for Oregon, and repaid his own firm for the time that he donated. In "The Living Law" (1915), an essay that reflected his successful defense of protective law, Brandeis linked his vision of the lawyer's role to the practice of sociological jurisprudence. Legal institutions, he contended, had not kept pace with the "rapid development of our political, economic and social ideals." He criticized the tendency of courts to upset the work of state legislatures, which represented the people, and the use of the Fourteenth Amendment and legal formalism to block reform, as in the 1895 *Ritchie* case, in which Illinois judges reasoned from "abstract conception." The modern corporate lawyer, Brandeis claimed, lacked "broad knowledge of present day problems" and showed distorted judgment. In contrast, he argued, the lawyer needed familiarity with economics, sociology, and politics. Judges, too, must be trained "to perform adequately the function of harmonizing law with life."[22]

To grasp the "facts" of a case, Brandeis examined the situation in which a problem arose, the remedies provided by existing laws, and the experience of other states or nations with the same or similar problems. The Oregon case offered a chance to pursue this method; it would also bring Brandeis a degree of professional prominence greater than what he had known thus far. In 1907, when he accepted the Oregon assignment, Brandeis decided what sort of case to prepare. One possibility, some analysts suggest, was to challenge *Lochner* directly. This option, which Brandeis did not consider, held risks: If the case for Oregon sank, the movement for protective laws might never recover. Instead of refuting *Lochner*, Brandeis took advantage of an opening that *Lochner* provided. According to the *Lochner* decision, "there must be ground, reasonable in and of itself, to say that there is a material danger to the public health or the health of the employees if the hours of labor are not curtailed." New York in 1905 had grievously failed to provide this "ground." But Julius M. Mayer's defeat in *Lochner* was Brandeis's opportunity. The challenge that Brandeis faced: to convince the Court that Oregon's ten-hour law was a reasonable exception to freedom of contract because it was directly related to—in *Lochner*'s words—"the public health or the health of the employees." That the Oregon law affected only women shaped his strategy.[23]

THE BRANDEIS BRIEF

When Brandeis accepted the NCL request to defend Oregon, he told his sister-in-law, Josephine Goldmark, head of the NCL committee on labor law, "what he would need for a brief, namely, *facts*, published by anyone with expert knowledge of industry in its relation to women's hours of labor." Goldmark gathered ten researchers, including her sister, Pauline Goldmark, an officer of the New York Consumers' League, and Florence Kelley. Using the resources of Columbia University, the New York Public Library, and the Library of Congress, the researchers found reports of British factory commissions and medical commissions, translated sources from western Europe, and collected information from states with maximum hours laws. In two weeks they had amassed the data for the 113-page Brandeis brief. Unlike a traditional brief, an argument based on precedent, that is, on citations from relevant court decisions, the innovative Brandeis brief cited the testimony of nonjudicial authorities: doctors, academics, factory inspectors, sanitary inspectors, legislators, bureaucrats, and other investigators. It relied extensively on foreign material, notably the reports of physicians and factory inspectors, some dating back to the early nineteenth century. A leading American source was the Massachusetts Board of Labor Statistics, started in 1869 and directed by Carroll D. Wright, pioneer in social science research and later the first head of the Bureau of Labor Statistics; the bureau had been collecting data on women workers since the 1870s.[24]

Two pages of concise legal argument, written by Brandeis, began the brief. Citing *Lochner*, Brandeis explained that a law restricting freedom of contract must have "a real or substantial relation to the protection of the public health and safety"; that "when the validity of a statute is questioned, the burden of proof, so the speak, is upon those who assail it"; and finally, that the Oregon law must be sustained unless (again citing *Lochner*) the Court "could find that there is no 'fair ground, reasonable in and of itself, to say that there is material danger to the public health . . . or to the health of the employees (or to the general welfare), if the hours are not curtailed." In a few sentences, Brandeis placed the burden of proof on his opponents and set forth his own assignment—to do what New York's lawyers had failed to do in *Lochner*, to convince the Court of a link between the law in question and public health. The data to follow, he said, constituted the "facts of common knowledge of which the Court may take judicial notice." A succinct phrase, perhaps a descendent of the reference to a "matter of universal knowledge" in *State v. Buchanan* (1902), "facts of common knowledge" seems to embrace both commonplace information (what everyone already knows) *and* more specific types of information (sociological studies, scientific data, and expert opinion).[25]

The "facts of common knowledge" supported the brief's contention that sexual difference justified special treatment. The first part of the "facts" section offered precedents for single-sex maximum hours laws: the brief listed legislation limiting women's working hours in European nations and in twenty American states.[26] The second segment of the "facts" presented "The World's Experience." In this largest and most innovative segment of the brief, Brandeis and Goldmark shaped a discursive argument bolstered by citations from European and American legislative, governmental, medical, and scholarly reports. The citations, in which experts and nonexperts melded observation and interpretation, bolstered the brief's main argument, that "overwork is more disastrous to the health of women than of men," not only because of "the speed and hazard of modern industry" but mainly because of women's "special physical organization."[27]

How did long working hours harm women workers? Long hours, declared observers from Europe and the United States, caused many ailments, ranging from indigestion and insomnia to lead poisoning, misshapen joints, and tuberculosis. Women "compelled to work in factories," New York physician George M. Price noted, suffered "general debility" and "increased susceptibility . . . to industrial poisons and to diseases." The overlong workday also affected "childbirth and female functions." It led to pelvic disease, menstrual problems, miscarriage, premature births, infant mortality, and enfeebled offspring. "[W]oman's ill health and drudgery in a factory may affect her progeny in a way that the statistician cannot estimate," a doctor stated in 1895. European protectionists, explained German reformer and social welfare expert Alice Solomon in 1907, sought to "preserve the health of women . . . as wives and as the mothers of future generations." Long hours not only injured women as individuals, the brief contended, but through their offspring or potential offspring injured the entire community. As one of the experts, Jules Simon, a member of the French senate and leading protectionist, asserted in 1891: "[I]t is not only of the women that we think; it is not principally of the women, it is of the whole human race. It is of the father, it is of the child, it is of society."[28] A shorter workday, in contrast, provided advantages, the brief argued: When hours were reduced, the generations that followed showed "extraordinary improvement in physique and morals" and "the tone of the entire community is raised." Observers reported the benefits that a curtailed day (of ten hours or even more, in some instances cited) brought about. Shorter hours, said an inspector for Upper Bavaria in 1905, gave the young, single woman "the opportunity to learn the art of homemaking, because upon this the health, welfare, and prosperity of her whole family will depend."[29]

In progressive fashion, Brandeis and Goldmark tried to stake a middle position between labor and management. Maximum hours laws would not handicap the interests of business owners, they argued, for instance. To the contrary, such laws affected employers only in positive ways. Shorter hours increased efficiency, raised productivity, lowered costs, and improved the quality of goods, as experts from Europe and America attested. How would curtailed hours affect businesses that depended on long workdays during rush seasons? "Foresight and management" would decrease the need for irregular hours. Did employers share these findings? "The good done by the Factory Acts has quite outweighed any evils or hardships," a British employer stated in a 1904 study of women in the printing trades. In that study, the employers surveyed "admit candidly enough that legislation allows them to be more humane . . . than they could otherwise afford to be." Would shorter hours harm the women worker by "contracting the sphere of her work?" Some foes of protection, Beatrice Webb reported, carped that factory laws annoyed employers and made them "inclined to get rid of women altogether and hire men." But an essay by British reformer Clementina Black in a 1901 book that Webb edited, *The Case for the Factory Acts*, offered a cogent reply: "Where women can be employed, their labor is so much cheaper than that of men that there is no chance of their being displaced."[30] Low pay, as British protectionists explained, would protect women's jobs.

Finally, the Brandeis brief discussed the particular hazards of labor in commercial laundries, places full of steam, harsh chemicals, big vats, hot irons, and perilous machinery, such as mangles. Such a work environment imperiled workers. Upright labor in damp conditions over long hours caused varicose veins, leg ulcers, rheumatism, bronchitis, and "all forms of internal disease." Dangers to labor lurked in the industrial workplace, in short, the brief took care to explain, not merely in the liabilities of workers. The section on laundries was an important part of the Brandeis/Goldmark argument.[31]

At the end of the brief, after one hundred pages of "facts" spanning many nations and six decades, Brandeis reiterated his main point of argument: "[I]t cannot be said that the Legislature of Oregon had no reasonable ground for believing that the public health, safety, or welfare did not require a legal limitation on women's work in manufacturing and mechanical establishments and laundries to ten hours in one day." With this famous triple negative, Brandeis declared that the Oregon legislature had acted reasonably in limiting women's hours and that the lawyers for Curt Muller would be unable to prove otherwise.[32] In a recent article, lawyer Clyde Spillenger points out that the much-cited triple negative includes one negative too many—and that Brandeis's grammatical error in fact negates his obvious intent. But everyone knows his obvious intent![33]

Oregon lawyers also submitted another, more traditional brief, signed by state officials and by Brandeis. The second brief was almost identical to that which Oregon's lawyers had submitted to the Oregon Supreme Court in 1906; a few new lines mentioned *Williams v. New York* (1907). The second brief for Oregon called the insistence on freedom to contract "gilded sophistry" and denied that the Oregon law was class legislation. Unlike the Brandeis brief, which cautiously skirted any mention of women's rights or lack of rights, the second brief argued that women were disadvantaged under law: a woman "only enjoys a limited citizenship." (Oregon denied women the vote in five referenda between 1884 and 1910 and finally granted it in 1912.) Unlike the Brandeis brief, again, the second brief conceded that the ten-hour law might "work a hardship" on individuals, a concession that the Brandeis brief never made. The "welfare of the individual" mattered less, the second brief contended, when "placed in the balance against the welfare of the state at large." Unlike the Brandeis brief, finally, the second brief relied solely on precedent and on argument; it did not present data (studies, statistics, expert testimony). But like the Brandeis brief, significantly, the second brief voiced concern for mothers of future generations:

> [W]hen we consider the case of a woman, unfitted as she is for most kinds of manual labor, remembering the keenness of competition for the places she can fill . . . and knowing the duty she owes to the home and the family and that she is the mother of the citizens of a coming generation, can we say that a law restricting the number of hours in which she may labor, in certain classes of hard work is not a law involving the safety, the morals, nor the welfare of the public.[34]

This section of the second brief, a document that lawyers for Oregon prepared for Muller's first appeal in 1906, a year before Brandeis entered the picture, suggests the currency of the mothers-of-the-race argument. The Brandeis brief alone, however, won the attention of the justices—and that of more recent commentators as well.

Feminist critics of the 1970s and 1980s attack the Brandeis brief for both the inaccuracy of its "facts" and for the devaluation of women in its argument. The opinions and contentions of random commentators, mainly in the nineteenth century, are not necessarily "facts," much less scientific facts, critics charge. The expertise of the authorities cited, from members of the House of Lords to Belgian factory inspectors, seems dubious. The views of women workers rarely appear, and only indirectly, as reported in the investigations of others. Overwhelmingly, feminist critics of the 1970s and 1980s attack the brief's argument, with its stress on sexual difference and sex-linked deficiency. The Brandeis brief, its critics point out, treats all women as mothers or potential mothers; it either fuses the needs of women with those of children, families, and society, or gives priority to the latter. Above all, the brief depicts women as weak and defective. It stresses, in Nancy Erickson's words, not the hazards of modern work but the vulnerability of the workers.[35] To its critics, the Brandeis brief seems at best a feeble argument and at worst reprehensible.

A previous generation of feminist critics—veterans of the early twentieth-century wave—also found fault with the tactics employed in the Brandeis brief and its successors. According to lawyer Blanche Crozier in 1933, Brandeis "introduced the potential mothers-of-the-race argument, which, from the inevitability of its popular appeal and its imperviousness to embarrassment on the grounds of scientific inaccuracy, was nothing less than a stroke of genius."[36] Crozier erred only in part. Brandeis had not introduced the mothers-of-the-race argument; it was already floating around the legal system. Lawyers for Illinois had brought the argument into play in 1895, when they sought to defend the state eight-hours law of 1893; it had emerged again in state decisions on women's hours laws in 1900 and 1902, and more recently in Oregon's brief before the state supreme court in 1906. But Brandeis and Goldmark gave the mothers-of-the-race argument its greatest visibility. Moreover, Crozier correctly identified the "inevitability" of the Brandeis brief's "popular appeal" and its "imperviousness" to attack. On what did the brief's popularity and invulnerability rest?

First, the "difference" argument appealed to Brandeis's contemporaries, to whom female difference *was* common knowledge—or as Brandeis later told his law clerk, Dean Acheson, the Brandeis brief should have been called "What Every Fool Knows." The "facts" that strike recent critics as unconvincing evoked less skepticism among turn-of-the-century Americans; interest in social science was a recent development, and Progressive Era citizens respected expertise, such as that of doctors and state officials. In addition, the receptivity then prevalent for evolutionary ideas sustained a concern with women's reproductive roles that, though suspect to contemporary readers, carried weight at the time; the "future mothers" argument of the Brandeis brief conveyed scientific authority. Nor did the contention that women were weaker than men even seem to demand scientific proof. Finally, as lawyer David J. Bryden points out, the mindset of Brandeis's contemporaries made the brief plausible. "To refute Brandeis's facts would have been a great challenge," Bryden argues. "To refute the ethos that made the facts intuitively persuasive would have been impossible."[37]

Just as important, according to Brandeis, the "facts" in the brief did not have to be correct or true. Brandeis had shifted the burden of proof to those who attacked the law. All that he had to show was that Oregon legislators had reason to act as they did when they approved the 1903 law. His talent, in *Muller* as well as in subsequent protective law cases, was to formulate the legislature's assignment and to define a standard of rationality that suited his purpose. "The question under this standard was not whether social and economic legislation was of dubious worth," lawyer Alexander Bickel notes. Rather, was the law "supported by reasoned and informed opinion? If it was, it benefited from a presumption of constitutionality that could not be easily rebutted." As a Supreme Court justice after 1916, Brandeis applied the same principle. Was the judgment of the legislature arbitrary or reasonable? The facts did not have to be accurate; their validity was not in question. Nor did the courts needed to examine the facts that the legislature actually considered but rather the facts that they should or might have considered at the time they passed a law. Brandeis explained his stance about the "truth" of the facts in oral argument for an Oregon minimum wage law of 1913 in December 1914 (see chapter 4). It did not matter, he then stated, "whether the remedy adopted was wise" or even what the facts actually were. "The decision of such questions lies with the legislative branch of government."[38] Brandeis gave the justices in 1908 a legal reason to do what no doubt seemed reasonable to them in the first place. He also thrust a formidable challenge at his opponents.

Curt Muller's lawyer, William D. Fenton, though prominent in Portland, entered the case with neither the eminent reputation of Louis D. Brandeis nor with a prestigious legal education. A graduate of Christian College in Monmouth, Oregon, in 1872, Fenton had read law in Salem, Oregon, from 1874 to 1875, when he was admitted to the state bar. Thereafter Fenton built up a corporate practice and entered Democratic Party politics. He served briefly as a member of the Oregon legislature in 1876, as a nominee for Congress in 1882, and as a presidential elector in 1884. His successful work for Portland businesses led to his long-term post as general counsel for the Southern Pacific Railroad lines (1891 to 1917). A plum position in the new and profitable field of corporate law, the railroad job enabled Fenton to travel without cost by rail to Washington, DC, in 1908—a not inconsequential saving for the laundry owners who employed him. To present Muller's case to the Supreme Court, Fenton and his current associate, Henry Gilfry, submitted an energetic thirty-two-page brief. Lawyer E.S.J. McAllister, who worked on Muller's case until mid-1906, had no doubt contributed to the brief as well.[39] The *Muller* brief attacked the Oregon law of 1903 and promoted equal rights for women.

CURT MULLER'S BRIEF

The brief for Muller built on the Illinois *Ritchie* decision of 1895. Women, like men, were entitled to equal protection of the law, Muller's lawyers charged. All women were "persons and citizens" and "as competent to contract with reference to their labor as are men." Oregon's law of 1903 defied the Constitution because it violated the equal protection clause of the Fourteenth Amendment, because it was not a valid exercise of the police power, and because it did not "affect equally and impartially all persons similarly situated" and was "therefore class legislation." Muller's lawyers also claimed that the kind of work the law curtailed did not endanger workers' health or morals; that no reasonable connection existed between hours limits and public health, safety, or welfare; and that the reasoning behind the law "would lead to ultimate state socialism."[40]

To challenge the Oregon law, Muller's lawyers put forth a slew of assertions and rhetorical questions. A woman could not be deprived of "the right to dispose of her labor" however she wanted, they argued. "Upon what theory can the state become her guardian," they asked, "and interfere with her freedom of contract and the right of employers to contract with her, freely and voluntarily, as if she were a man?" What if the law had forbidden employment for more than ten hours a day to "all persons of white color"? That is, what if the law imposed classification by race? Here, Muller's lawyers introduced a race-sex analogy of sorts. Certainly, they claimed, no one would argue that such a race-based statute "was reasonable or one that would be sustained." What if the law discriminated by age? What if it applied solely to "all persons over forty years of age"? Surely such a law would be found "arbitrary, unreasonable, and invalid." Why did the law single out women in laundries and factories, "when women in all other useful vocations may contract freely"? What about nurses, domestic workers, and stenographers? Why set an arbitrary limit of ten hours? Why not six hours? "What magic is there in the limitation of precisely ten hours and no more"? What if the woman employee was a widow in charge of dependent children? "In what way does the restriction in her case ... preserve the public health?" What if she were a single woman without children? Could the Court claim that "in the distant and remote future the possible children which she may bear will need the protection of this statute?" Most important, why did the law exclude men? "What conditions of employment exist in a laundry that endanger a healthy woman do not apply alike to a healthy man?" Muller's lawyers asked. What differentiated the situation of a woman at work in a laundry and that of a man employed as a baker? "Certainly conditions are as favorable in a laundry as in a bakery." Men and women held the same rights under law, declared the *Muller* brief: "Difference in sex alone does not justify the destruction of impairment of these rights."

Finally, Muller's lawyers warned about the hazard of state legislatures that interfered with constitutional rights. "The question involved is far reaching," they declared. If a law such as the Oregon law could be upheld "merely because the employe[e] is a woman," and if a woman's employment "in a healthy vocation" might be limited and restricted, "there is no limit beyond which the legislature's power may not go." Muller's lawyers had recognized an "entering wedge." They then summed up their commitment to female equality. "Women, in increasing numbers, are compelled to earn their living," the lawyers for Muller pointed out. But a woman entered the employment market "handicapped by centuries of tutelage" and by current convention.

> Social customs narrow the field of her endeavors. Shall her hands be further tied by statute ostensibly framed in her interests, but intended perhaps to limit and restrict her employment, and whether intended so or not, enlarging the field and opportunity of her competitor among men? The extortions and demands of employers, if any such exist, should not be made the cover under which to destroy the freedom of individual contract and the right of individual action. It is respectfully submitted that the judgment of the Supreme Court of Oregon should be reversed.

Did the spirited support for equal rights expressed by corporate lawyer Fenton and his associates represent a genuine commitment to equality of the sexes or was it merely a tactic to defend employers' prerogatives? Most definitely, Muller's lawyers' foremost goal was to protect the freedom of employers to do whatever they wanted, a goal to which Fenton had devoted his career. The job of the lawyers for laundryman Muller was to protect *his* rights from state intrusion, just as Oregon's major purpose was to enhance the state's authority. In both instances, the power of the state was the main issue at hand. In both instances, assertions about women's role under law were subsidiary concerns. Fenton easily fused the rights of women workers and their employers when it served his purpose; the briefs for Oregon just as easily conflated the needs of women, children, families, and societies. Lawyers on both sides used contentions about women's needs or rights to serve their primary ends.

Still, the women's rights argument of the *Muller* brief was logical as well as functional. Employers' rights and women's rights were natural confederates with common roots. Both represented individualism and classic liberalism. The nineteenth-century movement for women's rights involved expanding women's freedom as individuals, specifically their right of freedom to contract, as in the early nineteenth-century campaign for married women's property rights, or, as in Myra Bradwell's case in 1873, the right to practice law. To women who strove for legal rights as individuals, as to employers, the Fourteenth Amendment was crucial. At first, as in the *Bradwell* case, conservatives did not grasp the potential utility of women's rights. But now, as the twentieth century began, the threat of women-only protective laws spurred employers and their lawyers to develop a proclivity for ideals of sex equality, even before those ideals won a widespread constituency among women. Confluence of feminist goals and business interests was neither a fluke of 1908 nor a mere ploy of argument but rather an ongoing possibility, a potentiality. The companionate relationship between employers' rights and women's rights—and consequently between conservative lawyers and egalitarian feminists—would reappear in the controversy over single-sex protective policies.[41]

When Brandeis and Fenton presented their cases to the Supreme Court in January 1908, NCL leaders had cause for optimism. The *Lochner* court had been closely divided, and Justice Brown of the *Lochner* majority had retired. His replacement, William Henry Moody, a 1906 nominee of Theodore Roosevelt, had been Roosevelt's attorney general and a trustbuster; he had prosecuted the Standard Oil trust and meatpacking monopolies. This seemed a hopeful sign for Oregon. Since the *Ritchie* case, moreover, the legal tide had been turning in favor of women-only hours laws. Four state supreme courts, including that of Oregon, had recently upheld such laws. After oral argument, at which he excelled, Brandeis "felt pretty cheerful about the result," Florence Kelley reported to her son Nicholas.[42] Still, the outcome held surprises. On February 24, 1908, a unanimous Supreme Court upheld the Oregon law. Speaking for the Court was David J. Brewer (1837–1910), a noted conservative who had long defended the "sacred right" of private property, denounced state interference in the economy, and opposed labor protest.

THE *MULLER V. OREGON* OPINION

A member of an old New England family, David J. Brewer was a nephew of associate justice Stephen J. Field, who had written the dissent in the *Slaughterhouse Cases*. After attending Wesleyan, which he had entered at fourteen, and Albany Law School, Brewer moved west and began his legal career in Leavenworth, Kansas. An active Republican, he became a probate judge and swiftly rose. In 1871 he joined the Kansas Supreme Court and in 1889 the United States Supreme Court. On the Kansas bench, Brewer wrote several decisions that advanced women's rights. An 1876 decision upheld a woman's right to hold elective office, for instance (the office in question was county school superintendent); an 1881 decision held that a woman's property could not be seized to pay her husband's debts. By the start of the twentieth century Brewer had endorsed woman suffrage as desirable and inevitable.[43] But such concerns were not central to his reputation. Rather, Brewer won prominence in the 1890s as an outspoken defender of laissez faire at bar association meetings and other gatherings. "The acquisition, possession, and enjoyment of property are matters which human government cannot forbid," he declared at the Yale Law School commencement in June 1891; the police power, he added, was "the refuge of timid judges to escape the obligation of denouncing a wrong." In 1893, he told the New York Bar Association meeting that judges needed support "to restrain the greedy hand of the many filching from the few."[44]

Brewer's opinions from the bench reflected his conservative slant. "The paternal theory of government is to me odious," he had declared in an 1892 dissent. In *In re Debs* (1895), he had voiced the Court's unanimous opinion upholding an injunction against the leaders of the 1894 Pullman strike in Chicago. He had dissented in *Holden v. Hardy* (1898), joined the *Lochner* majority in 1905, and most recently, early in 1908, in *Adair v. United States*, had joined a five-justice majority to kill a federal ban on yellow dog contracts (agreements by workers not to join unions).[45] However, as Brewer's biographer, David J. Brodhead, points out, it is likely that Brewer appreciated Brandeis's approach to the "facts." Brewer believed that judges were capable of dealing with specialized knowledge beyond the law, as in patent cases, and that courts had the duty to look beyond judicial sources. Moreover, in his last decade on the court, Brodhead suggests, Brewer modified his ultraconservative stance slightly and became less doctrinaire. Or, as Alan F. Westin observes, Brewer was "a conservative whose ideological bark was a bit worse than his decisional bite."[46] In a concise opinion, Brewer handed the reformers a victory: he praised the Brandeis brief, accepted its primary argument, and elaborated with conviction on one of its implicit premises.

First, Brewer declared that the Court would accept "opinions" from nonjudicial sources ("We take judicial cognizance of all matters of general knowledge"). Praising the Brandeis brief, Brewer even mentioned Brandeis by name, a mention that is unusual in court opinions; a footnote listed all the laws Brandeis had cited and credited him with presenting excerpts from over ninety reports. Although Brewer dismissed the notion that "a consensus of present public opinion" could decide constitutional questions, he conceded that a "widespread" and "long-contended belief" merited consideration. In reformers' eyes, Brewer's receptivity to social and economic "facts"— to opinions from nonjudicial sources—cleared a path for protective laws as well as for sociological jurisprudence. Legal historians have been less certain on the latter point. According to Owen Fiss, the unusual reference to the Brandeis brief at the start of the decision may have been—rather than praise—a "distancing technique" that pushed the brief aside. The insight on "distancing" is salient. Brewer swept a great deal—Brandeis and his exceptional skill, the brief and its extraordinary contents—off to the margins. The Brandeis mode of sociological jurisprudence would have influence but perhaps less than reformers liked to think it did.[47] With Brandeis out of the way, Justice Brewer alone seized center stage.

Next, Brewer accepted a pivotal argument in the Brandeis brief, that the overwork of women injured the general welfare. The brief had shown that "woman's physical structure and the performance of her maternal function place her at a disadvantage in the struggle for subsistence"; that even without the "burden of motherhood," prolonged work on the feet had injurious effects on women's bodies. In conclusion, Brewer stated that, "[A]s healthy mothers are essential for vigorous offspring, the physical well-being of women becomes an object of public interest and care in order to preserve the strength of the race." In this section of the decision, following the argument of the Brandeis brief, Brewer affirmed rather than repudiated the *Lochner* decision. Oregon had convinced the court of a valid link between state law and public welfare, as New York had failed to do in *Lochner*. Brandeis, in short, had secured an exception to freedom of contract, but he had not changed the terms of debate or inspired a significant change in judicial policy. Brewer might well have stopped right here. But he continued.

Third, Justice Brewer put forth a doctrine of female exceptionalism or immutable sexual difference. Here, in a crucial section of the opinion, he expounded on social theory in ways that had not been mentioned in the Brandeis brief. Woman, said Brewer, was inherently and permanently dependent on man; she had innate psychological differences from men that prevented her from implementing her rights. Therefore, "some legislation to protect her seems necessary to secure a real equality of right." Because woman was in a "class by herself," Brewer argued, "laws designed for her protection may be sustained," although similar laws for men could not. In this section of the opinion, Brewer argued that Oregon's maximum hours law for women was acceptable as "class legislation" because women differed from men. He also moved beyond the arguments of the Brandeis brief to present a principle of immutable sexual difference. The principle embraced several points: that women were by nature dependent, and even legal rights (including suffrage) would not change their nature; that innate psychological differences ("disposition and habits of life") barred women from fully asserting whatever legal rights they possessed; that women needed compensatory laws in order to function as equals ("to secure a real equality of right"); and that protective laws, while acceptable or "necessary" for women, were unacceptable for men.

This section of the decision was stunning and historic. Deft and agile, Brewer moved quickly. While Brandeis had offered a narrow legal argument (that Oregon lawmakers acted reasonably), Brewer, pouncing on the Oregon argument as a springboard, seized the opportunity to make a very broad legal point. Women were a class apart, in a place remote from that of able white men, a place where all the justices agreed they belonged—a place beyond the "borders of belonging," a term introduced by legal scholar Barbara Young Welke.[48] "Distancing," again, is the crucial descriptive term. With perfect pitch, Justice Brewer clarified a point in legal geography. Even if enfranchised (as he thought they would be), even if further endowed with rights, women would always be distinct from men. They existed someplace *else*, as they always had.

The conviction about immutable sexual difference conveyed in the Brewer opinion drew a favorable response from Americans of 1908, to whom the *Muller* decision seemed benevolent, humanitarian, and public-spirited. A suggestion of eugenics—concern about "the race"—held appeal. Far from catering to fears of "race suicide" (meager population growth among the middle and upper classes), however, the *Muller* opinion included working-class women, or at least white working-class women, in the "future of the race." Headlines announced that the "Supreme Court Holds Women above Men." Editorial columns praised the justices' efforts "that the race may be preserved, that the health, vigor, and soundness of posterity be assured." Suffragists endorsed the decision in the *Woman's Journal*; editor Alice Stone Blackwell found nothing in it incompatible with woman's enfranchisement.[49]

Yet women's publications revealed some profound objections, though few in number compared to the positive comments the decision generated. One suggestion of female suspicion of single-sex protective laws had emerged in Portland two years earlier, as Muller's case made its way to the Oregon Supreme Court. It came from suffragist Clara Colby, onetime correspondent of Florence Kelley (in the 1880s) and editor of Portland's *Woman's Tribune*. "The State has no right to lay any disability upon woman as an individual," argued suffragist Colby in 1906, "and if it does as a mother, it should give her a maternity pension which would tend to even up conditions and be better for the family."[50] (In Chicago that year, lawyer and reformer Sophonisba Breckinridge pointed out that protective laws were "not enacted exclusively or even for the benefit of women themselves"; men, children, and families were the beneficiaries.[51] Unlike Colby, Breckinridge did not oppose protective laws; she merely noted their characteristics.) In 1908, attacks sharpened. Iowa suffragist Louisa Dana Harding, in an article in the *Woman's Standard*, the mouthpiece of the Iowa Suffrage Association, declared the Muller decision "abominable." Curbing women's hours, she declared, "practically amounts to confiscation of whatever amount would have been earned during the forbidden hours."[52] In the *Woman's Tribune* a month later,

Harding argued that the true aim of single-sex labor laws was not protection of women but rather to prevent women from being "enabled in some manner to enjoy the pleasure of an independent life."[53] In March 1908, the *Woman's Journal* published a letter from a group of New York women, members of the Henry George League, who denounced the *Muller* decision as "unjust and humiliating to women; as tending to sex slavery; as opposed to economic freedom, and as inimical to the best interests of present and future generations."[54]

Feminist commentators vary as to what extent Brandeis bore responsibility for the "dependent woman" in the Brewer opinion, but criticism settles mainly on Brewer. Analysts offer many illuminating points. To Frances E. Olsen, the "altruism" of the Brewer decision was linked to hierarchy. Although the case might have "seemed to exalt women," she points out, "it effectively degraded them by treating the asserted differences as evidence of inferiority."[55] Sociologist Susan Lehrer considers who benefited from the decision. The *Muller* decision, she suggests, represented a mediation between the needs of families and those of employers for women's services, a compromise between women's productive and reproductive capacities.[56] To historian Alice Kessler-Harris, the decision reflected the "gendered imagination" that prevailed at the time, habits of thought that recognized men as individuals and women as family members. Justice Brewer's opinion "so clearly and unapologetically denied women their status as persons under the law."[57] Legal historian Barbara Young Welke, who analyzes the mindset of nineteenth-century jurists, shows how their decisions separated able white men from those who differed from them in race, gender, or ability. "Courts and lawmakers dressed subordination in the language of privilege and protection," Welke observes. "Belonging for some is achieved through the subordination of others."[58]

How did the justices arrive at their decision in *Muller*? They left no records of discussion. It is unclear if they thought the case a challenging or significant one; or which of the justices, if any, actually read the Brandeis brief or how much of it; or what they thought of the "facts" in the brief (though as Brandeis later explained, the truth of the facts was irrelevant). It is unknown why Justice Brewer volunteered or was chosen to write the opinion—perhaps because of his interest in woman suffrage or his previous opinions on women's rights—and unknown if any of the justices voiced doubts before the group reached unanimity or if any had second thoughts subsequently. Justice Brewer is the exception. At the end of 1908, when Justice Brewer defended the *Muller* decision in an article in *Charities and the Commons*, a publication that catered to progressive reformers ("A Weekly

Journal of Philanthropy and Social Advance"), he revealed more of his rationale and supplied further grist for feminist analysts.[59]

Justice Brewer explained how he distinguished between the *Lochner* and
Muller cases. In *Lochner*, New York's ten-hour law violated the rights of able-
bodied men, with whom Justice Brewer identified.

> We held that the law could not be sustained because both employer and em-
> ployee had the right to contract for more hours than those prescribed. . . .
>
> And why should it not be so? Here is a man: strong, vigorous, healthy. Why
> should he not be permitted to contract for more than eight hours' labor—for
> nine, ten, or a dozen, if he wishes? There is scarcely a man in charge of any
> department at Washington who does not work over ten hours a day. There is
> not a justice of our court who does not work longer, and all of us look reason-
> ably healthy. The Declaration of Independence and the Constitution give us
> the right to determine these questions for ourselves. As Mr. Justice Peckham
> well said, any other rule is mere meddlesome interference.

Justice Brewer then turned to the *Muller* opinion. Here he referred to his
suffragist stance, distinguished his views from those of antisuffragists who
disparaged women, and defended his vision of women's "place and work in
life." The *Muller* decision, he made clear, was not precisely about women; it
was about the needs of society, the needs of posterity, and, again, the status
of able-bodied men.

> That language [of the opinion] was used in no disrespect to the other sex—nor
> in the sneering spirit in which it has been sometimes said, that women, like
> infants and lunatics are unfit to vote. It was written with the utmost respect for
> them, by one who knows the blessings which come from the sex, and in the
> firm belief that there was something in her place and work in life which justi-
> fied the legislature in forbidding her to contract for factory work beyond a
> limited time. The race needs her; her friends need her, in a way that they do not
> need the other sex. I had and have no doubt that the decision was correct. To it
> the Supreme Court unanimously assented. But while that is so, it is equally
> good law that a man in full health and strength is at liberty to contract to
> perform any ordinary healthy work, for as many hours as he sees fit.

Barbara Young Welke's analysis suggests what Justice Brewer was doing: he
was patrolling one of the nineteenth-century "borders of belonging." The
border soon crumbled slightly. Justice Brewer, who retired in 1910, was no
longer present when the Supreme Court upheld a ten-hour law that affected men in *Bunting v. Oregon* (1917), but it is fair to assume that he would
have joined the dissenters.

Would the Supreme Court have reached the same decision on the 1903 law without the Brandeis brief and Brandeis's shaping of Oregon's argument? Critics of Brandeis suggest that it might have done so. The *Lochner* decision of 1905, which progressives saw as a massive obstacle, had been a singular case; the replacement of Justice Brown with Justice Moody alone (it can be argued) might have insured Oregon's victory in *Muller*. Would the potential dissenting justices (Justices Fuller, Peckham, and Brewer) have provided a unanimous decision for Oregon without the Brandeis brief? Would the brief by the Oregon lawyers, which offered no sociological "facts," have sufficed to convince them? Again, considering the singularity of the *Lochner* case and the hope of a more sympathetic vote on the Court, could Brandeis have challenged *Lochner* directly in 1908 and succeeded?[60] These remain open questions.

In the event, the *Muller* decision offered a reward to each of the interested parties in the case, that is, to reformers and to employers. Reformers saw the decision as a critical victory that expunged the loss inflicted by *Lochner* and as a precedent for future achievement. The business community lost little, however. The decision specifically excluded male workers, who constituted the bulk of the industrial labor force, and in any case posed little threat to business owners. Employers whose enterprises depended on women workers might come to terms with ten-hour laws, cope with them without problems, ignore them, dodge them, or find substitute labor sources. Curt Muller, for example, closed the Grand Laundry in 1906, opened a new one in another part of town, and remained in the laundry business until 1940; presumably, after 1906, Emma Gotcher and her unionist coworkers were no longer his employees.[61] Major problems with single-sex hours laws were that they were weak and undemanding, and even so, difficult to enforce. Oregon's 1903 law serves as one example.

ASSESSING THE LAW OF 1903

In 1908, the year of the *Muller* decision, a young college alumna named Caroline J. Gleason (1886–1962) arrived in Portland to teach Latin and English. A recent graduate of the University of Minnesota, Gleason was drawn to social reform. After college she had worked as a volunteer in eastern city slums, and in 1910 she began graduate study at the University of Chicago's School of Civics and Philanthropy. Soon the Oregon Consumers' League tapped her talents. First the league engaged her to survey family living costs and wage rates, material used to promote a pioneer state minimum wage law in 1913. Thereafter, Gleason explored housing and laundry work in Portland, investigated labor conditions by working in a paper box factory, joined the OCL's board of directors, and served on Oregon's Industrial Welfare Commission, formed in 1913.[62] Her many studies of Portland's women workers in the Progressive Era, plus a subsequent survey of Oregon's protective laws for women workers, shed light on a major question: To what extent did single-sex hours laws affect women employees? In what ways did the Oregon law of 1903 do so?

Like women's hours laws in other states, the Oregon law had built-in frailties; the law had no doubt appealed to legislators because it was expected to have little impact (especially compared to the more threatening eight-hour general law that labor leaders had discarded). Many factors fostered such low expectations. First, as Gleason pointed out, the 1903 law provided for merely a ten-hour a day limit, with no mention of a sixty-hour a week limit. Although Oregon had a Sunday closing law, which should have insured a six-day workweek, employers could easily ignore this limit by citing "emergencies." In practice, Gleason contended, Oregon's ten-hour law of 1903 meant that women could legally work a seventy-hour week. Second, many employers of women had managed to win exclusion from the law; the owners of restaurants, hotels, and retail stores had successfully pressed legislators to whittle away the areas of employment the law covered. Canneries, moreover, typically the most exploitative of women workers, had been exempt from the outset. Finally, as sociologist Elaine Zahnd Johnson points out, the ten-hour limit for women in factories and laundries was not exceptional in Oregon in 1903. Men and women who labored at seasonal jobs in canneries, and men in some other occupations, including lumber work, iron and steel plants, and bakeries, worked longer hours, but the ten-hour limit was already widely established in Oregon in laundry work and the garment trades. According to Caroline Gleason, local laundry workers suffered mainly not from overlong workdays but rather from curtailed workweeks, curtailed work years, and irregular employment. Most laundry workers were unemployed for several weeks of the year, and outside of the rush season (June to September) had workweeks of inadequate duration.[63]

The women's ten-hour law's modest demands on employers were not the only factors curbing its impact: enforcement was hit or miss. Initially, the state labor commissioner tried to avoid the expense of prosecutions by issuing only warnings to first offenders. Many employers who received such warnings escaped indictment and prosecution (as did Curt Muller, at least once). In 1911–12, the commissioner dropped the warning policy and indictments rose. But convictions proved elusive. Of twenty-seven offenders accused of violations in 1912, Caroline Gleason reported, only twelve paid fines. Three forfeited bail, six received suspended sentences, and two were dismissed because the state lacked enough evidence to convict. It is likely, too, that (unlike Emma Gotcher) many workers hesitated to complain, although complaints were anonymous, for fear of losing their jobs. Even if poorly enforced, of course, the very existence of the law might have prevented exploitative behavior that never occurred and therefore cannot be tabulated. Still, Elaine Zahnd Johnson contends that the positive impact of Oregon's ten-hour law on women workers between 1903 and 1913 was minimal. Moreover, she concludes that the law "indirectly retarded" the unionization of women, that the NCL and the OCL limited women's unionization by preferring protective measures, that these measures led women to expect protection from the state rather than from unions, and finally, that Oregon's protective laws did nothing to curb patterns of sex segregation in the labor force but rather added to them. "The cost of special legislation for women," Johnson contends, "surpassed the benefits."[64]

But the goal of single-sex hours laws, like Oregon's 1903 law, was not merely—or not primarily—to benefit women workers but to create precedents for future laws and thereby to extend the scope of protective policies. Seen solely in this light, the Oregon law did its job well. Judicial victories gave reformers in Oregon new leverage to remedy the deficiencies of the 1903 law, to pass new protective laws, and overall to strengthen the fabric of protection. This process began as soon as the Oregon Supreme Court upheld the 1903 law in 1906. In 1907 the state legislature extended the hours limit to women working in "mercantile establishments, hotels, or restaurants." An exemption provided that women could work in retail stores up to twelve hours a day for the week preceding Christmas, a concession to department store owners. Then, a year after the *Muller* victory, a second amendment extended the ten-hour limit to telegraph and telephone work and to express or transportation companies, and imposed a sixty-hour a week limit. Finally, in 1913, when Oregon legislators provided a minimum wage law for women and minors, they established an Industrial Welfare Commission (IWC) whose curbs on women's work hours superseded those of the 1903 law. Subsequently, the IWC set hours for women in specific occupations, dropped the Christmas week exemption for store clerks, and continued to reduce the number of hours that women could work. For instance, by 1914, according to Caroline Gleason, the IWC had cut the workweek for women laundry workers to fifty-four hours, barred night work after 8:30 p.m., and imposed a minimum wage.[65] Oregon reformers also enacted in 1913 a precedent-setting ten-hour law for men (to be examined in the next chapter).

Thus the 1903 law and the decisions that upheld it led to further success for Oregon reformers.

The 1903 law and the *Muller* decision had national ramifications, too. After the crushing defeat in *Lochner* in 1905, the movement for protective laws could have been crippled or derailed. Instead, the *Muller* decision revitalized it by providing a window of opportunity. Single-sex laws could now pass muster with legislatures and courts as "general" laws usually could not. The viability of women-only laws, at least compared to general laws, secured their place at the front of the reformers' agenda and also ensured clout for women reformers, the major proponents of such laws, notably those at the NCL. The Brewer opinion, which the NCL widely publicized, along with the Brandeis brief, made the distinction between single-sex laws and "general" laws absolutely clear. As Brewer stated, a type of maximum hours law similar to the 1903 law could *not* be passed for men. Characteristically, while praising the decision and publicizing it, Florence Kelley overlooked the restriction that Brewer had imposed and drew another lesson entirely. "Henceforth," she declared in the *Woman's Journal* in 1908, "both men and women need only show a clear relation between their working hours and their good or bad health in order to get hours legislations sustained by the Supreme Court."[66] This statement was astounding. With it, Kelley defiantly ignored Justice Brewer's placement of woman in "a class by herself"; the Brewer opinion was for Kelley just a stepping-stone. In the decade after the *Muller* case, the NCL moved forward on two fronts, first, and most successfully, to extend the range of single-sex laws, and also, with substantially less impact, to attain general laws that would affect men.

· · · · ·

Twists and turns pervade the history of Oregon's ten-hour law of 1903. The bill for hours limits sprang out of a newly formed labor organization, the Oregon State Federation of Labor, whose leaders suddenly switched from a proposal for a general eight-hour law to one for a ten-hour law for women only. The ten-hour bill moved through the state legislature in a climate full of labor protest, including a 1902 strike of laundry workers and a 1903 lockout by laundry owners that crushed the laundry workers' union. Curt Muller's defiance of the law in the fall of 1905 reflected the strategy of laundry owners, who, having recently united to break the laundry workers' union, tried next to attack the law. By 1906, when Muller's case reached the Oregon Supreme Court, two important mutations had occurred. First, the demand for a "general" law had become a demand for a women-only law.

Second, the NCL had replaced the labor movement as the main proponent of laws to limit hours of work.

In court, the single-sex nature of the 1903 law shaped its fate. When the case reached the Oregon Supreme Court in 1906, the state's lawyers presented the "mothers-of-the-race" argument that had first emerged in Illinois in 1895—that overwork would injure women "who are the mothers of succeeding generations" and thereby harm the general welfare. NCL leaders and Louis D. Brandeis reiterated this contention in 1908. To attack the conservative "legal fiction" that employer and employee wielded equal strength in bargaining, reformers laid the groundwork for a countervailing legal fiction, that women were innately weak and dependent. Muller's lawyers responded that women deserved equality in life and in the labor market; the cause of sexual equality became linked with the stance of employers. Reformers, in contrast, fused gender-based distinctions with the promotion of labor standards. Accepting the reformers' main argument about mothers of "succeeding generations," Justice Brewer, writing the court's unanimous opinion, elaborated on it. Woman, declared the Supreme Court in 1908, was legally "in a class by herself," a conclusion that echoed through court decisions for decades to come and secured women's place beyond the "borders of belonging."

For over half a century, historians gave *Muller v. Oregon* an overwhelmingly positive spin; a long trail of scholarship, launched by progressives themselves, praised the Brandeis brief and the *Muller* opinion. Well into the 1960s, the decision seemed (in the words of legal historian Thomas Alpheus Mason) a "legal landmark unscarred by criticism." In law school in the late 1950s, future justice Ruth Bader Ginsburg learned that *Muller* was a response to oppressive working conditions and a "decision to applaud." A little over a decade later, as she embarked on cases to win for women equal protection, Ginsburg "assessed *Muller* differently." Protective laws, she now saw, treated women as "less than full persons" and "could operate to protect men's jobs from women's competition." Thereafter, Ginsburg remained "instinctively suspicious of women-only protective legislation." A few decades later she slightly softened her stance on *Muller*. When she presided over a reargument of the case at an event organized by the Supreme Court Historical Society in 2008, Justice Ginsburg underscored the other facet of the *Muller* case—as an "opening wedge" to wage-and-hour laws "protecting all workers."[67]

In a recent discussion of *Muller*, Justice Ginsburg asks whether the justices of 1908 ruled in Oregon's favor because they were impressed with the extraordinary quality of the Brandeis brief or whether the brief "seemed to confirm their preconceptions about the relationship between the sexes, the physical superiority of men, women's inherent vulnerability, and society's interest in 'the well-being of women' as actual or potential mothers."[68] It is more likely of course that the brief confirmed what the justices already believed. Still, undeniably, Brandeis had invented a fruitful legal tactic: the triumph of Oregon's ten-hour law bolstered if not salvaged the "entering wedge" strategy of progressive reformers. After the *Muller* decision, the movement for protection surged forward with new vigor, and the canopy of protective laws—especially the part that covered women workers—vastly expanded. The era between 1908 and World War I would represent the high tide of protectionist success.

4

Protection in Ascent, 1908–23

"I, WITH A NUMBER OF OTHER GIRLS, was in the dressing room on the eighth floor of the Asch Building, in Washington Place, at 4:40 o'clock on the afternoon of Saturday, March 25, when I heard somebody cry fire!" wrote Rosey Safran, one of seven hundred women workers at the Triangle Waist Company in downtown Manhattan in 1911. "I got out to the street and watched the upper floors burning, and the girls hanging by their hands and then dropping as the fire reached up to them. It was an awful, awful sight." Because of locked doors and inadequate fire escapes, 146 women perished; some leaped out of windows and some were incinerated. Only eighteen

■ ■ ■

The Triangle Fire, 1911. Crowds gathered at the scene of the fire at the Triangle Waist Company in New York City on March 25, 1911, when 146 workers perished. The "three top stories had turned into red furnaces where human beings were . . . incinerated," a journalist reported in the *New York World*. "They jumped with their clothing ablaze. . . . Thud after thud sounded on the pavement." Library of Congress.

months before, in October 1909, many of the Triangle employees, including Rosey Safran, had joined thousands of fellow garment workers in a massive strike to protest unsafe factory conditions and unfair labor practices. The strike failed; by mid-February 1910, most of the picketed factories had re-opened and most of the strikers had returned to work, with few concessions from employers. But after the Triangle fire, amid public outrage, prominent New Yorkers urged the state to gather evidence on industrial abuses and recommend remedies. In May 1911, the state legislature passed a resolution, sponsored by state senator Robert Wagner and assembly minority leader Al-fred E. Smith, to create the Factory Investigating Commission (FIC), whose nine commissioners included Wagner, Smith, Samuel Gompers of the AFL, and Mary E. Dreier of the New York Women's Trade Union League. For the next four years, the commissioners held hearings all over the state; heard testimony from hundreds of workers, union leader, employers, and reform-ers; and drafted sixty bills dealing mainly with health, safety, sanitation, fire prevention, and also with wages and hours. Fifty-six of the bills became state law, including, in 1912, a law that limited women's hours in factories to nine a day and fifty-four a week, and in 1913 a new night work law.[1]

The threefold sequence of events—the shirtwaist strike of 1909–10, the Triangle fire of 1911, and the well-publicized investigations of the FIC from 1911 to 1915—spurred a surge of concern for the woman worker and an impetus for labor reform, not just in New York but nationwide. Reformers capitalized on the moment. Empowered by *Muller v. Oregon* and a favorable political climate, the campaign for protective laws gained momentum; gen-dered laws assumed priority. By World War I, reformers had made solid strides. Many states had enacted maximum hours laws for women workers or enhanced old laws, some states had passed night work laws, and the courts had upheld both types of laws. In some instances, reformers even at-tained minimum wage laws for women workers and maximum hours laws for men. At the peak of the protectionist push, the Supreme Court on April 7, 1917, left in place two crucial Oregon laws, a ten-hour law that affected men in industry and an Oregon minimum wage law for women workers. The heady achievements of the post-*Muller* years, culminated by the double victory of 1917, signaled a triumph for reformers, especially for the ambi-tious women leaders of the NCL. Disfranchised but not without power, they had won legislators, judges, and opinion makers over to their cause.

World War I slowed but did not end the reformers' success. Protection-ists' most enduring coup of the World War I era was the start in 1920, just after the war's end, of the United States Women's Bureau. A part of the De-partment of Labor and an outgrowth of a wartime predecessor, the Woman in Industry Service, this agency gave women reformers a beachhead in the federal bureaucracy from which they could pursue and defend protectionist goals. The war era, however, also brought less auspicious developments for reformers that undercut their agenda, including the rise of antiprotectionist sentiment among women. By the early 1920s, the newly reorganized National Woman's Party proved an obstacle; so did a major Supreme Court case of 1923, *Adkins v. Children's Hospital*, where protectionists met a grievous setback. The hurdles that arose in the war era and soon after were not accidental. Rather, they reflected flaws in protectionist strategy that had been lying in wait; warning signals infiltrated even moments of triumph. Still, as the 1920s began, the protectionists had managed to make their mark in every state. They had also begun to revamp their arguments to meet changing times.

MAXIMUM HOURS CASES

After *Muller*, the status of the NCL rose exponentially. The league's main purpose was now to promote and defend protective laws. The Brandeis brief served publicity purposes. Lawyers, colleges, reform organizations, and state commissions requested copies of it, which the NCL provided. The Russell Sage Foundation, founded in 1907, funded publication and distribution of the brief as well as new research on worker fatigue, undertaken by Josephine Goldmark. Headquartered in New York City, the NCL profited from other fortuitous circumstances, including, after 1912, a forum for their views at the New York State FIC hearings, at which Kelley and Goldmark testified. Year by year, the NCL's influence expanded. As states passed new protective laws, Brandeis and Goldmark collaborated to defend them. Brandeis briefs, which proved formidable weapons in court, grew in girth as the data mounted.[2]

Galvanized by both reformers and local labor organizations, state legislatures surged into action, and laws to protect women workers held center stage. Between 1908 and 1917, nineteen states and the District of Columbia passed women's hours laws, and the twenty states that already had such laws enhanced them. Sometimes legislators lowered the hours limits (as in New York, for instance), or extended the laws to affect women in nonfactory jobs such as stores (as in Illinois, for instance) or in hospitals (as in California). Entrepreneurs affected by protective measures—such as box makers, candy makers, lock makers, milliners, hotel owners, and others—relentlessly challenged them. The typical challenger was an employer who had intentionally defied a law, often joined by one or more employees; together they contended that limits of women's hours of work violated their rights.[3]

An Illinois case paved the way. In 1909, Illinois for the second time enacted a women's hours law, less stringent than the eight-hour law of 1893, which the state supreme court had rejected. The new law, passed after a vigorous campaign by the Illinois labor movement and local reformers, provided a ten-hour limit for women workers. To test the 1909 law, the Chicago paper box manufacturer W. E. Ritchie, who had challenged the law in 1893, challenged it again. This time, two employees joined the suit, Anna Kusserow and Dora Windeguth, ages forty-five and thirty-two. Factory owner Ritchie, who employed 750 women (in a well-lit and well-ventilated factory, he claimed), argued that he needed far more than ten hours of work a day in the rush season. Brandeis and Goldmark produced a six-hundred-page brief, which included new data on women workers that Goldmark had collected. In *Ritchie v. Wayman* (1910), the Illinois Supreme Court upheld the law, reversing the 1895 *Ritchie* decision, which Florence Kelley had so vehemently denounced. The court accepted the premise of the Brandeis brief about common knowledge: "It is known to all men (and what we know as men we cannot profess to be ignorant of as judges) that woman's physical structure and the performance of her maternal functions place her at a great disadvantage in the battle for life." Had the NCL done nothing else beyond its victory in *Ritchie v. Wayman*, Kelley told league members in 1910, "our eleven years existence would be justified by this alone." To publicize the Illinois brief, the NCL raised funds from its branches plus donations from the Illinois Women's Trade Union League and from the Illinois section of the American Association for Labor Legislation (AALL).[4]

Ritchie v. Wayman led to further victories. In 1910 challenges to women's hours laws arose in Virginia, Michigan, and Louisiana. State courts upheld all the laws. "The effect has been electrical," declared Josephine Goldmark in an NCL report. Most state decisions cited the very expansion of women's hours laws as a factor that legitimized them. Judges also confirmed the legislative prerogative. "It is for the legislature to determine when conditions exist calling for the exercise of the police power," proclaimed the Illinois Supreme Court in 1912. That year women's hours cases arose in Ohio, California, Washington, and again in Illinois, which had broadened its law in 1911 to cover the hours of women employees in stores, telephone and telegraph service, hotels, restaurants, transportation, and public utilities. Brandeis and Goldmark prepared the Ohio and Illinois briefs, and Brandeis argued the Illinois case before the state supreme court. The California eight-hour law, passed in 1911 and extended in 1913, covered not only women in factories but also women workers in hotels and hospitals, among other venues. Brandeis and California's attorney general successfully defended the law in two cases that reached the Supreme Court in 1915. In all instances, protection triumphed. Even in cases not argued by Brandeis, state lawyers made use of arguments developed by reformers. Similarly, judges relied on the *Muller* decision, usually by reiterating the mothers-of-the-race theme or sometimes by mentioning other points Justice Brewer made, such as the issue of compensatory justice.[5]

A minor New York case, the only challenge to the state's nine-hour law, illustrates the trend in women's maximum hours cases. In 1912, the owner of a candy factory in Brooklyn challenged the new state law that limited the hours of women and minors in factories, other than canneries, to nine hours a day and fifty-four hours a week. To defy the law, the factory owner, William Hoelderlin, employed three workers (a male minor, a female minor, and an adult woman) overtime. When convicted and imprisoned, he launched a habeas corpus proceeding in state court against the prison warden who held him in custody. Hoelderlin protested the exemption from the 1912 law of canneries, which he held were far more hazardous places of work than candy factories; he claimed that the *Williams* and *Lochner* precedents, which had both upset New York laws limiting hours of work, invalidated the current law, and he argued that freedom of contract was sacred from legislative intrusion. In *Hoelderlin v. Kane* (1913), Judge Abel E. Blackmar dismissed the factory owner's claims. "The power of the legislature to create a class, consisting of women only, and limit their hours of labor, is established in *Muller v. Oregon*," the judge declared. Women and minors, he explained, lacked access to freedom of contract because they faced competition with men, who were "physically better qualified for the struggle." Women's disadvantage had "compelled them to submit to conditions and terms of service which it cannot be assumed they would have freely chosen," Judge Blackmar continued. "Their liberty to contract to sell their labor may be but another name for involuntary service created by existing industrial conditions. A law, which restrains the liberty to contract, may tend to emancipate them by enabling them to act as they choose and not as competitive conditions compel." Finally, Judge Blackmar touted legislative authority: "All these questions are for the legislature, and for the legislature alone." His writ of habeas corpus denied, William Hoelderlin returned to jail, and in 1914, the Appellate Division affirmed his conviction. The Brooklyn district attorney's office informed Josephine Goldmark at the NCL of the court's decision.[6]

Even as reformers succeeded, potential trouble spots arose; the laws affected women factory workers unevenly. As in New York, state legislatures excluded canneries from women's hours laws. Claiming special needs as seasonal industries that dealt with highly perishable crops and other food products, canners pressured lawmakers to provide loopholes. Typically, women's hours laws either exempted canneries, totally or for a two to three month season, or else offered looser rules for them. Under New York's fifty-four-hour law of 1912, women could be employed up to sixty hours during the canning season (the season for peas, which ripened rapidly, for instance, ran from June 25 to August 6) and up to sixty-six hours for limited periods. According to economist Elizabeth Brandeis, workweeks for women in New York canneries during the canning season could reach eighty or ninety hours. In state after state, women in industry who faced the longest hours gained no respite from the law.[7] Nor, of course, did domestic workers. Employment in private homes fell outside the perimeter of protective law or reformers' concern.

As women's hours laws extended their reach beyond the factory to other workplaces (such as hotels, hospitals, and stores), courts assessed the relative hazards of different types of employment, drew distinctions among different categories of women workers, and considered instances in which the laws might impose injury. Two cases arose in California, which in 1911 passed an ambitious law requiring an eight-hour limit and a forty-eight-hour week for women workers in many workplaces (factories, laundries, stores, hotels, restaurants, telephone and telegraph offices). Support for the law came from trade union women, wives of trade union men, and most emphatically from the state federation of labor, which, unlike the AFL, endorsed laws to limit hours and indeed initiated them. A challenge arose when the proprietor of the Glenwood Hotel in Riverside, California, defied the law by requiring a chambermaid to work overtime. The law, claimed F. A. Miller, violated the state constitution, which prohibited discrimination between the sexes in pursuit of business or professions; it arbitrarily invaded freedom of contract; and it was "repugnant to the Fourteenth Amendment." It also discriminated against hotels, while excluding rooming houses engaged in the same sort of business; similarly, it ignored clerical workers in offices, food processing workers, and domestic workers in homes. The US Supreme Court eventually upheld the law in *Miller v. Wilson* (1915); the eight-hour day was not unreasonable, said the Court. Meanwhile, in response to attacks on the law, California unionists secured an amendment in 1913 that went yet further, extending the hours limit to women working in public lodging houses, apartment houses, hospitals, and places of amusement (canneries continued to escape). The labor movement also sought but failed to secure an eight-hour law affecting men.[8]

The enhanced California law of 1913 drew another challenge from employers. This second case, *Bosley v. McLaughlin* (1915), the last case that Brandeis argued before the Supreme Court, revealed the predicament of women professionals. Three trustees of the Samuel Meritt Hospital in Alameda, California (among them William B. Bosley), joined by Ethel E. Nelson, a hospital employee and a licensed pharmacist, challenged the state's eight-hour-a-day / forty-eight-hour-week law of 1911, which had been extended in 1913 to women in nonindustrial workplaces, including hospitals. A final proviso of the law made it inapplicable to "graduate nurses" in hospitals, that is, to women who had pursued a course of study in a nurses training school or hospital and received a diploma or certificate (as opposed to student nurses who were still engaged in such training or untrained women who worked as nurses). As they were specially qualified, these "graduate nurses" earned much more than women nursing students who worked in hospitals. The trustees, however, argued that all nurses, including student nurses, and indeed all women hospital employees, should be excluded from the hours limit, just as graduate nurses were. The hospital employed over eighty women and eighteen men. Of the eighty women, ten were "graduate nurses." The rest, mainly student nurses, included a bookkeeper, a matron, a housekeeper, a seamstress, and pharmacist Nelson. These eleven women, the trustees contended, "performed work that was in no manner different from that done by persons engaged in similar employments . . . and not employed in hospitals." The trustees defended their practice of imposing long hours on student nurses: the hospital gave the nurses free board, lodging, laundry, their course of study, and a monthly stipend. Their work was part of their training; their hours, therefore, should be determined by the "exigencies of the cases they were treating." Were the eight-hour day enforced for student nurses, claimed the trustees, the hospital would have to either close its school or take on far many more student nurses at far greater expense. Like pharmacist Nelson, who argued that the eight-hour law impinged on her freedom of contract, the trustees claimed that their freedom to contract had been violated in an arbitrary way.[9]

The Supreme Court once again upheld the law, decided the same day as *Miller v. Wilson*. Using a bulletin about nursing study from the US Department of Education, presented by California, as its "facts," the Court decided that the limit on student nurses' hours was not arbitrary. Whether the hours of women pharmacists or nurses in hospitals could be limited was "a matter for legislative not judicial control," the justices declared. The Fourteenth Amendment did not prevent the California legislature from imposing an eight-hour limit. Nor was the exemption of graduate nurses from that limit "so arbitrary... as to make the statute unconstitutional." Pharmacist Ethel Nelson's request for exclusion from the law was denied. No decision could be made about women doctors and surgeons, the Court explained, as "the question was still 'merely an abstract one.'"[10]

The case left open questions about the distinctions among women's vocations. Should pharmacist Nelson, a trained professional who also filled "storekeeping" functions, according to the Court, be classified with domestic workers? Would a woman physician have been classified along with "graduate nurses," who fulfilled administrative functions, and male doctors, or treated like pharmacist Nelson? Why were women domestic workers in hospitals and hotels subject to the eight-hour limit as opposed to domestic workers in private homes? Was it the nature of women in general or the qualifications of a particular type of woman worker or the circumstances of a specific type of job that determined the rationale for hours limits? The California cases suggested that maximum hours laws for women workers, though steadily upheld, might not be problem free. They also suggest the energy with which the state labor movement sought to preclude competition from women workers.

The Supreme Court again upheld classification by sex in 1912 in the case of Quong Wing, a Montana man who ran a hand laundry. The state law that imposed a quarterly tax on laundries exempted steam laundries, that is, laundry businesses run by white people, and women who worked alone or in pairs, also white. The law in effect taxed Chinese men. Quong Wing sued the county treasurer who collected his tax on grounds of sex discrimination. Like the state courts, the Supreme Court upheld the Montana law. "If the state finds a ground of distinction in sex, that is not without precedent," said Justice Holmes in *Quong Wing v. Kirkendall* (1912). "The Fourteenth Amendment does not interfere by creating a fictitious equality where there is a real difference." The *Quong Wing* decision reinforced classification by sex as set forth in *Muller*. Still, the law could be upset if "attacked in a different way," Holmes suggested. The Supreme Court sent the case back to Montana where state courts in 1913 declared the laundry tax unconstitutional on grounds of race discrimination: it targeted only the Chinese. Quong Wing's plight led to a legal situation in which issues of race and sex converged. In this instance, race discrimination, barred by the Fourteenth Amendment, disqualified the Montana law; classification by sex remained in place.[11]

The challenges that single-sex maximum hours laws posed detracted little from their triumph. By 1920, forty-three states, the District of Columbia, and Puerto Rico had maximum hours laws for women workers; in thirteen of these places the laws required eight-hour days or forty-eight-hour weeks

or both.[12] Night work laws, in contrast, were from the outset more problematic, both for their proponents and for the women they affected.

NIGHT WORK LAWS

Night work laws excluded women from factory work from 10:00 p.m. to 6:00
a.m. and sometimes for longer periods, or else limited the hours that women
could work at night and/or the type of work they could do. After 1900, the
anti-night-work crusade gained force. An international convention on night
work for women in Berne, Switzerland, in 1906 and the widespread acceptance of night work bans in western Europe—twelve European nations
signed the night work ban at Berne in 1906—galvanized the cause. By 1920,
twelve states barred women from working at night in specific occupations;
six states (Delaware, Kansas, Maryland, Nebraska, New Hampshire, Wisconsin) limited the numbers of hours (to eight or twelve) that women could
work at night. The laws, as historian Alice Kessler-Harris shows, created a
crazy quilt of rules; the rules varied in both the types of work covered and
in the degree of restrictions on hours.[13]

Far fewer states enacted night work laws than maximum hours laws. But
night work laws played a vital role in the reformers' agenda; they were useful if not imperative to enforce maximum hours laws. With a night work
ban in place, a woman could not work two shifts in succession at the same
place or split shifts (well-paid short shifts of five or six hours late at night
between day and night shifts) without detection. "When inspectors find
women at work at a late hour in the evening they cannot tell the total duration of hours that the woman has been working," Josephine Goldmark told
New York's Factory Investigating Committee in 1912. "Unless they remain
on the premises all day long they cannot tell how long the work has been
going on." Without night work bans, in Goldmark's view, "the difficulties of
inspection become almost insuperable." Moreover, she noted, "when the law
had been violated, the statements of neither employer nor employees can
be relied on." In Pittsburgh, researcher Elizabeth Butler found that inspectors could not enforce Pennsylvania's twelve-hour law because the state had
never imposed a night work ban.[14] Night work laws did not guarantee enforcement of maximum hours laws; still, they seemed to help factory inspectors, reformers believed.

But the practical need for night work laws rarely surfaced in protectionist arguments. More often, reformers contended that night work imperiled
women workers' health and morals. Night work, they claimed, increased

morbidity and mortality, lowered vitality, and led to "loss of appetite, head-ache, anemia, weakness of female functions." It ruined not only women workers' health but also that of their children. Night work bans were needed, Josephine Goldmark claimed, to insure adequate rest at night; daytime sleep lacked "restoring power." Did the hazards to health from work at night affect men as well? Sometimes Goldmark argued, as in 1912, that night work should be banned entirely for both men and women, a proposal that if effected would shut down entire sectors of industry. Before the FIC, in contrast, a year later, Goldmark contended that women who worked at night in candy factories and bookbinderies could be replaced by men. Florence Kelley agreed. "There are enough men in this country to work at night," she told the FIC in 1912. "Some of the men who can't take care of their wives and children could do their work at night, and they ought to have a monopoly of it, because they can influence legislation for their protection, and they can organize.... They can take care of themselves.[15]

Whatever reformers' rationales, night work laws marked a tipping point between protection and restriction, or rather a sharp slide into restriction. For several groups of women workers, night work bans clearly inflicted hardships. In some instances, night work represented an opportunity to pursue a well-paid trade, such as printing, or a chance for high tips, as in the case of waitresses. In far more instances, night work made paid work possible for mothers of young children, who cared for those children during the day. In study after study, reformers found that night workers were mothers. The pattern emerged among mill workers in a New York state twine factory explored by the New York's Factory Investigating Commission in 1913. Of the one hundred women surveyed, eighty-two were married or widowed; seventy-five had children, most of them under school age; and mothers worked at night in order to take care of children during the day. "N. D. wants to do night work on account of baby," researchers reported. "N. T. is nursing her baby now and would rather work nights so that she can feed the baby in the daytime." Mothers' desire for night work, however, the FIC reported, was misguided. Commission investigators saw only dangers to health, such as those of the cannery worker who labored seventeen hours in a row or the practice of early shifts that started at midnight so that workers—such as one at a New York bookbindery—worked a complete shift on each of two days consecutively. The FIC blamed both the workers (for ignorance) and their employers (for greed): "Ignorant women can scarcely be expected to realize the dangers not only to their own health but to that of the next generation from such inhuman usage."[16]

The link of mothers and night work emerged again in 1918 to NCL researchers who surveyed wage-earning women in nineteen textile mills in Rhode Island, where legislators had rejected three successive night work bills. Visiting 244 women at home, the investigators asked what circumstances had led them into night work. Among the respondents, 135 were married, eighty single, and twenty-nine widowed, deserted, or divorced. The reason given for employment was the high cost of living; the reason given for working at night was to be with children during the day. Of the married women, only sixteen lacked children. One hundred and sixty women had children under school age. Night work caused neglect of children, Florence Kelley claimed. "These children are not only not mothered, never cherished, they are nagged and buffeted," she wrote. "Their mothers are not superwomen." But children were the reason most women worked at night in the first place. In Chicago, Mary McDowell, a University of Chicago settlement worker, studied forty-six mothers, 90 percent with children under school age, who worked at night in packinghouses. Laboring for ten-hour shifts, the women used their hours at home to do housework and to care for husbands and children. Causes of taking night work included "insufficient earnings of the husband to maintain the family in food," "sickness of the husband, resulting in his unemployment," and "debts due to sickness in family." These women were desperate. McDowell concluded that if mothers of under-school-age children were fired, it would be a good step. Dismissal would not solve their problems but it would let them conserve their health and strength.[17] The critical attitude toward mothers who worked at night reflected a conservative streak in protectionist sentiment that spurned the prospect of working mothers, day or night.

New York reformers sought a new decision on night work laws, which had been invalidated by *People v. Williams* (1907). That case had upset a state law of 1903 that barred women in factory work between 9:00 p.m. and 6:00 a.m. on the grounds that "men and women now stand alike in their constitutional rights" and because nothing in the language of the law suggested "the purpose of promoting health." Several factors, however, revived reformers' hopes for a night work ban—the *Muller* decision; the subsequent campaigns of New York reformers, especially Josephine Goldmark at the NCL and Mary Van Kleeck at Russell Sage; and the investigations of New York's Factory Investigating Commission. All provided new data about night work hazards. In 1913, spurred by an FIC report, New York passed a law that banned night work in factories between 10:00 p.m. and 6:00 a.m. A test case soon arose. Factory inspectors targeted the Charles Schweinler Press, a thriving downtown Manhattan corporation with over nine hundred employees, men and women, and a block-square ten-story plant that printed and bound popular magazines, among them *McClure's Magazine*, a leading muckraking publication. The lawyer who took Charles Schweinler's case, a former city magistrate, represented a dozen large printing firms.[18]

Charged with violating the law, the Charles Schweinler Press was convicted at a Court of Special Sessions of New York City and given a suspended sentence. A second charge against Schweinler began moving through the state courts in 1914 and soon reached New York's highest court, the Court of Appeals. Brandeis and Goldmark added four hundred pages to a brief prepared by the state's attorney general. The expanded brief summarized night work research and showed "how fully the act is in line with worldwide legislation." It explained the dangers of night work for all workers, such as the problem of sleep in the daytime and the ill effects of lack of sunlight, a factor that had made no impact on the Supreme Court in the *Lochner* case. The state's brief then focused on damage specific to women workers, from "neglect of household duties during the day" to impairment of reproductive capacity ("effects on future generations"). Schweinler's lawyer responded with vigor. He attacked the social science approach of Brandeis/Goldmark brief. The data in the brief was "worthless," he charged; "the 'Facts' are not up to date." Schweinler's lawyer also argued that night work laws imposed hardship, curbed opportunity, and aroused antagonism among women workers. The New York Court of Appeals upheld the night work ban in *People v. Charles Schweinler Press* (1915), which reversed the *Williams* decision of 1907. The night work law, said the court, protected women workers' future offspring, who would "almost inevitably display . . . the unfortunate inheritance conferred upon them by physically broken-down mothers." The decision noted, however, that the law might "inflict unnecessary hardship on a great many women who neither ask [for] nor require its provisions." The US Supreme Court refused to hear an appeal, a major victory for reformers. Florence Kelley attributed the *Schweinler* triumph to the "thorough investigation" of the FIC.[19]

But the fight for night work laws presented a challenge. State legislatures resisted passing such laws, sometimes repeatedly, as in Rhode Island. Where night work bans did exist, as in New York, exemptions for a miscellany of vocations (elevator operators, reporters and writers on newspapers, some types of waitresses) peppered the legislative record. Within a few years, protest against night work bans arose among women employees who held (or had lost) well-paid jobs, such as New York's public transit company conductors after World War I. In the end, the battle for gendered night work laws remained precarious. As Schweinler's lawyer charged, the laws evoked continual opposition among women workers; in addition, the night work issue undercut the potential of single-sex law as an "entering wedge" for general law. The reformers' campaign to extend protection to men, waged concurrently, faced yet other problems.

PROTECTING MEN

While preparing the brief for Oregon in 1907, Josephine Goldmark began to amass data on men's health that Brandeis had excluded from the original Brandeis brief. In *Muller*'s wake, Goldmark, financed by Russell Sage, continued her research. The summary of her investigation, *Fatigue and Efficiency* (1912), drew widespread attention. Here, Goldmark pursued the "entering wedge" strategy—she offered data to justify the extension of maximum hours laws to men. But the book revealed a dilemma: It celebrated women's hours laws, with their gender-linked defense, *and*, at the same time, promoted new laws to affect all workers. The type of protection that benefited women workers, Goldmark argued (Justice Brewer's warning to the contrary), was needed by men in industry, too.

Goldmark presented her findings about men as "a new basis for labor legislation." Pushing beyond the reliance of the first Brandeis brief on impressionistic observation, Goldmark turned to physical science. The daughter of a doctor and research chemist, she entered the realm of science with confidence. Invoking chemistry, physics, and physiology, she sought to "show what fatigue is," to "explain the phenomena of overwork in working people," and to "bridge the gap between laboratory and factory." To bolster its scientific aura, so appealing to progressives, *Fatigue and Efficiency* presented statistics, charts, and case studies. The crux of the book concerned the nature of fatigue and its applicability to men. Goldmark discussed the increasing pace and complexity of industrial work; the impact of overwork on both women and men; problems of law enforcement; and finally, the hazards of night work, which, she now argued, should be imposed on neither women nor men. Some of the trades that Goldmark discussed were those in which women predominated or else labored in significant numbers—textiles, the needle trades, telephone work, shoemaking. Other studies referred solely to male workers—to coal miners in Pennsylvania, Ohio, and Illinois, for instance, who, in eight-hour days, performed more than miners elsewhere with ten-hour days. Goldmark cast a global net. Similar studies of male workers in Europe—ironworkers in Manchester, England;

chemical workers in Liege, Belgium; and workmen on optical lenses in Jena, Germany—supported her argument for shorter hours.[20]

A model progressive document, *Fatigue and Efficiency* relied on expertise; in the preface Columbia University physiologist and professor Frederic Lee, whose research on toxicity had appeared in the first Brandeis brief, offered words of support. In the progressive spirit, Goldmark also tried to mediate between employers and employees. Taylorism, or "scientific management," a scheme for industrial productivity embraced by progressives, might serve the interests of both, she suggested. (Brandeis had endorsed Taylorism in 1910.) Maximum hours laws, too, would serve the needs of labor and management. Overwork, Goldmark claimed, not only destroyed worker health but also impeded production. Hours regulation, she argued, would not ruin industry, as manufacturers' associations insisted. On the contrary, "Shorter hours improve health," and "improved health and efficiency" led to "higher output." Why did this occur? Because "within certain limits the workman adapts himself automatically to the shortened day by increasing his speed and efforts, without noticeably increasing his exertions." Thus, Goldmark concluded, "Economic efficiency rises and falls with workers' physical efficiency, and whatever contributes to the latter tends to support the former." Employers stood only to gain. Hours limits would invigorate workers, boost productivity, and increase profits.[21]

Similarly, Goldmark sought to defuse the claims of potential foes, including the claim that men and women deserved equal rights. Goldmark found this a bogus argument against protective laws. "Superficially viewed, the great movement to obtain for women, in all fields, rights from which they have been debarred, might appear inconsistent with the efforts to protect one sex as contrasted with the other, but this is a fundamental misconception," she contended. "It ignores the fact that protection of health has never been held a bar to the efficacy of men as citizens.... Why, then, should similar restrictions—wider and more inclusive for women—operate against their dignity or value as citizens? Their physical endowments and special functions make the protection of their health even more necessary than the protection of men's health." To Goldmark, science justified hours laws for all workers, but women remained a more vulnerable class; their protection was more imperative. "Shortening the work day is something that legislation can effect for women and children today," she concluded, "for men doubtless in the future."[22]

As Goldmark collected her evidence, maximum hours laws for men in industry multiplied. By 1912, most states had passed laws to protect at least *some* categories of male workers—first, those in jobs that threatened their own safety or public safety. Many laws limited men's hours in mines, saw-mills, blast furnaces, and on railroads, for instance; *Holden v. Hardy* paved the way for such laws. Men who worked in telegraph offices, which served the public, also fell under protective rules. A second category of laws affected men employed by state or federal governments. Laws that fell into this category, though irrelevant to health or safety, were "easy to secure," economist Elizabeth Brandeis (Louis D. Brandeis's younger daughter and an astute analyst of protective laws) later explained; legislators and the public shared doubts as to "whether strikes to secure shorter hours could be used against the government." But *Lochner* cast a long shadow: states avoided enacting maximum hours laws for *all* men in industry. Exceptions occurred. Even as the labor movement lost interest in general hours laws, West Coast unions (California, Washington, and Oregon) pressed strongly for such laws. In January 1913, the Oregon legislature passed a general hours law. The law, supported by progressives and the state labor movement, provided a maximum ten-hour day for all industrial workers (all "persons" in manufacturing) but allowed employees to work overtime for another three hours if their employers paid them time and a half.[23]

The overtime provision, a seeming afterthought, was crucial. First, this provision embodied a specific intent: to deter employers from demanding long hours. "Time and a half" was an enforcement strategy. The threat to employers was weak—they risked little—but it was present. Second, "overtime" had longtime roots in labor law, mainly in laws that applied to men. Nineteenth-century maximum hours laws for laborers and mechanics permitted contracts for longer hours. Laws that affected employees at public works, such as a New York law of 1870, mentioned extra pay for overtime hours; so did some laws affecting labor on railroads and street railways. Most recently, calls for overtime pay had arisen briefly among strikers at the Lawrence, Massachusetts, textile mills in 1912 (mill workers at one point included double pay for overtime hours among their demands) and in 1913 among Oregon timber workers, who called for an eight-hour day with time and a half for overtime. "Overtime" was a labor demand suddenly catapulted into a "general" law. Third, although the Oregon law seemed to be gender neutral—that is, to apply to all "persons" in manufacturing—it soon applied almost entirely to male persons. Why? In June 1913, about six months after the Oregon legislature passed the 1913 law, lawmakers established an Industrial Welfare Commission, with the power to set maximum hours for women workers at or under the maximum set by statute. The IWC at once lowered maximum hours for women workers in industry to nine hours a day and forty-eight hours a week, with no loopholes for overtime at time and a half; the IWC regulation took priority over the "general" law. Thus the "general" law of 1913, with its option of extra pay for overtime work, applied virtually only to men. Ironically, while "extending" protection to men, Oregon legislators in 1913 in fact insured a distinction between men and women workers.[24]

Finally, the 1913 law underscored a shift in the meaning of the word "overtime." To Josephine Goldmark in *Fatigue and Efficiency* in 1912, "overtime" had only harmful connotations. It meant compulsory extra hours of work, "too long a stretch of working hours," imposed by employers on powerless employees. It also connoted specters of irregular work, of uninterrupted stints of long hours followed by underemployment or a slack season with no work. It involved no extra pay. With the Oregon law of 1913, the meaning changed. Thereafter "overtime" usually referred to time-and-a-half pay, as it did when inscribed in New Deal laws. The goal of "overtime" in 1913 persisted through midcentury: to discourage extra hours of work by raising their cost to employers. But eventually, in World War II and after, contrary to reformers' expectations, the gist of "overtime" would mutate again; it came to represent a convenience for employers and an opportunity for workers. The addition to Oregon's 1913 law was thus (unexpectedly) a concept in transition. The distinction it provided between men's work and women's work would be enduring.[25]

Not surprisingly, a challenge to the unprecedented 1913 law arose at once. Franklin Bunting, owner of a flour mill, was convicted of violating both sections of the law; his mill had employed a worker over thirteen hours without overtime pay. Bunting's lawyers charged that the law was less an hours law than a wage law—it was not a ten-hour law but a "thirteen hour law designed solely for the purpose of compelling the employer . . . to pay more for labor than the actual market value thereof." Defeated in the Oregon courts, Bunting appealed to the Supreme Court. The NCL now had the opportunity to put to use the new evidence about men and overwork that Josephine Goldmark had collected. Acting on behalf of Oregon, Brandeis, again with Goldmark as coauthor, produced a 1021-page brief on the damage wrought by overwork. When Brandeis joined the Supreme Court in 1916, Felix Frankfurter (1882–1965), a protégé who had joined Brandeis in his NCL work and who now taught at Harvard Law School, took over his role as NCL counsel. Frankfurter added a preface to the brief and argued the case.[26]

Instead of dwelling on the liabilities of workers, the theme that dominated cases involving maximum hours for women workers, Frankfurter stressed the hazards of industry. "Science has demonstrated that there is no sharp difference in kind as to the effect of labor on men and women," he wrote in a 1916 article. There was only a difference in "degree": both sexes needed protection if for different reasons. "[O]nce we cease to look upon the regulation of women in industry as exceptional, the law's graciousness to a disabled class, and shift the emphasis from the fact that they are *women* to the fact that it is *industry*, and the whole relationship of industry to the community which is regulated, the whole problem is seen from a totally different perspective," Frankfurter contended.[27] The "totally different perspective" was crucial; Frankfurter had vaulted over the gender gap. Industry endangered all workers! He promoted the new insight in his preface to the *Bunting* brief, as well as in oral argument.

Using Goldmark's data from *Fatigue and Efficiency*, the *Bunting* brief promoted a shorter workday for men. Citing the many laws that already limited men's hours in hazardous workplaces and government jobs, the brief sought, through "facts and statistics," to show the toll of overwork on worker health and thus on American "vitality, efficiency, and prosperity." Health was the foundation of the state, the brief declared. "No nation can progress if its workers are crippled by overexertion." Overlong hours of factory labor injured the nerves and senses; induced degenerative ailments and premature old age; caused industrial accidents, especially at the workday's end; and led to moral degeneration. The shorter workday, in contrast, curbed intemperance, improved health, helped Americanize the foreign-born, and fostered an educated electorate. "If democracy is to flourish," the brief declared, "the education of the citizen . . . must be a continuous process to enable men to understand great issues as they arise." In the *Muller* brief, the overwork of women injured generations yet unborn; in the *Bunting* brief, the overwork of men thwarted the democratic process. In passing, finally, the *Bunting* brief made another salient point: the ten-hour day was virtually in place in Oregon. In 1909, 93.7 percent of the state's workers were employed ten hours a day or fewer. Thus the law would "make compulsory a schedule of hours which the great majority of employers have already adopted of their own accord." The widespread adoption of the ten-hour day, claimed the brief, coincided with "the remarkable development of Oregon's industrial prosperity."[28]

In oral argument, Frankfurter underscored Oregon's contention that the law of 1913 was an hours law, not a wage law. The majority opinion in *Bunting v. Oregon* (1917) returned to this question: Was the state regulation a wage law in disguise? No, said the Court. The purpose of the law was not to set wages but "to deter by its burden." "It may not achieve its end, but its insufficiency cannot change its character from penalty to permission." Moreover, the law imposed "only a mild penalty." Beside that, "New policies are usually tentative in their beginnings [and] advance in firmness as they advance in acceptance." The *Bunting* decision ignored Frankfurter's claim that industry imperiled worker health. Instead, the decision quoted the conclusion of the Oregon Supreme Court that the law was not arbitrary because "the custom in our industries does not sanction a longer service than ten hours per day." According to the US Supreme Court, the Oregon law of 1913 was reasonable (as the reformers' brief had pointed out) because the ten-hour day already existed in Oregon. Indeed, the Court noted, the ten-hour day existed throughout the western industrial world.[29]

By affirming the Oregon law, the Supreme Court in *Bunting v. Oregon* (1917) fulfilled the reformers' long-sought goal: it extended protective law to men in all sorts of industrial work. In so doing, the Court had tacitly overruled the *Lochner* decision, or seemed to have done so. This was an extraordinary precedent. According to reformers' plans, *Bunting* should have encouraged other states to enact similar laws that protected men in industry. But none did. In 1914, state federations of labor in California, Oregon, and Washington promoted eight-hour laws "to cover all industries," but these efforts all sank in referenda. Thereafter, states enacted no "general" laws to curb working hours. Only in the 1930s did Congress do so. *Bunting*, thus, unintentionally, marked the end of a campaign, not a beginning; maximum hours laws for women had served as an "entering wedge" for *one* "general" law, but they failed to inspire any similar laws. Why not?

Economist Elizabeth Brandeis tackled this question in the 1930s. The Oregon ten-hour law was a feeble general-hours law, she noted, one that "scarcely provided a firm precedent for stronger laws." In addition, the public viewed the prospect of men's hours laws with apathy. For the most part, Brandeis wrote, with understatement, "the general public was never particularly interested in hours legislation for adult men." Yet another factor was the aversion of organized labor to "general" laws. Until 1914, the AFL (which by then endorsed hours limits for women and children) had paid lip service to eight-hour laws for men, long a goal of the labor movement. But in 1914 the AFL reversed itself; it claimed that its support had been only for public works laws and in 1915 reiterated its opposition to "general" hours laws. AFL animosity to such laws, as Elizabeth Brandeis contended, reflected the views of Samuel Gompers and of skilled workers, such as those in printing and construction: "Many of the skilled trades which had secured shorter hours through trade union action were strongly opposed, fearing that such legislation would weaken their unions." Were the skilled workers of the AFL selfish in their opposition to "general" laws? Not necessarily, Elizabeth

Brandeis answered: "They may have realized that statutes limiting hours are of all labor laws the most difficult to enforce; that inspection in this field has rarely proved an entirely effective instrument; that workers (lured by overtime pay) are altogether too apt to connive with employers in violating hours laws." The skilled workers, she concluded, were "in a measure correct, in their belief that the protection apparently secured for unorganized workers through hours laws might prove somewhat illusory."[30] To skilled men, Elizabeth Brandeis pointed out, maximum hours laws seemed at once futile and potentially harmful.

Bunting gratified reformers and eventually proved a valuable precedent—a mainstay of the "entering wedge" strategy—but more immediately, it lacked impact, and reformers veered off into another campaign. Here lay Florence Kelley's talent—to attack at once on several fronts. If one effort stalled, another beckoned. The new campaign involved the far more controversial cause of the minimum wage.

THE MINIMUM WAGE

Miss B. works at the 5c, 10c, and 15c store, earns $4.50 a week. Said that her salary was so small that she has to work for her room and board. Gets up in the morning and gets breakfast before she goes to work, washes dishes when she comes home at night, does family's washing and ironing on Sunday. Her people are unable to help her. . . .

Miss I., working in candy factory, $5 per week, states that after standing on her feet for ten hours at her work, she is required to sweep the floor in the evening. Lives with her mother; says that if she didn't, she could not work at this salary. . . .

Miss K., . . . in fruit cannery, earns $4.50 per week. She lives 15 blocks from working place, but walks back and forth because she can't afford to ride. . . .

Miss N., working in department store at $7.50 per week, gives a moderate, reasonable list of expenditures. Said that if she didn't have help, she would starve, or what is worse, get her living some other way.[31]

These "Personal Stories" and many others culminated researcher Caroline J. Gleason's report of 1913 for the Oregon Consumers' League on the need for a minimum wage law for women workers in Oregon. Like her counterparts in other states, Gleason employed the latest social science techniques. To gather data, her team of field-workers distributed questionnaires to women workers in Portland's factories, stores, and offices. They requested from employers wage data and views about the feasibility of the minimum wage. They became undercover workers themselves in twelve factories to verify the data they had assembled. Gleason, for instance, took a job for several days in a Portland paper box factory, where she glued labels onto shoeboxes. Finally, to determine the cost of living, the researchers visited boarding-houses, priced clothing in department stores, and set up subcommittees to collect data in Oregon towns. Overall, the Oregon research team reached 8,736 workers, mainly in Portland. Gleason's report concluded that $10 a week was "the least on which the average girl can support herself decently." Women workers in Oregon, however, earned far less. "The average girl receives wages which are inadequate to her support, and consequently would face the end of the year in debt if she does not receive support from her family or some outside source," Gleason concluded. "This shows the extent to which industries employing women are parasitic in character."[32]

Minimum wages for industrial workers, men and women, first arose in New Zealand (1894), Australia (1896), and Great Britain (1906). In the United States, the minimum wage crusade targeted only women. The NCL began studies of women's wages in 1907; in 1908–09, Florence Kelley explored the issue with British reformer Beatrice Webb; in 1909–10, Kelley adopted the minimum wage as an NCL goal; in 1911, the NWTUL joined the campaign. In 1912, Massachusetts enacted the first minimum wage law, a wary, non-compulsory law for women workers; the legislature chopped off the law's enforcement provisions. In 1913, eight western states enacted the minimum wage for women workers—California, Oregon, Washington, Colorado, Utah, Nebraska, Minnesota, and Wisconsin. Seven more states and the District of Columbia followed. Some states set a fixed minimum wage; most states, like Oregon, set up commissions that then established minimum wages.[33]

The Oregon law of 1913, drafted by the NCL and AALL, and endorsed by the Oregon Consumers' League, established the state's Industrial Welfare Commission (IWC), defined its powers, and provided for the setting of a minimum wage, maximum hours, and other labor standards. To Oregon reformers the minimum wage was imperative to protect women workers from employer exploitation. "In any justly and reasonably organized society each industry should support the people who are employed in it," declared Rev. Edwin O'Hara, an OCL leader and minimum wage crusader. In "parasitic industries," in contrast, "the burden is placed upon the shoulders of the very portion of society least capable of bearing it," that is, workers and their families. Although Caroline Gleason found that $10 a week was the least upon which the average woman worker in Portland could "support herself decently," the Oregon Industrial Welfare Commission ignored this target.

The IWC recommended a nine-hour day, a fifty-six hour week, a lunch break, and a minimum wage of $8.64 a week for women workers in Portland factories and laundries. Here was the trademark, the selling point, of the Progressive Era minimum wage: humble and unassuming, it always fell short of what workers needed to get by. Following the Oregon precedent, state commissions set minimum wages that typically failed to cover the basic living costs determined by surveys.[34]

To NCL reformers, minimum wage laws for women workers were vital companions to maximum hours laws; without a minimum wage, some women workers who labored shorter hours lost income. Like gendered hours laws, moreover, the single-sex minimum age law was a stepping-stone to "general" law. It set a precedent that could be extended to men. Kelley envisioned a minimum wage law for all workers, and in a 1912 article, urged conserving the family and the home with the male breadwinner as its economic support. NCL leaders urged that the Oregon law of 1913 apply to men as well, but the Oregon league refused to promote such a broad measure. Reformers typically shifted back and forth between reasons why women workers needed the minimum wage and reasons why all workers needed it. "There is no logical reason for fixing it for the women," wrote Barnard College economist Emilie Hutchinson in 1919. "If the principle is sound for women's wages, it is also sound for men." But in the United States, she explained, minimum wage advocates saw "the question of wages, not primarily as a labor problem but as a sex problem." Reformers could not abandon a strategy that worked. The reform machinery was in place to push for a single-sex minimum wage; as scholar Theda Skocpol points out, women-only arguments had thus far been effective. Surely, as Kelley argued, courts were "more likely to sustain a new application of state intervention if it were confined to women."[35]

But even in its gendered form, the minimum wage drew more animosity than maximum hours laws; legislators, labor leaders, and employers distrusted it. To the AFL, which had approved maximum hours for women workers, the minimum wage would undercut collective bargaining and, more ominously, might lead to (or even *be*) a maximum wage. "[W]hen government compels men to work for a minimum wage scale that means slavery," AFL leader Samuel Gompers declared. In several states, such as Massachusetts, labor supported reformers in their minimum wage campaigns, but typically wariness exceeded approval. In California, women garment workers voiced suspicion of the minimum wage and so did the state labor movement.[36] To employers, the minimum wage, an unprecedented danger, was far more ominous than maximum hours laws, which rarely involved serious costs (especially since the latter were difficult to enforce and often violated). Government tampering with wages, however, impinged on profits and undercut control. Wage fixing, said critics, was as illegitimate as price fixing. States might regulate the *conditions* of labor, such as hours of work, they conceded, but not the *cost* of labor; the *Bunting* court had made this same point. Moreover, the minimum wage reflected not the value of the work but the alleged need of the worker. Finally, to its foes, the minimum wage promoted the interests of one class (workers) at the expense of another (employers). "This sort of legislation is a new expression of the paternalistic and socialistic tendencies of the day," charged Rome G. Brown, the lawyer who challenged the 1913 Oregon law. It represented "the division of property between those who have and those who have not, and the leveling of fortunes by division under government supervision."[37]

Testifying before New York State's FIC in 1914, just after appearing before the US Supreme Court, Rome G. Brown worked his way into the anti-minimum-wage argument gradually, as if climbing a flight of stairs. At the start, on the bottom stair, he avowed his approval of noncompulsory minimum wage statutes, as in Massachusetts, that encouraged employers to take "voluntary" action. The compulsory minimum wage, in contrast, Brown claimed, would never work; it was "absolutely futile to enforce a spirit of cooperation, benevolence, or any other good quality on the part of the employer by legislation." (The call for "voluntary" action by employers remains a conservative tactic.) Moreover, the minimum wage made "the amount of the wage to be paid entirely independent of the . . . work that the employee does." Furthermore, giving the state the power to enforce a minimum wage also "established the power to fix a maximum wage" and thereby, "you have established a principle under which it is possible to create what is slavery." (Samuel Gompers, he noted, agreed with him.) Climbing higher on his staircase of argument, Brown turned to the damage that the minimum wage would foist upon workers, employers, and the public. It would reward poorer workers at the expense of better ones—"officially increase the wages of the lower class of labor to decrease the wages of the higher class of labor." It would force employers to contribute the "difference between what persons earn and what it costs them to live." Why should employers bear such a burden? "It does not reason out." Finally, the minimum wage would injure the public: The higher cost of labor would increase prices and thus the cost of living, leading to further hikes in wages, and finally making it necessary for the state to control prices. Thus the minimum wage would lead to "fixing the maximum price." Brown had one last point: Low wages did not cause immorality among women; rather, the minimum wage itself was immoral, insofar as it deprived low-paid workers of employment. Reaching the pin-

nacle of his argument, Brown declared the minimum wage a "social menace," a "compulsory division of property," and a prelude to socialism.[38]

Oregon's 1913 law, which Rome G. Brown challenged, led to the first test
case of the minimum wage. Frank Stettler, a paper box manufacturer who
had repeatedly violated the law, applied for an injunction against its enforcement; the Industrial Welfare Commission, he claimed, assumed powers that
belonged to the legislature. (Stettler had a special grievance against the law;
investigator Caroline Gleason had taken a job in his factory in order to collect data to support it.) One of Stettler's workers, Elmira Simpson, also sued
the state, because, she claimed, if the state imposed the minimum wage of
$8.64, she would lose her $6 a week job. The implication of her claim: any
employer could find any worker unworthy of the minimum wage and dismiss her. In 1914 the Oregon Supreme Court upheld the minimum age law.
It was common knowledge, said the court, that low wages demoralized the
public and the individuals concerned. The Oregon court announced the
Stettler and *Simpson* decisions (the cases traveled together) on the same day
that it announced the *Bunting* decision, a crucial victory for reformers. Stettler appealed.[39]

To defend Oregon, Brandeis and Goldmark prepared a 968-page brief on
the minimum wage. The *Stettler* brief argued for a "living wage," which meant
enough money to cover basic expenses plus a small amount for recreation
and saving. "No one can maintain health whose earnings are too small to
afford the necessities of existence," the brief declared. As in the *Muller* brief,
Brandeis and Goldmark discussed the scope of the problem, explained the
effectiveness of the remedy, and sought to rebut potential critics. The minimum wage, they argued, would not lead to the dismissal of women workers
and their replacement by men, nor would it injure employers. On the contrary, it would impel efficiency, spur use of new machinery, revitalize management, boost worker strength, increase output, enable "the enlightened
employer to pay higher wages without fear of underbidding by competition," and "bring industry up to the best prevailing standards in each trade."
As a US government agency quoted in the brief declared in 1916, "high
profits are not dependent on low labor costs.[40]

The *Stettler* brief relied in part on the winning argument of the *Muller*
brief. "[W]hen the health of women has been injured in industrial work,"
the *Stettler* brief contended, "the deterioration is handed down to succeeding generations." Like the *Muller* brief, the *Stettler* brief presented the opinions of authorities abroad, going back to the early nineteenth century. But
in the *Stettler* brief, Brandeis and Goldmark included many excerpts from
the most recent studies of state industrial commissions and federal agencies.

The new up-to-date "facts" from modern authorities, the data from social workers, bureaucrats, and academics, supplied statistics about the plight of underpaid workers, especially women; the need for food, shelter, and medical care; and the positive impact of the minimum wage.[41]

What impact did the updated nature of the "facts" have on the outcome of the Oregon minimum wage cases? Perhaps none. In his oral argument, one of the last he would make before the Supreme Court before his appointment to it, Brandeis explained his contention that the nature of the "facts"—and even their veracity—was irrelevant. The explanation arose toward the end of oral argument when a justice asked whether the Brandeis brief in *Stettler*, which contained all the data supporting minimum wage legislation, also contained data opposing it. "I conceive it to be absolutely immaterial what may be said against such laws," Brandeis responded.

> Each one of these statements contained in the brief in support of the contention that this is wise legislation, might upon further investigation be found to be erroneous, each conclusion of fact may be found afterward to be unsound—and yet the constitutionality of the act would not be affected thereby. This court is not burdened with the duty of passing upon the disputed question whether the legislature was wise or unwise, or probably wise or unwise, in enacting this law. The question is merely whether . . . you can see that the legislators had no ground on which they could, as reasonable men, deem this legislation appropriate to abolish or mitigate the evils believed to exist or apprehended. If you cannot find that, the law must stand.

With this argument, Brandeis presented his opponent-proof defense of protective laws: the burden of argument was on those who assailed the law. The only test of a law's legitimacy was whether the state legislature had a "reasonable" cause to believe that the act in question would have a desired effect on health, safety, or morals. Did the "facts" presented in reformers' briefs need to be true? Not necessarily. The truth of the facts did not matter.[42]

Reluctant to cope with the Oregon minimum wage cases in 1914, the Supreme Court let them marinate for three years. When Brandeis joined the Court in 1916, Felix Frankfurter added to the brief and reargued the case. On April 7, 1917, the same day it decided the *Bunting* case, the Supreme Court issued a split decision in the *Stettler* and *Simpson* cases, with no written opinion.[43] The 4–4 vote (Brandeis withdrew from deliberations) let the Oregon law stand. The minimum wage survived for the moment, though only barely; the decision did not set a binding precedent elsewhere (beyond Oregon), which meant that similar cases were bound to arise. The quasi-victory should have alerted reformers that the minimum wage was on precarious ground. But they pushed forward. Members of the NCL, the NWTUL, and women's clubs campaigned for the minimum wage in most of the jurisdictions where it was enacted. The impact of the minimum wage was muted. The states that passed minimum wage laws were not the most industrialized states; the wages set by state commissions never reached subsistence levels; and in the five states that had set the level of minimum wages in law, inflation soon sabotaged the wages imposed.[44] Foes of the minimum wage eagerly awaited their next chance to squelch it. Meanwhile, World War I disrupted the political climate that had thus far brought protectionists so much success.

WAR AND PEACE

"The gain made in the war was the practical demonstration of women's unsuspected industrial capacity," wrote reformer Mary Van Kleeck in 1921. "Hundreds of jobs ... became sexless." During World War I, women found work in the aircraft industry; in munitions factories; in iron, steel, and chemical plants; in public transit; and in other nontraditional fields. They also took white-collar jobs, in the federal civil service, in telegraph and telephone companies, and as bookkeepers and office workers. Women's labor in heavy industry was short-lived, as Van Kleeck observed. "Prejudices were laid aside ... but not shaken out of men's minds permanently." Women reformers, in contrast, secured a permanent gain: a fief in the federal government. In July 1918, fifteen months after the United States entered World War I, Congress established the Woman in Industry Service, an office in the Department of Labor, to "meet the needs of war production," to recruit women workers, and to "safeguard their health and efficiency" in "new and unaccustomed tasks." Like many other wartime agencies, the Woman in Industry Service reflected the Wilson administration's desire to cater to labor's demands. The new agency's underlying goal was to defend protective policies. "[T]he emergencies should not be met by sweeping away state labor laws," declared Van Kleeck, the agency's director.[45]

Van Kleeck (1883–1972) brought over a decade of experience to her job. A graduate of Smith, '04, impelled by Social Gospel impulses, she had worked as a member of New York's College Settlement on Rivington Street; then for the YWCA and its Industrial Work Program; and then for the Russell Sage Foundation, as director of its Department of Industrial Studies. A devotee of Taylorism and of social science research, Van Kleeck sought to explore "the effects of industrialization upon civilization" and "the status of women in industry." At Russell Sage, she had overseen investigations of working conditions, night work, and unemployment among New York City's women workers—milliners, bookbinders, and artificial flower makers—and promoted night work laws. As administrator of the Woman in Industry Service (and the highest woman employee in federal government), Van Kleeck faced contradictory demands: to speed up production, for instance, especially in hazardous occupations that suddenly lacked an adequate male labor pool, and to protect women workers' health. Mediating between conflicting requirements and commitments, Van Kleeck often made statements that moved simultaneously in opposing directions. The rapid surge in female employment in wartime, for instance, constituted the "peculiar problem of the war," she declared, and then immediately asserted that the war brought "wider public recognition of the need for female labor." Staking out a middle ground, the service might commission a study of night work laws (on one hand) and (on the other) consider wartime reprieves from such laws for states that no longer wanted any part of them.[46]

Under Van Kleeck's direction, the Woman in Industry Service shaped its distinctive identity and that of its successor, the US Women's Bureau. Beyond its primary mission—to protect protective laws for women workers—the new agency voiced concern with women's wages. Fearful that if women took on work once done by men for lower pay that female employment would be seen as a "menace," the Women In Industry Service pursued an equal pay agenda. "Women doing the same work as men should received equal wages," the agency declared. "Wages should be established on the basis of occupation and not on the basis of sex." Innovatively, the new agency announced an interest in the problem of race and in black women newly employed in World War I. It included in its staff a black woman "to work on the race problem from the point of view of women in industry." Concern with black women workers would continue with the wartime service's successor, the federal Women's Bureau (WB). Wage equality, declared a WB publication of 1922, should not rest "on the basis of either sex or race." The Woman in Industry Service also established a reputation as a watchdog, alert to women's health problems, as in the wartime Niagara Falls chemical industry, where it explored the impact of lead production on women workers. Finally, it sought to deal with "readjustment to peace," which meant the loss of profitable jobs for women workers (but renewed opportunity to impose protective laws).[47]

Significantly, the new agency—a federal "policy-making" body that lacked leverage over the states—had no real power. It coped with this handicap ingeniously, as would its successor, the Women's Bureau. First, the Woman in Industry Service regarded every minor gain as a major victory. Second, it interposed itself, wherever it could, even if powerless to make changes (as was typically the case), just to establish the habit—and prerogative—of interposition. Third, when action was impossible, as it usually was, it made studies and convened conferences. Fourth, it wove a chain of network affiliations—with tentacles in the states and in the federal executive departments, and with women's groups—its sisters in the NCL, WTUL, universities, women's clubs, and other venues. Above all, the Woman in Industry Service's paramount achievement was to perpetuate its own existence—to secure permanent status for a women's outpost in the federal government. When the US Women's Bureau began on July 1, 1920, without fanfare, it continued the mission of its predecessor, "to investigate and report . . . upon all matters pertaining to the welfare of women in industry." The exhaustive surveys and investigations of the WB would be phenomenal. Retiring from her post to care for her mother, Van Kleeck ceded her place to labor leader and NWTUL alumna Mary Anderson, who inherited her protectionist mantle. The Women's Bureau, though a federal agency and distinctive from the NCL, was its close relative; in the 1920s it opened a new front in the battle for protective laws.[48]

Beyond the auspicious founding of the Woman in Industry Service and the Women's Bureau, however, other World War I–era developments brought new problems for protectionists. Women workers made only temporary wartime gains in manufacturing; new opportunities arose mainly in white-collar work. But state legislators, prodded by an alarmed labor movement, enacted scores of new restrictive laws. Weight limits curtailed the types of jobs women might take; night work laws extended their reach to additional occupations. Exclusionary laws, which previously barred women mainly from mines and core industries, expanded to other types of work. Some new laws reflected NCL concern for safer workplaces and pressure from local consumers' leagues. New Jersey in 1917 barred women's employment on assembly lines that worked with dangerous chemicals. Elsewhere legislators sought to preserve jobs for men. Ohio in 1919 barred women from work as crossing watchmen, section hands, express drivers, molders, bellhops, taxi drivers (that ban failed in court in 1928), jitney drivers, and gas or electric meter readers; from work in blast furnaces or smelters, mines and quarries (except in offices), shoeshine parlors, bowling alleys, pool rooms, barrooms, saloons, and delivery services (wagons or automobiles); from operating freight or baggage elevators; from baggage or freight handling and "trucking of any kind"; and from jobs that involved frequent or repeated lifting of weights over twenty-five pounds. Ohio demonstrated the vast potential of single-sex laws to marginalize women workers.[49]

Opposition to protective laws, notably night work laws, arose among women workers. New York's women printers and streetcar workers denounced state laws that curtailed opportunity. In wartime, women had taken jobs on New York's street railways as conductors, ticket agents, and ticket collectors. After the war, the railway employees' union promoted a law to limit women workers to consecutive nine-hour days and to ban work after 10:00 p.m. In May 1919, over half of the 1,500 women street railway employees lost their jobs. Women printers in New York also assailed the state's night work ban. The remnant of women railway workers won exemption from protection, as did the women printers, eventually. But disgruntled workers of both groups mobilized in new organizations to support equal rights. The Women's League for Equal Opportunity (1915) and the Equal Rights Association (1917) declared their opposition to protective laws.[50]

Another obstacle to protectionist progress followed the ratification of the Nineteenth Amendment, which enfranchised women, in 1920. Suffragist Alice Paul reorganized the National Woman's Party (NWP), the wing of the suffrage movement that had picketed the White House in 1916 and had pressed for a federal woman suffrage amendment. The goal of the postwar NWP, Paul announced, would be legal equality for women. In 1921, Paul proposed a "blanket bill" to end sex discrimination in federal law and similar bills on the state level, all of which threatened protective laws. When the NWP began to draft an equal rights amendment (ERA), it sought several times to add a "saving clause" to exempt protective laws, it claimed, but each effort failed. By the end of 1921, the NWP had declared its opposition to single-sex protective laws.[51]

To Alice Paul and the NWP, woman suffrage represented a first step toward legal equality. To Florence Kelley, a member of the NWP until 1921, Alice Paul offered only "empty phrases about equality of opportunity." The factions of the women's movement split over strategies for change and colliding goals: labor standards and equal rights. A minimum wage case in the federal courts soon sharpened the division.[52]

ADKINS V. CHILDREN'S HOSPITAL (1923)

In 1918, after an NCL campaign, Congress enacted a minimum wage law for the District of Columbia. Clara Mortenson Beyer (1892–1990), a young academic, served as secretary of the district's Minimum Wage Board, headed by lawyer Jesse Adkins. After graduate work in economics at Berkeley, Beyer had taught at Bryn Mawr in 1916–17 and was scheduled to take a new appointment at Barnard when Felix Frankfurter recruited her service on the wartime Labor Employment Board. Finding public service more exciting than college teaching, Beyer moved on to the minimum wage job, joined by Elizabeth Brandeis, just graduated from Radcliffe, whom she recruited; the two young women shared the job and the salary. "As secretary, I started right out to assess the wages that were being paid to women in the District," Beyer recalled. "All that I had to support me was the Minimum Wage law. . . . I was given $5,000, the statute, and an office and I was told to put the law into effect." The two cosecretaries investigated women's wages in stores, hotels, offices, and factories; most of women workers in the trades they explored earned less than the $16 a week cost of living standard. By 1921 the board reported that it had collected thousands in back pay for 341 employees from ninety-nine firms and had reported three cases of violations to be prosecuted; the prosecutions were later dropped and the effort to collect back pay collapsed. Still, the experience of the DC Minimum Wage Board was a high point of social feminism.[53]

But as in Oregon, two challenges arose to the DC minimum wage law. An employer, Children's Hospital, sought an injunction against the DC Minimum Wage Board to restrain it from imposing the minimum wage of $16.50 per week for women workers in hotels, hospitals, restaurants, clubs, and apartment houses. In a companion lawsuit, Willie Lyons, a twenty-one-year-old elevator operator at the Congress Hall Hotel, challenged the minimum wage because she wanted to keep her job (which paid $35 a month plus meals); when the board forced the hotel to pay the minimum wage, which was higher, Lyons was dismissed.[54]

The District of Columbia Supreme Court upheld the law in June 1920, as did the DC Court of Appeals in June 1921. A woman worker, said the majority opinion, needed "a sufficient wage to supply her with necessary food, shelter, and clothing"; were she "compelled to subsist upon less," her health would suffer. In dissent, Justice Josiah Alexander Van Orsdel declared that the fixing of wages represented "paternalism in the highest degree." But the District of Columbia law faced an unexpected pitfall. Justice Charles Henry Robb, a conservative who had missed the 1921 appeal because of illness and had been replaced by another federal judge, returned to the bench and in October 1921 requested and was granted a new hearing. At the second hearing, in November 1922, the DC Court of Appeals upset the law. Justice Van Orsdel, who now wrote the majority opinion, denounced the violation of freedom of contract, Willie Lyons's loss of livelihood, the hazard of wage fixing, and the potential consequences of the minimum wage. "The tendency of the times to socialize property rights under the subterfuge of police regulation is dangerous," he declared, "and if continued will prove destructive of our free institutions."[55]

In 1923, when *Adkins v. Children's Hospital* reached the Supreme Court, defenders of the minimum wage faced a less receptive roster of justices than they had in 1917; recent appointments made in wartime or soon after had produced a more conservative court. The NCL legal team, which represented the District of Columbia's Minimum Wage Board and its head, Jesse Adkins, had changed as well. Josephine Goldmark left her position at the NCL to begin a study of the nursing profession. Molly Dewson, who replaced her, joined Felix Frankfurter to prepare the brief for the *Adkins* cases. A Wellesley graduate of 1897, Dewson had long experience as a social worker and reformer. She had served as secretary of the Massachusetts commission that explored a minimum wage; her report had been the basis for the state's pioneer law. Starting in 1919, Dewson and Frankfurter composed three briefs for the sequential *Adkins* cases, "each one more elaborate than the last," according to Dewson's biographer, Susan Ware. The final version of 1,138 pages, the longest of the NCL "Brandeis" briefs, not only cited recent data, mainly from minimum wage commissions in various states, but also conveyed a modernized form of the protectionist argument that developed in the 1920s.[56]

Like all earlier Brandeis briefs, the *Adkins* brief made claims about women's health. "The dangers to the health of women from low wages," wrote Dewson, created a "descending spiral into the regions of destitution." As in earlier briefs, "the deterioration is handed down to succeeding generations." But the *Adkins* brief replaced the dependent woman of the *Muller* brief with an updated counterpart who supported herself and others. "[T]he bulk of the girls living at home, work to support themselves, not for extra spending money," the *Adkins* brief contended; many women supported "aging parents or other dependents." The *Adkins* brief, historian Sybil Lipschultz contends, reflected the revised ideas of women reformers in the 1920s: "It argued for the minimum wage not primarily to protect women's health or the future of the race but to redress women's economic disadvantage." Women needed a "living wage," according to the *Adkins* brief, not because they were dependent but because they were self-supporting—and in many cases, provided for others. Molly Dewson had modernized the arguments of earlier Brandeis briefs to suit the new ideal of economic independence that characterized the 1920s women's movement.[57]

Representing Children's Hospital and Willie Lyons were the lawyer-brothers Wade H. Ellis and Challen Ellis, who also found a way to modernize *their* argument. The Ellis brothers acquired an expert advisor from the women's movement: Alice Paul, who had met with Challen Ellis in the early 1920s to discuss the wording of an Equal Rights Amendment. Now she supplied him with National Woman's Party literature about the danger protective laws posed to women's rights; his brother cited this material in oral argument. Thus the affinity between freedom of contract and women's rights that had first appeared in the *Ritchie* decision of 1895 and had reappeared in William Fenton's brief for Curt Muller now reappeared. "Challen Ellis helped forge the critical link between equal rights for women and the liberty of contract principle," historian Joan G. Zimmerman writes. "Paul's talk of rights provided the Ellis brothers with a way to revive an old doctrine in the new guise of equal rights." Communion with the Ellis brothers, Zimmerman shows, also affected Alice Paul. For Paul, legal formalism would serve as an instrument to achieve the reforms she sought for women.[58]

In oral argument, Wade Ellis discussed the NWP stance against sex discrimination and used the case for equal rights to discredit the single-sex minimum wage. "Can it be that the women of the country favor such laws, and especially for them alone?" Ellis asked. On the contrary, his investigations revealed "an overwhelming sentiment just the other way":

> All over the country today thoughtful and progressive women are contending for industrial equality which follows as a natural and logical sequence to political equality.... The women of this country ... want, and they deserve equal rights with men. They believe in self-reliance, independence, and character. And they believe that the right to make their own bargains will result ultimately in better pay, a finer sense of self-respect and a higher quality of citizenship. They are learning from experience that minimum wage laws are not discriminations in their favor but discriminations against them.

Ellis then impugned the "entering wedge" strategy. "Where will this legislation lead?" he asked. In his view, it was "perfectly obvious that if the state or the nation ... may fix the wages of women, they may fix the wages of men." Were not women-only laws intended to carve a path for general laws? But once again, said Ellis, reformers claimed that the woman worker's distinctive circumstances—"considerations of her life and morals"—made a single-sex law necessary. "I submit that such an alleged distinction is unreal and fanciful," Ellis charged. In the hundreds of pages of extracts that Frankfurter and Dewson provided, Ellis argued, he found "scarcely the slightest hint of a distinction between men and women"; all the authorities cited in the brief "believe in the minimum wage for both men and women." To Ellis, the minimum wage for women workers was merely a ploy to achieve minimum wages for all workers. He concluded with the ultimate impact of the minimum wage: "the leveling of all men and women to an industrial army working for the state" and "the experience of Russia under communism."[59]

The Supreme Court in 1923 failed to sustain the District of Columbia minimum wage law by a 5–3 decision (once again Brandeis withdrew, this time because his daughter held a post with the DC Minimum Wage Board). Justice George Sutherland, a prominent conservative who had joined the Court in 1922, wrote the majority opinion. In 1916, as a senator from Utah, Sutherland had opposed Brandeis's confirmation; the same year he had established his credentials in women's rights by urging the Senate to adopt a woman suffrage amendment. Division "by the line of sex," he told his fellow senators, was "purely artificial" and "certain to disappear, just as the other superstitions which in the past have denied women equal opportunities for education, equality of legal status, including the right to contract, and to hold property—and all the other unjust and intolerant denials of equality have disappeared, or are disappearing from our law and customs." Before his own appointment to the Supreme Court, he had, like Challen Ellis, advised Alice Paul on the drafting of an ERA.[60]

In the *Adkins* decision, Sutherland reiterated his women's rights views. Revolutionary changes in women's status had brought "the ancient inequality of the sexes" and the differences between men and women "almost to the vanishing point," Sutherland wrote. Now enfranchised, women were no longer a dependent class but equal to men. Nor was there a link between women's health and the minimum wage, he claimed; the evidence offered by Frankfurter and Dewson, though "interesting," was only "mildly persuasive" (although according to Brandeis's oral argument in *Stettler*, that should have been enough to sustain the law). But the gist of the case for Sutherland was not women's rights or health but the minimum wage, which affected "the heart of the contract, that is, the amount of wages to be paid and received." A maximum hours law burdened the employer, but a minimum wage law injured him. The "living wage" formula used by the District of Columbia Minimum Wage Board had "no relation to the capacity or earning power of the employee," Sutherland stated. The DC minimum wage law was "simply and exclusively a price-fixing law, confined to adult women . . . who are legally as capable of contracting for themselves as men." Moreover, if the police power could justify a minimum wage, it could also justify a maximum wage: "The power to fix high wages connotes . . . the power to fix low wages." Finally, Sutherland revived the *Lochner* decision, presumed dead since 1917 but evidently still alive. "Subsequent cases in this court have been distinguished from that decision," he declared, "but the principles therein stated have never been disapproved."[61]

The *Adkins* decision suddenly disrupted the long string of protectionist triumphs. The decision upset only the District of Columbia minimum wage law, but it stifled protectionist effort in the states, where minimum wage laws now languished, their future unclear. *Adkins* rested on the fragile assumption that the start of woman suffrage had at once transformed gender relations. As Joan G. Zimmerman points out, the *Adkins* decision posited an "equal woman" who did not exist: women in industry had no more freedom of contract in 1923 than they did in the nineteenth century. The decision had used the newly won right to vote as a weapon to deny new women voters a living wage. "Most ominous part of the decision," Frankfurter telegraphed Kelley on April 23, 1923, "is suggestion that the Muller decision has been supplanted by the Nineteenth Amendment." Woman suffrage, it seemed, came with a cost. Finally, and most significantly, the *Adkins* decision derailed reformers' hopes of extending the minimum wage to all workers. The courts—the very institutions that reformers had sought to appease with their women-first plans—had rejected them: the "entering wedge" strategy had floundered.[62]

But the *Muller* decision survived the *Adkins* decision. Although it had been "supplanted," as Frankfurter claimed, in regard to minimum wage, it lived on. Differences between the sexes, as Justice Sutherland soon explained, might still justify regulations that applied solely to women; thus, single-sex maximum hours laws, night work bans, and occupational restrictions remained legitimate. Within a year of *Adkins*, in *Radice v. New York* (1924), the Supreme Court approved a New York law, an amendment to the law upheld in *Schweinler*, that barred women's work after 10:00 p.m. in restaurants in large cities (though not in smaller ones). Citing *Muller*, Justice Sutherland affirmed that the law fostered women's health and welfare. Could *Adkins* and *Muller* prevail at once? Political scientist Judith A. Baer suggests how Sutherland effected this maneuver. Except for "wage-fixing," he stated, the Court was willing to defer to legislatures. To Florence Kelley, the *Radice* decision signaled a commendable change of heart ("volte face") on Justice Sutherland's part; modern readers are more skeptical. To use scholar Frances G. Olsen's terms, false paternalism (which, under *Radice*, deprived some New York waitresses of high tips at night) and false equality (which, under *Adkins*, denied Washington, DC, women workers a minimum wage) could now coexist. The Court, too, had trouble with *Radice*; the justices had at first been divided on the case. "[Y]ou might have been certain, but it was not at all certain," Justice Brandeis told Felix Frankfurter in a postdecision conversation, according to Frankfurter's notes. The decision had been one of those 5 to 4 that was teetering back and forth for some time. The man who finally wrote—Sutherland was the fifth man & he had doubts & after a good deal of study (for whatever you may say of him he has character & conscience) came out for the act & then wrote his opinion. That swung the others around to silence. It was deemed inadvisable to express dissent and add another 5 to 4. The doubt as to the statute turned on unequal protection, which now looms up even more menacingly than due process, because the statute omitted some night work & only included some. The whole policy is to suppress dissents.... You may look for fewer dissents.[63]

Wary of a reputation for division, the justices forged unanimity on New York's unwieldy night work ban. Sutherland sought to distinguish the law in *Radice*—it banned a policy "detrimental to health"—from the law in *Adkins*, which, he claimed, had no relation to health. In *Radice*, he turned to "the facts," which he had rejected in *Adkins* as "only mildly persuasive." He also urged courts to "be cautious" about challenging legislatures.

The *Adkins* decision evoked widespread criticism in law journals, where the doctrine of legal realism held sway. "Minimum wage legislation is not and was not predicated upon political, contractual or civil inequalities of women," declared an article in the *California Law Review*. "The problem is one of economic fact, not of political, contractual or civil status." But supporters of *Adkins* saw a defect in the reformers' case: If economic affliction was the prerequisite for the minimum wage, then men could meet this criterion as well. "[I]t is difficult to see how a low or high wage can affect women as a class to a greater extent than men," wrote an *Adkins* defender in *Law Notes*. "Good wages are as conducive to health in men as in women, and poor wages would be equally detrimental to both classes."[64] Debate over the minimum wage and over single-sex laws would continue through the 1920s, but with *Adkins* reformers had suffered a crushing setback.

· · · · ·

Between 1908 and 1917, when the United States entered World War I, the crusade for protective labor laws enjoyed a golden age. Protective laws proliferated in the states and prevailed in the courts. Women's maximum hours laws led the way; the mode of argument that Brandeis had used in the *Muller* case insured legal victory. It proved effective even as reformers sought to extend their success to night work laws, men's hours laws, and the minimum wage. Each new campaign brought new risks. Night work laws, never widely endorsed, suggested the restrictive and discriminatory potential of gendered laws. "General" hours laws that affected men, adopted only in Oregon, won no support anywhere else. The single-sex minimum wage, only sporadically effective, enraged employers and faced a shaky future. Still, advocates of protection had laid the groundwork for their "entering wedge" strategy. They had also gradually shifted from arguments about women's innate disabilities to circumstantial arguments that could potentially apply to men as well. Paradoxically, the single-sex minimum wage, initially the most radical and contested of reformers' proposals, would ultimately achieve the most enduring success as a "general" law. But this lay decades ahead.

The post-*Muller* decade was also the golden age of Brandeis briefs, as produced by Brandeis, Goldmark, Frankfurter, and a few years later Molly Dewson. These ever-expanding compendia of data, with their catalogs of evidence—some of it expert opinion, some scientific reports, and much miscellany—exude progressive zeal ("as if the contents of a great cosmopolitan bank of file drawers had been tipped into legal argument," writes historian Daniel T. Rodgers). Notable for their attention to international sources ("The World's Argument") as well as for their deluge of details, the huge briefs enabled lawyers to present "facts" once unfathomable in legal settings. The briefs drew imitators. Margaret Sanger's lawyer, Jonah Goldstein, a Brandeis admirer, submitted a Brandeis brief of his own to New York's Court of Appeals when he pressed Sanger's defense for opening a birth control clinic in 1915 in violation of state law. The brief for Sanger presented health data from several nations to show that use of birth control prevented many diseases among women, beyond venereal disease. In 1919 Goldstein won his case: the Court of Appeals acceded to Sanger's plea for a broader interpretation of state law. The tradition of sociological jurisprudence and lawyers' involvement with social science remained important if contested parts of law.[65]

After US entry into World War I, the pace of protectionist victory slowed and new roadblocks emerged. At the war's end, outspoken hostility to protective laws erupted among women. The federal Women's Bureau, a beachhead for protectionists, sprang into life in 1920 just as the campaign for protective laws began to falter in the courts and as opposition among women found voice. In the early 1920s, foes of protection won mounting attention. The new National Woman's Party revealed its enmity to single-sex protective laws; the *Adkins* decision of 1923 crippled the minimum wage campaign and stymied the "entering wedge" strategy that had served reformers so well in the past. In the 1920s, the battle for protective laws bifurcated. Although a fight for the minimum wage continued in the courts after *Adkins*, it made slow progress (until 1937). The argument over single-sex protective laws now shifted to the women's movement, where a dramatic clash arose. A secondary debate arose as well, over the effectiveness of protective policies.

Different versus Equal: The 1920s

"[O]UR MEMBERSHIP WAS ALWAYS VERY TINY," recalled Alice Paul of the National Woman's Party in the 1920s. "We didn't go in for a big membership because we thought there were enough organizations by this time in the country, of women, and all of them had to spend *enormous* amounts of time and money on just organizing. We thought the easiest way to get the [Equal Rights] amendment through was to get each one of the national organizations to come out for it with its membership, not to try to build up a

■ ■ ■

Alice Paul, 1918. Alice Paul, leader of the National Woman's Party, during the campaign for woman suffrage. At first the proponent of a federal woman suffrage amendment, the NWP remobilized after 1920, when women won the vote, to campaign solely for equal rights. In 1923 Alice Paul drafted and proposed the first equal rights amendment; thereafter NWP members challenged protective laws for women workers. Library of Congress.

duplicate membership." The early 1920s had been a time of hope for the NWP and for its vision of an ERA, Paul remembered. "[W]e had expected universal support," she told an interviewer five decades later. "We were astonished that we didn't get such support." ERA foes included "people who feared alimony would be imperiled, or support from husbands ended, or the people who thought we were going to endanger the health of women of opening up to them tremendous working hours—all night and so on."[1]

The main adversary, in Alice Paul's view, had been the National Consumers' League, a group whose goal she claimed to grasp only vaguely: "It was people who were consumers, I understood. . . . [T]hey were a group of women consumers who had been organized by Florence Kelley to use the power of women to benefit women in industry." Paul saw the battle between her constituents and the NCL as a crucial event of the 1920s. "The Consumers' League objected to the Equal Rights Amendment on the ground that they'd worked very hard to get protection for women and this would be wiped out," she recalled. "We said it *wouldn't* be wiped out because equality in laws affecting industry could be made by every state to apply equally under the Equal Rights Amendment, to men and women employees."[2]

The clash between friends and foes of the ERA—and over the protective laws for women workers that it would surely invalidate—fueled women's politics in the 1920s. Both sides claimed precedent-setting accomplishments. In 1923 the National Woman's Party proposed the historic ERA, which incurred conflict that lasted for decades; the battle took shape in the early 1920s. The social feminist contingent, larger and more powerful, gained favor briefly among congressional lawmakers, expanded the number and strength of state laws, saw the minimum wage gain a foothold, and promoted protection through the federal Women's Bureau. Neither faction, however, achieved the advances it sought. Instead, a fight between factions underscored competing contentions about single-sex protective laws and their effect on women workers.

ALICE PAUL, THE NATIONAL WOMAN'S PARTY, AND THE ERA

Born in 1885, Alice Paul came from a New Jersey Quaker family in comfortable circumstances; her father was a business owner and bank president. Paul attended Quaker schools and Swarthmore College, an institution that her maternal grandfather had cofounded with abolitionist Lucretia Mott; Paul graduated in 1905. After college Paul followed a social feminist route. She studied social work at the New York School of Philanthropy, later the Columbia School of Social Work; volunteered to work on New York's lower east side; worked on a project sponsored by the NWTUL and the Henry Street Settlement, to urge labor unions to accept women; and helped form a milliners' union. Paul received a master's degree in sociology in 1907 at the University of Pennsylvania, and in 1908 enrolled in the London School of Economics. While in England, she lived among the poor in London's East End; she also worked in England and Scotland for a militant woman suffrage group, the Women's Social and Political Union, founded in 1903 by suffragist Emmeline Pankhurst. The Union's members risked imprisonment and went on hunger strikes; so did Alice Paul. These activist months made women's rights the central goal of her career.[3]

Returning to the United States in 1910, Paul earned a PhD in economics at the University of Pennsylvania in 1912 and began to campaign for a federal amendment for woman suffrage. She led a small faction in the National American Woman Suffrage Association (NAWSA) that became in 1914 the Congressional Union and in 1916 changed its name to the National Woman's Party. Pressing the cause of the federal amendment—as opposed to NAWSA, which campaigned for state enfranchisement of women—Paul's NWP followed English tactics, attacked the party in power (the Democrats), picketed the White House, and courted indictment. Arrested in 1917, along with other suffragists, Alice Paul was sent to a prison in Virginia, went on a hunger strike, and endured forced feeding.[4]

In 1919, Congress passed a woman suffrage amendment, ratified by the states on August 26, 1920. With the vote attained, the NWP, which had until then been committed solely to woman suffrage, reshaped itself for the "new era"; at a crucial executive committee meeting in September 1920, it resolved to pursue equality and confirmed its allegiance to Alice Paul's leadership (at that moment, Florence Kelley was part of the NWP executive committee). In February 1921, a new NWP replaced the old one. Its goal: to achieve equal rights for women and to remove all disabilities based on sex. The vote alone would not achieve equality, Alice Paul told readers of the *Suffragist* in early 1921. Women still had "far to go," she declared; the NWP would now struggle "to remove the remaining forms of subordination."[5]

In 1921, Alice Paul proposed a "blanket bill" to bar sex discrimination in federal law and similar bills on the state level. Would the NWP's egalitarian goals—specifically its demand for an equal rights amendment to the Constitution, the "blanket amendment"—erode protective laws for which women reformers had long campaigned? At the NWP's September 1920 executive committee meeting, attended by Florence Kelley, the potential clash between legal equality and protective laws had not yet arisen. Briefly, for two years, Paul tried to bypass the hurdle of protective laws. When the NWP began to draft an ERA, it made several attempts to add an escape clause, a "saving clause," to exempt protective laws, but each try failed, and Alice Paul straddled or evaded the issue. In public she claimed to have no position on protection; on occasion she claimed to supporters that the proposed amendment would not "affect labor legislation for women"; and on other occasions in private correspondence with supporters condemned it: "I do not believe in special protective labor legislation for women but believe that protective labor legislation should be enacted for women and men alike in a trade or in a geographical district and not along sex lines," she wrote to a supporter. By the end of 1921, Paul told supporters that she had abandoned "hope of aid" from her opponents. Her antagonism to protective laws was probably strong and continuous. "I'll wager anything I possess that Alice Paul herself is fundamentally opposed to labor legislation for women," wrote Ethel M. Smith, legislative secretary of the National Women's Trade Union League (NWTUL) to Florence Kelley in October, 1921. Paul's NWP colleagues discussed protection's liabilities. As NWP member Gail Laughlin (Wellesley, 1894, and Cornell Law School, 1898) argued in April 1922, "If women can be segregated as a class for special legislation, the same classification can be used for specific restrictions along any other line which may, at any time, appeal to the caprice or prejudice of our legislators."[6]

Gail Laughlin's argument was prescient: For NWP egalitarians, conciliation with protective goals was self-defeating. Battle lines hardened. In March 1921, Kelley resigned from the NWP's executive committee. The National Woman's Party, she declared in *The Survey*, "will not be every woman's party." In early 1922, the NCL resolved to oppose an ERA, and the vast bulk of women's organizations mobilized to oppose it, too, even with an escape clause. By then Alice Paul had abandoned any hint of concession. In November 1922, the NWP decided to focus on a federal ERA, regardless of what the states did. Within a few years of the achievement of woman suffrage, the NWP had once again become an embattled minority in the women's movement.[7]

These early years of the 1920s were a busy time for Alice Paul. She earned a law degree in 1922 from Washington College of Law (later a part of American University) and took the bar exam in June 1923. She aided the lawyers for Children's Hospital in the *Adkins* case, which had been moving through the federal courts since 1918 (see chapter 4). She consulted steadily with NWP lawyers—with Shippen Lewis, who had presented an NWP equal rights bill to Congress in 1921, and with Albert Levitt, a recent law school graduate who married NWP leader Elsie Hill (thereby, he said, he had "married the Woman's Party") and whose advice Paul sought on ERA wording. On December 10, 1923, after the *Adkins* decision had been handed down, the NWP had an ERA introduced in Congress, by Congressman Daniel Anthony, nephew of Susan B. Anthony, and Senator Charles Curtis, Republican whip and later Hoover's vice president. The amendment stated: "Men and Women shall have equal rights throughout the United States and every place subject to its jurisdiction." Conciliation with social feminists was now impossible. Florence Kelley saw her former colleague, Alice Paul, as a "fiend" who would hinder the women's movement and reverse protective laws. ERA supporters, in contrast, agreed that protective laws injured women workers; women should be treated as individuals under law, not as members of a suspect class.[8]

The factional feud reflected a sharpening divide in the female workforce of the 1920s. New trends included rising numbers of married women workers, an influx of women into office jobs, and growing opportunities in facets of the business world—such as sales, real estate, communications, copywriting, bookkeeping. By the decade's end the proportion of women workers in white-collar work outweighed the share employed in the next largest sector, manufacturing. Rising expectations, concern with aspiration and career, and hope for "economic independence" fostered the sense that women were, in one feminist's words, "invading every field that had once been the province of men."[9] The new competitive mood boosted the message of the NWP. For the rest of the 1920s, the NWP strove to remove women's legal disabilities in the states, to win support among business and professional women, to challenge supporters of single-sex protective laws, and to secure the future of the ERA.

THE NCL, SOCIAL FEMINISM, AND THE MINIMUM WAGE

The NCL began the 1920s with confidence. It claimed forty thousand members, though it was run by a small leadership in the states and at its New York headquarters. The ten-year program that the NCL adopted in 1919 (the eight-hour day, night work laws, a child labor bill, establishment of minimum wage commissions in all states, and health insurance in industry) was underway. It drew support from the social feminist network—notably from the NWTUL, the only middle-class women's organization with a partially working-class membership. The NWTUL moved more firmly into the protectionist camp, if only because unionization of women had proved unfeasible. The cause of protection also drew support from the League of Women

Voters (LWV), which represented the largest remnant of NAWSA; from the YWCA, a growing social feminist stalwart; from the Women's Joint Congressional Committee (WJCC), started in 1920, a lobbying arm for twenty-one women's organizations; and from the Women's Joint Legislative Conference (WJLC), a New York State pressure group formed in 1918 that lobbied for a shorter workday and a minimum wage. Finally, the NCL depended on the new federal Women's Bureau (1920), which urged an identical agenda and had in part assumed the NCL's role as coordinator of research and chief proponent of protective laws. A cauldron of enthusiasm, the WB of the 1920s published reports, ran conferences, communicated with women's organizations, and maintained a brisk pace of activity.[10]

Protectionists had much to celebrate on the NCL's twenty-fifth anniversary in early 1923. Most states had women's hours laws, the WJCC had pushed through Congress the Sheppard-Towner Act of 1921 (medical services for women and infants) and a child labor amendment; further gains seemed imminent. But problems arose: in the 1920s the pace of achievement slowed, child labor law ran into trouble, the minimum wage hit a roadblock, and opposition grew—not just from industrialists and manufacturers, not just from unreceptive judges, not just from the NWP, but from a political climate hostile to reform.[11]

Right-wing attacks plagued social feminists throughout the 1920s. By mid-decade, according to historian Jan Doolittle Wilson, the WJCC devoted more time to refuting political critics than to promoting legislation. Social feminism, to critics on the right, represented communism, socialism, pacifism, and subversion "under the guise of reform, peace, and child welfare" (according to Henry Ford's Dearborn Independent in 1924). Critics from the War Department, resentful of World War I pacifism, also assailed social feminist groups. Business associations, opposed to child labor law and other protective measures, were prime critics. The National Association of Manufacturers (NAM) in 1926 created a "Women's Bureau" in its department of industrial relations to attack protective laws. The NAM bureau targeted for conversion women workers, to whom it addressed antiprotectionist literature, and members of women's clubs, always a weak link in the protectionist chain of support. Modern employers, the NAM "Women's Bureau" head, Marguerite Benson, told a chamber of commerce, "have learned to be as ardent as the reformers in looking after the health and welfare of employees."[12]

Problems with child labor law suggest the sort of resistance that social feminists would meet. By World War I, over half the states had passed laws to moderate child labor—that is, to bar the work of children under ten, twelve, or fourteen and to regulate hours and working conditions for employed youngsters. Poor enforcement undermined the laws. The National Conference on Child Labor (NCCL), a pressure group started in 1904, won a federal child labor law in 1916. In 1918 the Supreme Court upset the law, 5 to 4. NCCL pushed Congress to pass another law in 1919 and supported other measures to aid children—child welfare provisions and mothers' pensions—in the Sheppard-Towner Act of 1921. In 1922, the Supreme Court again declared the federal child labor law unconstitutional. Reformers then proposed a child labor amendment, sponsored by the NCL and WJCC and passed by Congress in 1924. But ratification proved impossible. Of forty-two state legislatures that met in 1924 and 1925, only four ratified the amendment—and by 1930, only six had done so. State laws remained in effect, but efforts to end child labor in federal law capsized until the 1930s.[13]

The fate of the Sheppard-Towner Act underscored another facet of resistance to social feminism. Enacted in 1921 to cater to women voters, Sheppard-Towner provided maternal and child medical care, mainly in rural areas. The first federally funded health care law, Sheppard-Towner drew the enmity of the American Medical Association; doctors disliked the encroachment of outsiders—federal agents, public health nurses—in the health care field. Congress let the law expire in 1929. In its brief life, significantly, the law reduced maternal and infant death rates. Sheppard-Towner is also significant for what it failed to include: maternity benefits for working women. The last hope for such benefits had been the AALL health care proposal in New York State, which sank for a final time in 1920. By 1921, six states had passed laws to bar employers from "knowingly" keeping women at work for several weeks before and after childbirth and which, if enforced, meant job loss without benefits. European nations, in contrast, provided maternity benefits. Germany mandated paid maternity leaves in 1911; France started similar policies in 1910. In 1919 the International Labour Organization, formed as an agency of the League of Nations after World War I, adopted an international standard, the Maternity Protection Convention; it called for compulsory leave after childbirth, optional leave before childbirth, benefits to maintain worker and child through public funds or insurance plans, and prevention of worker dismissal for pregnancy. When it came to maternity benefits, the United States became the outlier among industrialized nations.[14]

Protective laws for women workers in industry made modest progress in the 1920s, but the peak of advance for this type of law had been 1911 to 1919. Thereafter, momentum slowed. In 1921, five states and the District of Columbia had laws that provided for a forty-eight-hour week, and in 1931, four more states signed on. In 1921, only nine states plus the District of

Columbia insured an eight-hour day for women workers, and in 1931 another state joined the list. Thirteen states had passed night work laws by 1921 and sixteen ten years later. Minimum wage laws were in place in 1919 in fourteen states, the District of Columbia, and Puerto Rico. After *Adkins v. Children's Hospital* (1923), progress faltered; minimum wage boards hesitated, their budgets shrank, and their support wavered. Repeals by legislatures and derailment by courts took a toll. By 1930, only six minimum wage laws remained. All were either unenforced or otherwise ineffective. In most states where minimum wage laws existed, efforts arose to have them declared unconstitutional.[15]

NCL problems of the 1920s soared with the *Adkins* decision, which enraged reformers. "Upshot would be adoption [of] Alice Paul theory of constitutional law plus invalidity of legislation affecting industrial relations of either men or women," NCL counsel Felix Frankfurter wrote to Florence Kelley in 1923. For Kelley, the decision seemed a return to "that stagnant period" between *Ritchie* and *Muller*, when the courts rejected protection for women. In her view, the *Adkins* decision gave "the unorganized, the unskilled, the illiterate, the alien, and the industrially sub-normal women wage-earners the constitutional right to starve," she claimed. "This is a new Dred Scott decision." Moreover, Justice Sutherland's use of NWP literature to shape the majority opinion underscored the alliance of equal rights proponents with business interests. "The women who pretend to be making heroic exertions to get 'equal rights' for all women are, in practice, the Little Sisters of the United States Chamber of Commerce [and other business organizations]," Kelley informed a 1923 correspondent. In October 1923, at Kelley's instigation, the NCL board of directors voted to press for a bill to require seven Supreme Court justices to concur in pronouncing federal or state legislation unconstitutional. Harvard law professor T. R. Powell, an NCL supporter, offered another version of protectionist arithmetic. Of all the votes ever cast on the minimum wage in state and federal courts, Powell computed, thirty-two judges favored it, and nine opposed it. But five of those nine were on the Supreme Court in 1923. Had the case been heard one year earlier, as it well might have been, the justices would have voted 5–3 to uphold the law, Powell claimed. The *Adkins* decision was an accident![16]

Adkins left a legacy of challenges for NCL leaders. Their argument for the minimum wage for women workers, as presented in the Frankfurter/Dewson brief, embodied a contradiction. If women deserved the minimum wage because of economic circumstances, did not men deserve it for the same reason? Was this the time for the NCL to promote a minimum wage for both women and men? Florence Kelley tilted back and forth on the question. Kelley had always embraced inconsistent views on women who worked, historian Vivien Hart observes. She preferred a "family wage" (earned by men) but advocated a minimum wage that recognized the needs of the working woman. Did not women work for wages at all, she asked, "ultimately because their men breadwinners are insufficiently paid?" Kelley vacillated similarly in her ideas for constitutional amendments, a lively topic in the early 1920s. In 1923 she discussed in an article an amendment to secure women workers' "right to differ . . . to cast off the yoke of uniformity with men." The next year, she joined Thomas Reed Powell to draft an amendment (that remained in her files) to protect the minimum wage "for any persons," male or female, from judicial scrutiny. The draft amendment at first applied solely to women workers, but Kelley changed it to apply to "all persons."[17] How best to press for a minimum wage—for women alone or for all workers—remained a point at issue among her colleagues.

NCL leaders faced a second post-*Adkins* tactical decision: should they shape a minimum wage bill that would survive judicial scrutiny or promote a constitutional amendment to legitimize a minimum wage? At first, Kelley and Frankfurter agreed to pursue an amendment. Kelley wrote to Frankfurter in May 1923 about her "impatience of furthering tinkering with legislation—What have I done but tinker for forty-one years?" Frankfurter then changed his mind. An amendment was "an extremely remote thing," he responded to Kelley. He preferred the "salvage of minimum wage legislation in the states." The NCL, moreover, should "concentrate upon things that are within their purview, and still more within their resources," Frankfurter told an associate, lawyer Benjamin V. Cohen. He also called on Cohen to take over his pro bono stint with the NCL. Cohen began to draft a minimum wage bill for women workers. Florence Kelley still supported the idea of an amendment to protect the minimum wage. Other NCL women leaders, starting with Molly Dewson, drifted away from the amendment idea. Frankfurter continued to advise Cohen by letter, thus staying out of the line of fire. "Mrs. Kelley is a very hard customer, as those of us who have been working with her for years well know," Frankfurter wrote to Cohen in June 1923. Still, Frankfurter retained admiration and compassion for Kelley, too. All of the causes to which she had devoted her life, such as a child labor amendment and the minimum wage, he told Cohen, were "turning to dust and ashes."[18]

Division over how to promote the minimum wage among NCL leaders and their lawyers persisted into the 1930s. Meanwhile, conflict with the NWP moved to the forefront. "Sooner or later in every country where women have won the franchise, this vexed question of equality versus protection is bound to arise," wrote NWP member Crystal Eastman in *Equal Rights* in 1924.[19] The United States was no exception.

FACTIONS COLLIDE: THE WOMEN'S MOVEMENT

"All modern-minded people desire, of course, that women have full political equality and also be free from the old exclusion from the bench, the bar, the pulpit, the highest ranges of the teachers' profession, and of the civil service," Florence Kelley declared in 1922. But an ERA, she charged, would clog the courts for years, cause "endless confusion," and negate all laws that benefited women, including mothers' pensions and the recent Sheppard-Towner Act. It would leave women open to new hazards, such as conscription or loss of financial support at home ("Will husbands continue to support their wives?" "Can deserting husbands be brought back and compelled to support wife and child?" "Could the state compel women to work for the maintenance of their child?"). Finally, an ERA would invalidate existing protective laws for women workers, preclude further protection, and leave wage-earning women nothing "to compensate the disadvantages which they everywhere suffer in competing with men—i.e. longer hours and lower wages." To Kelley, the ERA was a "dangerous experiment" that exposed women to risk and deprived them of benefit. "Cannot every desirable measure attainable through the amendment be achieved without it?"[20]

Kelley's 1922 attack spoke to the clash between factions in the women's movement, just underway, over the ERA and protective laws. To NWP members, single-sex protective laws defined women as weak and dependent, classified them with minors as wards of the state, kept them in low-level jobs, limited their earning capacity, and penalized the ambitious—those who competed with men for work. "Labor men wanted protective laws for women only, so that they could steal women's jobs away under cover of chivalry," charged the NWP journal *Equal Rights* in 1928. To ERA foes, in contrast, single-sex protective laws served a compensatory, equalizing function. To remove them would destroy years of progressive achievement, sanction employer exploitation, and keep women in "industrial slavery." The proposed ERA, claimed its critics, was shaped by a professional elite that lacked knowledge of women in industry; its defenders were tools of the business class; and it goal was pernicious, or, as Kelley claimed, "insane." "It deals with abstract rights, not real rights," stated WB head Mary Anderson. Women with "neither experience in or contact with the industrial struggle are often unable to see that social and industrial inequalities are problems at least co-equal with the sex problem," argued Ethel M. Smith of the NWTUL.[21]

On the defensive, social feminists now stressed the compensatory facet of single-sex protective laws—the way they offset men's advantages in the workforce and promoted "industrial equality," or what has subsequently been called a level playing field. "Men have been in industry longer than women and have established their [labor] standards," argued Frieda Miller of the Philadelphia WTUL in 1922. "Genuine equality requires that [women] shall have such laws as will bring them nearer to the standard which men have won by their longer experience and stronger organization." Single-sex protective laws were "equalizing in their effect," wrote WB head Mary Anderson in 1925, "for the reason that they obtain for women certain economic rights and benefits which men have already in large measure attained." Rejecting "rigid application of abstract principle," Anderson claimed: "The worker prefers industrial equality, which is in this case *defeated* by legal equality." At the same time, while attacking "blanket" equality, social feminists endorsed the achievement of specific legal rights, piece by piece ("specific bills for specific ills") in a manner that would not "call into question" protective laws. The LWV in 1922 prepared its own roster of bills to "remove legal discrimination against women" and "establish equality of rights under law."[22]

Ideally, both factions declared, protective laws should be "extended" to men but neither assertion carried weight. The NWP claim was patently false. The possibility of extending maximum hours laws and minimum wage laws to men—when organized labor scorned such an extension, when state legislators rejected it, and when the Supreme Court had just scuttled the District of Columbia minimum wage—was remote, to say the least. Alice Paul, moreover, had only recently collaborated with lawyers who sought to destroy the minimum wage and had depended on her for much of their argument. Restraints on employers were clearly not NWP goals. That night work bans or occupational restrictions might be "extended" to men was even less likely. To "extend" night work bans to men would mean to abolish all work after 10:00 p.m., from printing to steel production, and thus to wipe out sectors of industry. Few took such a claim seriously. But reformers did not necessarily favor an immediate extension of protective laws to men any more than their rivals did. Such an extension would differ not at all from the *removal* of protection for women, argued Clara Mortenson Beyer, New York Consumers' League activist and officer of the District of Columbia Minimum Wage Board, in 1923: "The effect, in all probability, would be the same in either case—women would be left without the safeguards which are peculiarly necessary to their well-being and men would be in exactly the same position as before." Here was a conundrum: if single-sex protective laws were compensatory, as reformers claimed, their "extension" to men would defeat that purpose. The "entering wedge" strategy had tethered social feminists to gendered law, a dependence caused by legal necessity, and left them at an awkward impasse.[23]

The feud in the 1920s women's movement imposed on both factions a challenging problem: were women fundamentally different from men or equal to men, or, if both, where did the legal advantage lie? This question pitted the interests of one group of women—the ambitious, the high achievers, and bourgeois professionals, those most likely to compete with men—against the less advantaged, those lacking skill, influence, and alternatives, the group that social feminists sought to protect. Arguments in the women's movement echoed those in court. NWP members, speaking for themselves, embraced individualism; social feminists hoped to enhance the role of the state. Significantly, as the dispute concerned women's role under law, the dominant figures in each faction, Florence Kelley and Alice Paul, *were* lawyers; each was deeply involved with fellow lawyers committed to the goals they sought. Professional rivalry erupted. Alice Paul won the support of the National Association of Women Lawyers (1899); women lawyers' conferences of the 1920s proclaimed their close ties to the NWP and their zeal for NWP policies, from the "blanket equality bill" to the ERA. Florence Kelley posited her own weighty credentials in law against the lesser professional record of Alice Paul. "I was admitted to the Bar of Illinois and have been continuously active in the field of litigation ever since," Kelley told the editor of the *Woman's Home Companion* in an indignant letter of 1922. Alice Paul, in contrast, Kelley charged, was just an upstart. "Miss Paul . . . carries great weight with the uninitiated," Kelley continued. "In fact, however, as to the effects of statutes and judicial decisions, she is a newcomer fresh from the law school."[24]

Not every woman activist joined the factional feud. Historian Mary Ritter Beard, on the left wing of the NWP, voiced a defiant ambivalence, a refusal to take sides that still resonates. Beard's iconoclasm in women's politics had begun in the Progressive Era. An early NWP member, she could never fully adopt the party's woman suffrage stance because she had "labor commitments," as she wrote to Alice Paul in 1914. "I ought to be interested in suffrage first and labor second but I frankly am not," she declared. Before women won the vote, Beard saw herself as too radical to place "my whole absorption in the one fight for enfranchisement." When the NWP regrouped in the 1920s and shifted its single-issue focus to equal rights, Beard's defiance persisted. An ERA "would overthrow all protective legislation for women" and "might do things like conscript women for war," Beard (a pacifist) wrote to the NWP's Elsie Hill in 1921. "I am not an ultra-feminist," Beard told Hill, "because in my mind children do add a complexity to women that they cannot add to men and I see no way of removing it entirely for the best interests of both sexes as well as for the children." By the 1930s, Beard concluded that the NWP's equal rights stance paved the way for capitulation to conservative principles. Such a stance "ran the risk" of "supporting, if unintentionally, ruthless laissez-faire," she wrote to author and NWP member Alma Lutz, "of forsaking humanism in the quest for feminism." But social feminism could not sustain her allegiance either. "Nor could I throw my heart and energy into the mere struggle for a minimum wage, even for women." Mary Beard told Alma Lutz. "The protectionists satisfied me as little as the rightists."[25]

Mary Beard's refusal to commit and her appreciation of competing values—"the value . . . of the equal rights principle" and "the value of restraining exploitation"—remains compelling. The great battle among 1920s feminists had no solution. Each faction held justifiable suspicions—that classification by sex could impose injury or that blanket equality could have unequal ramifications. Neither faction had much immediate chance of moving toward its stated goals, even if the other vanished. At the same time, the conflict itself had positive import in that it shaped a "constitutional community," to use lawyer Reva Siegel's term; each faction of the women's movement negotiated conflict with "reference to a shared constitutional tradition." The negotiation, the constitutional conversation, was creative; the conflict *was* the women's movement. Finally, viewed either negatively or positively, the women's campaigns for labor standards and for equal rights had become too enmeshed in argument to disengage; their entanglement, forecast in miniature by similar disputes in European nations, had been inevitable and would persist, intransigent.[26] As in any war, the clash that split the 1920s women's movement fed on its own momentum.

CLOSE COMBAT: THE CONFERENCES

The feud over protection erupted at two Women's Bureau conferences, where delegates from women's organizations gathered to "develop policies and standards for the effective employment of women in industry" (that is, to promote protective laws). A 1923 conference hosted representatives from eighty-six women's organizations and addresses from many leaders in social feminism—Florence Kelley of the NCL, Mary Van Kleeck of the Russell Sage Foundation, Maud Swartz of NWTUL, Sophonisba Breckinridge of the University of Chicago, Melinda Scott of the AFL, Mary McDowell of the Chicago settlement movement, Grace Abbott of the Children's Bureau, and Clara Beyer of the District of Columbia Minimum Wage Board. The debate at the conference spilled over into the pages of the *Nation*. "The objection to special legislation is because . . . partial laws . . . have thrown women out of employment or crowded them into lower grades of work," declared Harriot Stanton Blatch of the NWP, prominent former suffragist and founder of the Equality League (1907), a working women's suffrage organization. "Legislatures would do more for children if adult women ceased to hang on their necks." Clara Beyer, in response, attacked "theoretical equality." Single-sex protective laws, she claimed, brought women "up to the point where industrial equality with men is more nearly possible."[27]

Confrontation recurred at the Women's Bureau conference of 1926 where a galaxy of activists defended protective laws, including Mary Van Kleeck, former head of the World War I Women in Industry Service. "She [Van Kleeck] said that women are not picked out as weaklings when labor legislation is made to apply to them," noted the WB records. "She also stated that her investigation had shown that few women had really lost their jobs because of laws regulating their conditions of work." Problems arose when NWP delegates demanded a program change to provide a venue for debate over labor laws. Supporters of protection—the vast majority—voted down a change in schedule but agreed to a special evening session when activists debated labor laws. Here, NWP delegates voiced their views (according to the Women's Bureau records):

> Miss Gail Laughlin, delegate from the Woman's Party, was the fourth speaker, and opposed the necessity for labor legislation for women, because she said it was a handicap in getting a job, and that the restrictions of the law made women workers "clock watchers." "Labor laws started first," she said, "in the minds of men who did not want women as competitors." She also stated that there had been no conclusive test of the comparative health of men and women, and that there are no convincing figures to show that a woman is not as strong as a man. She concluded her address with the statement that if the future generation is to be considered a justification for labor laws it should not be forgotten that the condition of the fathers is as important as that of the mothers.

A dozen more delegates joined the fray: Josephine Goldmark of the NCL, Agnes Nestor of the Glove Workers Union, and AFL delegate Melinda Scott weighed in among defenders of protective laws; foes included NWP delegates Burnita Shelton Matthews, Sue Shelton White, and Doris Stevens. After much debate, the next morning, the conference resolved to recommend "that the Women's Bureau make a comprehensive investigation of all the special laws regulating employment of women to determine their effects" and the formation of an advisory committee with representatives on both sides "with whom the [WB] director will take counsel concerning the scope of the investigation." Each piece of the resolution signaled a triumph for the Women's Bureau—for whom the extensive investigation and advisory committee were reliable partisan tactics.[28]

The advisory committee comprised three NWP representatives: Alice Paul, Doris Stevens, and Maud Younger, and three WB stalwarts: representatives of the AFL, the NWTUL, and the LWV. The committee met four times from January through March of 1926 before acrimony prevailed. According to Mary Anderson's report for the year (not an unbiased account), the committee dissolved after the withdrawal of the three members supporting labor laws, who "felt that they could no longer serve to good purpose with the other members of the committee." The WB report of 1928 further explained the disagreement. NWP representatives, the report claimed, had urged public hearings on protective laws for women workers; their foes, who supported the laws, claimed that those who testified at such hearings might lose their jobs and "could not be relied upon to bring out all the facts." NWP delegates then urged NWP members to pressure their congressmen; this last move, a public appeal, impelled the labor law supporters to withdraw. According to the WB, the friends of protection, who strove for reconciliation and met only obstruction from the NWP, were forced to bring the committee to an end. "[M]y experience with the National Woman's Party," declared Sara Conboy, the AFL representative on the committee, "has shown me that is composed mostly of women who never knew what it meant to work a day in their lives."[29]

Alice Paul's recollection of the 1926 conference, unsurprisingly, differed from the WB report. Paul seethed with contempt for the WB. "The Women's Bureau was the enemy camp, one of the great enemy camps of the Amendment," she told an interviewer in 1976. "They were having these conferences *all* the time you know," she declared. "They had all the financial backing of the United States government, they could send letters everywhere and get people to come down to conferences, and this [conference] was just one of many, many, many." Paul claimed not to recall Mary Anderson's name, but she remembered in detail the pivotal role of NWP delegate Gail Laughlin— who "was out there campaigning against special labor laws for women, long before we ever knew there *was* such a problem." According to Paul, Laughlin "was a great speaker, and of course a lawyer, and knew all about parliamentary law and how to hold the floor." Thereafter, Laughlin "kept on capturing the whole meeting with a protest against the Women's Bureau." Alice Paul saved special venom for the WB's advisory committee, which, she claimed, duplicitously dismissed the NWP's view. She found the WB representatives on the committee uninformed, unprepared, and obstructionist. "[T]hey didn't know what the labor laws were, they didn't know what *anything* was, apparently from what they said. . . . [O]ur people seemed so superior to these people who were all sitting there with their nice big salaries and just *breathing* incompetence . . . So we didn't really, I think, get anywhere. . . . What they were always doing was opposing the Equal Rights Amendment." Alice Paul concluded that the WB had not "come off with glory."[30]

The feud between factions crossed the Atlantic in 1926 to reach an international gathering, a congress of the Woman's Alliance (1911), an organization formed to oppose "all legislation called protective of women's work." "Rival Suffragists Take Row to Paris," declared a headline in the *New York World* in May 1926. "Feminism Is Real Issue."[31] At home, the WB, with wider support than the NWP, had for the moment scored a point. It had staved off NWP efforts to derail protective laws for women workers, and it had put forth a new goal: its big investigative report.

By the end of 1926, the WB report on protective laws was well underway. Researchers finished their work between March and December. Luminaries of social feminism took leading roles. In addition to the initial committee, from which social feminists withdrew, the WB had ingeniously set up a backup committee, a "technical advisory committee," full of its own stalwarts, to supervise the investigation. Mary Van Kleeck chaired the technical advisory committee, Mary N. Winslow directed the research, and other WB loyalists directed fieldwork. The investigation sought "to discover in what way legislation applying to women only has affected their employment in industry, and how extensive any effect has been." More specifically, WB researchers strove to study "conditions of women's employment before and after the laws went into effect" and "to find out what actually happened in a selected number of industries in different states before and after the enactment of laws in those states which had them, compared with what actually happened in the same industries in states not having the same laws."[32]

THE WOMEN'S BUREAU REPORT OF 1928

In 1928, the Women's Bureau's five-hundred-page report on the impact of maximum hours laws appeared. According to the WB, 8.5 million women held jobs, and protective laws covered one-third of them. Surveying five industries in nine states (box, hosiery, garments, boots and shoes, and electrical products), the bureau narrowed its inquiry to one main question: Did single-sex protective laws lead to the replacement of women workers by men? This was a loaded question, designed to evoke a negative answer. Three of the main industries surveyed (box, hosiery, garments) relied on female labor in a sex-segregated market; in the other industries surveyed (boots and shoes and electrical products), the minority of workers that were women performed specific types of work. In all of these cases, low pay protected women's jobs; replacement by men was not a pressing issue. Researchers collected additional data on waitresses and store clerks, and also on core makers, streetcar conductors, ticket agents, elevator operators, pharmacists, and workers in printing plants and the metal trades—occupations that typically involved small minorities of women who competed for work with men.[33]

The WB, not unexpectedly, found that maximum hours laws did not decrease female employment in industry or curb women's opportunity. Indeed, by banning "overtime" (overlong workdays), the report claimed, hours limits increased opportunity for *other* women workers ("One of the most important effects of hours legislation on women's opportunities is, therefore, to increase the number of jobs available for them"). Night work laws and exclusionary laws, the report conceded, "restricted women's opportunities in a small number of cases"—though women had little interest in the dangerous jobs excluded by law, the report contended. But among women who had held jobs when single-sex maximum hours laws went into effect (another loaded proviso), "not one woman found that such legislation [limiting working hours] had handicapped her or limited her opportunity in industry." That is, among the few women interviewed in 1926 whose terms of labor in industry had spanned the years since maximum hours laws had been enacted in the states where they worked, typically between 1909 and 1919 (at most 1,200 out of 660,000 women workers), none said that they experienced handicaps under such laws. Most (not all) said wages had been unaffected, too. Thus, according to the WB, among this very tiny and insignificant sample, maximum hours laws did not injure women workers. The laws also acted to "raise the standards of working conditions of their fellow male employees."[34]

To modern readers, the WB's huge report quivers with qualifications. As factory payroll records failed to distinguish workers by sex, the WB explained, it found it could not rely on statistics; rather, it depended on "interviews [with plant managers and workers] supplemented by statistics." In short, the report was in part impressionistic and in part based on whatever samples the researchers obtained. Moreover, a series of special considerations hampered the investigation, according to the WB. "[C]ountless qualifications and limitations . . . must be made before any conclusion can be reached," the report declared. "The subjects for study and measurement are both intangible and inconsistent." Indeed, the possible effects of single-sex labor laws were "almost countless and can not be measured completely at any one time." A final caveat in the report's summary stressed protective laws' minimal effect across the board: "In almost every kind of employment, the real forces that influence women's opportunity are far removed from legislative restrictions from their hours or conditions of work," the WB claimed. In manufacturing, technological progress, the nature of the labor supply, and "the general psychology of the times" played significant roles in determining women's position, the WB argued. In nonmanufacturing occupations, "other influences have been dominant [such as] a breaking down of prejudices against women's employment on the part of employers and of male . . . employees. [Such forces] will play the dominant part in assuring to women an equal chance in those occupations for which their abilities and aptitudes fit them." Overall, to its credit, the WB put forth only qualified conclusions; it claimed that protective laws neither injured women workers nor really affected them much at all (compared to "real forces" and "other influences").[35]

The WB's caveats were justifiable. The main problem of the report, as the WB readily conceded, was that its researchers faced limits. Their opportunities to obtain reliable data were few. Thus they asked narrow questions that could be answered more or less honestly but lacked salience. They also failed to seriously pursue inquiries about protective laws that could lead to negative conclusions. Still, surprisingly, many sections of the report revealed lively pockets of resistance to protection and views that clashed with those of researchers. Night work bans *did* cause substitution of men for women, as a section on night work conceded. Women who escaped such bans and worked at night in newspaper offices and printing plants, for instance, were "enthusiastic" about their opportunities: "[F]rom their standpoint night work was far from being a hardship." Women pharmacists provided another pocket of resistance. Among those surveyed in New York, California, and Wisconsin, sixteen of 194 declared maximum hours laws a problem. Or, in the WB's grudging concession, it found "a residue of what seemed to be actual experience of handicaps from hours restrictions." The WB had many explanations for women pharmacists' discontent: They competed directly with men; employers preferred male pharmacists; so did male coworkers and pharmacy customers. The basic problem for women pharmacists was not hours limits, the WB declared, it was that women *became* pharmacists: "Women are still pioneers in this occupation and are facing the difficulties with which pioneers must meet in almost every line of work."[36]

A review of the WB report by economist Elizabeth Faulkner Baker (1885–1973) identified some of its drawbacks. Baker, who taught at Barnard from 1919 to 1952, had graduated from the University of California in 1914 and received a PhD from Columbia in 1925. Her doctoral dissertation, a study of protective laws in New York State, remains a pivotal source on the subject. In her review of the WB report, Baker stressed the role of some 60,000 women workers, whom, she claimed, the WB had "largely overlooked." Such workers entered occupations dominated by men; they labored on "little industrial frontiers," served to "make way for the many to follow," and were "cramped or cut off" by protective laws.[37]

Baker's conclusions in her 1925 study in part anticipated those of the Women's Bureau. As the WB would do, she stated that for those who assessed the effect of women's labor laws, research problems abounded: "there exist practically no unquestioned facts on which to form an impartial judgment." Baker suggested, too, that women's status in the workforce rested on factors other than single-sex labor laws: "their occupations and plans of living are frequently results of a set of circumstances outside of their control and outside of legislation pertaining to them." The shorter workday, she argued, ultimately depended on worker organization, more humane employers, and a shrinking labor pool. But Baker's stance on the impact of single-sex laws was more critical than that of the WB. Maximum hours laws, she concluded, were an advantage in industries where women predominated—the industries where the majority of women workers were employed, such as garment work. Here, protective laws for women were "likely to protect both men and women." In trades in which women were a minority, however, Baker contended, protective laws curtailed opportunity:

> In occupations or industries where men greatly predominate, protective laws for women are likely to prohibit rather than protect their employment, or in other words, to relieve men of the competition of women. . . . For those minorities of women, legislation based only upon sex is of doubtful value.

Baker's sympathies rested with "the significant minority who have emerged from the mass into a more self-reliant position."[38]

Clashing assessments of the 1920s on the impact of protective laws for women workers bring up problems at issue then and subsequently. Did single-sex protective laws fulfill the goals of those who promoted them? What was their impact on women workers? Two economists of the 1980s assess the impact of maximum hours laws around 1920. The question at issue concerns solely maximum hours laws, because, from the standpoint of the 1920s, the minimum wage was too recent a change and minimum wage laws too rare to assess their effect.

According to economist Claudia Goldin, protective legislation "had virtually no adverse impact on female employment around 1920." Moreover, the drop in working hours affected men as well as women. "[S]tates with more stringent hours laws had greater declines for hours for all workers than those with less stringent laws." Certain women—such as those employed in printing, publishing, and streetcar railways—"were constrained by the laws," Goldin concludes. "But from the perspectives of a trade-union leader, a reformer, or a laborer who wanted lower hours, the benefits of maximum hours laws and other types of protective legislation were well worth the costs." Social feminists, to whom protective legislation was "an indispensable substitute for collective action for workers" were "probably correct that protective legislation was associated with reduced hours for all workers," Goldin states. "But the real costs of protective legislation began to mount almost immediately," Goldin contends. "The cause of protective legislation served to delay a national policy to combat discrimination against women through its definition of women as marginal workers and through the opposition it raised to real equality.[39]

Goldin's study (1990) reflects the findings of a 1988 article she wrote that asked: Did protective hours legislation have an impact on the scheduled hours of women and if so by how much? Here she concludes that hours declined for men as well as for women in states with maximum hours laws and that the employment share of women in manufacturing did not decrease with the restrictiveness of the legislation. Indeed, the employment share of women in another economic sector, sales, rose with increasing restrictiveness. Goldin also finds that among white women—native born, foreign born, or daughters of the foreign born, shorter hours were associated with higher workforce participation rates, most strongly among married women. In her article, Goldin takes issue with a 1980 article by Elisabeth Landes; both economists look at data from forty states and the District of Columbia. Landes argues that states with more restrictive legislation had a lower female employment share in manufacturing compared to a decade earlier and that most of the decline occurred among daughters of the foreign born and foreign-born women. She concludes that maximum hours laws greatly reduced the hours worked by women in 1920 and reduced their employment share in manufacturing.[40]

Economists' studies suggest problems that arise in assessing the impact of maximum hours laws: Each study reflects an aspect of ideas about protection that emerged in the 1920s debate. In Landes's article, the laws curbed women's share of the labor market—as foes of protection contended they might. In Goldin's assessments, the laws shortened hours for men as well as women—as advocates of protection argued they would and as the WB report of 1928 stated that they did. Neither conclusion precludes the other. Recent analysts often return to the view economist Elizabeth Faulkner Baker presented in 1925—that protective laws were an asset to women workers in fields they dominated but were a liability in fields in which they were a minority.

Overall, the impact of maximum hours laws remains elusive, and as Baker emphasized, night work laws and other restrictive laws remain the problematic factor. It is difficult to compute the negative effect of laws that curb opportunity. One critic of the WB report, an NWP activist, made this point in the 1940s. "The debit side is not at all susceptible to accurate bookkeeping," lawyer Rebekah Greathouse argued. "How can we know how many women would work at night if they were permitted to do so, or what jobs they were obliged to accept in lieu of night work? . . . How can we know how many are kept from promotion by such laws or what new work may never be opened to women because of them?"[41] The "debit side" remains a matter of guesswork. Another obstacle to assessment is a factor much discussed by reformers in the early twentieth century: the difficulties in enforcing protective laws.

DID THE LAWS WORK? ENFORCEMENT AND EFFECTIVENESS

"Laws do not enforce themselves," declared Ohio's chief factory inspector in 1888. "There must be an active, energetic, and vigilant force behind them." But inspection systems lagged behind legislation. In the nineteenth century, state laws lacked provision for enforcement. Employees were expected to redress grievances themselves by private civil actions or by urging the state's attorney to prosecute complaints. "Provision for the enforcement of the factory acts did not keep pace with factory legislation itself," wrote the International Labour Organization in 1923. "The theory was that injured employees would make complaints on their own initiative, and police, attorneys, and officers of the court were expected to prosecute upon complaint."[42]

Industrial states gradually began factory inspection systems, which sometimes started in state bureaus of labor statistics. Massachusetts, the first state to pass factory laws, began factory inspection in 1866 to enforce child labor laws; subsequently, responsibility for inspection moved to the police, the state board of health, and in 1913 to a state industrial board. New York appointed a few inspectors in 1886 and created a state department of labor in 1901. After the Triangle Fire of 1911, New York's State Factory Investigating Commission started an industrial board, chaired by a labor commissioner, to enforce labor laws, and in 1915, a five-person Industrial Commission. Pennsylvania in 1889 began a system of factory inspection. Wisconsin appointed two inspectors in 1887 and in 1911 turned law enforcement over to a special commission—the first state to put an industrial commission into practice. Ohio followed this example in 1917 and so did Pennsylvania. Illinois began factory inspection to enforce its law of 1893; Florence Kelley was one of the first inspectors.[43]

But even with inspection systems in place, obstacles to effective inspection and enforcement abounded. Flagrant escape hatches, weak penalties, overburdened inspectors, noncompliant employers—and on occasion evasive employees—made enforcement precarious throughout the Progressive Era and beyond. In some instances, loophole-laden laws begged for violations. A Maine law of 1887 limited the number of working hours of minors and women in manufacturing to ten in one day—except when it was necessary to repair machinery or to compensate for shorter days, a provision that seemed to undercut the law at the outset. In no case could working hours for minors or women exceed sixty a week; "however, any female of eighteen years of age or over may lawfully contract for any number of hours in excess of 10 hours a day, not exceeding six hours in any one week or sixty hours in any one year, receiving additional compensation therefore." When found violating the law, both employers and employees found refuge in the sixty-hours-a-year loophole; lawbreakers claimed that "I am working my extra sixty hours."[44]

Pennsylvania's twelve-hour law of 1897, upheld by a state court in 1900, also eluded enforcement. Surveying women's work in Pittsburgh industries (a "factory-to-factory investigation") in 1908, Elizabeth Beardsley Butler, former secretary of the New Jersey Consumers' League, found that manufacturers persistently evaded the law. Poor enforcement of this feeble statute rested in part on loopholes: the law provided a twelve-hour limit with no fixed closing hour (that is, no night work ban) and limited total working hours to sixty a week. An amendment to take effect in 1910 would limit girls under eighteen to a ten-hour day and bar their labor after 9:00 p.m.,

Butler noted. Still, for women over eighteen, the law remained "elastic"; employers could extend work any given day on the pretext of requiring only a short day later in the week. "Overtime" (which then referred to hours of work beyond the legal limit, not to time-and-a-half pay as in current usage) might be irregular, as in industries where customer demand suddenly rose, such as laundries, or seasonal, as in factories that made candy or paper boxes, where holiday seasons heightened demand. Employers reported collusion with factory inspectors. "The inspectors don't interfere with us," the manager of a candy factory—where the Christmas rush meant frequent night work—told investigators. "They usually come in around September and then again after the holidays, and they never see any overtime." In the canning industry, "overtime" prevailed year-round, night work was frequent, and workweeks ran seventy-two hours from May through September; employees seldom lasted over two years in their jobs.[45]

Progressive Era Oregon presented an array of problems: too few inspectors, lenient inspection policies, and recalcitrant employers—who variously claimed ignorance of the law, used ruses to evade it, sought exemptions from it, and showed a willingness to risk fines. Oregon's embattled labor commissioner had to enforce the law of 1903 single-handedly for four years and then gained only three deputies for the rest of the decade, sociologist Elaine Zahnd Johnson observes. Investigating factories all over the state, the overworked commissioner prepared cases against violators and wrote two-hundred-page biennial reports for the Oregon legislature. To avoid expensive litigation "as much as possible," the commissioner initially gave only warnings for first offenses. In 1912, when he began to prosecute first offenses, only half of employers charged paid fines. Employers found ways to evade the law. First, they sought exemptions from it. Retail stores, hotels, and restaurants escaped restriction until 1907, when mercantile firms won a "Christmas week clause," an exemption to employ saleswomen twelve hours a day over holiday seasons. When accused of defying the law, employers claimed to be unaware of it and seemed willing to risk the fines imposed. Canneries routinely violated the ten-hour law, according to the Oregon Consumers' League in 1913—and were then exempted from the state's minimum wage law. Other repeat offenders, like F. C. Stettler's paper box factory, were fearless in court. When fined, Stettler appealed, and then challenged the state's minimum wage law. Employers also resorted to tricks. Some evaded the ten-hour law by firing workers and replacing them at lower cost ($1 or less a week) with apprentices, who performed limited tasks and were dismissed if they asked for training on the job or higher pay. Finally, despite assurances of confidentiality, employees feared reporting on employers.[46]

In New York State, as of 1925, enforcement of maximum hours laws had been dismal, economist Elizabeth Faulkner Baker claimed. Factors that impeded law enforcement included exhausted inspectors, recalcitrant employers, gross violations, bungled prosecutions, dismissed charges, inadequate penalties, unpaid fines, and intimidated employees, who, out of "ignorance, inefficiency, or fear" of dismissal, hesitated to complain about abuses. The "long-entrenched custom of homework by women" endangered New York's important fifty-four-hour law of 1912; women who worked in factories for nine or ten hours took work home with them overnight and on Sundays. Owners of canning factories, when affected at all by state law, consistently violated it and escaped punishment; laundries demanded consideration for "seasonal and sporadic trade." Overall, Baker charged, among factory laws in general, "the extent to which laws are enforced is almost impossible to trace" and of violations, "only a small per cent are discovered." In the case of protective laws for women workers, "[W]e are told that the difficulty of enforcement is frequently owing to the opposition of workers themselves."[47]

By the mid-1920s, states enforced protective laws in several ways. New York, the most highly industrial state, had an appointed industrial commissioner, an industrial board, and 183 inspectors (thirty-one were women). Pennsylvania followed a similar system with eighty inspectors, nine of them women. In California, the commissioner of labor statistics, the Industrial Accident Commission, and an Industrial Welfare Commission shared responsibility for enforcement. Virginia had five factory inspectors, female. In Wisconsin, the first state to put in practice an Industrial Commission, "Woman and Child Labor" was one of seven departments. In most instances, industrial commissioners or other executives appointed inspectors whose terms expired frequently. In every state, health measures (factory safety and sanitation) consumed the attention of law enforcement, the ILO reported. Laws that affected women's hours remained minor considerations, and few resources fell their way.[48] Enforcement remained a work in progress that awaited federal action in the 1930s.

Evidence about the fragility of enforcement systems usually came from reformers who promoted protective laws and sought improvement in their impact. Their zeal for research, though mainly local, extended to Europe. New York physician George M. Price, whose studies were quoted in the Brandeis briefs and who served the state Factory Investigating Commission, set the pace in the summer of 1913 with a whirlwind four-month inspection tour of six nations. European factory inspectors were superior to those in the United States, Price declared; well trained, they enjoyed merit promotions and tenure in office. European factory inspection systems, in contrast, he stated, might be less effective than American counterparts. In France, a special trouble spot, employers were uncooperative, inspectors incompetent, police unavailable, and departmental administrators a bureaucratic nightmare. Employers everywhere, even in Germany and England, where inspection systems worked best, routinely whisked underage labor out of sight as inspectors approached. Finally, Price concluded, no inspectors could successfully enforce labor laws "unless those provisions are based on the needs of the workers themselves and call forth their support."[49] When women workers in the United States joined the battle over protective laws in the 1920s, they offered support for both protectionists and equal rights advocates.

WORKING WOMEN'S VOICES

"My dear Mrs. Kelley," wrote Philadelphia factory worker Emma Hess in 1922. "I would be very sorry to see any Amendment passed that would infringe on any laws that stand for the betterment of women in any way, particularly the industrial laws as they stand now in our state of Pennsylvania." Emma Hess worked eight hours a day or a forty-four-hour week but remembered "when as a small girl" she labored a sixty-hour week. "I hope that for the sake of women and girls, that the influence of yourself and all the good women working so hard will prevail upon the men who make our laws," Emma Hess concluded. "Because we all know that upon the health of women depends the increase of the population of our country."[50]

Emma Hess's letter was one of many that protectionists amassed as the battle over a proposed ERA took shape in the early 1920s. Like most workers who voiced opinions for or against protective laws, Emma Hess responded to an agency that sought—if not shaped—her views. The NCL, its local branches, the NWTUL, the WB, and independent researchers recorded workers' opinions of protective measures, as did summer schools for women workers and legislative hearings. Women employees who opposed protection typically worked on what Elizabeth Faulkner Baker called "industrial frontiers"—trades dominated by men. They were printers, streetcar conductors, elevator operators; sometimes office workers or professionals; and most often foes of night work laws. Both groups of employed women included those who had in the past or "until recently" been factory workers and had subsequently moved on to other vocations.[51]

Conflict among women workers arose in 1919 when the Women's Joint Legislative Conference in New York State held hearings in Albany in the assembly chambers to debate six measures then under consideration. Speakers included defenders of protective laws, manufacturers who opposed them, and supporters on both sides, including employers and employees. Bette Hawley, until recently a Buffalo waitress, claimed to represent three hundred women restaurant workers. "My girls, every one of them . . . working girls, not uplifters, advocate and approve an eight-hour law and we positively disapprove working at night because the waitresses at Buffalo have worked harder at night than any other class of girls in the United States." "I do not think it is fair to say we can do the same work that men do," claimed Miss Berrigan, a factory worker in Poughkeepsie. "If 29 states in the Union can have what we are asking [an eight-hour day] for here today why not the great state of New York?" Anna Merritt, who worked as a subway guard ("conductorette") for the Brooklyn Rapid Transit Company, described ten-hour shifts beginning before 5:00 or 6:00 a.m. plus a "swing run" in the evening during rush hour. "[W]e were supposed to work ten hours a day but [i]f we worked ten hours a day we were lucky," Anna Merritt declared. "We always had to work ten, eleven, twelve, thirteen, fourteen hours." Those who complained were suspended or risked layoffs for four days. "We worked seven days a week," stated Anna Merritt. "I had no time to myself. . . . I do not think it fair to a girl to have to work at night." Anne Hogan, a unionized factory worker and then a clerical worker, claimed that office workers needed single-sex labor laws: "We need protection as much as the factory worker and the girl in the mercantile establishment."[52]

Women workers opposed to protective laws at the 1919 hearings spoke out, too. "I started running an elevator when I was 17 years old in an apartment house," Stella Jackson declared. "They say it is dangerous to run elevators in apartment houses for girls working nights. It is not. . . . Night work is not injurious to a girl's health. . . . If this [night work] bill goes through it means I will not work for the same amount of salary I am earning now; it means I will have to go back to housework." The proposed night work bill for elevator operators, Stella Jackson concluded, will "mean taking away my bread and butter." Business and professional women joined the antiprotection speakers. "For the last fifteen years I have been self-supporting, working up from a small clerical position to an executive post," stated office executive Miss Thompson, "and I have never wanted any special legislation . . . further than the same protection accorded to men. . . . I am opposed to any legislation that discriminates in any way against women." Amy Wren, president of the Brooklyn Women's Lawyers Association, who had recently surveyed the views of disgruntled transit workers, endorsed the case against protection.

"We want the same laws for men and women," claimed Wren, who had worked for twenty-nine years. "They [audience members] don't hear the other side of it, but it is a lot of Consumers' Leagues or somebody like that who are not the real working women. Now we feel you should hear the working women and take their view of the matter."[53]

Conflicting views among employees appeared in the NWTUL magazine *Life and Labor* in 1920. Marguerite Moers Marshall, a journalist and foe of single-sex protective laws, attacked the New York WTUL for it's "anti-feminist" attitude. At issue: An exemption to New York's single-sex night work law won by reporters in 1919, now in question. Protective laws, Marshall claimed, kept women "from meeting men on the ground of equality." As a journalist, Marshall concluded that night work "in no way injured my health, either physical or mental." To quibble about night assignments, she claimed, would have supported prejudice against women reporters. A stenographer, in contrast, she suggested, might enjoy her social life more than her career. "Why penalize, for her sake, the ambitious woman in newspaper or business office ... who is willing to do extra, to stay after hours," and to work for promotions? Rose Schneiderman, former cap maker, founder of a women's local of the Cap Makers' Union, activist in the ILGWU, and officer of the New York WTUL responded. "I daresay that if Miss Marshall had to sort dirty linen for nine hours a day, instead of sitting in a nice, airy office, feeding the minds of working women with a lot of sob stuff ... she would be ready to be protected by legislation," Schneiderman wrote. "I think the whole mistake Miss Marshall makes is in the idea that there is a career in industry or in the department store. Those of us who have worked in the factory or store know that there is only room for one at the top and the rest must struggle until they get married or die." Schneiderman continued: "Frankly speaking, the average working woman does not want a factory career, as there is no such thing. She is looking forward to getting married and raising a family."[54]

The Women's Bureau captured a diversity of views in several reports; one was its 1921 study of women transit workers—streetcar conductors and ticket agents—in Detroit, Kansas City, Boston, and Chicago. Replacing men during World War I, women transit workers voiced mixed views about protective laws afterward. Detroit workers in January 1920 responded to questions about a maximum hours law: of thirty-two women that the WB interviewed, twenty-six expressed approval of the law and six objected, each group with some qualifications. "Ten hours a day and 54 hours a week are long enough for anyone," one woman said. "If there were not laws to limit the hours of work for women, some employers would work them to death." "Believe women should have equal rights with men," another Detroit worker countered.

> Some of the women working here have had to give up money they needed badly by being forced to cut their hours. When you are strong and have children to support it is rather difficult to understand why such restrictions are placed, especially when you know of many women working two shifts in restaurants so as to increase their pay. Some work 16 hours, six and seven days each week. So why pick on the streetcar women?[55]

The massive WB report of 1928 conveyed the results of interviews with hundreds of women workers, though use of the third person ("thinks all women would be benefited by an even shorter week if they have a family to care for") distanced readers from workers. Most summaries of interviews with workers reflected the WB stance, but in interchanges with women in cutting-edge jobs—transit workers, women in newspaper offices—the WB conceded that some employees held protection in low regard. A series of interviews with twelve night workers (half on newspapers and half in printing plants) yielded mixed results. A proofreader on a New York newspaper who lost her job because of state law but regained it when the law was repealed preferred night work to day work because "working at night enabled her to look after her children during the day. . . . This woman was convinced that special laws for women were a hindrance to them in the industrial world."[56]

The threat of an ERA in the early 1920s led social feminist leaders to solicit supportive correspondence from women workers. "It is as working women, and wives, mothers and daughters of Union men that we are opposed to the Blanket Legislation favored by the National Woman's Party," wrote the secretary of a midwestern WTUL branch, Anna A. Carlson, to Maud Swartz of the NWTUL. "[I]t is not for the best interest of working women." A York, Pennsylvania, branch of the YWCA offered Florence Kelley support: "[P]olitical and legal equality for women may be secured more safely by the slower process of legislation against specific laws and . . . the existing protective and welfare laws for women and children will certainly be endangered by the Blanket Equality Amendment." In California, Katherine Philips Edson (1876–1933), suffragist, clubwoman, protectionist, and head of the state Industrial Welfare Commission (IWC), received letters to support the state's eight-hour day (1911) and minimum wage (1918). "Use all your influence to show the National Women's [sic] Party that the greater majority of working girls wanted and need the legislation that is now being enforced," wrote Louise Jacobs, a San Francisco saleswoman. Another San Francisco employee, Ida Lockhart, an assistant buyer at a department store, praised California's laws to Florence Kelley. "I am for the Masses," Ida Lock-hart declared. "We have better service now, than before we had the eight-hour day, and the minimum wage." Women trade unionists in California, in contrast, who supported the state maximum hours law, took issue with Katherine Edson's IWC and attacked the minimum wage. "Let the women get their wages as men do by collective bargaining and organization," declared labor leader Sarah Hagan, an officer of San Francisco's United Garment Workers' Local 131. To Hagan, single-sex protective laws made women workers "wards of the state" and impeded unionism. "[T]hey lean too much on the minimum wage and the eight-hour day, which make them feel protected without organization and the employers have it their own way."[57]

The most forceful voices of women workers in the 1920s came from former workers in industry who assumed leading roles in the NWTUL. Former workers—Rose Schneiderman, Pauline Newman, Maud Swartz, Agnes Nestor, Elisabeth Christman, and Mary Anderson (as of 1920 head of the WB)—had long dominated the executive boards of NWTUL and the New York branch. Unionization of women workers had always been primary to NWTUL. But to organize women, with meager support from the AFL or from local union leaders, had been difficult. The Triangle Fire of 1911 made worker safety laws a priority; after World War I, NWTUL interest shifted toward single-sex protective legislation—not as a substitute for unionization but rather as a spur to it. "If we organized even a handful of girls and then managed to put through legislation which made into law the advantages they had gained, other girls would be more likely to join a union and reap further benefits for themselves," declared Rose Schneiderman. NWTUL also found it easier to win protection from the state than endorsement from male union leaders, historian Annelise Orleck points out. Finally, the voices of former workers at NWTUL became stronger as the passage of time distanced them from their experience as workers. Those at the New York branch gained special influence. Eleanor Roosevelt's involvement in their work brought an influx of funds that kept the group alive in the 1920s and empowered its leaders in the decade ahead. Among social feminists in general, Eleanor Roosevelt became a crucial figure. Unexpectedly, access to this gifted colleague—socially prominent, politically skilled, and strategically placed—would be a far greater asset to social feminists in the 1930s than proximity to a working-class base.[58]

. . . . .

"We appear, then, to have arrived at the crossroads in the legal protection of women in industry," wrote economist Elizabeth Faulkner Baker in 1929.

"Which way shall be our next turn? One voice is toward more and more laws for women; another leads to none—to the abrogation of laws which do not apply alike to men and women." Baker recommended the "retention of present laws" and a drive "for the extension of these laws to include men as well." The Women's Bureau regularly totaled the achievement of single-sex protection. At the end of 1931, forty-three states had women-only maximum hours laws, though most affected only small proportions of women workers. Sixteen states barred night work for women in specific industries or occupations. Almost half of the states had prohibitory laws of some sort—seventeen states, for instance, excluded women from jobs in mining; almost all states had laws providing rest periods or seating regulations; fourteen states banned or regulated homework; and nine states had minimum wage laws, which were operative in only six (California, North Dakota, Oregon, South Dakota, Washington, and Wisconsin).[59]

The great battle over protective laws among women activists in the 1920s—a classic confrontation that split the women's movement and endured for decades—represents a critical era of women's engagement with legal questions and political process, an era in which feuding factions of the women's movement became embroiled in constitutional issues and shaped a "constitutional community." The conflict was spirited, unavoidable, and unresolvable. It generated crucial documents in the history of protective laws, including the internal debates of the NWP in the early 1920s, Elizabeth Faulkner Baker's study of protective laws in 1925, and the massive Women's Bureau report of 1928. Hopes of both factions faded around mid-decade—about the same time that woman suffrage, to observers, seemed to have little impact on politics. The NWP succeeded in proposing an equal rights amendment to Congress in 1923. But the NWP remained a minority faction; after proposing the amendment, supporters made no further progress with it. Reintroduced in Congress in 1924, 1925, and 1929, the proposed ERA failed to move out of committee. Social feminists retained dominance in the women's movement but faced problems as well. An unfavorable political climate cut their momentum and diminished their ranks. They also suffered failure after failure—failure to achieve influence with Congress, failure to retain the Sheppard-Towner law, failure to pass a child labor amendment, and failure to make progress with the minimum wage. By the fall of 1930, the NCL had only seventeen branches, down from sixty-four in 1903.[60]

Setbacks, however, do not invalidate social feminist achievements in the 1920s. Reformers sought to create a fabric of protection and set precedents on which more widespread protective measures could rest. Single-sex protective laws were a means to this end; their retention and efforts by the states to enforce them maintained pressure for broader and more effective "general" laws. Single-sex laws also assumed a symbolic function. They embodied a challenge to domination by business values. Ironically, in contrast to the setbacks that protectionists experienced in the 1920s, the Great Depression suddenly provided opportunity for progress. Ironically, too, it was the minimum wage—the most controversial of protectionist proposals, feared, derided, and barely operative—on which progress in the 1930s hinged. The six minimum wage laws in place at the end of the 1920s were the cutting edge of protective policy. The despised *Adkins* opinion set forth the challenges that reformers would have to meet.

6

Transformations: The New Deal through the 1950s

"I HAVE ALWAYS FELT THAT IT WAS not I alone who was appointed to the Cabinet, but that it was all the women of America," declared Frances Perkins in the fall of 1933. FDR's choice for secretary of labor, Perkins sought a rationale for accepting the job. Years later she still defended her decision: "[T]he door might not be opened to a woman again for a long, long time," she wrote in 1945. "I had a kind of duty to other women to walk in and sit down on the chair that was offered." Yet another defense struck Perkins in retro-

■ ■ ■

Elsie Parrish, 1937. Chambermaid at the Cascadian Hotel in Wenatchee, Washington, Elsie Parrish sued her employer, the company that owned the hotel, for violating the state law that mandated a minimum wage for women workers. The Supreme Court unexpectedly found the law constitutional in *West Coast Hotel v. Parrish* (1937). Photo courtesy of Wenatchee Valley Museum and Cultural Center, #87–169–1.

spect. She personally had not been selected for the post, she told an audience in 1939, "but it was the Consumers' League who was appointed ... I was merely the symbol who happened to be at hand, able and willing to serve it at the moment." Perkins's reflections resonate, especially the last. She served as a bridge between the National Consumers' League and the state. Long certain that protective laws surpassed whatever unions might achieve, she used her new position to advance protectionist goals. To her New Deal colleague, Molly Dewson, another NCL veteran, who had avidly urged the Perkins appointment, "[H]ere was the golden opportunity for pushing ahead the labor legislation program for which I had worked for so many years."[1]

NCL leaders' hopes were realized. In contrast to the setbacks of the 1920s, the New Deal revived the prospects of protective laws and of their proponents. The stunning victory of the minimum wage for women workers in federal court in 1937 and the passage in 1938 of the Fair Labor Standards Act (FLSA), which extended labor standards to men, represented a peak of protectionist achievement. This achievement rested firmly on the precedent of single-sex labor laws for which social feminists—led by the NCL—had long campaigned. The victory of the 1930s was double-edged: as it advanced the cause of labor standards for all, it helped to undercut the long-term prospects of single-sex laws, in which protectionists retained a vital interest. Suspended in war and restored in peace, single-sex protective laws remained in place, long after FLSA opened up a second route to labor standards. Social feminists, the Women's Bureau, and women unionists defended them; to supporters, the benefits of single-sex laws continued to outweigh their liabilities; their dismantling lay far ahead in the late 1960s. But "equal rights" gained momentum in the postwar years, 1945–60. A gamut of changes transformed their prospects. By the start of the 1960s, single-sex protective laws had resumed their role as a focus of contention in the women's movement.

NEW DEAL WOMEN

To women reformers, the New Deal showed that the state could act to provide relief, aid families, protect workers, and enact a social feminist agenda. Eleanor Roosevelt exemplified social feminist concerns. She had entered public life and party politics in the 1920s as an activist in the NWTUL and NCL, and in the Democratic Party's women's wing in New York State when FDR was governor, 1928–32. By the time FDR became president in 1933 she had honed her political skills. Lobbyist, publicist, moralist, and partisan, ER filled an unprecedented space in public affairs. An advocate for the less advantaged—for women, blacks, youth, and the unemployed—she reached the public through her Monday morning press conferences and through newsreels, magazine articles, newspaper columns, radio talks, and lecture tours. In continual motion, she publicized women's projects, lobbied for women's causes, and served as White House liaison for women's groups. By the 1936 election, ER had created a unique sphere of influence. "I am sure, Eleanor dear, that millions of people voted with you in their minds, also," wrote Rose Schneiderman of the New York WTUL after the campaign.[2]

The early New Deal saw a women's upsurge in government and politics. Social feminists made unprecedented inroads in appointive office. Concentrated in Frances Perkins's Department of Labor, where Mary Anderson and Katherine Lenroot led the Women's Bureau and Children's Bureau, respectively, women also found jobs in newly formed federal agencies and advisory boards. Emily Blair, Mary Harriman Rumsey, and suffragist lawyer Sue Shelton White, for instance, served on the Consumers' Advisory Board of the National Recovery Administration (NRA), and Rose Schneiderman on the NRA Labor Advisory Board; Ellen Sullivan Woodward and Hilda Smith were administrators at the Federal Emergency Relief Administration (FERA) and the Works Progress Administration (WPA). Mary McLeod Bethune, a black educator, friend of Eleanor Roosevelt, and in 1935 founder of the National Council of Negro Women, headed black programs at the National Youth Administration (NYA). After 1935, White and Woodward served on the three-person Social Security Board, as did Molly Dewson, head of the Democratic National Committee's Women's Division. Clara Beyer in 1938 became associate director of the new Bureau of Labor Standards. "Those of us who worked to put together the New Deal," Frances Perkins later told Molly Dewson, "are bound by spiritual ties that no one else can understand."[3]

Most of the New Deal's high-level women appointees and party activists, like Eleanor Roosevelt, shared backgrounds in women's organizations and social welfare. Historian Susan Ware identifies a network of twenty-eight women, linked by a history of "personal friendship and professional interaction," that moved into jobs in politics and national government in the 1930s. The network had roots in suffrage, progressivism, and social reform. Born around 1880, network members were usually well off and well educated. They knew each other from the NWTUL, NCL, and Democratic politics of the 1920s; about half were relatives of male politicians. Their interaction, Ware shows, served to "maximize their influence in politics and government." Unlikely to call themselves "feminist," a label now claimed by NWP members, they saw themselves as social reformers. Network members some-

Frances Perkins and Clara M. Beyer, 1938. Secretary of labor Frances Perkins, the first woman cabinet member, and Clara M. Beyer, associate director of the Bureau of Labor Standards in the Department of Labor, confer in 1938. Both officials were veterans of years of activism in the National Consumers' League. Library of Congress.

times supported an ERA, as did Sue Shelton White and Democratic representative Emma Guffey Miller. But most shared social feminist bonds and endorsed protective legislation. When Eleanor Roosevelt defended single-sex laws in 1933, her qualified support reflected the always-tentative NWTUL stance: protective laws were a temporary expedient. "I think women have a right to demand equality as far as possible, but I think they should still have the protection of special legislation regarding certain special conditions of their work," she wrote. "[U]ntil we actually have equal pay and are assured of a living wage for both men's and women's work, I believe in minimum wage boards and regulating by law the number of hours women may work."[4]

The NCL shaped several dominant New Deal women. Molly Dewson first worked for a Boston social reform club, the Women's Educational and Industrial Union, where she studied the homes of working families, and then in 1911 as executive secretary of the Massachusetts Minimum Wage Investigative Committee. Her report to the Massachusetts legislature led to the first state minimum wage law in 1912. As research secretary for Florence Kelley at the NCL, 1919–24, Dewson focused on minimum wage laws for women and children; she joined Felix Frankfurter to write the brief defending the District of Columbia Minimum Wage Board in *Adkins v.*

Children's Hospital, and served as president of the New York Consumers'
League from 1925 until 1931. A likely candidate to head the NCL after Florence Kelley's death in 1932, Dewson instead turned to New Deal politics.
She mobilized women voters in FDR's presidential campaigns, led the Wom-
en's Division of the Democratic National Committee from 1933 to 1937,
promoted women's appointments, and in 1935 helped draft the Social Security Act. Throughout her New Deal career, Dewson strove for federal
labor standards. "Mary Dewson and I were both people committed to the
Consumers' League," Perkins declared.[5]

Like Molly Dewson, Frances Perkins had long championed the NCL. As
a Mount Holyoke student, she had formed an NCL chapter; after gradua-
tion in 1902, she joined the settlement movement in Chicago. A Russell
Sage fellowship in 1909 led her to the New York School of Philanthropy
(1904), later the Columbia University School of Social Work. Perkins moved
on to Columbia for a master's degree in sociology and then to the New
York City Consumers' League, as its executive secretary. In 1912, after the
Triangle Fire, Perkins worked for the New York State Factory Investigating
Commission, and in 1919, New York governor Al Smith appointed her to
the Industrial Commission of the State of New York. Florence Kelley saw
this leap into state bureaucracy as a crucial step. "Glory be to God!" she told
Perkins. "You don't mean it. I never thought I would live to see the day
when someone we had trained, who knew about industrial conditions,
cared about women, cared to have things right, would have the chance to be
an administrative officer." Perkins's rise in public office had just begun. In
1929, FDR, then New York governor, made Perkins head of the state's labor
department, where she administered workmen's compensation, expanded
factory inspection, and opposed child labor. "[T]here will be less death, misery, and poverty because you are at the helm," Florence Kelley wrote to Perkins upon her induction.[6]

Frances Perkins's New Deal post was a tinderbox of controversy. As the
first woman cabinet member, Perkins was suspect. Congress called on her
relentlessly to testify, more than any other member of the executive branch.
She lost administrative battles continually. She faced attacks in the late
1930s that she supported communists from Martin Dies, head of the House
Un-American Activities Committee. Labor bills always evoked dispute. Organized labor distrusted Perkins, in part because she had never been a union
leader or even a union member. "Labor can never become reconciled to the
selection," declared AFL president William Green in 1933. Perkins clung to
her preference for legislation over unionization, an NCL tenet that she reiterated in her oral history of the early 1950s. "This I know to be true," Perkins

told historian Dean Albertson. "The trade unions in this country have never at anytime, either then or later taken the lead in labor legislation. It's always been done by the so-called reformers." Dismissive of strikes, Perkins defended "the mass protections that come out of law, of legislation . . . I'd much rather get a law than organize a union, and I think it's more important." Labor representatives, unsurprisingly, in the words of Women's Bureau head Mary Anderson, "thought of her as a social worker, not a real labor person."[7]

Perkins's strained relationship with Mary Anderson was a frayed link in the New Deal women's network. A Swedish-born immigrant, Anderson began work as a domestic servant ("I was not a success at it") and then as a stitcher in a Chicago shoe factory. She joined the Chicago branch of the WTUL in 1905, became a salaried league organizer, served on an AFL subcommittee on women in industry, and then became assistant director under Mary Van Kleeck of the World War I Women in Industry Service. A staunch friend of women workers, Anderson headed the WB from 1920 to 1944. In the 1930s, the WB—an outpost in the labor department with some sixty women employees—shrank while the Children's Bureau grew. Perkins sought to consolidate the two bureaus but backed down. Anderson charged Perkins with lack of attention to women workers. According to Anderson, Perkins "leaned over backwards" not to favor women, "minimized the importance" of women's issues, and "did not want to be thought of as a woman too closely identified with women's problems." When Anderson sought special funds for a WB study of domestic workers, a primarily black constituency, her proposal could not get past the House Appropriations Committee ("the whole subject got mixed up with the race question"), and Perkins, she claimed, did nothing to help. The labor secretary told her "the colored people were alright as they were," Anderson charged, and said, "Don't ever bring that up again."[8]

The WB faced many problems in the 1930s. It "had been and continued to be on the edges of power," writes historian Judith Sealander, "its advice ignored or accepted without acknowledgement." Still, under Anderson, the WB started to replace voluntary organizations as the advocate of women workers. It also extended its network to a growing constituency, women in unions. Women's numbers in unions began to rise in 1933. Section 7A of the National Industrial Recovery Act (NIRA) protected labor's right to organize, as did the National Labor Relations Act of 1935. Women's membership mushroomed; the International Ladies' Garment Workers' Union (ILGWU) quadrupled in 1935 alone. An important advance for women was industrial unionism, which took hold in 1935, first under the industrial union committee of the AFL and then, after 1937, under the new Congress of Industrial Organizations (CIO). The CIO focused on heavy industry with mainly male employees; it also moved into northern textile plants and the West Coast canning industry. Between 1930 and 1940, women's union membership more than tripled; the main surge was yet to come in World War II when women constituted over a third of the workforce. The growing number of organized women would revitalize social feminism: Union women became the WB's main constituency.[9]

As unions rose, support for Progressive Era women's groups fell. The NWTUL's budget shrank, and the last of its Washington lobbyists resigned. The NCL remained active in the 1930s under its new general secretary, Lucy Mason, but membership dropped.[10] Volunteerism ran adrift; defense of protective laws shifted back to the courts.

THE MINIMUM WAGE AND THE REVOLUTION OF 1937

In *Adkins*'s wake, when protectionists of the 1920s regrouped to salvage the minimum wage, Florence Kelley and Felix Frankfurter favored different strategies. Kelley sought a constitutional amendment to protect the minimum wage from judicial review. Frankfurter found such an amendment "a remote thing"; he sought instead a loophole in the *Adkins* opinion. Division between NCL leaders and protectionist lawyers continued after Kelley's death in 1932. Her legatees—Elizabeth Brandeis, Molly Dewson, Frances Perkins, Josephine Goldmark, and Clara Beyer—hoped to win the minimum wage for both women and men. Frankfurter favored a women-first policy; he wanted to see the courts uphold a single-sex minimum wage "before we bring the men in." To cope with "the Ladies," Frankfurter had turned to his colleague Benjamin V. Cohen, after 1932 a major New Deal advisor. The lawyers seized the initiative. Hold-out Clara Beyer, who had first suggested "that we cover men, too," pursued that goal into 1934, she recalled, until "the wrath of the drafters of the new [women-only] standard. . . . came down on my head." By then her NCL colleagues had conceded to the lawyers' women-first scenario. "Molly Dewson, my dear Molly Dewson, said she was sorry to have to [agree to the lawyers' proposal]," Beyer told an interviewer. She remembered "the Goldmark sisters and all running in apologizing for objecting to my proposal to cover men."[11]

When Cohen and Frankfurter shaped a New York State minimum-wage-for-women bill in 1933, they pursued a due process strategy on which they had worked since the 1920s. The goal: to satisfy Justice Sutherland's demand, in the *Adkins* decision, for a "fair wage." To achieve this, the lawyers revised the rationale for a minimum wage and built the new rationale into the law. New York's law of 1933 defined "an oppressive or unreasonable wage" as one "both less than the fair and reasonable value of the services rendered and less than sufficient to meet the minimum cost of living necessary for health." Such a law, the lawyers hoped, would meet Sutherland's criteria. Like Brandeis in 1908, the lawyers hoped to navigate around an adverse ruling; they had found what historian Jeff Shesol calls "a little room to maneuver." The new strategy, historian Vivien Hart points out, meant abandoning the police power, on which protectionists had always relied, and the concern that it embodied for workers' health.[12]

In the last stage of the feud between lawyers and NCL leaders, in 1932–33, the New York legislature passed two minimum wage bills that were the same, save for three points in dispute. Benjamin V. Cohen's biographer, William Lasser, describes the distinctions. One bill, drafted by Molly Dewson, applied to men as well as to women and minors. Dewson's bill was limited to the "emergency" (of the Great Depression) and provided for enforcement solely through publicity about the employers who violated it. The second bill, drafted by Ben Cohen, with the consultation of Frankfurter, applied only to women and minors. It did not refer to the "emergency" and it provided penalties for violators. New York's governor (still FDR at the start of 1933) had to choose the bill most likely to get past a hostile Supreme Court; he signed the bill drafted by Cohen. Five other states enacted similar laws. The New York law would soon play a major role in New Deal history.[13]

A challenge to the New York law arose when Joseph Tipaldo, manager of the Spotlight Laundry in Brooklyn, violated it; although he paid the minimum wage on the books, Tipaldo took kickbacks from workers and ended up in jail. His lawyers charged that the minimum wage was unconstitutional. To defend the law, Frankfurter and Cohen devised a two-ploy argument. The specially designed New York law of 1933 could be distinguished from the DC law of 1918 at issue in *Adkins*, they contended. At the same time they asked the justices for a "reconsideration" of *Adkins*. Their strategy: both to get around *Adkins* and overturn it. Chief Justice Charles Evans Hughes appreciated the first argument but rejected the second; he alone favored both the New York law and *Adkins*. Five other justices, including Owen Roberts, rejected the New York law in *Morehead v. New York ex rel. Tipaldo* on June 1, 1936. The Frankfurter/Cohen strategy, it seemed, had failed.[14]

Tipaldo dismayed New Dealers and fed dissent. On February 5, 1937, after his second inauguration, FDR announced the court-packing plan, a scheme to end Supreme Court rejection of New Deal measures (for every justice who reached the age of seventy and refused to retire, the president could appoint another justice, up to six). As Congress began to consider the plan, a new case that had arisen in the state of Washington moved forward. The case involved a single-sex minimum wage law of 1914.

Elsie Parrish, a thirty-six-year-old mother of six, recently remarried, worked as a chambermaid at the Cascadian Hotel in Wenatchee, Washington. In 1935, Parrish, with her husband, sued her employer, the company that owned the hotel (the West Coast Hotel Company), for $216.19, the difference between what she had been paid and the state minimum wage ($14.50 per forty-eight-hour week). After *Tipaldo*, no one expected such a case to reach the Supreme Court. Moreover, the Washington State law differed from the carefully designed New York law. Rather, it resembled the Oregon law of 1913 that had just squeaked by in *Stettler* (1917) and was identical to the DC law that had failed in 1923 in *Adkins*. But the Supreme Court voted to hear the case. Unexpectedly, Justice Owen Roberts, who had sided with the majority in *Tipaldo*, agreed to do so. The Court heard arguments in December 1936, reached an informal decision soon after, and on March 29, 1937, in *West Coast Hotel v. Parrish*, announced this surprise decision. The Court upheld the Washington law. "Liberty under the Constitution is . . . subject to the restraints of due process," said Justice Hughes, "and regulation which is reasonable in relation to its subject in the interests of the community is due process." Justice Roberts voted to uphold the law. With Justices Brandeis, Benjamin Cardozo, and Harlan Stone, the minimum wage now had a majority of 5—4. Justice Roberts's "switch in time" had changed the court's direction. "Just to think that silly Roberts should have the power to play politics and decide the fate of minimum wage legislation," Molly Dewson exulted. "But, thank God, he thought it was politically expedient to be with us!" "Overruling Adkins case must give you some satisfaction," Brandeis wrote to Frankfurter right after the decision. The 1937 victory made Brandeis look back to his own argument of 1914 in the *Stettler* case. A week later he noted to Frankfurter that "[t]he fight for the minimum wage really began 30 years ago with *Muller v. Oregon*."[15]

Elsie Parrish recalled the event with less exuberance. "[N]obody paid much attention at the time," she complained in 1972 to an interviewer, journalist Adela Roger St. Johns, "and none of the women running around and yelling about Liberty and such have paid any since."[16]

Justice Roberts's motivation has been at the center of historical debate. Years later, in 1945, Roberts explained his switch in a memorandum that he left with Justice Frankfurter, who published it in a law journal a decade later. Roberts claimed that his position had been consistent. When deciding *Ti-*

paldo, he had rejected only the Frankfurter-Cohen argument that New York's minimum wage law differed from the District of Columbia law as disingenuous. New York's lawyers should have directly challenged *Adkins*, he stated. (They did indeed do this, Jeff Shesol points out, by asking for a "reconsideration" of *Adkins*.) Roberts also wrote in his memo that he should have presented his own narrow concurring opinion but had not done so. "Who knows what causes a judge to decide as he does," Roberts once commented, looking back on *Parrish*. Shesol posits that probably both Hughes and Roberts were influenced by the rising tide of public antipathy to *Tipaldo*. Did a summer visit from Justice Hughes influence Roberts's thoughts on the minimum wage? Frances Perkins, another summer visitor—Perkins was a girlhood friend and college classmate of Roberts's wife, Elisabeth Rogers—thought that she detected a change in Justice Roberts's ideas in the fall of 1936 when *Parrish* was en route to the Supreme Court. Roberts told her he could differentiate the two cases, Perkins recalled, but she didn't grasp exactly why.[17]

Parrish was of course a monumental triumph for New Dealers. President Roosevelt labeled the decision a "clearcut victory." "The Court Yielded. The Court Changed," he wrote a few years later. "The Court began to interpret the Constitution instead of torturing it." FDR declared the 1937 decision "a turning point in our modern History." It was a well-timed turning point. The justices had reached their informal decision on *Parrish* in December 1936, before the presidential message that announced the Court-packing plan (February 5, 1937); the formal decision was handed down afterward, in March. On July 22, 1937, the Court-packing plan died in the Senate, its underlying goal fulfilled. From *Parrish* forward, the Supreme Court upheld all the New Deal measures it reviewed. Within five years, FDR had appointed all of the Supreme Court justices save two, Justices Stone and Roberts. One of his appointees was Felix Frankfurter, who joined the Court in 1939.[18]

The legacy for protectionists—and for the history of labor standards—was huge as well. The single-sex minimum wage was the lever on which this crucial episode in jurisprudence rested. Here was a moment when a social feminist achievement took center stage. As it did so, however, the legal scenery changed. The *Parrish* decision was grounded in the due process clause, formerly used to attack protective labor laws. At the very moment that the minimum wage triumphed, the police power vanished from judicial consideration. Historian Vivien Hart observes: "The social critique reasoning inherent in police power reasoning was lost when the issue became due process." For social feminists, a degree of loss accompanied gain.[19]

Yet another critical legal tilt soon followed. Two weeks after *Parrish*, the Supreme Court upheld 5–4 the National Labor Relations Act (NLRA) as a legitimate use of the power of Congress to regulate commerce. "These two decisions," wrote economist Elizabeth Brandeis, "gave hope that the court might uphold a general federal minimum wage and maximum hours law, like NRA, on the power to regulate commerce." What workers would such a new federal labor standards law reach? "I think it should include everybody, men and women," FDR told the press corps in 1937, when the Supreme Court upheld *Parrish*. "Why not go the whole hog?"[20]

FLSA: PROTECTION TRIUMPHANT

The National Recovery Administration (NRA) codes of 1933 had provided labor standards for women and men and regulated industrial homework, a longtime social feminist goal, but the Supreme Court invalidated the National Industrial Recovery Act (NIRA) in *Schechter v. U.S.* (1935). Sometime in 1935, as NRA's fate pended, Frances Perkins reminded FDR that she had two bills "locked up" in a desk drawer that would put "a floor under wages and ceiling over hours." The first bill, drafted by Benjamin V. Cohen, now a presidential advisor, and his associate, Tom Corcoran, became the Walsh-Healey Public Contracts Act, signed into law in June 1936. A forerunner of FLSA, the Walsh-Healey law provided a minimum wage and maximum hours (forty hours) for contractors manufacturing supplies for the government and banned child labor in such an activity. Like NLRA, Walsh-Healey rested on federal power to regulate interstate commerce. The claim: the commerce clause allowed regulation of economic activity, even activity indirectly affecting interstate commerce. The second bill, a more far-reaching wage-and-hours bill, also based on the commerce clause, would become FLSA. It reached Congress in May 1937.[21]

Again drafted by Cohen and Corcoran, the new wage-and-hours bill evoked dispute. Frances Perkins, who opened the bill's defense in Congress, stressed employer benefit and the public interest. FLSA would stabilize employment, production, markets, and prices. Business was divided. Some employers, who already paid living wages, hoped to bring low-wage-paying southern competitors into line. Southern employers voiced hostility; their legislators insisted on exclusion of agricultural labor and domestic workers from labor standards and, during debate, expanded the scope of exemption. Without such "fine tuning," historian Ira Katznelson observes, FLSA would have "shaken the political economy of segregation." The National Association of Manufacturers leveled other charges. FLSA, said the NAM, would cause "doubt, uncertainty, confusion." Labor was split, too. The new CIO endorsed the bill. The AFL, ever hostile to the minimum wage, attacked it, but was forced to make concessions. New Dealers argued that FLSA would protect employers from unfair labor practices and facilitate commerce. The cause of labor standards, once promoted to protect women's health, now served the nation's economic health.[22]

Passed in 1938, FLSA provided minimum wages, maximum hours (a forty-four-hour week, to fall in two years to forty hours), and overtime pay rules for various categories of women and men engaged in the production of goods for interstate commerce; it also banned child labor, though with exemptions. The federal government could now begin to fulfill goals that social feminists and other progressives had long envisioned: it could impose health and safety measures, enforce wage and hour standards, curb exploitation of school-age youngsters, and even obviate the need for a child labor amendment. Frances Perkins defended the law's limitations. "The original touch should be light and the movement gradual," she stated, "so that you do not immediately get disturbing factors." Members of the New Deal women's network were in place to support the fight for FLSA. NCL alumna Clara Beyer, since 1934 at the Bureau of Labor Standards, was pivotal. "More than any other network woman, Beyer saw that depression conditions made it possible to include men under labor standards," historian Eileen Boris points out. NCL head Lucy Mason spoke at congressional hearings, and New Jersey Democrat Mary V. Norton took over as head of the house labor committee and of its hearings in 1937 when the chairman died. "Everybody claimed credit for it," Frances Perkins declared. "The AF of L said it was their bill . . . The CIO claimed credit for its passage." But in her view, "The President and I . . . thought we had done it."[23]

The Supreme Court soon agreed that FLSA passed muster. In 1941, four years after upholding the minimum wage for women workers in *Parrish*, the Court upheld the minimum wage provisions of FLSA in *United States v. Darby*. "It is no longer open to question that the fixing of a minimum wage is within the legislative power," said the majority opinion. As in *Bunting v. Oregon* (1917), which extended maximum hours laws to men, most of the *Darby* decision involved a single and apparently ungendered issue: Did wage and hour provisions fall under the interstate commerce clause? Yes, said the Court. With no Brandeis briefs and no mention of the police power, now no longer a consideration, the Supreme Court upheld the minimum wage for men. The decision was a momentous turning point. As in 1917, the "entering wedge" strategy worked. The precedent of the single-sex minimum wage played a vital role in its success. Could protectionists have won this crucial victory without the women-only precedent? No. The single-sex minimum wage, points out historian Alice Kessler-Harris, "had kept alive the possibility that all workers deserved state protection."[24]

With FLSA, the gears of modern labor standards cranked into place. Subsequent amendments expanded the law's coverage, though FLSA reached its potential only gradually. Its immediate impact on wages and hours was small. The law excluded employees in agriculture and domestic service, that is, most black employees in the South, and elsewhere. It covered only a portion of industrial workers, mainly men. FLSA reached only about a quarter of employees when it began, almost half in the 1950s, and by the 1970s, about 90 percent of wage earners. States did not rush to pass gender-neutral minimum wage laws and did not start to do so until the mid-1950s. Indeed, after a brief flurry of protectionist activity in 1937, the states resisted the new options FLSA opened. "[T]he state legislatures, in almost every instance, are dominated by farmers and big business," Clara Beyer reported in 1939. "Very little labor legislation will be enacted." With FLSA's passage, Beyer, a staunch protectionist, withdrew her one-time qualms about legal equality. "I wouldn't have argued against the Equal Rights Amendment after that," she recalled.[25]

How did FLSA affect women workers? "Interstate commerce," scholars point out, was not a gender-neutral term. As historian Vivien Hart observes, "the concept of interstate commerce itself discriminated." In a reversal of previous policy and in contrast to previous protective laws, the majority of employees that FLSA reached were men, primarily white men with little need for the minimum wage. Among women workers, FLSA affected mainly textile, shoe, and garment workers. It did not include women workers with the lowest pay, who were covered, if at all, by the states. Although men who were covered surpassed women in number, percentages of men and women were similar. FLSA minimum wage provisions, scholar Suzanne Mettler points out, reached nearly equal proportions of the male and female workforce (35 percent of men and 32 percent of women workers, according to 1940 statistics). Still, the impact of FLSA differed according to sex. Among workers exempt from FLSA, 35.6 percent of men earned wages below the minimum wage and 62.1 percent of women. Among male workers who were exempt, 22.8 percent were low-paid agricultural workers; a majority of excluded male employees were skilled workers, professionals, and business and government managers who earned much more than the minimum wage. "For most men, exemption from FLSA was irrelevant," Mettler writes. For women, not so: "The vast majority of those who could actually have benefited from the minimum wage had been eliminated from the jurisdiction of labor standards."[26]

The most grievously excluded women employees were domestic work-ers, mainly black and mainly southern, who constituted three of ten women wage earners. When Mary Anderson sought to collect data on domestic labor in the 1930s, she found the topic a "hot potato." According to WB re-search, three out of five African American women workers in 1930 held jobs in domestic and personal service; the number of black women in house-hold jobs had leaped over 80 percent in the 1920s. Almost no state wage-or-hour laws reached domestic workers. WB and NCL leaders began cam-paigns to include such workers in FLSA, though this took decades to accomplish. An NCL campaign in 1939 under economist Mary Dublin (Keyserling), who briefly led the league, introduced bills to extend the mini-mum wage to domestic workers in seven states and to provide maximum hours laws in five cities; none passed. Even a bill to limit domestic workers to a sixty-hour week failed. Eventually, in 1945, at the instigation of WB head Frieda Miller, New York State finally passed a workers' compensation measure for domestic workers. But there progress stopped; wage-and-hour laws remained out of range. Only in Wisconsin did a state minimum wage law include domestic labor. Lawmakers hesitated to invade the home, a pri-vate space that defied inspection, and protectionists, who may have shared such reluctance, rarely made domestic workers a priority. As *Muller* had long made clear, contends historian Vanessa H. May, "'work' took place in facto-ries and shops—and not in private homes." Thus, with FLSA, those most in need of labor standards failed to get them. "All legislative measures pass us by," sang domestic workers at a 1938 YWCA summer conference."[27]

When FLSA *did* affect women workers, however, its impact could be con-voluted. Although Congress had finally passed a "general" law and *Darby* soon upheld that law, no branch of government discarded the rationale for single-sex protective laws; women-only laws remained in the states and con-tinued to affect women workers in factories, stores, and offices. Such laws would compensate for gaps in FLSA, reformers argued. "[T]he need for state minimum wage laws remains as great as before," the WB declared in 1938. "The majority of women workers are employed in occupations not covered by the Federal minimum-wage provisions." A main gap in FLSA: the service sector. Excluded workers, said the WB, included "saleswomen, laundry and dying and cleaning operatives, cannery and allied workers, waitresses, other hotel and restaurant employees, beauty operators, agricultural laborers, household employees, and clerical workers in industries not interstate in character." Even in interstate industries that FLSA covered, the WB stated, state minimum wage laws might "establish rates for factory workers higher than those provided under the Federal law." If a state provided a "higher" standard, such as a higher minimum wage, than FLSA, the state standard "took precedence."[28]

But state maximum hour laws also took precedence over federal law, and FLSA combined with state hours limits could impose a new variant of gender difference in law. For men in industry, under FLSA, the limit on hours represented the point at which overtime pay (or premium pay) began; the federal law specified that overtime pay meant time and a half of regular pay. For women, however, state maximum hours laws barred overtime and kept them out of jobs that required overtime. In a sense, this new disparity defied reformers' original intent. They had hoped that time-and-a-half wages would make overtime too expensive for employers, decrease its incidence, shorten hours for all workers, and spread jobs around a larger pool of workers; the WB continued to view premium pay as a deterrent to employer exploitation. But employers, it turned out, preferred the cost of overtime pay to the expense of hiring and training new workers, and wage earners increasingly sought the added pay. Single-sex state laws thus imposed a disadvantage on women workers unanticipated by protectionists. The disparity was limited: only sixteen states in 1938 legislated eight-hour days for women workers. Most states had less restrictive single-sex hours laws that would not impede FLSA (or none). Moreover, states might enact special rules to permit overtime in specific lines of work. Many state laws enabled women and minors to secure permits to work overtime for time and a half "only in emergencies"; states briefly capitalized on such loopholes in World War II. Still, exclusion from overtime distinguished women's status under FLSA from that of men; the discrepancy remained a protectionist blind spot. Employed women might view overtime—depending on circumstance—as either voluntary (an opportunity for high pay) or compulsory (an employer prerogative and a form of exploitation). Union women often preferred the mandatory hours limits of state laws. No wonder the WB avoided the issue; it was another "hot potato."[29]

Finally, the protectionist victory in FLSA and *Darby* undercut a social feminist goal: empowering women bureaucrats. Since the Progressive Era, single-sex laws had carved out space in state employment for women, mainly as factory inspectors. As far back as 1889, Pennsylvania's maximum hour law had required the state to hire two women inspectors; women eagerly sought such jobs. Single-sex minimum wage laws, though always precarious, provided yet more bureaucratic space. Some early laws required a woman to serve on state minimum wage boards, as did the pioneer law in the District of Columbia; Ethel Smith of NWTUL had served on the DC board (and NCL stalwarts Clara Beyer and Elizabeth Brandeis had enforced the law). But once federal law included men in wage-hours standards, women bureaucrats ran into resistance. "Contrary to NCL expectations, the passage of the FLSA made the position of women wage-hour officials more precarious than before," writes historian Landon R. Y. Storrs. "[O]nce labor standards affected men, and received federal funding, men began competing for posts as bureaucrats." At the Bureau of Labor Statistics, Clara Beyer had to train new state inspectors and administrators ("some of the most impossible people"). Some women lost leverage; some lost their jobs. It was not "the sex of the inspector" that mattered, an aggrieved Kentucky NCL activist observed, but rather "the capabilities to see that the laws are enforced." "My whole heart is in the minimum wage work," a North Dakota woman, forced out of her job, declared. Women who had promoted protective policy, Storrs notes, were "sidelined from administering it."[30]

Overall, FLSA opened up a new route to labor standards, beyond single-sex laws. It was another beachhead, one with potential to affect a growing pool of workers. But victory brought complications for social feminists. Protectionists retained their separate sphere of influence in the states, but it was now more difficult to enact or defend single-sex state laws. The WB coalition also faced continued enmity from NWP loyalists. Although the NWP had opposed FLSA, its members now claimed the federal law and the *Darby* decision as a validation of their own demand for sex equality. Finally, social feminists faced the challenge of war.

THE 1940s: WAR AND POSTWAR

"Today women—hundreds of thousands of them—are at work in war industries," the WB told employers in 1944. "Unafraid of the hard, tedious, and dangerous jobs, they are working in shipyards, in aircraft and instrument factories, in arsenals and steel mills." About six million women joined the workforce in World War II. The number of women workers rose by half and the proportion of women who worked soared from 27 to 37 percent. The defense industry saw the biggest influx; by mid-1943 women constituted 32 percent of its employees. Women migrated to war production centers for well-paid jobs. They ran cranes and lathes, repaired engines, and cut sheet metal; in auto plants one out of four workers was female. The number of unionized women skyrocketed; the proportion of women workers in unions surged from 9.4 percent in 1940 to 21 percent in 1944. As job opportunities rose, black women moved away from domestic work and up the occupational ladder. The composition of the female workforce changed; three out of four new women workers were married. By the war's end, married women were almost a majority of women workers.[31]

At the war's start, the WB expected no change in single-sex protective laws, but from 1942 to 1944, states modified the laws to meet the need for labor, especially the need of defense contractors. The states relaxed maximum hours laws, removed some exclusionary laws, and modified night work laws or suspended them, as in Delaware, Indiana, and Ohio. Almost all changes were "for the duration of the war." State legislators occasionally passed new laws, but there were easier ways to proceed. In most cases, protective laws already contained provisions for "emergencies" or were so lenient about hours of work that no change was needed. In other instances, legislators empowered state agencies to grant permits to employers to evade protective laws "for the duration." As states relaxed maximum hours laws, by whatever means, barriers fell to overtime pay. Some states already permitted it. In Oregon, for instance, the law that provided a forty-four-hour week for women allowed extra hours at "overtime pay." Elsewhere, some states changed the rules. A Texas law authorized extra hours in the "emergency" and required "payment of double time for such employment."[32]

Women war workers greatly appreciated good jobs, good wages, and premium pay for overtime. Income, they claimed, was their main motivation in the workforce. But access to overtime drew a mixed response; women workers were alert to the hazard of "forced overtime." Some refused to take jobs that required long workweeks. Most factories adopted a six-day, forty-eight-hour week and ran two or three shifts. Workers with household chores and families, with few social services available, sometimes quit jobs or just took time off. A survey in Detroit concluded that women workers who stayed home to do laundry missed 100,000 hours of work a week. As one worker concluded, "Eight hours of that is enough."[33]

Relaxation or suspension of state protective laws in wartime suggested (to their foes) that women workers didn't need them, want them, or appreciate them, and bolstered demands for an ERA. "Nearly all the states have suspended their protective laws for the war emergency," wrote New Orleans lawyer Rebekah Greathouse. "And the women are getting along extremely well. They are holding hundreds of jobs that were formerly supposed to be unsuitable for them. They are belonging to unions. They are drawing excellent pay. And they are liking it." Greathouse had submitted an amicus brief against the single-sex minimum wage in *Tipaldo* in 1936; her coauthor was Burnita Matthews, her NWP colleague and one-time law partner. Single-sex laws had served their purpose as a launching pad for general laws, Greathouse argued; in her view, the decision in *Darby* made an ERA more likely.[34] This was the NWP stance.

The wartime WB, in contrast, strove to retain its protective domain in the states—to preserve "this great body of beneficial social legislation built up by great effort over ... many years"—and to carve out some wartime authority. Conceding that labor shortages necessitated an extension of women's working hours, the WB sought ways to enlarge its advisory role. It sent emissaries to counsel employers on hiring women; strove to coordinate federal policy on women workers, though with little success; and collected data on women's wartime employment. It also developed an interest in equal pay. WB observers charged that in many wartime plants women who took jobs traditionally held by men received lower wages; employers simply changed the job titles. From 1944 on the WB coalition made equal pay a prime concern. "Wage rates should be based on occupation, not sex," Mary Anderson declared. Anderson also recounted in a WB document of 1945 a remark she made to union men about equal pay: "I appealed to their selfishness in preserving their own jobs." Equal pay, historian Alice Kessler-Harris notes, carried "a subverted or hidden" meaning.[35]

As the end of the war neared, the WB urged the states to restore protective laws to avoid the "ever-present danger" of employer abuses. Single-sex protective laws returned including maximum hours laws that barred overtime, night work bans, limits on weights that women might bear, and exclusions for jobs considered immoral or hazardous. In some instances, the WB found, restrictions made gains. As of 1944, laws to remain in effect in peacetime included fifteen laws that barred night work in one or more industries and nine laws that regulated weights to be lifted. Nine states targeted "unhealthful workplaces or hazardous working conditions," and barred women from cleaning moving machines, handling lead substances, and work in core rooms or in unventilated basements. Prohibited jobs in twenty-nine states included work in mines, especially coal mines. Twelve states, by either state law or municipal ordinances, excluded women from bartending.[36]

The return of single-sex protective laws was never in doubt. But other circumstances changed radically. The war years left a unique legacy in women's history; women had enjoyed employment options, good pay, and few restrictions. They "had a taste of freedom, of making their own money, making their own decisions," a retired schoolteacher told interviewer Studs Terkel for his oral history of the war years. "I think the beginning of the women's movement had its seeds right there in World War II."[37] The war's end was yet more momentous. The postwar years brought new factors into play.

Their interaction in the next two decades undercut support for single-sex laws and realigned protectionist goals. The end of the 1940s was a crucible, not least for the Women's Bureau, now the most significant protectionist bastion.

"We can expect the flood tide of women in the labor force to recede rapidly with the coming of peace," Mary Anderson wrote in 1944. Women did not want to "advance at the expense of veterans," Frieda Miller, Anderson's successor, added, although they hoped to retain "some if not all of the gains of the war years." Before the war ended, the Department of Labor issued recommendations to sever women from wartime jobs, provide work for returning veterans, and ensure a smooth transition. When war production plants closed or converted to civilian production, most women lost jobs. The numbers of women in aircraft and shipbuilding dropped; in auto plants, women's proportion of work fell from 24 percent in 1944 to 7.5 percent in mid-1946. High pay and wartime opportunity vanished; the WB could not save women's jobs. But the war's end only briefly halted the long-term growth of the female workforce; a countervailing trend started almost at once. The postwar economy provided new space for women workers, and in 1947 the numbers of women at work began to climb. By 1950, 31 percent of women were employed, though no longer in heavy industry. Pink-collar work was the new frontier; women took jobs in offices, stores, and services, all growing fields. The postwar female workforce retained some wartime characteristics. It was predominantly married, older, and middle class, a trend that had begun in the 1920s but became more visible in the 1940s. The postwar era provided new jobs for the working wife. A second income helped to maintain a middle-class lifestyle; women's roles as consumers made them wage earners.[38]

Frieda Miller mobilized the WB to meet postwar challenges. A labor economist trained at the University of Chicago, where she studied from 1911 to 1915, and the lifetime companion of ILGWU leader Pauline Newman, Miller taught at Bryn Mawr before joining the Philadelphia branch of WTUL. In the 1930s she had served as industrial commissioner for the state of New York, the job Frances Perkins held a decade earlier. The WB under Miller continued to support protective laws. "Though state wage and hour laws are far from adequate, they do represent years of progressive action," Miller told a WTUL conference in 1944; such laws "must be improved and extended." As she pragmatically explained in 1950, "You never give up a tool that is useful in furthering your purpose until you have a better one to substitute for it." But the postwar WB shifted course; single-sex protective laws took a back seat to new priorities. Swayed by its largest constituency, trade

women, the WB focused on job opportunity, workplace rights, and
pay. Traditional concerns about protective laws now shared space
her concerns.[39]

postwar WB depended on women in labor unions. In 1939 about
women belonged to unions; by the early 1950s, three million women
of organized labor. Under Mary Anderson's lead, the WB had
its new constituency since the 1930s; Frieda Miller continued the
the war's end, the WB secured union women's support with two
ces, of April 1945 and November 1946, and also set up a "Labor
sory Committee" composed of women labor leaders. Women in unions
usually supported the WB stance on protective laws. But they endorsed protection selectively and also adopted the language of "rights." Union women
were aware that they were "part of the permanent labor force," declared
Elisabeth Christman of NWTUL at a 1948 WB conference. "They cannot be
denied the right to work, the right to equal pay, the right to job seniority, the
right to legal safeguards on the job."[40]

Equal pay surged into a central spot in the WB agenda. Speakers at WB
conferences sometimes spoke of equal pay laws as a component part of
"protective labor standards" and sometimes as one of a group of "rights"
that included labor standards. Each view was viable; mercurial and elastic,
the equal pay policy fell into both categories. Either way, calls for equal pay
bolstered the WB's tactical stance in its fight against an ERA. House and
Senate committees reported an equal pay bill favorably in 1946—the bill
was to bar wage discrimination by private citizens in interstate commerce—
but neither house acted on it. In the states, however, the popularity of equal
pay soared. The number of states with equal pay laws, two in 1940, leaped
to twenty by the end of the 1950s. The laws applied in few circumstances,
rarely included provisions for enforcement, and failed to disrupt job segregation by sex. Equal pay laws meant little without equal employment opportunity laws. Or, as Mary Anderson observed, "Equal pay for equal work
did not mean much when we came to apply it in a practical way."[41]

As equal pay gained traction, WB allegiance to the more problematic
facets of single-sex protective laws wavered. Night work laws now posed a
trying problem; those women who had just lost their wartime jobs needed
no further hurdles in finding new ones. In 1946 the WB Labor Advisory
Committee urged a study of night work laws. The WB surveyed hotel and
restaurant workers but hesitated to reverse its night work policy. Such a
shift, said an internal memo, might start a "toboggan toward eliminating
other and far more vital standards" and harm workers "in the weakest position for bargaining." Night work research continued. In 1946–48, the WB

surveyed service workers' attitudes toward night work bans in twenty cities and towns with mixed results. WB researchers conceded that "many women now need to work at night, so that their days can be open for family and household responsibilities," but again equivocated. The Labor Advisory Committee assessed the new data, too. In a 1949 position paper, it stated that night work laws no longer fit women's needs or conditions in the workforce, and that health issues were irrelevant. Still, the committee could not discard such a long-term plank of protective policy. Night work legislation, it finally concluded, was a "means of control" over industry, to be "supported and bolstered." To snip any thread in the protective fabric might unravel the whole cloth.[42]

As the WB regrouped, the Progressive Era protectionist coalition that had held together through the New Deal slowly faded. In World War II, when the numbers of unionized women surged, the NWTUL declined and finally dissolved in 1950; the New York branch held out five years longer. By 1950 the NCL represented only eight local leagues and within a decade, only two. The AALL folded in 1944. New Dealers had adopted its commitment to workers' compensation and unemployment insurance in the Social Security Act. The New Deal women's network endured attrition. Mary Anderson resigned in 1944. Molly Dewson retired, as did Frances Perkins, who saw her mission as complete. "The program is almost accomplished," she wrote to Felix Frankfurter in 1945. "Everything except health insurance, dear Felix, that I had on my original list . . . because the climate was right for social change."[43]

The rationale for single-sex protection faded, too. Since 1938 FLSA had opened up an alternative avenue to labor standards. After the war, doubts arose about parts of the protectionist package. In the late 1940s, Rose Schneiderman and Elisabeth Christman abandoned their long-held support of night work laws; such laws, they feared, contributed to women workers' forced displacement from wartime jobs. "It's enough to drive a fellow into the ranks of the Woman's Party," wrote Schneiderman, who retired from the New York WTUL in 1949. Some leading protectionists spurned single-sex laws completely. Clara Beyer, who had changed her stance when FLSA became law in 1938, now saw women-only laws as a barrier to labor standards. "I can't get excited any more about separate legislation and believe we are losing a lot of the push for real improvement of conditions by the emphasis on sex," she wrote to Molly Dewson in 1946. To emphasize the need for separate facilities for women only did "a great disservice to women in general," Beyer claimed. "In the same way the movement for wage and hour legislation for women has certainly held back the possibilities of getting such laws for all."[44]

Eleanor Roosevelt began to modify her protectionist stance in the 1940s, albeit quietly, and gradually moved away from debate over it. According to her biographer, Blanche Weisen Cook, the shift began after FLSA in 1938. Rose Schneiderman's continued opposition to ERA prevented Eleanor Roosevelt from endorsing it in 1941, Cook states. But ER consented to the Democratic Party's endorsement of ERA in 1944, though she declined to take a public stand on it and withdrew her opposition in 1946. Other historians support this timeline with variations. In early 1944, historian Brigid O'Farrell points out, Eleanor Roosevelt proposed to Frances Perkins that the labor department survey sex-based laws to determine whether protective legislation was still necessary. Perkins assured her such a study was underway. At the same time, ER told Rose Schneiderman that ERA foes needed to adopt new tactics. Women were "better able to protect themselves," she wrote to Schneiderman, "and they should, in all but certain very specific cases, which are justified by their physical and functional differences, have the same rights as men." But ER's loyalty to Schneiderman and other old friends insured the first lady's silence on the 1940s equal rights debate. Historian Lois Scharf, too, discovers signals from Roosevelt in the early 1940s that her enmity to ERA was not immutable. Widowed in 1945, she began work at the United Nations and led a committee that shaped the Universal Declaration of Human Rights, adopted in 1948. While engaged in human rights, her stance on women's rights shifted. Scharf finds that ER definitively changed her mind in a syndicated article of 1951, and even there, equivocated; single-sex laws continued to hamper women more than a federal ERA would help them, she stated. But she edged a notch further toward equal rights: "I can see that perhaps it does add a little to the position of women to be declared equal before law and equal politically and in whatever work a woman chooses to undertake." Finally, ER refused to be bulldozed by the NWP. When asked by the NWP president, in the wake of the 1951 article, to endorse ERA, Roosevelt declined: "While I am not going to fight the Equal Rights Amendment, I really do not feel enthusiastic enough about it to write you a letter in its favor." She would not discard support for labor standards, betray old friends, or capitulate to NWP demands. Instead, by midcentury (even though she had more or less reversed her stance), she had simply withdrawn from debate on the issue.[45]

When the NCL reached its half-century mark in 1949, Josephine Goldmark celebrated the league's contribution to FLSA and to the newly hiked minimum wage. "Eternal vigilance remains, however, the price of progress," Goldmark wrote. "Trucks still rumble in the dawn carrying children from towns and cities to nearby commercial farms; new poisons in industry threaten the workers from year to year." The new welfare state was fragile, Goldmark stressed. "[I]t does not operate in a vacuum." Labor standards of any kind remained precarious; employers disliked them and Republicans challenged them. The Taft-Hartley Act of 1947 showed that labor's foes could stifle New Deal gains. Under such circumstances, Goldmark found single-sex protective laws "indispensable."[46] But the protectionist ship now sailed in a postwar sea.

What changed in the postwar economy, 1945–60? Protectionist policy now directly affected men. As FLSA spread, use of overtime soared. Postwar inflation—the same pressure that spurred the rise of working wives—led to surging overtime rates among workers with access to it, overwhelmingly male. "Workers' conception about the purpose of overtime changed entirely in the postwar era," labor historian Ronald Schatz reports in his study of the electrical industry. No longer a tactic to spur employers to limit hours of work, overtime was now a way to raise earnings. Employed men relied on premium pay to keep up with inflation. Rising use of overtime widened the chasm of difference between employed men and women. Similarly, state laws for equal pay, doubled-edged and "equal" only in name, protected employed men from women competitors, as federal bureaucrats well knew. Equal pay "discourages the employer from hiring women cheaper," wrote Dorothy S. Brady, a labor bureau statistician, in 1947. The laws were "designed to protect men, to prevent the degradation of the wage structure." The shifting impact of protective policy in the postwar era advantaged men.[47]

So did the Supreme Court. The discriminatory effect of single-sex protection probably rose most sharply in the late 1940s, when the economy revived and when veterans sought jobs. Just then, in 1948, the Supreme Court decided a labor standards case: it upheld a Michigan exclusionary law. Throwing a spotlight on protective policy, the decision suggests (in retrospect) just the opposite of what the justices decided—that single-sex laws faced a finite future.

BARTENDING: *GOESAERT V. CLEARY* (1948)

"Union men!" declared San Francisco's Local 41 in the 1930s. "Do not patronize taverns that have women behind the bar." Before World War II, bartending locals endorsed laws to exclude women from bartending and picketed bars that had hired them. In wartime, with male labor scarce, the International Union of Hotel and Restaurant Employees and Bartenders, which itself excluded women, supported the hiring of women in bars if their contracts guaranteed that their work would "only be temporary." At the war's end, bartending locals sought to restore exclusionary laws; they hoped "to enable our members to get back to work." The states complied. In 1945 Michigan passed a law to bar women from obtaining licenses as bartenders (in cities over 50,000), unless they were wives or daughters of owners of "a licensed saloon." Under the law, women might still work in bars as waitresses who circulated drinks among customers. But they could not work behind the bar as bartenders, or "barmaids," who mixed drinks. The bartenders' union promoted the law's passage and prodded its enforcement.[48]

As soon as the state liquor commission began to enforce the law on May 1, 1947, two women who owned bars and two women employees challenged it. Valentine Goesaert, a widowed bar owner in Dearborn, Michigan, and her daughter, Margaret, the bar's main employee, sued the Michigan Liquor Control Commission, along with two unrelated Detroit women, tavern owner Caroline McMahon and bartender Gertrude Nadroski. The plaintiffs, represented by Detroit lawyer Anne R. Davidow, pressed a class action suit on behalf of themselves and others in the same position. Their main argument: The law imposed on women an "arbitrary hardship" and violated their rights of "equal protection" under the Fourteenth Amendment. It discriminated against women owners of bars and women bartenders, between daughters of male and female owners, and between waitresses and female bartenders. Whether they owned bars or worked in them, women could no longer pursue their vocations.[49]

Twenty-four other women, who either owned bars or worked for pay as bartenders ("barmaids"), swore affidavits to support the plaintiffs. Bartending did not involve hazard, the deponents claimed; they had tended bar for four to seventeen years without incident. Moreover, they stated, women workers in bars had a "civilizing influence" on customers and were "an asset to the business." The state law, however, caused them economic hardship. Some deponents tended bar to care for sick husbands and support children. One woman lived with an invalid husband in a room adjoining the bar and needed income from the bar to care for him. Others could not get by on the low pay of waitresses. Some who worked in bars had moved up from lower-paid jobs as waitresses, had trained to be bartenders, and had no other way to earn a living. The deponents' statements conveyed desperation.[50]

Michigan courts upheld the law. Two members of the three-judge district court found the legislature entitled (quoting a Brandeis opinion in a banking case of 1923) to "direct its police regulations against what it deems an existing evil, without covering the whole field of possible abuses." The third judge, Frank Picard, who, as chairman of a state commission of the early

1940s to study Michigan liquor control legislation, had recommended the licensing of bartending, wrote a spirited dissent. Citing the idiosyncrasies of the Michigan law ("palpably arbitrary, capricious, and unreasonable"), Picard focused on the predicament of Valentine Goesaert.

> [T]his is not a new venture for Mrs. Goesaert. She is not just now going into the liquor business under this new law. She started business, bought property, and incurred obligations under a law that permitted her to do exactly what her license said she could do—own and operate a business. . . . [H]aving granted her a license, can the legislature arbitrarily and unreasonably change the rules in the middle of the game as against her alone because she happens to be a woman licensee?
>
> Where is the "equal protection" for her? . . .
>
> She not only has lost her husband but neither she nor her daughter may help run the family business as they did when the main breadwinner was alive. Across the street her male competitor may permit his wife and daughter to run his business even if he works in a factory miles away. . . .
>
> Has not this woman by every test of reasoning been deprived of the equal protection of the laws?

Judge Picard concluded with an allusion to the start of the "rights" revolution that was underway. To uphold "this type of discriminatory legislation," he charged, "opens the door for further fine 'distinctions' that will eventually be applied to religion, education, politics, and even nationalities." Sex discrimination, said Judge Picard, imperiled constitutional rights in other areas.[51]

The plaintiffs appealed. In *Goesaert v. Cleary* (1948) the Supreme Court upheld the law 6–3. Justice Frankfurter, appointed to the Court in 1939, wrote the majority opinion. Bartending by women, Frankfurter stated, might "give rise to moral and social problems." Adopting a tone of jest, Frankfurter mocked the notion that the Michigan law had been generated by "an unchivalrous desire of male barkeepers to monopolize the calling." He found no change in women's social and legal position to "preclude the states from drawing a sharp line between the sexes, certainly, in such matters as the regulation of the liquor traffic." According to the majority opinion, the state did not "play favorites among women without rhyme or reason." Michigan could reasonably assume that supervision of a woman bartender by a male relative would reduce the "hazards that may confront a barmaid without such protecting oversight." The Court, Frankfurter stated, was "not situated to cross-examine either actually or argumentatively" the mind of Michigan legislators. Three dissenters (Justices Wiley Rutledge, William O.

Douglas, and Frank Murphy) argued that the Michigan law violated the equal protection clause of the Fourteenth Amendment. Like the majority opinion, the dissent focused on women bar owners, not on unrelated women employees. The law imposed invidious distinctions and arbitrarily discriminated between male and female owners of bars, stated the dissent. A male owner, even if absent, could employ his wife and daughter as barmaids; the female bar owner could not.

> A female bar owner may neither work as a barmaid nor employ her daughter in that position, even if a man is always present in the establishment to keep order. This inevitable result of the classification belies the assumption that the statute was motivated by a legislative solicitude for the moral and physical well-being of women who, but for the law, would be employed as barmaids. Since there could be no other conceivable justification for such discrimination against women workers of liquor establishments, the statutes should be held invalid as a denial of equal protection.[52]

The *Goesaert* decision marked a low point in the history of protective laws. It underscored the bias against women that prevailed in the postwar job market; full employment of veterans was the nation's priority. The Michigan law insured advantage to male bartenders by enhancing their options for work and protecting them from competition. The decision showed the potential of protection to injure women workers and reminded even long-term protectionists of the inherent flaws in single-sex laws. Along with *Bradwell* and *Muller*, *Goesaert* was one of a quartet of major Supreme Court cases that curtailed women's rights. The fourth case, *Hoyt v. Florida* (1961), permitted gender difference in jury service.[53]

The *Goesaert* decision was also a low moment in the career of Justice Frankfurter. Protectionists had long benefited from his energy, ambition, and intellect. It was Frankfurter who in 1916 reminded reformers that there was "no sharp difference in kind as to the effect of labor on men and women"; rather, emphasis should shift to "the fact that it is *industry*, and the relation of industry to the community that is regulated." It was Frankfurter who had argued the protectionists' cases in *Bunting*, *Stettler*, and *Adkins*, and who had corresponded for years with social feminists such as Frances Perkins and Alice Hamilton. But he had clung to a philosophy of judicial restraint when the liberal tide had turned against it. "[H]aving made a career arguing against judicial interference in the majority's decision, Frankfurter chose to stick to his guns," Noah Feldman explains. By the 1940s he had lost some of his former allies among protectionists. Benjamin V. Cohen's support of civil rights and civil liberties in the early 1940s had led him away from Frankfurter's stance of judicial restraint. Frankfurter's relations with "the Ladies" had endured strains since the 1920s when he had fallen into conflict with Florence Kelley over minimum wage tactics. Clara Beyer, long alienated, disparaged Frankfurter. In retrospect, she found him a "self-promoter" and "never the man that the Justice [Brandeis] was." Finally, in the disdainful and faux-jocular language of the *Goesaert* opinion, Frankfurter had shown the legal equivalent of a tin ear.[54]

But the *Goesaert* case was also a turning point in the history of protective laws. This significant case against sex-based discrimination was distinctive; the plaintiffs argued that sex discrimination violates women's constitutional rights by denying them equal protection under the Fourteenth Amendment. The innovation of "equal protection" had a bright future. The challenge to the Michigan law presaged a new direction for women's rights, one that came to fruition in the 1970s.[55] The new direction (in retrospect) was as important as Frankfurter's intransigence.

Credit for *Goesaert*'s equal protection claim goes to attorney Anne R. Davidow (1898–1991), who practiced law in Detroit with her older brother, Lazarus "Larry" Davidow. Anne Davidow had always been an activist; as a young woman she had campaigned for suffrage on a soapbox outside factories. The Detroit College of Law, from which Larry graduated, rejected Anne; she attended the University of Detroit, graduated with a law degree, and passed the bar exam in 1920. In the 1930s, Davidow and Davidow served as general counsel to the Reuther brothers and to their new union, the United Auto Workers (1935) (UAW), by 1945 the nation's largest union. Larry Davidow had a long history as a socialist and sometime political candidate; in the 1930s he assumed a contentious role in AUW disputes and veered to the political right. Anne Davidow, in contrast, retained progressive beliefs. Her major public commitment was to the Women Lawyers' Association of Michigan, in which she was a life member, frequent officer, and fourth president (1925–27). Women lawyers' associations, notably the National Federation of Women Lawyers, were active pockets of resistance to protective laws and held strong views on equal rights, nurtured since the 1920s. Unlike most ERA proponents of the 1940s—that is, NWP members—Anne Davidow came from a left-of-center background. In this regard, she resembled activists of the 1960s.[56]

With *Goesaert*, Anne Davidow shaped the case of a lifetime. Still, the case was singularly ahead of its time. Six years later, in *Brown v. Board of Education* (1954), the Supreme Court stepped forward and changed the legal landscape. With *Brown*, the climax of a long campaign by civil rights lawyers, equal rights based on the equal protection clause triumphed. *Brown* opened new pathways for equal rights arguments, pathways not open to Davidow in 1948. Still, the legal impact of *Brown* was gradual. Only in the late 1960s, only after the passage of Title VII of the Civil Rights Act of 1964, were women's rights advocates able to capitalize on the *Brown* precedent and by drawing analogies to civil rights law successfully claim equal rights for women. Anne Davidow's case had come up too soon.[57]

To what extent were those involved in the *Goesaert* case alert to the concurrent campaign for black civil rights? In 1939 attorney Charles Hamilton Houston, dean of Howard Law School, had formed the Legal Defense and Education Fund, a legal arm of the National Association for the Advancement of Colored People (NAACP) (on whose board Florence Kelley had served for over two decades, from the NAACP's start in 1909 to her death in 1932.) Led briefly by Houston and then by Thurgood Marshall, the Legal Defense Fund sought to dismantle the separate-but-equal policy of *Plessy v. Ferguson* (1896) and to desegregate schools. NAACP lawyers pursued a two-part plan, not totally dissimilar from the protectionists' "entering wedge" strategy; they demanded "equal" schools under the separate-but-equal ruling and simultaneously challenged school segregation under the equal protection clause, starting with law schools. In 1938 the Supreme Court decided its first modern civil rights case, argued by Houston, *State of Missouri ex rel. Gaines v. Canada*, one of the last cases in which Justice Brandeis participated. Joining the majority, Brandeis voted that Missouri had to provide an in-state legal education for Lloyd Gaines, a black applicant to the state university's law school. The decision did not explicitly desegregate the all-white law school, but it pushed the Supreme Court to start a reconsideration of *Plessy*. The dissenting justices in *Goesaert* cited the *Gaines* decision when they mentioned equal protection. NAACP lawyers pressed forward to win other cases, culminated by *Brown* in 1954. Lawyer Pauli Murray, who, after *Gaines*, urged Thurgood Marshall (in vain) to take on her own effort to desegregate the University of North Carolina, would serve in the 1960s as a bridge between the civil rights and women's equal rights campaigns. But that lay in the future. Little linked the two campaigns in 1948, beyond a footnote in the *Goesaert* dissent.[58]

Anne Davidow's argument in *Goesaert* had repercussions in Michigan. To new lawmaker Martha W. Griffiths, who served in the state legislature from 1948 to 1952, the issue was clear: when the officer of a county labor federation asked her to support a ban on women bartenders, she refused to be a "traitor" to women. In 1949 the legislature amended the state law to allow female bartenders and their daughters to tend bar, and in 1955 lawmakers rejected the entire section of the law on licensing bartenders. Still, seventeen states prohibited women from tending bar in 1948, and the *Goesaert* decision encouraged more to do so. Women's numbers in bartending grew slowly; in 1940, women were under 3 percent of bartenders and in 1960, under 11 percent. Bartending, historian Dorothy Sue Cobble shows, was an especially contested area for women and remained so until the early 1970s, when Title VII opened the field to women. Waitresses' unions of the 1940s, Cobble notes, generally accepted the exclusions that bartenders' locals promoted. Their acceptance suggests the complexity of working-class women's stance on protective laws. Women who worked, Cobble contends, "juggled economic, gender, and class considerations." They balanced "desire for higher wages and increased employment options" against "desire for economic security," the "advantage of female community," and "societal approval."[59] Union women generally supported protective laws, but in a selective way and for their own reasons.

WOMEN IN UNIONS

Unionized women were a vital component of postwar protectionism. By the mid-1950s, 35 percent of nonagricultural workers were union members. Despite the crippling effects of the 1947 Taft-Hartley Act and other antiunion laws, union membership surged; over three million women were organized. Women in unions shared the optimism and energy of the postwar labor movement. They also shared gendered concerns, voiced at their own meetings and WB conferences, ranging from equal rights in the workplace to maternity benefits. For women in unions, paid work was no longer a temporary phase but an enduring one; they sought ways to fuse work roles and family roles. Overall, union women embraced strategies of both "equality" and "difference," Dorothy Sue Cobble explains, and "did not think of the two as incompatible." Usually—though not always—they endorsed single-sex protective laws, if sometimes with qualifications.[60]

The postwar WB at once established a mutually beneficial relationship with union women through special conferences in 1945 and 1946 and through its Labor Advisory Committee, set up in 1945, comprising about fifteen women labor leaders and led by WB head Frieda Miller. The WB relied on union backing. Unions in turn profited from WB attention; women activists met one another at WB conferences and on the Labor Advisory Committee, which nurtured a new generation of women labor leaders. In 1946, for instance, committee members included, besides NWTUL activists Pauline Newman and Elisabeth Christman, Esther Peterson, a rising star of the Amalgamated Clothing Workers of America (ACWA); Mildred Jeffries, educational director and executive secretary of the United Auto Workers (UAW); and Ruth Young, an officer of the United Electrical Workers (UE). At WB gatherings, such as the WB conferences of 1945 and 1946, concerns about "rights" merged with support for protective laws. The conferences announced efforts to end the discrimination women workers faced; union women sought to "ensure equal rights for women on and off the job, equal pay, equal opportunities for promotion and advancement, adequate maternity leave, and protection against discrimination in hiring and firing." Labor standards coexisted with other goals.[61]

Union women's support for protective laws reflected in part whether they worked in trades dominated by women (garment manufacture, food processing plants, cotton mills, laundries) or in trades in which they faced competition with men. Most union women shared beliefs that put them in protection's camp. Protective laws were part of a bulwark against employer prerogatives, they agreed; to discard every law that recognized difference risked harm to women workers. Union women also differentiated among types of single-sex laws and felt free to reject laws they saw as restrictive, whether weight limits, night work bans, or occupational exclusions. They urged case-by-case review of single-sex laws to discard those that imposed "unfair" or "invidious" treatment of women. Maximum hour and minimum wage laws, in contrast, provided "benefit." Union women appreciated hours limits that enabled women to fuse wage work and family life. Mandatory curbs on hours, they believed, provided better protection than FLSA, which used overtime pay as a disincentive to discourage long hours. At the same time, they claimed, they wanted state laws made more "flexible" and to extend them to men. Overall, union women who endorsed protection voiced views closer to those of the fading NWTUL than to those of the NCL, though distinct from both. Pragmatism ruled: union women balanced rights and protection, union contracts and legislation. Difference-based strategies, they argued, could foster equality.[62]

Gladys Dickason of the Amalgamated Clothing Workers explained union women's selective pro-protection stance at a WB conference in 1948. Dickason voiced support for minimum wage laws as a "line of progress . . . adopted by the Federal government," but distinguished between beneficial protective laws and restrictive ones. She urged "not . . . giving up any of the protective regulations that we have put into effect which benefit women, but rather . . . extending these regulations so that they benefit men as well as women." Dickason next offered the social feminist defense of "difference." "The fact that men and women are equal does not make them identical," she declared. "[T]here will always be special problems relating to women. By recognizing that fact and making gains as we can through protective legislation, by clearing away all of those laws which interfere with equal status for women, women can be more assured of equality than they can by ignoring the differences and seeking a theoretical equality." Finally, Dickason launched into her most crucial argument: union membership brought women specific and tangible gains "outside of the legislative field." Unions raised wages. Union contracts often secured to women paid holidays and vacations; they provided for rest periods and maternity leave; "many of them now provide for insurance which is payable during sickness and for cash benefits for maternity." Concrete benefits in union contracts directly addressed women workers' needs, Dickason emphasized. Above all, trade unions gave women "the opportunity . . . to exercise their capacity for leadership."[63]

Dickason's qualified, nuanced, and carefully-worded speech conveyed union women's distinctive stance and mixed allegiances: they interpreted "different" and "equal" to suit themselves; they appreciated protective laws, though only laws that "benefit women;" and they appreciated unions even more. Dickason's references to protective laws in fact slightly distanced union women from those laws ("the legislative field"). Dickason also conveyed a final, practical point: Changing circumstances made protective laws less relevant. The greatest current benefits to union women in garment production, Dickason claimed, were a labor shortage that insured jobs, higher wages, and recognition of skilled work.

Pockets of support for equal rights developed among union women. Women in the United Auto Workers formed their own "Women's Bureau" to end sex-based employment practices. In the late 1940s, UAW women lobbied to abolish separate seniority lists. African American women often endorsed equal rights strategies. Among waitresses, for instance, black women disputed the sexual division of labor; as protective laws rarely reached them, black women had less inclination to defend them. Finally, though generally friendly to policies that reflected "difference," union women could still be alert to the potential hazards of such policies. At the 1945 WB "Conference of Union Women," when delegates considered an endorsement of paid maternity leave and disability pay during pregnancy, a dissenting representative of electrical workers noted that "inequality can come in the back door as well as the front."[64]

Historian Dennis Deslippe, who posits a gradual slide away from loyalty to protective laws, finds some antecedents of equal rights convictions among postwar unionists. For instance, unions with large groups of women workers, such as the UAW, ACWA, ILGWU, and Textile Workers Union of America (TWUA), decried lack of federal and state benefits for pregnancy and supported their own insurance plans, as Gladys Dickason mentioned. They based their campaign on *Muller* arguments about "separate spheres," not on "rights," but in essence, Deslippe argues, their concerns antedated "equal rights" campaigns of the 1970s. Changing circumstances also dented women workers' fealty to protection. Automation, Deslippe shows, removed job elements that formerly justified job segregation, fostered the replacement of male workers with women, and increased shift work, which made night work bans more burdensome. Union women, Deslippe notes, "did not abandon protective laws as much as subordinate their importance to a new set of priorities." By the late 1950s, in Deslippe's account, unionized women among electric workers and packinghouse workers started to "inch" toward an egalitarian stance. Still, the "inching" was subtle. Union women's views in the 1950s remained ambivalent and contradictory. Reluctance to discard protective laws prevailed.[65]

"It is true that not many women are in top places in the unions," Elisabeth Christman of NWTUL observed at a 1948 WB conference. "But many women without benefit of title or recognition are a power behind the throne, and it is simply a matter of time . . . until women get the official recognition they deserve." By the end of the 1950s, a core of women leaders had emerged, many of them participants in the WB Labor Advisory Committee. Most came from large unions affiliated with the CIO in which women were prominent (20 percent to 60 percent of members). Some rose up through the rank and file, including Caroline Davis, Catherine Conroy, and Dorothy Haener of UAW. Davis, who began work in an Indiana auto parts plant in the 1930s, served as director of the UAW Women's Bureau from 1948 to 1973. Addie Wyatt, an African American who began work at Chicago's Armour Meatpacking Plant in 1941, was by the 1950s a vice president of the (mainly male and white) Packinghouse Workers' union. Myra Wolfgang, who organized hotel and restaurant employees in Detroit in the 1940s and 1950s, later became a union vice president. Other women union leaders were college graduates, with backgrounds similar to those of social feminists at NCL, NWTUL, and the WB. Gladys Dickason, with a master's degree from Columbia (1924), taught economics at Sweet Briar and Hunter Colleges before becoming research director of ACWA in 1935. Katherine Ellickson, a Vassar graduate of 1926, studied economics at Columbia before taking a staff job with the United Mine Workers staff in the 1930s; by 1942 she moved on to the CIO research department. Esther Peterson, who attended Columbia's Teachers College, taught at Bryn Mawr's Summer School for Women Workers, began a stint as legislative representative for ACWA in

1945, and in 1958 became the AFL-CIO's first woman lobbyist. Vital to the WB in the late 1940s and 1950s, labor leaders served on the National Committee for Equal Pay (1953–65), endorsed alternatives to the ERA, and participated in the feuding women's movement.[66]

THE WOMEN'S BUREAU AND THE NWP

"Women must become more conscious of themselves as women and of their ability to function as a group," Eleanor Roosevelt wrote in a *Good Housekeeping* column in 1940. "At the same time they must try to wipe from men's consciousness the need to consider them as a group, or as women, in their everyday activities, especially as workers in industry or the professions." An enduring tension between women as "individuals" and as "a group" remained the clash over an ERA and single-sex protective laws. In the New Deal years, social feminists had overshadowed the NWP, which endured internal schisms. Still, the amendment advanced. In the 1920s and 1930s it won approval from women's business and professional groups; women lawyers' associations became staunch advocates. The ERA also drew support from men in Congress: the phrase "equal rights" was "hard to beat," Mary Anderson noted. In 1936 a House subcommittee approved the ERA and in 1938 the Senate Judiciary Committee reported it to the floor. In 1940 the Republican Party endorsed an ERA, though Republican women held mixed views. An ERA, declared the Federation of Women's Republican Clubs in 1943, was "premature, unwise, and unnecessary." In 1944 the Democratic Party bestowed its support, after a zealous campaign by Emma Guffey Miller, who assumed a leading role in the by-now tiny NWP.[67]

ERA foes mobilized. In 1945 a coalition of forty-three organizations united to defeat the "Unequal Rights Amendment," including the League of Women Voters, the American Association of University Women, the YWCA, the New York branch of NWTUL, the national councils of Catholic and Jewish women, and twenty-five trade union groups. ERA foes included major names of social feminism such as Carrie Chapman Catt, Alice Hamilton, Mary McLeod Bethune, Frances Perkins, and Frieda Miller. When the Senate considered an ERA in July 1946, the amendment failed to win a two-thirds majority, with thirty-eight in favor and thirty-five opposed. Congress rejected an equal pay bill that year as well. In 1947, the WB coalition proposed a Women's Status bill, an alternative to ERA that accepted distinctions on the basis of sex if "reasonably justified by differences in physical structure, biological, or special functions." The bill failed. In 1950 the Senate approved an ERA with a rider excluding protective laws. This bill failed, too. By now, the issue was stalled, though the rage of the factions that debated it endured; their mutual antagonism was volatile.[68]

Small, embattled, and self-involved, the NWP made little progress. ERA steadily won endorsements, from the Federation of Business and Professional Women in 1937, from the (now conservative) General Federation of Women's Clubs in 1943, from the American Association of University Women in 1953, and from women lawyers and their organizations. Lawyer Marguerite Rawalt, an important recruit, recalled how she made her way to the NWP in 1943 through a roster of supportive organizations, especially women lawyers' groups. But the NWP failed to capitalize on mounting support for ERA. Internal feuds arose in 1947 and again in 1953, mainly over the leadership of Alice Paul, whose single-minded devotion to cause could alienate potential followers. With each schism, membership sank. The NWP counted 627 "active" members in 1947 and only 200 in 1953. In the 1930s, NWP lawyers had battled in court for equal rights, for instance, to make jury service for women a federal right; in the contentious postwar schisms, in contrast, NWP factions sued one another. Beset from within and without, the NWP earned its reputation as querulous, even among Republicans. Republican women's leader Marion Martin, pressured by NWP members in the 1940s, saw them as "pains in the neck." Social feminists were yet more aggrieved. Frieda Miller attacked the NWP in 1945 as "a small but militant group of leisure-class women" and "women of property with conservative economic ideas." ERA supporters, Pauline Newman added, were "numerically insignificant, industrially ignorant, politically theoretical, and socially muddled." Animosity between factions of the women's movement, note historians Leila J. Rupp and Verta Taylor, "persisted long after the protective legislation issue lost its salience."[69]

Political antipathy underscored the longtime rivalry of factions. "[A]lmost all of our members seem to be of the conservative school," Alice Paul told an interviewer in the 1970s, and her postwar critics would have agreed. The NWP won the support of conservative legislators, capitalized on anticommunist sentiment, and identified the labor movement—especially the CIO—as an archfoe. "Our big enemy is organized labor," declared the head of the Connecticut Committee for the ERA, an independent equal rights group founded in 1943. In the early 1950s, the NWP denounced the WB, endorsed a bill to reduce its funding, and forged alliances with labor's foes. "We were convinced that in some cases the Woman's [P]arty was used as a front by the employers' associations that wanted to kill legislation for women," wrote Mary Anderson in 1951. Social feminists found the NWP reactionary.

To compound their grievances, prominent women associated with the New Deal and/or the labor movement faced accusations of communism or communist leanings, including Frances Perkins, Ellen Woodward, and Hilda Smith. Those who remained in public life, states historian Landon R. Y. Storrs, had to prove their anticommunist credentials in the late 1940s and 1950s, as did Esther Peterson and Mary Dublin Keyserling, who had briefly led the NCL in 1939–40. "Few of the accused women had actually joined the Communist Party," writes Storrs, "but many, like Mary Dublin Keyserling, had been more active in Popular Front social movements than has been generally understood."[70]

Protectionists of the postwar era staved off NWP attacks but made no gains; defections seemed to flow toward equal rights. Eleanor Roosevelt, as we have seen, withdrew from the debate over protective laws, though silently and without abandoning social feminist convictions. She remained a vice president of the NCL and referred to her long experience as an NCL officer in 1959, when she pressed Congress to extend FLSA to farm laborers. Unlike Eleanor Roosevelt, who dismissed NWP demands to endorse an ERA in 1951, Alice Hamilton, longtime protectionist and former NCL officer, changed her stance more definitively. Hamilton had attacked the prospect of an ERA since the 1920s and continued to do so into the 1940s. "We know that women would lose more than they gain," she wrote in the *Ladies' Home Journal* in 1945. She announced her change of heart in a letter of 1952 to an NWP member who published it in the *New York Herald Tribune*. "My long opposition to ERA has lost much of its force during the thirty years since the movement [for ERA] started," Hamilton wrote. The health of women in industry, she claimed, was now "of concern to health authorities, both state and Federal, to employers associations, insurance companies, trade unions." NWP members voiced delight.[71]

Protectionists also lost a major bastion, the Women's Bureau. When the Eisenhower administration began in 1953, the WB's special relationship with labor unions ended. The bureau's new head, Republican Alice K. Leopold, held a new title, "Assistant to the Secretary of Labor for Women's Affairs," that distanced her from the WB under Democrats. Republicans hoped to terminate the bureau entirely, which never occurred. A Connecticut businesswoman, Leopold belonged to the Connecticut Committee for the Equal Rights Amendment. She entered public life through the Connecticut League of Women Voters, became a state legislator, and rose to secretary of state in Connecticut, acting governor, and in 1952 an Eisenhower advisor. Unlike her predecessors, Alice K. Leopold had ties to business. "Before entering politics [she] was a businesswoman," explained the narrator of a WB skit sponsored by the National Association of Manufacturers. "She was personnel director in two large department stores and when her boys were small, she manufactured toys." Under Leopold, the WB sought involvement with chambers of commerce, not labor unions. The Labor Advisory Committee became a Women's Advisory Committee and welcomed business representatives, with whom Alice K. Leopold identified. "We must accept women," she told a conference of industrialists in 1957. "We must make adjustments so that they can enter the fields of industry. We must encourage them by promotion and recognition."[72]

The theme of Alice K. Leopold's reign was "womanpower," a World War II term that she applied to women in the workforce, the family, and volunteer roles. In a 1955 WB conference on "The Effective Uses of Womanpower," experts analyzed women's opportunities in the professions, technical vocations, and jobs that needed advanced training. Star performer and agile partisan, Leopold reached out to women in business, the professions, and women's clubs. She told a Pasadena women's club of the achievements of the older woman who, when her children went to school, "returns to work because she wants to." Addressing the National Association of Woman Lawyers ("Are Lawyers Leaders?") she endorsed equal pay, urged activism in government, and praised women who entered "so-called men's professions." Leopold never mentioned the WB's former alliance with union women. As she told a Republican women's group in Pennsylvania, "It is my strong belief that Republicans are friends of Labor." Under Leopold, the WB established ties with the NWP. The bureau no longer opposed an ERA, Leopold announced, but would not endorse it either. This evasive stance was shrewd; outright rejection of protective laws would have antagonized the WB staff. Still, the bureau's role as bulwark of protectionism had been suspended.[73]

When Alice K. Leopold summed up the state of protective laws at the end of the 1950s, she put a positive spin on recent change. By 1959, aspects of worker protection were in flux. FLSA had expanded slowly and steadily, and as it did, the minimum wage rose. In 1949, Congress hiked the federal minimum wage to 75 cents an hour, though new stipulations made coverage more restrictive; the amendment excluded women in clerical and service jobs in firms that did interstate business. By the mid-1950s, FLSA reached over half of wage and salary earners. In 1955, the minimum wage rose to $1 an hour; in 1961, it rose to $1.25 and Congress added 3.6 million workers. FLSA would not reach agricultural workers until 1966, under pressure from the civil rights movement. At last, in 1974, under pressure from the women's movement, Congress would finally extend the law to cover retail, service, and domestic workers. By then, FLSA reached about 90 percent of wage earners. Once the most controversial part of the protectionist agenda, the minimum wage made phenomenal progress.[74]

The reach of minimum wage laws grew in the states as well. No progress occurred in the states from 1942 to 1955, economist Elizabeth Brandeis reported. Then three states—Idaho, New Mexico, and Wyoming—approved a minimum wage for men and women in limited lines of work. Thereafter state activity picked up dramatically. By 1959, among thirty-three minimum wage laws, fifteen covered both men and women, and the trend continued. A decade later, among minimum wage laws in thirty-eight states plus the District of Columbia and Puerto Rico, thirty-two affected men and women; the "entering wedge" strategy was still operative. Labor women continued to champion the single-sex minimum wage because, as Frieda Miller claimed in 1954, minimum wage laws failed to reach almost half of working women. Alice Leopold, in contrast, praised the few state additions to wage-and-hour regulations that provided premium overtime pay for women workers. Leopold also underscored the advance of equal pay laws. As of 1959, twenty states had enacted such laws, and the number kept rising.[75]

Maximum hour laws remained the most widespread type of single-sex labor law. As the 1950s ended, forty-three states and the District of Columbia regulated women's hours. Most provided for an eight-hour day and forty-eight-hour week, but some were higher; Kentucky's law, for instance, set a sixty-hour maximum. Twenty-two states provided a six-day maximum workweek for women. Most states insured meal periods on the job or meal and rest periods; almost all states (forty-six, plus DC and Puerto Rico) had seating laws. Restrictions continued, too, though states persistently tinkered with them. Twenty states and Puerto Rico prohibited or regulated night work for women in specified industries or occupations. North Dakota and Washington night work laws targeted only elevator operators. Ohio's law extended only to taxicab drivers. Utah barred from night work solely women workers in restaurants after midnight on split shifts. Nineteen states and Puerto Rico prohibited industrial homework, usually for both men and women. Six states and Puerto Rico barred employment of women for specified periods before and after childbirth, usually four weeks. Eleven states regulated the weights that women might lift. Twenty-six states prohibited women from employment in specified industries, mainly mining (seventeen states), or occupations considered hazardous to health; the most widely prohibited work was bartending (ten states). Each state offered its own restrictions. Georgia barred women from work in retail liquor stores. Other states barred women from jobs that involved constant standing, coke ovens, cores and foundries, or work with harmful substances. Missouri excluded women from jobs that involved cleaning or working between moving machines. New York barred women from jobs in the basements of mercantile establishments. Ohio still provided the longest list of precluded jobs, including that of crossing watchman, or work in shoe polishing parlors or poolrooms.[76] The Progressive Era legacy of single-sex restrictions lived on.

As the 1960s began, economist Elizabeth Faulkner Baker assessed changes that had affected the workforce since World War II—the trends toward economic growth, full employment, shorter work hours, shorter work life, advanced technology, diminished occupational hazards, and improved working conditions. "These developments . . . suggest that protective labor legislation may play a smaller role in the future than the past," Baker wrote. Still, it was hard to envision an end to such laws. "[D]oubtless there will always be less advantaged workers—more women than men perhaps—who will need legislative protection from employer abuse."[77]

• • • • •

"Our efforts have always been to protect both men and women," wrote Alice Hamilton in 1945. "[B]ut when legislators were willing to protect only women workers, then we gladly took what we could get." Protectionists of the 1930s, who for years had accepted "what we could get," suddenly surged toward their original goal. The Supreme Court in 1937 upheld a minimum wage for women workers in *West Coast Hotel v. Parrish*, a major triumph for protectionists. Another victory followed in 1938, when Congress passed FLSA, extending wage-and-hour laws to men, and again in 1941, when the Supreme Court upheld FLSA in *U.S. v. Darby*. FLSA opened up a major artery to labor standards. Its reach, though small at first, steadily grew. The 1938 law both validated protectionists' "entering wedge" strategy and at the same time offered a new, alternative "entering wedge." After 1938, protective laws ran on a double track. Within two decades, FLSA reached a majority of wage earners and continued to expand.

Even with FLSA in place, protectionists defended single-sex protective laws in the states. Such laws were needed, they argued, to cover the large majority of women workers that FLSA excluded, women in jobs unconnected to interstate commerce. In World War II, the states temporarily suspended protective laws "for the duration" and then quickly restored them. For women at work, the war was a watershed—a brief era of new options, good pay, and few restrictions. The major ground shift in the history of protective laws, however, came after the war. The postwar economy saw a sudden rise in protectionist benefit, including premium pay, to men. By the late 1940s, the volunteer movement that had once supported protective legislation was fading. So were the careers of New Deal women who had kept the cause in play. From 1945 to 1960, the Women's Bureau remained the leading bastion of single-sex protective laws.

The postwar WB under Frieda Miller reached out to a new constituency, trade union women. "Labor feminists," historian Dorothy Sue Cobble's term, pragmatically accepted single-sex laws; difference-based strategies, they suggested, could foster equality. Their endorsement revitalized protectionism and social feminism. With labor women's support, the postwar WB sustained a successful holding pattern. It continued to support single-sex protective laws. To discard any of those laws, such as night work laws, might have a "toboggan" effect and injure labor standards in general. Protective laws, WB personnel declared, stood for "years of progressive action" and represented a "means of control" over industry. Finally, the WB insisted, FLSA never reached the most powerless workers. Frieda Miller's achievement was significant; she shifted WB priorities from protective laws to a focus on wages and to issues of workplace equality. Alice K. Leopold ignored protective laws but saved the WB from oblivion. Overall, the WB of the 1940s and 1950s preserved a constituency for single-sex laws and simultaneously preserved its own space in the federal bureaucracy.

By the 1950s, the conflict that had long dominated the women's movement, the feud between equal rights feminists and social feminists, reached Congress. It also reached stasis. Bill after bill—for equal pay, for ERA, for "Women's Status"—floundered and sank. Neither faction of the women's movement could move forward and neither would cede ground. In several ways, the foundation under single-sex protective laws had been crumbling since the 1930s. FLSA had made a dent. "Rights" were on the rise and laws based on difference could be in peril, as the dissent in *Goesaert* suggested. But single-sex laws were resilient. Moreover, as of the mid-1950s, state labor laws for women workers—notably minimum wage laws—continued to serve as springboards to "general" laws. As the 1960s began, single-sex protective laws were at once entrenched and vulnerable. Their fate changed suddenly.

7

Trading Places: The 1960s and 1970s

"WE WERE UP AGAINST THAT AWFUL Equal Rights Amendment situation," Esther Peterson recalled. A former official of the Amalgamated Clothing Workers, subsequently a lobbyist for the AFL-CIO, and longtime defender of protective laws, Peterson in 1961 was the leading woman appointee of the Kennedy administration. Offered her choice of jobs, she became head of the Women's Bureau as well as an assistant secretary of labor. She also requested and then led the President's Commission on the Status of Women

■ ■ ■

Pauli Murray and Esther Peterson, 1962. Pauli Murray, civil rights advocate and senior fellow at Yale Law School, and Esther Peterson, head of the Women's Bureau, assistant secretary of labor, and leader of the President's Commission on the Status of Women, pose together at a conference in New York City on October 11, 1962. Murray, who galvanized the PCSW's Committee on Civil and Political Rights, proposed a way to bypass the long-term controversy over protective laws and to achieve equal rights. The Schlesinger Library, Radcliffe Institute, Harvard University.

(PCSW) from 1961 to 1963. Peterson denied that the new commission was formed to foil ERA but conceded that enmity to the amendment "was a factor in it." Looking back on the early 1960s, Peterson recalled her mistrust of ERA supporters, with their ties to business and misplaced priorities: "These women were for the long distance things but not for the really gutsy immediate things," she claimed. A decade later, however, in 1971, Esther Peterson agreed to support an ERA. By then protective laws had floundered; courts had revoked them and states had repealed them. "After much soul searching I have come to the conclusion that . . . the enactment of the equal rights amendment would be a constructive step," Peterson wrote to member of Congress and ERA advocate Martha W. Griffiths. "It is difficult to make this statement. I realize that it will come as a disappointment to many individuals and organizations with whom I shared the opposite view for many years. However, much has happened in the past decade to improve the prospects for women." By the 1970s, equal rights had trumped protection. "History is moving in this direction," wrote Peterson, "and I believe women must move with it."[1]

When Esther Peterson jettisoned the cause of single-sex protective laws in 1971, reversing decades of support, she indeed kept pace with history. Between 1961 and 1971, a sequence of events brought protective laws to a virtual end. Two developments of the early 1960s—the PCSW and the Equal Pay Act of 1963—were just the prelude; they contained only hints of reversals to come. Change began abruptly with Title VII of the 1964 Civil Rights Act, which barred discrimination in employment on the basis of sex, and with the start of the Equal Employment Opportunities Commission (EEOC), the agency that enforced the law. After a few years of indecision, the EEOC in 1969 declared that single-sex protective laws violated Title VII. Protection's downfall rested not on EEOC, however, but rather on the courts—on women employees who sued for equal rights in federal courts under Title VII and the lawyers who represented them; on pressure from feminist organizations, notably the National Organization for Women (NOW), that supported the plaintiffs; on a series of court decisions that upset protective laws; and on a mounting consensus among judges in favor of equal rights. Also important, more generally, was feminist resurgence, which swayed conviction; shifts in public opinion culminated in the passage in Congress of an ERA in 1972. Single-sex protective laws were thus the first casualties of the new feminism. Once central to the women's movement, they became obstacles on the path to equal rights. The laws did not fall easily. But in retrospect they were sitting ducks.

THE EARLY 1960s: PCSW AND EQUAL PAY

Prospects for an ERA had held steady through the 1950s. The Democratic Party had endorsed an ERA in 1960; the new president, John F. Kennedy, promised, more ambiguously, "legislation [to] guarantee to women equality of rights under the law." Still, ERA foes found room to maneuver. Esther Peterson, the new WB head, urged alternative goals: extension of FLSA to cover more women workers, the minimum wage for women excluded from FLSA, and equal pay, long a WB cause. With Democrats in office, Peterson seized upon a tactic to keep ERA at bay. President Kennedy needed to compensate for a paucity of women's appointments to the new administration. The PCSW, formed in December 1961, served both the president's need—to mollify women constituents—and Peterson's goals, to navigate around the threat of an ERA. The "status of women" phrase, left over from a failed social feminist bill of the 1950s, signified an alternative to ERA. Peterson persuaded Eleanor Roosevelt to serve as chair of the new commission. Roosevelt had withdrawn from the conflict over single-sex protective laws back in the 1940s. "This may be the last thing I ever do," she said.[2]

The commission's twenty-six members were business and labor leaders, educators, and six members of the president's cabinet. The vast majority of about one hundred commission participants opposed ERA, save for NWP member Marguerite Rawalt (1895–1989), an IRS lawyer. A graduate of George Washington University's Law School, Rawalt had long experience in women's organizations. She had been president in 1942 of the National Federation of Women Lawyers, an ERA stronghold; president of the National Federation of Business and Professional Women's Clubs (1954–56); and the first woman president of the Federal Bar Association. Energetic and engaging, Rawalt would play a crucial role in protection's downfall. In PCSW, however, her stance was isolated. The commission sought to steer clear of controversy, find areas of agreement, and propose viable policy initiatives. Its final report, which fused recommendations from seven committees, was presented on October 11, 1963, and soon published commercially.[3]

Two committee sessions dealt with protective laws. The first, the Committee on Protective Labor Legislation, floundered on the issue of maximum hours laws. Members debated clashing proposals: the extension of hours limits to men versus premium overtime pay for men and women as a "deterrent" to longer work days. Debate was unresolved. Single-sex hours laws, the committee finally stated, still served a function: to protect women workers concentrated in the nonunion sector. Women-only maximum hours laws in the states "should be maintained, strengthened, and expanded." The committee saw FLSA, with its overtime provision, "as a complement rather than an alternative to maximum hours limitations." Farm workers and domestic workers, up to now exempt from protective law, should be included in it; women in executive, professional, or managerial jobs should be exempt. The commission (the governing body of PCSW), unsatisfied with the committee report and controlled by Esther Peterson, tilted the other way, toward extension of FLSA. Overtime pay, the commission declared in its final report, was at once "the best way to discourage excessive hours for all workers." FLSA standards should be extended to women workers who lacked them. In the interim, single-sex state laws should be "maintained, strengthened and expanded," as the committee had stated. But state laws would be only temporary measures. Moreover, "[p]rovisions for flexibility under proper safeguards should allow additional hours of work where there is a demonstrated need [undefined]." The commission's change, though subtle, was significant. So was the subtext: the problem of overtime versus maximum hours laws defied simple solution.[4]

A second relevant committee, the Committee on Civil and Political Rights, provided a forum for Pauli Murray, then a fellow at Yale Law School and a longtime civil rights activist. Murray, at this pivotal moment, began to channel lessons from the civil rights movement into the women's movement. While the labor legislation committee equivocated, the civil and political rights committee broke new ground.

Born in 1910, Murray, a Hunter College graduate, worked in a series of jobs under a WPA program in the early 1930s. She started to crusade for civil rights in 1939 when rejected from graduate school at the University of North Carolina because of her race. Never hesitant, Murray asked the Roosevelts to intervene to desegregate the university that had spurned her. "I understand perfectly," responded Eleanor Roosevelt, thereafter a friend. "But great changes come slowly." While attending Howard Law School in 1944, Murray led student sit-ins at segregated restaurants. When rejected by Harvard Law School for an advanced degree in law, this time because of her sex, she attended Boalt Hall. After a sixteen-year hiatus of intermittent law practice, labor organizing, writing, and civil rights activism, she moved on to the fellowship at Yale. Pauli Murray's extensive experience with bias shaped a special perspective, which she brought to PCSW. Murray had always supported labor standards for all workers, as had her heroine, Eleanor Roosevelt; she saw, however, that single-sex protective laws had "very little meaning" for black women, who worked mainly in jobs untouched by such laws. At the PCSW, Murray turned her attention to the women's movement.

"Ironically, if Howard Law School equipped me for effective struggle against Jim Crow, it was also the place where I first became conscious of the twin evil of discriminatory sex bias, which I quickly labeled Jane Crow," Murray wrote. "In my preoccupation with the brutality of racism, I had failed until now to recognize the subtler, more ambiguous expressions of sexism."[5]

Bringing her outlier status and bifocal perspective to the PCSW, Murray made a crucial contribution: she proposed a strategy for constitutional recognition of women's rights without an ERA. Murray contended that courts could interpret the equal protection clause of the Fourteenth Amendment to guarantee sex equality as well as race equality. She did not specifically reject an ERA. "Equality of Rights for all persons, male or female," she stated, "must be reflected in the fundamental law of the land." However, Murray argued, the Constitution already provided for legal equality. Therefore, as the committee concluded, "a constitutional amendment need not now be sought in order to establish this principle." Murray's proposal pacified supporters of single-sex protective laws, who believed the committee's conclusion left those laws alone. Marguerite Rawalt, the committee's lone ERA supporter, insisted on the "now" to preserve the possibility of an ERA if the courts failed to act as Pauli Murray proposed. Murray's legal strategy enabled the commission to propose an alternative to ERA; it bridged the chasm that severed ERA friends from foes. It also predicted by and large how the courts would eventually act. Murray had outlined an effective women's rights strategy based on civil rights strategy, or "reasoning from race." According to scholar Serena Mayeri, "No one did more than Murray to make race-sex analogies the legal currency of feminism."[6]

Before the PCSW could present its report to the president, the WB coalition achieved one of its major goals. Congress passed the Equal Pay Act in June 1963. An equal pay bill had failed in 1946; no hearings had been held since 1950. Business argued that state equal pay laws had already ended inequality and (conversely) that women cost more than men to employ due to absenteeism and higher turnover. The WB gathered statistics to foil both arguments. Congress limited the scope of the equal pay measure; it made the bill an amendment to FLSA—which meant that it excluded two-thirds of women workers, including most low-income workers (laundry, hotel, restaurant, domestic workers, employees of small stores, farm workers) as well as professional and administrative employees. The modified bill, moreover, applied only in the very few instances in which men and women performed exactly the same work; these instances were few in a sex-segregated job market. Without women's equal access to jobs, the equal pay law had little impact. An equal pay requirement might even increase workplace segregation

The Equal Pay Act, 1963. Supporters of the Equal Pay Act of 1963 surround President John F. Kennedy as he signs the law. At the left, with flowered hat, is Dorothy Height, president of the National Council of Negro Women and head of the PCSW's "Consultation on the Problems of Negro Women"; Mary Anderson, former head of the Women's Bureau, 1920–44; and Esther Peterson, current WB head and PCSW leader. At the right, looking away from the president, is Caroline Davis of the United Auto Workers Women's Department. Extensive hearings on equal pay exposed Congress to women's concerns about workplace equality. Cecil Stoughton/White House Photographs, John F. Kennedy Presidential Library and Museum, Boston.

by sex, opponents charged. The NWP, which lobbied against the bill, claimed that an ERA was needed to insure women equal access to jobs. But the WB coalition viewed equal pay as a major victory, not without reason. One positive consequence was less in the law's immediate impact than in the long fight to achieve it. The extended campaign for equal pay exposed members of Congress to sixteen years of argument over sex discrimination in wages— and to three sets of congressional hearings on the subject. This exposure no doubt softened up legislators for a far more consequential step on sex discrimination in employment some months down the road.[7]

The PCSW delivered its report in October 1963. "Not since World War II had women's issues received so much attention," historian Cynthia Harrison observes. The PCSW "pointed out problems of which the general populace had before been largely unaware." Shrewdly, the commission asked the president to establish two further bodies to continue along the path it had carved out: an ongoing committee, made up of executive officers and agency heads, and an "Advisory Council" of private citizens to continue the

PCSW's efforts, meet periodically, and report to the president to implement and reevaluate the commission's recommendations. The PCSW thus perpetuated itself; it made the shaping of national policy on women's status a continuing assignment. PCSW success was also a triumph for Esther Peterson, whom President Lyndon Johnson at once promoted yet again, this time to a White House post, as presidential assistant for Consumer Affairs. Ironically, the PCSW did not further Peterson's career in precisely the way she intended. In retrospect, an outsize player on the PCSW stage was Pauli Murray, who drew on her experience in civil rights to formulate a new legal strategy, the most original part of the PCSW's report. Another significant player, retrospectively, was lawyer Marguerite Rawalt, who soon spearheaded NOW's legal campaign for equal rights. The PCSW's main outgrowth, the "Advisory Council," soon backed equal rights as well. Within a year, the cause of single-sex protective laws, which the PCSW had so carefully preserved, would be fatally undermined.[8]

The short life of the PCSW and the triumph of equal pay played out against an eventful backdrop. As the commission mobilized in 1961, freedom riders began their forays into Alabama and Mississippi; during PCSW deliberations from 1961 to 1963, demands for civil rights gained momentum. The civil rights movement changed the political landscape for activist women. It created a climate of protest, provided models of pressure groups, posited equality as a positive good, and set precedents for ending discrimination under law. These developments each contributed to protection's demise. The process began in 1964.

TITLE VII, THE EEOC, AND PROTECTIVE LAWS

Title VII of the civil rights bill that Congress considered in 1964 barred discrimination in employment on the basis of race. In an apparent effort to derail the bill, eighty-one-year-old Virginia representative Howard W. Smith, chair of the House Rules Committee, proposed an amendment to Title VII that would bar discrimination in employment on the basis of sex. Smith opposed civil rights; to some, his proposal seemed a facetious stunt—a way to subject the bill to ridicule. Smith, however, was a longtime ally of Alice Paul and of the NWP; he had sponsored an ERA in Congress since 1945. In late 1963, expecting debate on the civil rights bill, NWP leaders decided to seek an amendment to end sex discrimination; two Virginia members of NWP had urged Smith to propose it. The ploy was not new. NWP had tried to attach provisions on sex to civil rights measures for years; so had Howard W.

Smith. That Congressman Smith intended primarily to defeat the civil rights bill seems evident; the move to end sex discrimination served his purpose. "I am a conservative and I have been scrambling around here for 32 years now," Smith told a reporter, "and I have always found that when you are doing that you grasp any snickersnee you can get hold of and fight the best way you can."[9]

Howard W. Smith's proposal delayed passage of the civil rights bill and evoked dispute. Liberal groups opposed Smith's amendment, as did Esther Peterson at the Department of Labor, the rest of the WB coalition, and the labor movement; these critics did not want to scuttle the cause of civil rights for African Americans by adding a new consideration. Other concerns arose, too. Brooklyn congressman Emanuel Celler argued in a speech in the House that equality of the type the Smith amendment provided might "endanger traditional family relationships" and deprive women of hard-won privileges such as alimony and child custody. "This is the 'entering wedge,'" said Celler. "The list of foreseeable consequences is unlimited." To the NWP the Smith amendment may have seemed retribution for the Kennedy commission's failure to endorse ERA. ERA foes, in contrast, saw it as a stepping-stone to ERA. But Democratic representative and NWP member Martha W. Griffiths of Michigan (1912–2003) promoted the Smith amendment; she was, she claimed, preparing an identical amendment. "Without saying anything to anyone, I decided to let him [Smith] offer it," she wrote to friends. "I used Smith." The Smith amendment passed the House handily, a "glorious victory" to Martha Griffiths. Representative Smith then voted against the civil rights bill he had amended; so did other southern Democrats who had endorsed his amendment. Esther Peterson, in contrast, after the House vote, changed her mind on the amendment on sex that she had formerly opposed and lobbied for its passage in the Senate. Historians weigh whether the success of the Smith amendment was an accident, an orchestrated plan to kill the bill, or an attempt by women's rights advocates to seize the moment; it was all at once. Congress passed the civil rights bill in the summer of 1964, its provision against sex discrimination intact; the law took effect one year later.[10]

Title VII changed the outlook for protective laws—or, in the words of historian Patricia G. Zelman, Title VII's link of race and sex discrimination "cast the debate about protective laws in a new light." The 1964 law provided that employment discrimination complaints could be sent for investigation to the Equal Employment Opportunities Commission (EEOC), a five-member panel appointed by the president. But the panel's ability to cope with complaints was limited. Republicans in both houses had undercut the bill by curbing EEOC power to enforce the law. In consequence, the federal agency empowered to enforce the civil rights law could only "investigate" complaints and "conciliate" opposing views. "The EEOC's teeth were pulled out one by one as the bill went through the legislative process," political scientist Jo Freeman observes. Although Title VII empowered employees to file job discrimination suits in federal court—and thereby gave the federal courts a major role in sex discrimination law—this long, costly process took time. For the moment, EEOC had little clout to enforce the law; employees had limited chance to profit from it.[11]

Sex discrimination claims faced further obstacles. EEOC members, who expected to deal mainly with race discrimination complaints, soon faced a slew of women's grievances; among charges filed at EEOC in its first year, about one-third involved sex discrimination. Viewing sex discrimination as less serious than race discrimination, the EEOC gave scant attention to women's complaints; it saw little cause to pursue such complaints without the insistence of pressure groups such as those that supported civil rights. Wary of upsetting a balance of power between federal and state governments, the EEOC also failed to address the impact of Title VII on protective laws. "At first glance Title VII appears to have the effect of superseding all state protective legislation," the EEOC noted in its first annual report. "However, there is nothing in the legislative history of Title VII to indicate that Congress intended any such far-reaching results." (That claim was true in part; that is, Congress had held no committee hearings on Title VII after "sex" was added to it.) The EEOC had further reason to skirt the issue; among sex discrimination charges filed at EEOC in its first year, only 12 percent involved protective laws—mainly hours restrictions and barriers to overtime, or premium pay. Most sex discrimination complaints concerned unequal benefits in union contracts and discriminatory seniority lists. Finally, Congress had added a baffling loophole to Title VII in the aftermath of the Smith amendment, one that distinguished sex discrimination from race discrimination. The loophole was an exemption for employers: the bona fide occupational qualification (BFOQ) defense. It allowed employers to make sex-based employment decisions by showing that sex was a "bona fide occupational qualification necessary to the normal operation of the particular business or enterprise." The employer hiring a bathroom attendant, for instance, might hire a person of the required sex. Beyond that, the boundaries of the BFOQ were difficult to determine. The possibility arose that protective laws fell entirely under the BFOQ.[12]

In November 1965 the EEOC announced its first sex discrimination guidelines without addressing the issue of protective laws; the guidelines concerned refusals to hire, classification of jobs, and separate seniority lists. Thereafter, EEOC shuffled back and forth on protective laws; a series of conflicting regulations reflected its wavering policy. At first, as in its first annual report, EEOC assumed that Congress did not intend to revoke state protective laws. In a regulation of December 2, 1965, the EEOC allowed "restrictive" state protective laws to be used as a BFOQ defense provided that employers acted in good faith and did not discriminate against women employees. Protective laws that provided "benefit" (minimum wage, overtime pay rules, rest periods, physical facilities), in contrast, could not be used as a BFOQ defense; such laws had to be extended to men. Key terms, such as "protective" and "discriminatory" were undefined. Within a year, on August 19, 1966, the EEOC announced in a press release that when Title VII and state protective laws clashed, it would refrain from making a decision. The reasons: EEOC interpretations could not protect employers against state liability for violation of state laws; nor could the EEOC start lawsuits to challenge state laws. "The commission cannot rewrite state law according to its own view of the public interest," EEOC declared. Instead, the EEOC urged aggrieved women workers to sue the state under Title VII; litigation, it said, was needed to resolve conflicts between Title VII and state law. It also urged state lawmakers to revise protective laws. Then, on February 24, 1968, EEOC revoked the 1966 policy and reverted to its 1965 guideline. The EEOC would decide if Title VII superseded state laws in cases where the effect of those laws was discriminatory rather than protective (again the terms were undefined).[13]

While the EEOC hedged, the women's movement sent out mixed messages. From the WB, Mary Dublin Keyserling, who had replaced Esther Peterson in 1964, defended protective laws. Critics, including status-of-women groups, issued rumbles of dissent. The Citizens' Advisory Council on the Status of Women urged states to revise their protective laws in light of Title VII. In December 1965 lawyers Pauli Murray and Mary O. Eastwood published a law review article that pushed the case against protection forward. Eastwood had served as the attorney general's deputy on the PCSW; she opposed protective laws, at first covertly, then more overtly. The Murray/ Eastwood article, which illuminated the "reasoning from race" strategy, marked another turning point.[14]

Murray and Eastwood made the link between sex discrimination and race discrimination explicit: "The rights of women and the rights of Negroes are only different phases of the fundamental and indivisible issue of human rights." Protective laws, they declared, contradicted Title VII and could not be harmonized with it. The conflict between Title VII and the laws would be brief, they predicted. In the view of Murray and Eastwood, the "tipping point" had been reached. Protective laws suffered from "waning utility." The number of women who benefited from such laws was small and shrinking. Single-sex maximum hours laws, at once the most common and controversial of single-sex protective laws, deprived women of "premium pay" for overtime. "Removal of inequities" was now the goal; equality of opportunity was the most compelling consideration. Equality did come without risk or cost, Murray and Eastwood conceded, but "relatively little harm would result." Women must "pay the price that must be paid for equal recognition in the world of work." Courts had "not yet fully realized that women's rights are part of human rights," the authors concluded, but "the climate appears favorable" for a judicial attack on sex discrimination. "We are entering the era of human rights," Murray and Eastwood declared. Like civil rights for African Americans, gender equality was imperative. "'Classification by sex' should now be shelved alongside the separate but equal doctrine."[15]

In Congress, Martha Griffiths reiterated the Murray/ Eastwood concerns. By now Griffiths (University of Michigan Law School 1940, elected to the state legislature in 1948 and to Congress in 1954) had seized the role of leading equal rights crusader in the House. In May 1966 she attacked EEOC on the House floor for "shilly-shallying" and "whining." EEOC's attitude toward sex discrimination, Griffiths charged, was "specious, negative, and arrogant"; sex discrimination should be treated like race discrimination. In June 1966 Aileen Hernandez, the sole woman EEOC member (and one of two African American members), resigned to join NOW. Spurred by EEOC recalcitrance, a core of twenty-eight activist women mobilized to press the commission into action on women's complaints. "[U]nless a powerful watchdog organization of women" arose, wrote Pauli Murray, "the sex provision of Title VII would not be enforced." Unable to win support among existing women's groups, the feminist nucleus began a civil rights organization for women "to take action to bring women into full participation in the mainstream of American society *now.*" NOW at once created a legal arm and brought suit against sex discrimination in labor practices.[16]

The EEOC still evaded a firm policy, but pressure mounted. In May 1–3, 1967, when the EEOC held hearings on protective laws, the women's movement remained divided, but the equal rights faction had won adherents. More important, from 1965 onward, aggrieved women employees used Title VII to press sex discrimination suits against employers in federal courts. Finally, in August 1969, EEOC reached a definitive stance on protective laws. It announced that single-sex protective laws by their very nature clashed with Title VII "and will not be considered a defense to an . . . unlawful employment practice, or as a basis for application of bfoq." The laws in question were "those that limit the employment of females . . . in certain occupations, in jobs requiring the lifting or carrying of weights exceeding certain prescribed limits, during certain hours of the night, or for more than a specified number of hours per day or week"—in short, in the terms of the 1965 regulation, "restrictive" laws.

> The Commission believes that such State laws and regulations, although originally promulgated for the purpose of protecting females, have ceased to be relevant to our technology or to the expanding role of the female worker in our economy. The Commission has found that such laws and regulations do not take into account the capacities, preferences, and abilities of individual females and tend to discriminate rather than protect. Accordingly, the Commission has concluded that such laws and regulations conflict with Title VII of the Civil Rights Act of 1964.[17]

By the time EEOC revised its guidelines in 1969, changes were under way in the states and in the courts. Since 1966, six states had repealed single-sex maximum hours laws; six more states had provided for exemption from maximum hours laws; in five states and the District of Columbia, attorneys general had ruled that single-sex protective laws were superseded by Title VII or state fair employment laws. Two states had curtailed prosecutions under protective laws because of uncertainty as to the effect of Title VII. State courts in Wyoming and California had overturned state protective laws that excluded women from bartending. In three federal women's employment cases, in the Fifth and Seventh Circuits, the EEOC had filed amicus briefs on behalf of the plaintiffs. Federal district courts in California and Oregon had declared that Title VII superseded single-sex state laws.[18] Debate on protective laws, meanwhile, percolated through government agencies, the labor movement, and political parties.

PROTECTION DEBATED: PRESSURE AND POLITICS, 1965–69

EEOC reluctance to upset protective laws reflected split opinion in the women's movement. Debate focused on a shrinking range of issues, or what the commission called "restrictive" laws: weight limits and hours limits (that is, the critical issue of overtime). Conflict emerged in the EEOC hearings of May 1967, where equal rights proponents seized a dominant role. Stressing the discriminatory impact of protective laws, they urged the EEOC to state that Title VII violated such laws. The equal rights faction included tradi-tional stalwarts, such as NWP, the National Federation of Business and Pro-fessional Women's Clubs, and employers associations, such as the Illinois state chamber of commerce. It also included NOW representative Margue-rite Rawalt, member of Congress Martha Griffiths, and significantly, repre-sentatives of several unions.

"[E]mployers have used these laws to circumvent our collective bargain-ing contracts and to discriminate against the women who are members of our union," stated a spokesman for the UAW. "[S]o-called 'protective' state laws—that is, those based on stereotypes as to sex rather than true biological factors—are undesirable relics of the past." In World War II, employers had been "more than happy" to hire women and ignore state laws, the UAW spokesman stated. But postwar, "when men were available again, employers resorted to the technique of combining two jobs into one so that it was beyond the state maximum weight law, or scheduling hours of work be-yond the statutory limit for women in order to avoid hiring women em-ployees." Employers thus used state law to "deprive women of jobs, promo-tions, and overtime." EEOC performance had been disappointing, the UAW representative charged. "Its lack of courage here has brought long neglected laws and regulations out of the woodwork." Marguerite Rawalt, on behalf of NOW, endorsed the UAW stance. "Such laws prevent women from being hired, promoted, transferred, and recalled to work after lay-off," charged Rawalt. "In addition to excluding them from jobs, such laws on hours de-prive them of overtime pay."[19]

The AFL-CIO voiced opposing concerns. Single-sex labor laws "served not only as a direct protection for women but also as means of abating abuses for men, increasing the availability of legislative standards for all workers," the spokesman for the AFL-CIO declared. Protective laws also pro-tected nonunion employees, the AFL-CIO stated; the "benefits" that women gained from protective laws should be "retained" and "extended to men to the maximum extent possible." Moreover, if "existing law serves a valid pro-tective purpose" but could not be directly extended to men (maximum hour and weight limits), "they should be retained for women alone." The AFL-CIO also disagreed with equal rights proponents on the importance of overtime pay; women workers, it stressed, had divergent interests. "We have no evidence that women *generally* prefer extended opportunity to overtime work to a clear hours limitation, even though obviously there are a number that do." Still, most women workers faced a "double day," said the AFL-CIO, and appreciated hours limits. "Except for the privileged few, this remains a current reality in American life." Defenders of protection now represented an old guard: the WB and its allies. The goals of working men and women differed, confirmed Katherine Ellickson, speaking for NCL. "While men may also require protection from overtime hours, as a group their need is less than that of women, who usually spend more time on family and home responsibilities."[20]

The statements at the EEOC suggested the shrinking arena of debate in the late 1960s. Feminists who urged an ERA seized the high ground—what Eastman and Murray in 1965 had called "the fundamental and indivisible issue of human rights." Sex discrimination must be treated like race discrimination. Protective laws were inherently discriminatory and could no longer be justified; they kept women from applying for jobs, from promotions, from overtime pay, and from competition with men. Any law that truly advantaged women workers (the minimum wage, factory safety rules) had to apply to men as well. Conversely, any mention in law of difference meant disadvantage. "A worker is a worker," Martha Griffiths wrote, "and should receive exactly the same consideration as any other worker, whether she earns all of the family income or merely subsidizes it." Supporters of protective laws conceded that some laws might impede equal opportunity (night work laws, exclusionary laws) and no longer defended them. They argued, however, that women had fought for years to gain maximum hours and minimum wage laws; that if any such laws discriminated, those laws should be dealt with on a case-by-case basis; that women workers played a double role, at home and at work; and that only through difference in treatment could equality be achieved. Legislators could not be counted on to extend "beneficial" laws to men, for instance; to repeal all such laws on that false assumption would not provide a meaningful equality. Nor did defenders and foes of protective laws agree on what overtime meant; to defenders of maximum hours laws, overtime seemed compulsory, not voluntary—an onerous job requirement more than an opportunity. Finally, defenders argued that protective laws were imperative for the least advantaged workers, those without union contracts or FLSA coverage. As Katherine Ellickson explained at the EEOC hearings, "The value of laws protecting those with the least skill and bargaining power should not be sacrificed because a much smaller number of highly skilled or favorably situated women and men may find them restrictive."[21]

The Women's Bureau under economist Mary Dublin Keyserling steadily pressed the EEOC to prevent Title VII from undercutting protective laws. A Barnard graduate and PhD in economics, Keyserling led the NCL from 1938 to 1941. She began her career in public service in World War II as an advisor to Eleanor Roosevelt at the Office of Civilian Defense. With her husband, economist Leon Keyserling, she formed the Council on Economic Progress, a pressure group committed to full employment, strong unions, unemployment insurance, and the minimum wage. When WB head Esther Peterson was promoted to a White House position in 1965, Keyserling replaced her. As WB head, Keyserling promoted equal rights in various ways: she strove to gain for women equal opportunity in government jobs, urged the inclusion of "sex" in state fair employment practices laws, disputed the labor department's characterization of women as "secondary workers," and sought to place labor union women on state commissions on the status of women—though these soon adopted an equal rights stance. But Keyserling staunchly defended protective laws even as the women's movement started to veer away from them and claimed that the laws did not conflict with Title VII. According to one critic, Dorothy Haener of the UAW, she was "just absolutely deaf to anyone who suggested that state protective laws didn't protect, that they did discriminate sometimes." By the late 1960s, feminist activism undercut WB claims to represent the women's movement; Mary Keyserling's stance became isolated. The EEOC's announcement in 1969 that Title VII invalidated protective laws left the WB stranded. When the Nixon administration took over in 1969, Keyserling left government work. Within months, the EEOC reversed its policy on protective laws, and within a few years most women's organizations that were part of the long-term WB coalition followed.[22]

Like Mary Dublin Keyserling, NOW leaders of the late 1960s sought to influence the EEOC. From 1966 on, NOW sought enforcement of Title VII, pressured the EEOC by monitoring it, and helped women workers file complaints. NOW also urged the Justice Department (in vain) to initiate Title VII lawsuits and then supported workers who did so. Most important, NOW dove into the process of litigation. Modeling its actions on those of the NAACP Legal Defense Fund, NOW mobilized a network of lawyers attached to its local chapters who volunteered their services to join Title VII lawsuits. It also appeared in amicus capacity in two early Title VII cases. Marguerite Rawalt headed NOW's legal committee from 1966 to 1969, aided by Mary O. Eastwood, whose article of 1965 with Pauli Murray promoted equal rights. In 1970, the legal committee became NOW's Legal Defense and Education Fund, a formal litigation unit, led by Rawalt until 1973. Other women's rights activists followed NOW's lead. In 1968 the Women's Equity Action League joined in, and later the Women's National Law Center and the ACLU Women's Rights Project; by 1970, historian Susan M. Hartmann shows, equal rights activists had swayed the ACLU to shift ground on protective laws. Equal rights campaigners thus brought the debate over protective laws back into the courts and shaped its outcome in a way that the WB could not. They also pursued the strategy of "reasoning from race"—of drawing a race/sex analogy unavailable to their opponents.[23]

While the clash between protective laws and equal rights absorbed women activists, political parties of the late 1960s sought to distance themselves. To get mired in this ceaseless debate would only alienate a portion of women constituents. Political timing favored the Democrats, who held the presidency through 1968. In the early 1960s President Kennedy relied on the labor movement; the AFL-CIO and the WB sought to keep ERA at bay, and the Democratic Party cooperated. Party platforms in 1960 and 1964 evaded mention of ERA; the PCSW in October 1963 stated that "an ERA need not now be sought." President Johnson handled women's issues deftly. He told a reporter in 1964 that he wanted "to make the upgrading of women in American life one of the major goals of his administration," claimed credit for including "sex" in Title VII, and catered to both factions of the women's movement. Mary Keyserling at the WB saw the Johnson years as "a time of unprecedented progress" for women wage earners. In 1967, at Martha Griffiths's urging, Johnson issued Executive Order 11375, which banned sex discrimination in federal jobs and by private firms with government contracts. Even in 1968, when antiwar protest eroded Johnson's popularity and his poll ratings plunged, his support among women remained high. By then equal rights feminists had made inroads among Democratic women and held sway over protectionists.[24]

Republicans, unlike Democrats, had no allegiance to protective laws, rather the contrary; antipathy to protection prevailed in the business world. Party platforms had endorsed ERA since 1940. With the rise of feminism from 1966 on, Republican women—who for decades had supported ERA—suddenly hesitated. Nixon took office in 1969 just as calls for an ERA escalated. But equal rights feminists had few representatives in the administration. A special task force on women's rights and responsibilities, appointed by Nixon in September 1969, urged the president to endorse an ERA because, it stated, protective laws were no longer an issue ("these laws are disappearing under the impact of Title VII"). It also urged the EEOC to enforce Title VII. Nixon did not release or comment on the report.[25] Presidential advisors, meanwhile, voiced varied attitudes toward women's rights.

Daniel Patrick Moynihan, who had caused consternation with his 1965 report on the black family, turned to women's rights in a memo to the president of 1969. The nation had "educated women for equality . . . but have not really given it to them," Moynihan told the president. "Inequality is so great that the dominant group either doesn't notice it, or assumes the dominated group likes it that way." The theme of gender would gain force in the coming decade, Moynihan predicted (accurately). Among Nixon advisors in general, in contrast, suspicion of feminism prevailed. Although the president "publicly supported" an ERA, advisor Charles Colson reminded advisor Ken Cole in early 1970, "[f]ortunately the good sense and ultimate wisdom of Congress has always kept this ridiculous proposal from being enacted." "It is good politics to talk about, I must admit," Colson added. Patrick Buchanan's memos to fellow staffers reinforced hostility to the prospect of an ERA. As he wrote to Nixon advisor H. R. Haldeman in 1971: "My view is that it is not good for the country." Nor was militant feminism. "As for the extremists in the movement, they are a target of opportunity so far as I am concerned," Buchanan told Haldeman. "Female militants are more of an object of ridicule and a pain in the butt than the black chauvinists."[26]

When Congress began to consider an ERA in 1970, debate on single-sex protective laws resumed, and politicians became enmeshed. By then the courts had made so great an impact that protection's death was imminent.

PROTECTION CHALLENGED: THREE LANDMARK CASES

Invalidation of single-sex protective laws began with Title VII. Foes of civil rights in Congress had crippled the EEOC's power from the start; the commission could only "investigate" and "conciliate." But Title VII enabled employees to bring charges about discrimination in employment to federal court. Women workers at once started lawsuits to challenge protective laws; women's rights advocates endorsed their suits, formed organizations to provide support, and served as counsel. The courts—like the EEOC—at first hesitated to grasp a conflict between Title VII and protective laws but quickly came around to it. Thus women litigants, their lawyers, and NOW took the lead in toppling protective laws; so did federal judges, especially in the district courts.[27] Three landmark cases shaped protection's fate. The plaintiffs worked in an aviation plant, for a telephone company, and for a railroad company; unable to win promotions, they challenged maximum hours laws and weight-lifting limits. The three cases moved through the federal courts from 1966 to 1971.

"Your gallant spirit is more than appreciated," lawyer Marguerite Rawalt wrote to Velma L. Mengelkoch in October, 1965. "[Y]ou are indeed the bearer of a banner of importance to all women." Mengelkoch, a widowed California mother of three, worked on the assembly line for North American Aviation, which rejected her application for promotion. With two coworkers, Mengelkoch sued the company; the plaintiffs said North American Aviation violated Title VII and also the equal protection and due process clauses of the Fourteenth Amendment. "[B]ecause overtime is required, they cannot be employed in better paying jobs for which they have the skills, such jobs as operating functional test equipment, final assembly work, or work as supervisors on the assembly line," Rawalt told the EEOC in 1967. "Secondly, they are denied opportunity to earn time-and-a half for overtime." North American argued that it complied with the state's maximum hours law, which limited women workers to an eight-hour day and forty-eight-hour week. Mengelkoch's case bounced around the lower federal courts for several years; the judges were not ready to grapple with Title VII. A three-judge court in 1968 claimed no jurisdiction and dissolved itself. The court pointed to *Muller v. Oregon* (1908) and *Miller v. Wilson* (1915), which had upheld a ten-hour law (Oregon) and an eight-hour law (California) for women workers; since those cases, the court argued, no intervening decisions suggested that the Supreme Court had rejected its stance. The same day a single district judge dismissed the case without prejudice. When Mengelkoch appealed both decisions to the Supreme Court, it claimed lack of jurisdiction and dismissed her appeals; the case fell to yet another three-judge lower federal court, which dissolved itself. Mengelkoch, by now the sole plaintiff, kept appealing. The case, long supported by NOW, finally reached a federal appeals court, which in 1971 issued an opinion favoring Mengelkoch. Federal policy, said the Ninth Circuit, was "too firm, and too urgent, to warrant such leisurely processing of civil rights actions."[28]

Velma Mengelkoch's challenge to a maximum hours law that prevented overtime was central to the ending of protective laws. "We want the right to be asked for overtime and the right to refuse it without detriment to our jobs," Mengelkoch told a reporter as she filed suit in the Los Angeles federal district court. Mengelkoch assumed that overtime would be voluntary, an option that an employee might turn down. "There's no chance of going back to forced labor and sweatshops," she declared. "Voluntary overtime" might be a possibility in limited circumstances (a union contract, achieved through collective bargaining, might provide for it). But the alternate possibility, compulsory overtime, was far more likely, if not inevitable. Mengelkoch's optimistic assumption was unwarranted. The first three-judge court to consider her case examined the issue:

> It has also been pointed out that the abandonment of limitations on working hours for women would place women on an equal basis with men in the matter of overtime pay, but at the same time would also make them subject to the

obligation to perform as much overtime work as that required of men. This is a mixed blessing. It is not a matter of making women earn overtime when they want to, but an obligation to work overtime whether they want to or not on pain of being discharged. . . . It is not so certain as plaintiffs assume that their position represents the will of many other women even if similarly situated.

To insure "voluntary overtime" would require state laws precluding employers from firing any employee for his or her refusal to accept overtime work.[29]

When Velma Mengelkoch first sued in federal court in 1965 she also complained to the EEOC. The commission evaded the complaint; it could not determine what impact Title VII had on protective laws. Only one commissioner, Aileen Hernandez, thought that Mengelkoch had met discrimination on the job; the other commissioners did not want to pursue the issue. Disgruntled, Hernandez soon resigned, joined NOW, and later became its second president. Pauli Murray, an EEOC consultant and a board member of the American Civil Liberties Union, tried in vain to get the ACLU California chapter to represent Mengelkoch. Murray also urged EEOC to file an amicus brief on Mengelkoch's behalf, a step opposed by the Justice Department, which, unlike the EEOC, had the power to file lawsuits but would not do so. Finally, Murray urged the EEOC to issue guidelines that Title VII voided protective laws. That effort failed, too. Mengelkoch then appealed for help to Marguerite Rawalt and to the National Association of Women Lawyers (NAWL), a longtime proponent of equal rights. Rawalt, who saw in the case the potential to become a "landmark decision similar to the school desegregation decision," steered it in 1966 to NOW, which was just starting a legal arm. Through NAWL, Rawalt found local counsel in Los Angeles, Evelyn Whitlow, who, with Rawalt, Murray, and Hernandez, drafted an amicus brief on behalf of Mengelkoch; Evelyn Whitlow remained on the case until its end in 1971. The women lawyers' network and NOW kept Velma Mengelkoch's case afloat for six years.[30]

While Velma Mengelkoch's case inched forward through the federal courts, NOW threw its support to another landmark case. The first Title VII sex discrimination case to reach an appellate court, *Weeks v. Southern Bell* set a precedent for using Title VII to upset a state protective law. Lorena Weeks, mother of three, who worked for nineteen years as a clerk for a telephone company in Louisville, Georgia, had applied for the job of "switchman." A switchman maintained, repaired, replaced, and tested equipment. When rejected on the basis of sex, she filed a complaint with EEOC and sued her company for violation of Title VII. The job had such rigorous physical demands, the company argued, that it constituted a legitimate BFOQ;

switchmen had to lift over thirty pounds and perform other "strenuous activity." Women "just don't need this type of job," Weeks's union told her; still the union supplied a lawyer. A federal district court in 1967 agreed with Southern Bell; it cited a Georgia law that restricted the weight women might lift. Nothing in Title VII suggested that Congress intended to nullify such a law, the court said; it was a legitimate BFOQ.[31]

Weeks appealed; she also dropped her union-appointed lawyer and reached Marguerite Rawalt. Thereafter, NOW supported the case, and Sylvia Roberts, a Baton Rouge lawyer, argued it. In 1969 the Fifth Circuit rejected the district court decision. The circuit court found "the burden of proof must be on Southern Bell" to show that the state law was a legitimate BFOQ; the "legislative history indicates that this exception was intended to be narrowly construed." The court did not need to upset the Georgia law because in 1968 the state had repealed it and replaced it with a vague, sex-neutral rule ("weight . . . shall be limited so as to avoid strain or undue fatigue"). But the court took the opportunity to explain Title VII. Title VII, said the Fifth Circuit, "rejects . . . this type of romantic paternalism as unduly Victorian and instead vests individual women with the power to decide whether or not to take on unromantic tasks." Weeks and Roberts spent two years seeking full compliance from Southern Bell. Finally, Weeks obtained the job she sought plus back pay; Roberts became the first general counsel of NOW's legal arm. The reversal in *Weeks* suggested a new turn in interpretation of Title VII.[32]

The BFOQ was also an issue in *Rosenfeld v. Southern Pacific Railroad* (1968). Leah "Rosie" Rosenfeld first worked in her teens as a clerk for a law firm. In the 1940s, after courses in telegraphy and clerical work, she became a telegraph operator for Southern Pacific. After her divorce in 1953—Rosenfeld was now a mother of twelve—she worked for the railroad in varied capacities—telegraph operator, clerk, station agent—mainly in remote one-person stations in the desert from California to Arizona. In 1955, Rosenfeld applied for an agent-telegrapher job at Saugus, California, and Southern Pacific turned her down; the railroad would not upgrade her status from telegraph operator to station agent. The reason: California law barred women from lifting over twenty-five pounds or working over eight hours a day. Rosenfeld, who had already done the same sort of work for less pay under her previous title, kept applying for new jobs; the railroad continued to reject her; and her union, the Transportation Communications International Union, would not help her. But as a former clerk for lawyers, Rosenfeld, a model plaintiff, knew the importance of keeping all her records. Title VII suddenly provided an option. In March 1966 Rosenfeld again applied for promotion, this time to a station agent job in Thermal, California, and again met rejection. When EEOC told her to sue on her own, she filed a sex discrimination suit against the railroad, her union, and the state of California. Appearing as amicus curiae, EEOC urged a decision in Rosenfeld's favor. Rosenfeld prevailed on November 25, 1968. A federal district court declared the California maximum hours and weight limits law unconstitutional. It was not a legitimate BFOQ; rather, it discriminated against women. Rosenfeld received her promotion "and the salary that went with it," she told a reporter, "just in time before I retired."[33]

The Rosenfeld decision in 1968 enabled EEOC in 1969 to announce that protective laws were not BFOQ exceptions to Title VII. A federal court of appeals affirmed the decision in 1971. "We conclude that Southern Pacific's employment policy is not excusable under the BFOQ concept or the state statutes," the Ninth Circuit said in 1971. "It would appear that these state limitations upon female labor run contrary to the general objectives of Title VII" and "are therefore supplanted by Title VII." The Ninth Circuit rejected the railroad's BFOQ defense. Employers must consider the "individual qualifications of the employee," not "subjective assumptions and traditional stereotyped conceptions regarding the physical ability of women to do particular work." The court ordered Southern Pacific to pay Rosenfeld's attorney fees, which it did in 1975.[34]

The Ninth Circuit in 1971 also ruled on *Mengelkoch*. The ruling returned to issues brought up by the first court that considered the case (and refused to rule on it) in 1968. Now, in 1971, the Ninth Circuit suggested that it was time to reconsider earlier decisions upholding single-sex protective laws. Without rejecting the earlier opinions, the court distinguished Velma Mengelkoch's stance in the 1960s from that of Curt Muller in 1908. "Unlike [the employer in] *Muller*, she invokes the Equal Protection Clause, and she does so not to preserve the right of employers to employ women for long hours" but to overcome discrimination against women workers. Turning to *Miller v. Wilson* (1915), when the Supreme Court upheld California's eight-hour law of 1911, the Ninth Circuit again distinguished Mengelkoch's case. The 1915 case "did not deal with the claim, asserted here by Mengelkoch, that the statute is repugnant to the Equal Protection Clause because it favors men employees over women employees." The Ninth Circuit distinguished the *Mengelkoch* case from *Goesaert v. Cleary* as well. *Goesaert* did not establish, "beyond reasonable debate," that a statute limiting women's hours "may not be so discriminating against females as to offend the Equal Protection Clause." Assessing the impact of Title VII, the Court found state law inconsistent with federal law.[35]

The landmark Title VII cases brought by Velma Mengelkoch, Lorena Weeks, and Leah Rosenfeld between 1966 and 1971—all supported by feminist advocates—catalyzed a major change in women's legal status. The cases, especially the *Rosenfeld* decision of 1968, enabled EEOC to confront the impact of Title VII on sex discrimination in employment and to issue its 1969 guidelines, which undercut protective laws. The landmark Title VII cases also paved the way for further landmark decisions on women's rights in the early 1970s and for an ERA, which Congress passed in 1972. More immediately, the landmark Title VII cases led to many more suits in federal and state courts upsetting protective laws.

PROTECTION DISMANTLED: THE COURTS AND THE STATES

"Our newfound collective strength, coupled with the potency of title VII, was overturning laws, challenging corporate giants," wrote Betty Friedan, looking back on the late 1960s. From 1969 on, every single-sex protective law challenged in federal court was eventually invalidated. In 1971 alone, district court judges upset protective statutes in seven cases in six states. After 1972, when Congress authorized EEOC to initiate discrimination suits in federal court, the commission became a litigant on behalf of women workers. This change made a difference. Title VII lawsuits were expensive for employees to pursue and costly as well for the women's groups that sought to assist them. Moreover, although the attorney general had the power to bring sex discrimination suits under Title VII, this did not occur. But the unleashing of EEOC made Title VII suits more feasible.[36]

Court decisions that upset protective laws from 1969 to 1972 prodded EEOC to reaffirm that Title VII invalidated the laws. In 1972, commission guidelines warned against any laws that "prohibit or limit the employment of females." These included exclusionary laws, weight limits, hours limits, bars to night work, and (a new addition) any laws imposing limits "for certain periods of time before and after childbirth." Such laws and regulations, the EEOC declared, "do not take into account the capacities, preferences, and abilities of individual females and, therefore, discriminate on the basis of sex." Accordingly, the laws "conflict with and are superseded by Title VII." At the same time, EEOC declared that "beneficial" protective laws (the minimum wage, laws insuring overtime pay, laws providing days of rest, lunch and rest periods, or employee seating) had to extend to men so as not to violate Title VII.[37]

Several decisions that spurred EEOC's 1972 announcement and hastened protection's death involved weight limits. *Bowe v. Colgate-Palmolive*,

which had been the first Title VII lawsuit to reach federal court, in 1966, addressed the complaint of a group of women workers at Colgate-Palmolive's
Indiana plant about the company's thirty-five-pound weight limit rule.
After a federal district court upheld the company in 1968, NOW organized
a boycott of Colgate products and picketed the company's New York headquarters ("Down the Drain with Ajax"). Within a year, the Seventh Circuit
reversed the 1968 decision; it held that a company's weight-lifting qualifications for a job might be retained "as a general guideline for all of its employees, male and female" only if it applied to both men and women a "highly
individualized test." *Bowe v. Colgate-Palmolive* (1969) was a triumph for the
women's movement. Volunteer lawyers from NOW and Human Rights for
Women, Inc. represented the women workers; the EEOC, the National Federation of Business and Professional Women's Clubs (NFBPWC), and the
UAW submitted amicus briefs. Just as the long, coauthored Brandeis brief
on behalf of states became the NCL's weapon of choice in the Progressive
Era, the amicus brief became a weapon for women's rights advocates in the
1960s and 1970s. A few months before *Bowe*, federal courts had upset two
other weight regulations. In May 1969, an Oregon district court had found
the state weight-limit regulation in violation of Title VII in *Richards v.
Griffith Rubber Mills*; in July 1969, an Alabama district court upset a private
company's weight regulation in *Cheatwood v. Southern Bell*. *Bowe*, in September, ended the issue of weight limits for women workers.[38]

In most (not all) protective law cases, as in *Bowe*, women employees sued
their employers because they had been denied access to better-paid jobs. As
in *Bowe*, these were class action suits, a new type of group litigation authorized by Congress in 1966 that enabled common citizens to take on large
businesses with legal resources; in such cases a few selected plaintiffs represented the "class." Most courts (not all) concluded that Title VII invalidated
single-sex protective laws and that such laws did not constitute a BFOQ. Use
of the Supremacy Clause (Article VI clause 2 of the Constitution states that
federal law takes precedence over state law) enabled courts to rely on Title
VII to upset protective laws without addressing precedents such as *Muller* or
Goesaert and without invoking the Fourteenth Amendment equal protection clause. A limit to Title VII: it affected only workplaces with fifteen or
more employees.[39]

Several cases suggest the ways in which worker-plaintiffs assailed protective laws in the early 1970s. In *LeBlanc v. Southern Bell Telephone and Telegraph* (1971) plaintiffs Gloria Kendall LeBlanc and Helene Jenkins Roig had
each been denied the position of test deskman, an employee who dealt with
a customer's complaint of telephone malfunction or "trouble ticket," analyzed

the complaint, dispatched a repairman, checked the repairs, and completed the trouble ticket. The issue: most deskmen worked over forty-eight hours a week, the limit that Louisiana law imposed on women. A federal district court upset the state's maximum-hour law. A few cases involved aspects of protective laws that provided women workers with "benefits" such as rest periods. In *Richards v. Griffith Rubber Mills* (1969), mentioned above, the company denied the application of stock cutter Diane Richards to promotion to one of two available jobs as press operator. Both jobs went to men with less seniority. The company's reasons (besides the weight limits on women workers that Oregon imposed): a union contract that gave women employees two ten-minute rest periods. The district court decided that federal law prevailed over state law, and that neither company nor union could impose different rules on women workers. Except in "rare and justifiable instances," said the court, "Individuals must be judged as individuals and not on the basis of characteristics attributed to racial, religious, or sexual groups." (The court agreed with the employer that it had acted in good faith—though as decisions upsetting protective laws piled up, this excuse would be short-lived.) In some instances, employees included unions in their lawsuits. In *Ridinger v. General Motors Corporation* (1971), workers at GM's Frigidaire and Inland manufacturing divisions who sought overtime work and better paying jobs sued both the company and their union, the IUE (International Union of Electrical Workers). While state laws in Ohio had been originally enacted "for the laudable purpose of protecting females," said the district court, they now violated Title VII by stereotyping on the basis of sex. The IUE, found liable, started a "model compliance program," an effort to secure nondiscriminatory labor contracts and to cooperate with the EEOC. The plaintiffs in *Ridinger* did not challenge an Ohio "benefit" law that required seats and lunchrooms for women workers, but GM asked for a ruling anyway; in this instance, the court ruled that the benefit type of law did not clash with Title VII.[40]

Women workers were not the only plaintiffs in suits against protective laws. Employers too challenged the laws, so as not to get caught between clashing demands of state law and Title VII. In *Caterpillar Tractor v. Grabiec* (1970), two Illinois employers, Caterpillar Tractor and Illinois Bell Telephone sued Illinois's state director of labor. Caterpillar employed 3,558 women (of 43,374 workers); Illinois Bell employed 17,000 women (of 41,000 workers). The employers challenged the state's historic maximum hours law, the Illinois Female Employment Act of 1909, which, to Florence Kelley's joy, the Illinois Supreme Court had upheld in 1910 in *Ritchie v. Wayman*. The law, the employers charged, deprived women workers of "additional compensation" male employees enjoyed and thus violated Title VII. Moreover, they claimed, women employees or their unions had filed or would soon file grievances against them if not given a chance for jobs that required overtime. The district court agreed. The law acted "to deprive such employees of employment opportunities because of their sex" and was invalid. In yet another instance, an employer and a union joined hands to challenge a Kentucky law. In *General Electric Co. v. Young* (1971), the company and union, again IUE, won the right to assign overtime hours and jobs involving overtime to women employees.[41]

One suit brought by employers drew special attention. Exclusionary laws sank with *Sail'er Inn v. Kirby* (1971), a landmark California case. The petitioners, several Los Angeles bars, sought to prevent the state's Department of Alcoholic Beverages from revoking their liquor licenses for hiring women bartenders. To obey the state exclusionary law, they argued, meant violating Title VII and the Fair Employment Practices Act. That Sail'er Inn, the lead petitioner, was a topless bar—it hoped to promote topless waitresses to be topless bartenders—did not deter the Boalt Hall Women's Association from addressing the case; two law students wrote an amicus brief on which lawyers for the bars based their oral argument. The California Supreme Court ruled that sex discrimination violated the equal protection clauses of both the US Constitution and the state constitution.

> The desire to protect women from the general hazards inherent in many occupations cannot be a valid ground for excluding them from those occupations. . . . Women must be permitted to take their chance along with men when they are otherwise qualified and capable of meeting the requirements of their employment.
>
> Laws which disable women from full participation in political, business, and economic areas are often characterized as "protective" or beneficial. These same laws applied to racial and ethnic minorities would be recognized as invidious and impermissible. The pedestal upon which women have been placed has all too often, upon closer inspection, been revealed as a cage. We conclude that the sexual classifications are properly treated as suspect.

The Supreme Court had not yet declared classifications based on sex as "suspect classifications" that require "close scrutiny," but the California Supreme Court asserted that they were, that "sex, like race and lineage, is an immutable trait, a status into which the class members are locked by an accident of birth." The extraordinary *Sail'er Inn* decision, announced by Justice Raymond Peters, had been drafted by his law clerk, Wendy W. Williams, who would take a leading role in the campaign against sex discrimination. The decision reversed a 1970 California district court decision, *Krause v. Sacramento Inn*. It pressed the Supreme Court to confirm its own conclusion about suspect classification; the Court would do so two years later.[42]

Law review articles of the early 1970s that assessed the tussle between Title VII and protective laws generally saw a "trend toward invalidating state law." Still, the situation seemed fluid. One writer constructed a relevant (if counterfactual) scenario: What if several women workers sought the "protection" of protective laws? What if widow Mary Smith, for instance, with three young children in day care and no further help, was told by her employer to work three extra hours a day for two weeks and refused to do so, citing her state's maximum hours law? "Her supervisor, however, sympathizes with 'women's lib', and tells her that the law is no longer valid since it denies her an equal employment opportunity. . . . She again declines and is fired." A second worker, Sally Jones, who is transferred by her employer to a job that involves lifting heavy weights, asks for her old job back, citing the state's weight limit law. The employer refuses and so does Sally Jones; she is fired. Finally, Peggy Brown is transferred from her day shift to a shift involving work until 1:00 a.m.; she refuses the transfer and is fired. In such instances, the writer posits, the state labor department might argue that "Title VII should not be construed to permit employers to take advantage of women." But the employer could point out that "all the recent cases invalidating state protective legislation have found them invalid on their face, rather than as applied." Moreover, state protective laws discriminated against men, who were also protected by Title VII. Finally, enforcing state law might make employers "generally reluctant to hire women." After arguing both sides, the writer, IBM lawyer Joseph P. Kennedy, concluded that the employer was likely to prevail. Indeed, he foresaw a "clean sweep" to invalidate all single-sex laws: "While some hardship may result, the common good of all women necessitates this conclusion."[43] The case of the three aggrieved workers is salient only as the type of case that did *not* occur; protective laws were in free fall.

By 1973, less than a decade after the passage of Title VII, federal courts had upset maximum hours laws in nine jurisdictions, three weight limit laws, and two exclusionary laws (bartending). No case involving a state protective law for women workers had reached the Supreme Court. Several lower federal courts had rejected plaintiffs' cases but appellate courts upset such decisions; all agreed that Title VII invalidated single-sex state laws.[44] Thereafter, women-only protective laws had no future in the federal courts. Supreme Court cases, however, remain relevant in the narrative of single-sex protection's decline.

The first sex discrimination case under Title VII that the Supreme Court considered, *Phillips v. Martin Marietta* (1971), dealt not with protective laws but with a company's policy toward some of its employees, mothers of young children. Ida Phillips sued her employer, the Martin Marietta Corporation (chemicals, aerospace, and electronics) over a company policy to bar the hiring of mothers with preschool children. The policy, she claimed, discriminated on the basis of sex and violated Title VII. The Fifth Circuit in 1969 denied Phillips's claim; the discrimination that occurred, said the court, was because of "sex plus" (sex plus another factor, in this case motherhood of preschoolers) and was not barred by Title VII. The Supreme Court, in contrast, in January 1971, unanimously declared that the corporation had discriminated against Ida Phillips. It dismissed the "sex plus" argument and sent the case back to the lower federal courts. Amicus briefs in the case came from Dorothy Kenyon and Pauli Murray at the ACLU and Sylvia Ellison of Human Rights for Women. The return of the case suggested that the corporation might be able to justify sex discrimination by using the BFOQ exemption. Justice Marshall's concurring opinion rejected this idea. "The Court has fallen into the trap of assuming the [Civil Rights] Act permits ancient canards about the proper role of women to be a basis of classification," Marshall stated. The majority opinion was less decisive. Its significance: the Supreme Court rejected the inventive and discriminatory "sex plus" argument, thus curbing the "gendered imagination" that corporations might otherwise have brought to employment policy. The Court also upheld Title VII.[45]

Would the Supreme Court treat sex discrimination in the same way as race discrimination? "[N]o woman litigant has ever stood before the Supreme Court and successfully argued that she is entitled to the 'equal protection of the laws' clause of the Fourteenth Amendment," wrote Martha Griffiths in 1970. But as single-sex protective laws faltered in court, equal protection cases arose. In 1971 law professor Ruth Bader Ginsburg won *Reed v. Reed*. The case involved an Idaho law giving preference to men in the appointment of administrators of estates. Ginsburg's brief stressed the race-sex analogy that feminists favored. The Court unanimously upset the law. A state's "drawing a sharp line between the sexes" violated the equal protection clause. *Reed v. Reed* did not directly affect protective laws; it did not explicitly overrule the *Goesaert* decision of 1948. But it came close to doing so. *Reed* suggested that single-sex protective laws were about to lose all legitimacy. At the end of the year Ginsburg formed the ACLU Women's Rights Project to pursue further equal rights litigation.[46]

Equal protection cases continued. In *Frontiero v. Richardson* (1973), air force officer Sharon Frontiero challenged a law providing dependency allowances for men in the uniformed services with no proof of economic dependency but permitted such allowances for women only if they could show that they paid half of their husbands' living costs. Ruth Bader Ginsburg presented an amicus brief and was allowed to argue the case before the Supreme Court. The justices rejected the law eight to one without sharing a rationale. Four justices found sex a suspect classification: "the sex characteristic frequently bears no relation to ability to perform or contribute to society." This stance gratified feminists. Three justices, who said they did not want to preempt passage of an ERA by judicial action, upset the law following *Reed*. In 1976, in *Craig v. Boren*, the justices overturned an Oklahoma law that barred the selling of beer to men under twenty-one but permitted its sale to women over eighteen. The Court stated that "classifications by gender must serve important governmental objectives and must be substantially related to achievement of those objectives." After *Craig*, the Court settled on "intermediate scrutiny." *Reed* remained the major turning point; equal protection now determined a woman's legal status. The early Title VII cases—and the derailing of protective laws—had cleared a path for the first landmark cases upholding gender equality.[47]

While courts upset protective laws, state legislatures, state officials, and state agencies followed in their wake or sometimes preceded them. Delaware had invalidated all of its single-sex protective laws in 1965. Most states repealed or modified maximum hours laws. Some states acted decisively and others with more caution; they exempted women workers covered by Title VII or FLSA, made provisions requiring employees' consent to modifications, changed laws to provide for voluntary overtime, or amended state Fair Employment Practices laws to bar sex discrimination, which might or might not change protective policies. The year 1969 set the pace. Nebraska legislators repealed the state's protective laws; Tennessee and Maryland exempted businesses covered by FLSA (which applied to most employees covered by Title VII too). New Mexico exempted "any female who signs a written agreement to work more than 8 hours a day or 40 hours a week," provided premium overtime was paid for the longer week. New York amended its laws to provide exemptions on the application of employers, with employee agreement. State officials grasped the initiative, too. Even before the EEOC offered its revised guidelines of 1969, the attorney general of South Dakota ruled that state laws "must yield to Title VII." North Dakota's attorney general announced that "recent developments," such as court decisions, might prevent prosecution of violations of protective laws. For the rest of 1969, state officials proclaimed that Title VII trumped protective laws. In Ohio, known for its many exclusionary laws, the Department of Industrial Relations declared that it would not prosecute alleged violators. In Oklahoma and Michigan, attorneys general found that state maximum hours laws clashed with Title VII and that federal law took precedence. Pennsylvania's attorney general ruled that the state's Human Relations Act of July 1969, which barred sex discrimination in employment, nullified the state's protective laws and that they would be considered repealed. In California, after *Rosenfeld*, the attorney general announced jointly with the state Department of Industrial Welfare that restrictive state laws (for example maximum hours and weight limits) would no longer be enforced, though "laws extending benefits to females" (minimum wage, rest periods) would continue to be enforced. States continued chipping away at protective laws into the 1970s.

That state legislators and attorneys general moved so swiftly to modify or discard protective laws reflects in part the crescendo of pressure from women's rights activists in the states. It also suggests the receptivity of the business community, which had always disliked the laws, to their decline. A law review article summed up the variety of state actions on maximum hours laws as of the start of 1972: twelve states retained hours restrictions unchanged since the passage of Title VII, seven states had recently amended their laws to make them less restrictive, two states said existing laws could not be enforced, nine said the laws would not apply to employees covered by Title VII (those employed in workplaces of fifteen or more), ten states explicitly repealed the laws, and the remaining ten states had no maximum hours laws when Congress enacted Title VII.[48] In 1973, only Nevada's maximum hours law remained unchanged since 1964.[49]

The process surged forward. By the mid-1970s the fabric of single-sex protective laws that had recently blanketed the states had been shredded. After *Rosenfeld* and similar cases, all states that had once imposed weight-lifting limits had invalidated them. Twenty states had repealed exclusionary laws that once kept women from working in mines, bars, and other off-limit workplaces. Twenty-one states had repealed maximum hours laws, four states had repealed their night work laws, and several had repealed laws that disqualified women from employment before and after childbirth. In many instances, following the EEOC regulations of 1972, states had extended their "beneficial" laws—minimum wage, rest periods—to include both men and women. Thirty-eight jurisdictions now had minimum wage laws that affected both men and women; twenty-five had sex-neutral overtime pay regulations (though not laws providing for "voluntary overtime"); and nineteen had rules about meals, rest periods, or seating requirements for all workers. The changes were a triumph for equal rights.[50]

Without question, a degree of chaos characterized protection's decline. The gradual development of EEOC policy, the continuous trail of court decisions, and the various contributions of state legislatures and state officials created piecemeal change. Many single-sex laws remained in place, unchallenged in court, untouched by lawmakers, unenforced or ignored. Night work laws, troublesome throughout their history, remained troublesome to the end, riddled with exemptions but still in place. As of the mid-1970s night work bans remained in DC, Kansas, and New Hampshire, though unenforced; in New Hampshire, a woman employee could request the state department of labor to enforce the ban. In Puerto Rico, the night work ban affected only some industries. Utah and Rhode Island permitted night work for women only if employers provided transportation. Straggling on, night work laws died slowly. Some states purposefully enforced the single-sex protective laws that remained. Illinois and Ohio enforced maximum hours laws for women in workplaces with fewer than fifteen employees and thus untouched by Title VII.[51]

Feminists hoped that an ERA would wipe away all remnants of single-sex protection. ERA, as a supporter declared in the *Women Lawyers' Journal*, would "bring to the already partially completed process of reform [a] mandate for adopting laws to meet the genuine needs of workers of both sexes." It would extend Title VII benefits to workplaces with fewer than fifteen employees. Most of all, supporters stressed, the ERA would move swiftly; within two years of ratification it would take full effect. This process, supporters claimed, was preferable to the slow pace of change that courts imposed. Marguerite Rawalt, who had done so much to promote Title VII cases, denounced "piecemeal" reform; even recent victories showed "that it would take a hundred years or more to eliminate thousands of existing discriminatory laws, one by one, state by state, lawsuit by costly lawsuit." Ruth Bader Ginsburg, who had just begun to win major women's rights cases in 1971, confirmed that without an ERA "major legislative revision" would probably not occur, "if past experience is an accurate barometer." Judges, Ginsburg pointed out, could not be counted on to advance sex equality. She cited a recent study by two law professors documenting judicial sexism; when it came to sex discrimination, the study contended, judges' judgment ranged from "poor" to "abominable." Without an ERA, revision of the law would be long delayed, Ginsburg concluded. Ratification of an ERA, in contrast, would "stem the tide" of sex discrimination suits underway in the 1970s. Martha Griffiths voiced a parallel thought in her own way. The Supreme Court remained a "bottleneck" for women's rights, she stated in the wake of *Reed v. Reed*. "They're just nine old idiots." By then an ERA was back in Congress.[52]

CLOSING ARGUMENTS: 1970

In 1970, Martha Griffiths reproposed an ERA and the Senate Judiciary Committee began considering it.[53] In May, a subcommittee on constitutional amendments met, led by senator Birch Bayh of Indiana, who favored the proposed amendment. The full Judiciary Committee held hearings in September, led by senator Sam Ervin of North Carolina, who was skeptical. The hearings provided a final chance for defenders and foes of single-sex protective laws to debate. With the momentum generated by feminism in general and by *Rosenfeld* and the EEOC stance of 1969 in particular, protective laws were fast sinking. But the conflict over them had by no means ended. Two arguments from the 1970 hearings suggest the tenor of debate.

Myra Wolfgang, embattled labor leader and vice president of the Union of Hotel Employees and Restaurant Employees (HERE), took the floor at both sets of hearings. Challenged by Senator Bayh or encouraged by Senator Ervin, Wolfgang defended protective laws with passion. "Protection is not obsolete at all—as is claimed by some—but still very much needed," she argued. The House had responded to the call for an ERA "like a herd of stampeded cattle," Wolfgang claimed. "Never have so few business and professional women been so effective and done such harm." Scorning the arrogance of ERA supporters, she mocked the concept of "liberation" in feminist rhetoric. Elitist equal rights advocates, claimed Wolfgang, lacked familiarity with working women's lives. "The Business and Professional Women of America don't bake the bread for Americans, nor package the meat, nor clean the hotel rooms, nor wipe the noses, nor change the diapers, nor man the production lines, nor ring up your retail purchase." Women who joined "liberation groups" were "white, middle-class and college oriented." They might rebel against social dictates that infantilized them but were in turn dictatorial themselves: "[T]he women's liberation groups wish to regulate the lives of other women and treat them as children telling them the job of wife and mother is unfulfilling and unsatisfying." Should a woman disagree, "she is immediately charged with having been brainwashed." Women workers, in contrast, Wolfgang claimed, were "too busy to be liberated." To such women, loss of protective laws brought disadvantage. "It would be desirable for some of these laws to be extended to men," she told the senators, "but the practical fact is that an equal rights amendment is likely to destroy the laws altogether rather than bring about coverage for both sexes." Loss of maximum hours laws, Wolfgang explained repeatedly, opened the door to compulsory overtime. Those who wished to work overtime were only a small minority; those not under FLSA, in contrast, could be compelled to work extra time without premium pay.

> Thousands of women, because of economic necessity, will submit to excessive hours without a law to protect them in order to obtain or hold a job. . . . They accede to this excessive overtime or quit the job. In the first instance, the children become the victims, in the second instance, the entire family suffers, from the loss of that income or the mother and the family become public charges. . . . Don't talk theory to me, tell me the practice.

Wolfgang reversed the terms that ERA advocates used: "The denying of excessive overtime to women who do not want it is not a discrimination." Equality, she argued, served "only a minority"; the majority would gain "an equality of mistreatment." "Laws that treat women differently than men are not necessarily 'discriminatory' or unfair," Wolfgang told the senators. "Conversely laws that arbitrarily call for sameness of treatment can be grossly unfair . . . and self-defeating."[54]

Myra Wolfgang spoke for women members of her union, which represented cooks, bartenders, food servers, dishwashers, and other hotel and restaurant workers (35 percent were women) and for other women wage earners who remained attached to hours limits. Wolfgang's constituency feared compulsory overtime; to her supporters, whether waitresses or factory workers, maximum hours laws offered stronger protection than FLSA, which provided premium pay for overtime. "The FLSA used the disincentive of overtime pay to discourage long hours but it did not forbid them," historian Dorothy Sue Cobble explains. "The FLSA approach to limiting hours was, in their minds, an inadequate check on employer power and on the competitive market's relentless drive to work longer hours." To those who supported Wolfgang's stance, still a majority of union women in 1970, maximum hours laws provided leverage and remained imperative.[55]

A ringing denunciation of single-sex protection came from one of its younger opponents. Susan Deller Ross, thirty years old and a recent graduate of NYU Law School, had recently been hired by the EEOC general counsel. Prior to that, she had been active in the formation of NYU's women's rights committee, and an intern at the ACLU (which at the time opposed an ERA). As an intern, Ross began a study of protective laws, which she presented at the Senate subcommittee hearings Senator Bayh led in

May 1970. Ross's critique of protective laws drew on the recent Title VII cases in federal courts and introduced new elements of feminist analysis. Her research, Ross claimed, showed that women-only protective laws, now rejected by the EEOC and the federal courts, were "discriminatory" and "harmful." "Protective legislation," said Ross, "often actively hurts women and fails to help where help is needed."[56]

Susan Deller Ross methodically denounced every facet of protective laws. Maximum hours limits, she argued, precluded the hiring of women, re-served higher-paid jobs for men, and excused employers who preferred to hire men ("offered a way out to employers bent on discrimination"). Laws that were supposed to be "beneficial" injured women as well. Employers could provide thirty-minute lunch breaks for women (as in one EEOC case) by creating different work shifts that meant lower take-home pay than men. Difference, Ross contended, always brought injury: "Such 'benefit' laws hurt women by denying them job opportunities and hurt men by denying them the benefit." Protective laws were duplicitous, Ross argued: "[W]hile women are chivalrously allowed chairs for rest periods in forty-five states, they are given job security for maternity leaves of absence in no states and maternity benefits in only two." Even single-sex minimum wage laws failed to serve a purpose. They did not "deal with the *real* problem for women—exploitation by being underpaid and funneled into the lowest-paying, most menial jobs of our society." "Real protection," Ross declared, would not bar women from overtime, "nor would it limit a family which prefers an arrangement whereby the father cares for [the] children and does not work overtime while his wife works at night, for instance, as a nurse." Overall, Ross concluded, "sex as a criteria cannot predict with sufficient accuracy who needs what protec-tion." "In fact, these laws do not protect women in the one area clearly ap-plicable to women only—maternity benefits and job security; they are inef-fective in dealing with the exploitation of women through lower pay than men; they are used to discriminate against women in job promotion and higher pay opportunities." Finally, Ross declared:

> [C]onditions today do not warrant support for state labor laws which dis-criminate against woman on the basis of sex. The EEOC, federal courts, wom-en's groups, labor unions and states have begun to recognize this fact. There-fore "protective" labor laws for women should no longer furnish any basis for opposition to the Equal Rights Amendment.[57]

Yet one more argument at the congressional hearings of 1970 compels attention. ERA supporter Leo Kanowitz, a law professor at the University of New Mexico who had given a pioneer course on "Women and the Law," discussed protective laws extensively when he testified before the Senate Judiciary Committee in 1970. Protective laws for women workers should be extended to men rather than repealed, Kanowitz advised. But in the case of maximum hours laws, he warned, male workers would see such an extension "as the imposition of a burden not a boon." Many women too now wanted premium overtime pay, he observed. To eliminate maximum hours limits for women, however, would be "deplorable and mistaken" and would lead to forced overtime. The only solution: state laws to embody the principle of "voluntary overtime." Such laws would bar employers from discharging any worker for refusal to work overtime, Kanowitz explained; they would meet the demands of women workers; and they would benefit men, whose collective bargaining agreements often stipulated that workers who refused overtime would be fired. Finally, voluntary overtime laws would make the court's concern in *Mengelkoch* moot.[58] Several states in the late 1960s had in fact amended maximum hours laws to provide voluntary overtime for women workers, but such efforts violated Title VII. The type of unisex voluntary overtime laws that Kanowitz envisioned, in contrast, would meet equal rights requirements. But his proposal made no progress; employers were not about to cede control over overtime.

Debate in Congress began later in 1970, when Martha Griffiths forced the ERA out of the Judiciary Committee with a "discharge petition."[59] Within two years, Congress had approved an ERA, yet another signal of protection's doom.

THE ERA AND THE WOMEN'S MOVEMENT

Protection's decline had cleared the way for an ERA. Passage of the ERA in March 1972, in turn, sealed protection's fate. In January 1971 Martha Griffiths reintroduced the amendment into the new Ninety-Second Congress, and equal rights momentum escalated. In February 1971, the Supreme Court decided the crucial case of *Reed v. Reed*. In October, the House endorsed an ERA with a vote of 265 to eighty-seven. On February 19, 1972, the Senate Judiciary Committee ignored its chair Sam Ervin, an amendment foe, and approved the ERA fifteen to one. On March 27, 1972, the Senate approved the amendment eighty-four to eight. Four days before, belatedly, President Nixon had explicitly approved the measure. Congress then sent it to the states. By the end of 1972, twenty-three states (of thirty-eight needed) had ratified the ERA. Its final ratification seemed a matter of time.[60]

ERA's 1972 triumph in Congress was a milestone for the new feminism and for equal rights. As Congress considered and passed ERA, a series of conversions shifted the balance of power in the women's movement from protectionists to the equal rights camp. The shift had started with the eruption of NOW in 1966. EEOC's rejection of protective laws in 1969 had been another turning point. By then, Nixon had appointed Elizabeth Duncan Koontz, a Democrat, African American, former teacher, and former officer of the National Education Association, to replace Mary Keyserling at the Women's Bureau. The WB reversed course on its fiftieth anniversary, February 26, 1970, when it endorsed an ERA. "[I]f protective legislation is gone or going," stated Koontz, "then gone also is one of the major reasons why the Women's Bureau has never supported the ERA." With some reluctance, WB publications of the early 1970s conceded that Title VII overrode protective laws. Or, in the tormented bureaucratese of WB staffers (who probably had mixed opinions), "Courts have held that laws designed in the past to protect women workers are discriminating in their present effect."[61]

With protective laws now "gone or going," the series of conversions swept into the 1970s. The Citizens' Advisory Council on the Status of Women had endorsed the ERA on February 7, 1970, "sensing that the time had come to advance the cause of justice and equality for men and women." Women's groups that had once shaped the WB coalition each announced a change of stance. The League of Women Voters had thrown its support to ERA in 1969. The American Association of University Women argued about the ERA into 1971, when almost 45 percent of AAUW members rejected it. But the AAUW leadership thought otherwise: "[I]f we do not change, we will die," one officer declared. At the year's end, the AAUW convention overwhelmingly endorsed ERA. The National Consumers' League dropped its opposition to ERA in the early 1970s. In October 1970, as states repealed single-sex labor laws, the NCL board of directors still held fast; it discussed "the development of a positive program re the Equal Rights Amendment and getting this out to unions." The *Reed v. Reed* decision of 1971 was a turning point. Once the Supreme Court had stated that "dissimilar treatment for men and women" violated the equal protection clause, the NCL's defense of protective laws silently folded.[62]

Leaders of the WB coalition (the group of bureaucrats and union women that historian Dorothy Sue Cobble calls "labor feminists") had been in partial retreat from protective laws through the late 1960s. Assistant secretary of labor Esther Peterson, ever alert to shifts in the political wind, had been bracing for a turnaround since 1966. Peterson backed off from protectionism in stages by toying with greater receptivity to an ERA. ERA need not "be viewed as the same disruptive force we once thought it was," she had stated in 1967, citing "changes that have come about and the gains women have made." In another statement of 1967, Peterson claimed to find the prospect of an ERA irrelevant. As she told the AFL-CIO, "It is foolish to spend our efforts debating the merits of the proposed amendment at a time when we have so nearly achieved its objectives." In 1970, Peterson suggested to NCL leaders "the need for creative thinking about legislation for everyone, not just women." Once the EEOC, the courts, and the states had effectively nullified protective laws, the coast was clear to change position. Peterson then wrote to Martha Griffiths to reverse herself ("History is moving in this direction"), while urging concern for "those who may still be exploited."[63]

Katherine Ellickson, AFL-CIO official, held out slightly longer. In 1967 Ellickson had asked the EEOC to safeguard protective laws, and in September 1970 she had testified to senators on behalf of the NCL, on whose board she served. But in the early 1970s Ellickson changed her position. She told an interviewer in 1976 that the shift occurred "when it became clear that state laws were going out anyhow and that the psychological effect of defeating the ERA might be bad." Former WB head Mary Dublin Keyserling held out the longest. As WB head from 1965 to 1969 Keyserling had urged the EEOC to save protective laws from Title VII, but by 1969, she had become isolated. Her loyalty to protection emerged in her 1970 Senate testimony: "Were existing laws nullified in the name of so-called equality," she testified, "many . . . women would find that overtime would be required as a condition of employment." But eventually Keyserling too gave up. "One by one the large majority of prominent organizations" that had once opposed ERA "shifted their positions," she later noted. "In the early 1970s, as I reviewed what had happened in the previous decade, I too, became strongly convinced that the ratification of the ERA had become an essential goal." For Keyserling, according to historian Landon R. Y. Storrs, *Reed v. Reed* in 1971 was a turning point.[64]

As labor feminist leaders shifted stance, union women remained divided. A minority supported an ERA: AUW women leaders—Caroline Davis, Dorothy Haener, Catherine Conroy—had been the first to leave the protectionist fold. They had been active in the founding of NOW, pressed the EEOC to reject protective laws, advocated equal rights at Senate hearings, and in 1970 convinced the UAW to support an ERA. Women in heavy industry like autoworkers had a distinctive stance. Less dependent on state laws, they were more likely to be covered by FLSA, to compete for men with jobs, and to resent hours limits that barred promotion and deprived them of premium pay. Even there, opinion split. Among women in the UAW's militant Local 3 at a big Michigan Chrysler plant in 1968, in historian Nancy Gabin's account, some opposed the repeal of the state's maximum hours law because it provided "a small measure of protection against inhuman work schedules." They hoped to retain the state law "until legislation made overtime voluntary on the part of the employee." UAW workers withdrew support for protective laws in 1970 when the union endorsed an ERA.[65]

But support for single-sex protective laws persisted among labor unions and their women members through the end of the 1960s. When Delaware legislators suddenly repealed all protective state laws in 1966, the president of the Communication Workers of America (CWA) warned members "that employer organizations all over the country are setting their sights on repealing or weakening [the laws] to the point of ineffectiveness" and called for a state of high alert. As 1968 began, Cornell labor expert Alice H. Cook found that union support for protective laws remained strong; union policies reflected "their current experience of where advantage for their members seems to lie." Women union members in workplaces insulated from competition with men might "actually welcome the limits" that protective laws provided. Many women in industry "valued job security over job opportunity," historian Dorothy Sue Cobble points out. "Others didn't want access to male jobs." Even as protective laws toppled, union women's hostility to ERA persisted. "Labor feminists" remained adamant at the senate hearings in 1970, as evident in the comments of representatives from the ILGWU, IUE, and CWA. Katherine Ellickson spoke on behalf of the NCL, Ruth Miller for CWA, and Anne Draper for the AFL-CIO. Myra Wolfgang, who campaigned for retention of Michigan's maximum hours law (and lost), summed up the resentment and suspicion of labor feminists for the Bayh subcommittee in May 1970. "Right-to-work" laws did not guarantee a job anymore than the ERA "will guarantee equality," Wolfgang declared. The ERA would destroy protective laws altogether rather than bring about protection for both sexes. "[F]requently we obtain real equality through difference in treatment rather than identity in treatment," she said. "[D]ifferent does not mean deficient." In October 1970 in Detroit, in a dispute with Betty Friedan at a Wayne State University event, Wolfgang labeled Friedan the "Chamber of Commerce's Aunt Tom." Anyone who urged repeal of protective laws, Wolfgang charged, was "doing the bosses' work and the women of America know it."[66]

The labor movement endorsed protective laws into the 1970s. "It has taken the trade union movement nearly half a century to build the protective laws," an AFL-CIO official told a correspondent in 1972, "and we do not intend to see them destroyed." But unions gradually shifted their positions. A UAW convention in April 1970 declared an ERA "essential." The American Federation of Teachers, the Newspaper Guild, and the Teamsters agreed. After passage of ERA in March 1972, union resistance wavered. The CWA endorsed ERA in June 1972; the IUE followed in December. An AFL-CIO convention in October 1973 adopted a resolution approving ERA as "an essential step towards meeting the nation's stated goal of equality." Union support for single-sex protective laws was over. "As an unprotected 'man' I work a little more than women and I earn almost twice as much money," a West Coast woman communications worker in a nontraditional job wrote in 1972 to AFL-CIO head George Meany. "Protective laws, sir, I do not need."[67]

Union lawyers, historian Susan M. Hartmann suggests, were pivotal in the switch to endorse ERA. Her example is the IUE (one-third female in the 1960s). Even after EEOC declared that Title VII invalidated protective laws in 1969, it lacked enforcement power until 1972; in this interval, Hartmann points out, union lawyers saw a chance to fight gender discrimination through lobbying, member education, and lawsuits. The IUE legal department, led by general counsel Winn Newman and associate counsel Ruth Weyand—both activists in civil rights since the 1940s—endorsed equal rights. Like other labor unions, IUE had long supported protective laws and opposed an ERA. But in 1967, influenced by Pauli Murray and Dorothy Haener, who addressed delegates on the need to enforce Title VII and abandon protective laws, IUE women narrowed their support to "beneficial" laws. In 1971, Newman and Weyand pushed union members further. The 1972 IUE convention, told by Newman that protective laws were "illegal," resolved to reconsider ERA; at a September meeting the union endorsed it. With protective laws invalid, capitulation to ERA became feasible. "An ERA is not going to change protective legislation," as IUE leader Mary Callahan observed in the late 1970s, "because protective legislation is already changed." By 1974, under the guidance of its lawyers, IUE members had filed EEOC charges against GE and Westinghouse involving 170 plants and launched six lawsuits against GE and three against Westinghouse. The lawyers, Hartmann finds, had been "engines of change." They grasped that union women's feminism differed from that of middle-class women—that "comparable worth," which IUE women endorsed, mattered more than upward mobility, which "lay beyond the reach of most working-class women." Even when shifting support to ERA, union women remained hostile to "women's liberation," with its connotations of radicalism. Thus, once protection was no longer an issue, the IUE came to rest in the ERA fold. In 1974 IUE women helped found the Coalition of Labor Union Women (CLUW) to combat at sex discrimination in the workplace.[68]

IUE officer Mary Callahan voiced the wary attitude of union women toward feminism. "Union women may be a little suspicious of women in other organizations that you would term 'feminist,'" Callahan told an interviewer in the late 1970s. "We don't see eye-to-eye yet on a lot of the ways to reach a goal." A worker in Philadelphia electronic plants since the 1930s, Callahan had joined the UE in 1936 and in 1946 became an officer of her local, Local 105. Electronics plants depended heavily on women. In Callahan's plant, IRC Volume Controls, women were 85 percent of employees. Local 105 broke with the UE in 1949 to join a new rival union, IUE. There, Callahan became an executive board member in 1959; in 1962 she served as the sole labor representative on the PCSW. In 1977 Callahan—now campaigning for an ERA—honed in on a salient difference between feminism and unionism.

> I think the feminist leaders are very snobbish. Sometimes they're suspect because I don't think they're for real. Some of them are looking at, "How can I become the Manager." Not, "How can we all get along and improve our lot in life?" It's "How do I get up there." This is the way businesses are run, unfortunately not just with females but with males too.[69]

Callahan was of course correct: "How do I get up there" had always been and remained a crux of equal rights. Mary Callahan defied the prospect of a work culture dominated by competition and corporate values; to accede to feminism was to accept the tenets of free-market individualism, "the way businesses are run."

By the early 1970s, when unions finally gave way on protective laws, a new women's movement had taken shape. Sources of energy that had been dominant for forty years had waned or vanished. The NWP, always elitist and vaguely libertarian, no longer flourished; social feminism too had faded. New feminists had created a double-pronged movement: the equal rights campaign, dominated by NOW and, to its left, the forces of women's liberation, clamoring for the removal of sexism from social institutions and less concerned about legal change. Women's liberation served the equal rights faction by providing pressure from the left. It also aroused the ire of conservative women, as did the movement for abortion rights. As the new factions of the women's movement coalesced and as a critique of feminism began among women on the right, the political parties traded places. The Republican Party, which had endorsed an ERA for decades and did so once again in 1972, looked askance at feminism and its demands. President Nixon vetoed the Comprehensive Child Development Act of 1972, which would have provided a national network of day care centers and aided working parents; the veto undercut the feminist agenda at its weakest link, where family role and vocational role intersected.[70] New feminists were overwhelmingly allied with the Democrats.

As single-sex protective laws faltered, labor standards expanded. In 1966 Congress extended FLSA to include a majority of employed women. The extension, recommended in the PCSW report of 1963, covered many retail and service workers (in hotels, hospitals, laundries, and restaurants) as well as agricultural workers. By 1970 FLSA reached between 80 percent and 90 percent of employees. On December 29, 1970, President Nixon signed a bill that established the Occupational Safety and Health Administration (OSHA) to enforce labor standards and issue workplace regulations. In 1974 Congress passed an amendment to FLSA that finally brought wage and hours benefits to domestic workers, a goal that had eluded social feminist leaders of the 1930s and 1940s. This development was "the first time that domestics had been included in any protective labor legislation," notes historian Vanessa H. May. After the FLSA extension of 1974, states began to add household workers to minimum wage, unemployment insurance, and workers compensation plans. As protective law finally reached domestic work, African American women moved out of such work into clerical, sales, and technical jobs previously out of range; new groups of more exploitable women workers, often undocumented, and less likely to join unions or challenge law-breaking employers, entered the market for domestic work. The extended FLSA still excluded home care workers, along with other categories such as independent contractors and public sector employees. The private household remained a holdout against worker protection.[71]

Title VII litigation, always challenging, became more so. By the end of the 1970s lawyers for employers grasped that many forms of workplace discrimination were difficult for plaintiffs to prove. "The opposition has gotten its act together," wrote lawyer Margaret A. Berger in a report to the Ford Foundation. "Title VII litigation is costly and getting costlier." Cases now centered not on constitutional issues but on disputes over facts. Employers, with greater resources for trials, could launch "paper wars" against plaintiffs, demanding more and more information. Forced to undertake the cost of extensive discovery, plaintiffs needed statistical analysis and expert witnesses. Title VII lawyers also faced the difficulties of mounting class action suits. They had to find "willing plaintiffs" whose interests represented those of a larger group but who would tolerate the risk of employer retaliation and the hazards of trial. Courts at times failed to grasp workplace experiences in which race discrimination and sex discrimination intersected. Finally, Title VII lawyers feared judicial bias against their clients, whom judges sometimes characterized as overbearing, oversensitive, or delusional. One plaintiff, declared an appellate court decision of 1974, "envisions herself as a modern Jeanne d'Arc fighting for the rights of embattled womanhood."[72]

ERA failed in June 1982, when its deadline for ratification expired, only three states short of its goal. "As I look back more than twenty years later," Pauli Murray observed, "none of us in 1963 could have foreseen that the ERA would emerge as one of the foremost issues of the women's movement or that it would fail of ratification by only three states." ERA's failure reflected less the "Stop-ERA" campaign of conservative women than the recalcitrance of the southern states; southern hostility to feminism and to federal encroachment on states rights brought the ratification process to an end. ERA's failure was the final moment in the long feud between factions of women activists that had started in the 1920s. Both factions of the midcentury women's movement had failed to achieve their goals; protective laws for women workers had faltered in the 1970s, and now in 1982 ERA capsized, too. But both factions had succeeded as well. Labor standards had been extended throughout the 1960s and the principle of equal rights survived the 1982 capsize of ERA, in a form similar to what Pauli Murray had suggested two decades before. When Murray first proposed "the fourteenth amendment approach" to the PCSW in 1962, it had seemed "a practical intermediate step," she reflected later. "If successful, it might achieve on a case-by-case basis the same objectives as ERA supporters envisioned." That is approximately what happened.[73]

· · · · ·

Inclusion of "sex" in Title VII was a plunge into the unknown. "If sex is not included, the civil rights bill . . . would not protect Negro women from discrimination on the basis of sex," Pauli Murray wrote to Marguerite Rawalt in April 1964. Martha Griffiths had a different concern. "I will be . . . darned if I am going to sit there while white women come in last at the hiring gate," she informed Myra Wolfgang as Congress passed the Smith amendment. Not only was the addition of "sex" to Title VII unexpected, but, in addition, its consequences could not be foreseen. Still, accident that it may have been, the addition of sex to Title VII—Congressman Smith's "snickersnee"—set off a cascade of transformations. Title VII brought the women's movement into the path of change carved out by the civil rights movement and into the powerful force field of equal rights. It provided the courts with a legal instrument to dismantle single-sex protective laws, a process that began in the late 1960s and continued into the 1970s. By making gender equality in employment a federal policy, Title VII ended or at least reconfigured the different versus equal conflict that had split the women's movement since the 1920s. It legitimized the goal of equal rights, reshaped the women's movement into a campaign for equal rights, and pressured defenders of single-sex laws to shift their allegiance to equal rights, because, as in Esther Peterson's words, "history is moving in this direction." Overall, the inclusion of "sex" in Title VII served as an "entering wedge," much as Congressman Celler feared that it would in 1964. By catalyzing the process that ended single-sex protective laws, Title VII cleared the way for use of the equal protection clause of the Fourteenth Amendment to secure equal rights, the "intermediate" strategy Pauli Murray proposed in 1962 at the PCSW. Title VII opened a window of opportunity to pursue an egalitarian agenda.[74]

When exactly did protective laws for women workers end? A crucial turning point was sometime between 1968 (the first *Rosenfeld* decision) and 1971, when the Fifth and Ninth circuit courts declared that Title VII supplanted protective laws and when the Supreme Court decided *Reed v. Reed*. Cases in process continued for a few years, but protective laws had no future. Among issues that divided supporters and opponents of protective laws, "overtime" was the most enduring. Would loss of maximum hours laws mean compulsory overtime? A subject of debate in the PCSW in the early 1960s, the overtime issue defied resolution. "Voluntary overtime" remained a fantasy. Courts could not impose it, legislators rarely bothered with it, and history barreled right over it.[75]

At what point did single-sex protective laws start to handicap more than help the women workers they were intended to benefit? What was the "tipping point"? In the 1920s, economist Elizabeth Faulkner Baker had suggested that the vast majority of women workers affected by protective laws around 1920 profited from them; only a minority, workers on the "cutting edge," those who were more likely to compete with men, did not. Baker's division of women employees into two groups, the helped and the harmed, evokes echoes over the decades. In 1965 Pauli Murray and Mary O. Eastwood suddenly claimed that the "tipping point" had been reached. The laws had "waning utility"; the number of women who benefited from them was "small and shrinking." Protective legislation, claimed Murray and Eastwood, had outlived its usefulness. The death of protective laws would involve a degree of loss, they noted, but "relatively little harm would be done." Exactly when a "tipping point" occurred, among whom, or what it might mean, remains a challenge to determine. It is possible that a "tipping point" had occurred earlier, perhaps in the 1940s, after FLSA took effect, or, alternatively, that it had not yet occurred. But the preconditions for dismantling protective laws at any earlier time were absent.[76]

In the 1960s, in contrast, the preconditions suddenly materialized. What were they? Structural and technological change had transformed occupations, demand for two-income families had reshaped the economy, two-thirds of new workers were women, and almost half of adult women earned wages. Beyond that, five factors vie for primacy. The first was opportunity; a favorable political climate, the crucial civil rights precedent, and the fortuitous accident of Title VII made equal rights demands viable. A second factor: the persistent activism of women wage earners, both as complainants to the EEOC and as determined plaintiffs in long-running lawsuits, such as Velma Mengelkoch, Lorena Weeks, and "Rosie" Rosenfeld. A third factor: a successful campaign effected by women lawyers (among them Pauli Murray, Mary O. Eastwood, Martha W. Griffiths, Margaret Rawalt, Ruth Bader Ginsburg) who seized the opportunity that Title VII offered and shaped a strategy built on civil rights precedent. A fourth factor: The rise of the new feminism, a mass movement that created a visible constituency for legal change and swayed public opinion in the direction of equal rights. Although the women's movement was not unified—the women's liberation branch of it voiced disinterest in legal change, and many labor activists objected to losing maximum hours laws—the clamor for equal rights prevailed. A fifth factor, perhaps less visible, was just as important: the judicial ground shift toward protection of "rights," well underway before the 1960s, became irreversible. Judges, legislators, and other officials had no vital interest in maintaining single-sex protective laws once such laws lost a forceful constituency among women. Economic inequality faded in the 1960s and 1970s, sociologist Robert Max Jackson observes, "when state officials decided discrimination against women in the workplace was more trouble than it was worth."[77]

Yet protection's death—and the triumph of equal rights ideology—carried elements of loss and risk, as Pauli Murray and Mary Eastwood had predicted in 1965. Equal rights arrive with a built-in undertow; equality tends to favor those best equipped to claim it. Political scientist Jo Freeman (as a graduate student) pointed to part of the undertow in 1970, even as she summed up the liabilities of protective laws. "The lesson that 'protective' legislation teaches is that law that specifies caste will inevitably reinforce caste," Freeman wrote. "Sex specific legislation will become sex restrictive." An ERA, in contrast, would "sweep away the legal deadwood of the sexual caste system." But equal rights, once achieved, could not be expected to confer benefits equally. The ERA was "quite limited because it can only remove sex per se as a barrier," Freeman observed. "The women who will benefit most directly from this are those who can most easily adopt male life styles and responsibilities." Nor would "legal neutrality" suffice, Freeman predicted. "To ignore the caste system is to reinforce it."[78] Activists in the women's movement confronted the nuances of equality in the 1970s and 1980s as they coped with pregnancy law, a last vestige of protective policy.

8

Last Lap: Work and Pregnancy

"WE DO NOT ACCEPT MRS. COHEN'S PREMISE that the regulation's provision which denies her, with the advice of her doctor, the right to decide when her maternity leave will begin is an insidious classification based upon sex," declared Judge Clement Haynsworth of the Fourth Circuit in a 1973 decision. A high school social studies teacher, Susan Cohen had challenged a compulsory pregnancy leave imposed on her by her school board in Virginia. The forced leave was sex discrimination, Cohen claimed, and violated her Fourteenth Amendment rights. A bare majority of the circuit court joined Judge Haynsworth to reject her claim and support the school board. "Only women become pregnant," Judge Haynsworth continued, "only women become mothers."

■ ■ ■

Lillian Garland and Betty Friedan, 1986. Los Angeles bank receptionist Lillian Garland lost her job, in violation of California law, after she took an unpaid leave in 1982 for workers disabled by pregnancy. She sued her employer; the bank challenged the state regulation. Garland with Betty Friedan, on the right, met the press after the Supreme Court upheld the law. The challenging case, *California Federal Savings and Loan v. Guerra* (1986), in which feminists voiced diverse opinions, prodded Congress to enact the Family and Medical Leave Act of 1993. ©Bettmann/Corbis Images.

But Mrs. Cohen's leap from those physical facts to the conclusion that any regulation of pregnancy and maternity is an invidious classification by sex is merely simplistic. The fact that only women experience pregnancy and motherhood removes all possibility of competition between the sexes in this area. No man-made law or regulation can relieve females from all of the burdens which naturally accompany the joys and blessings of motherhood. Pregnancy and motherhood do have a great impact on the lives of women, and, if that impact be reasonably noticed by a governmental regulation, it is not to be condemned as an invidious classification. . . .

Pregnancy and maternity are sui generis, and a governmental employer's notice of them is not an invidious classification by sex.[1]

Susan Cohen's case, among others, opened an era of contention in pregnancy law. In 1908, when the Supreme Court decided *Muller v. Oregon*, concern with women's reproductive lives loomed large. "The overwork of future mothers . . . directly attacks the welfare of the nation," the Brandeis brief had declared, and the Court had unanimously agreed. Convictions about sexual difference and "the performance of maternal function" had sustained decades of single-sex protective laws. In the 1970s, with equal rights in ascent, the legal status of the pregnant worker posed challenges. To what extent could employers treat women workers differently than men because women were capable of childbearing? Was pregnancy unique as a medical condition or disability? Was it "sui generis," as Judge Haynsworth contended in 1973, or was pregnancy similar to other medical conditions or disabilities? Overall, how would pregnancy and childbearing fit into the feminist agenda for equal rights? Could pregnant women facing discrimination rely—as feminists hoped—on the equal protection clause? The charged issue of workplace pregnancy opened a minefield of questions. Courts, legislators, and feminists wrestled with such questions through the 1970s and 1980s. Debates about workplace pregnancy revived clashes about difference and equality that had vexed the women's movement for decades. Paradoxically, pregnancy, a badge of difference, served as a springboard to advances in equal rights. As that happened, the new direction in pregnancy policy underscored the doom of single-sex protective laws.

PREGNANCY CASES: THE 1970s

Protective laws had never offered special benefits to pregnant workers, but some laws noticed childbirth. In 1970, laws in six states and Puerto Rico prohibited the employment of women in one or more industries and occupations for periods before and after childbirth. Passed between 1910 and 1920, the laws barred work for periods (usually) of two to four weeks before childbirth and four to six weeks afterward. No laws in 1970 stopped employers from terminating pregnant workers or imposing unpaid leaves of absence. Thirty-five states excluded pregnant women from unemployment insurance; the handful of states with disability insurance plans either excluded pregnancy from their programs or restricted pregnant women's benefits. Legislative efforts to offer paid maternity leave, starting with the AALL proposal of 1916, had always floundered. As in preceding decades, pregnancy in 1970 usually meant that women left the workplace; when they did, their losses included pay, benefits, and seniority. Complaints that reached the EEOC in the late 1960s claimed that employers treated pregnancy differently than other disabilities and that this constituted sex discrimination. But EEOC support for pregnant workers was limited. EEOC guidelines did not yet (until 1972) address pregnancy. Title VII did not yet cover pregnancy discrimination nor did it reach public employees, whose only recourse was federal court. Legal challenges to pregnancy regulations began with schoolteachers who protested mandatory maternity leaves.[2]

In Cleveland in 1971, junior high teacher Jo Carol LaFleur and seventh grade French teacher Ann Elizabeth Nelson challenged their school board's policy of mandatory leave after four months of pregnancy. A teacher could not return to work, the school board stated, before the start of the first semester after the baby was three months old. In Chesterfield County, Virginia, high school social studies teacher Susan Cohen challenged a similar policy. The Virginia school board regulation imposed leave at the end of the fifth month of pregnancy; the leave ended at the start of the semester after birth, with a doctor's certificate on the mother's fitness to work. Cohen requested an extension to the period she could teach before childbirth; she provided the written opinion of her obstetrician that she might teach as long as she chose. Mandatory leaves, the teachers claimed, violated their equal protection rights. Their employers saw things differently; the school boards claimed that pregnant teachers disrupted the educational process. The Cleveland district's concerns included mother and child health, continuity of instruction for children (thus the restart provision), and classroom propriety. The Virginia school board hoped to avoid disruptions caused by students "pointing, giggling, laughing, and making snide remarks."[3]

In February 1971 a federal district court in Ohio found the claims of the Cleveland district board of education reasonable.[4] In July 1972, however, the Sixth Circuit reversed the first ruling and decided in favor of LaFleur. The school board's policy, "inherently based upon classification by sex," was arbitrary and unreasonable.[5] Susan Cohen's challenge in Virginia followed a reverse trajectory. Cohen's lawyer demanded equal protection, and in May 1971 a federal district court agreed. "There is no medical reason for the board's regulation," said the court. The maternity provision "denies pregnant women such as Mrs. Cohen equal protection of the laws because it treats pregnancy differently than other medical disabilities."[6] A three-judge panel of the Fourth Circuit also decided in Cohen's favor. Then in January 1973 the entire Fourth Circuit, sitting en banc, reversed the two previous decisions by a 4–3 vote. Justice Haynsworth, speaking for the majority, was well known as a conservative. When President Nixon had nominated him to the Supreme Court in 1969, labor unions and civil rights groups had opposed the nomination; during the confirmation debate he had been accused of ethics violations (voting in two cases in which he had a financial interest). In the end the Senate had rejected Haynsworth 55 to 45. Four years later, Haynsworth rejected Susan Cohen's equal protection claim. "How can the state deal with pregnancy and maternity in equal terms with paternity?" he asked. "It cannot, of course."[7]

Judge Haynsworth staked out a position in pregnancy policy that fellow conservatives would share. By 1973, when the Fourth Circuit spoke on Susan Cohen, federal judges accepted that Title VII expanded women's workplace rights. But to conservatives, the pregnant worker—awkward, unwelcome, and invariably demanding—remained a special case, a class apart. Their language kept this worker at a distance.

As 1973 began, two circuit courts had issued clashing opinions on workplace pregnancy. By then the legal status of the pregnant worker was in flux. On April 6, 1972, the EEOC declared that policies discriminating against pregnant women were sex discrimination and violated Title VII. Susan Deller Ross, the lawyer whose critique of single-sex protective laws supported the ERA campaign in 1970, had written the new EEOC guidelines on pregnancy. The EEOC in 1972 also extended Title VII to cover public employees, such as schoolteachers. At the same time, feminists pushed forward with other parts of their legal agenda. In early 1973 the Supreme Court had decided *Roe v. Wade*, which upheld a woman's right to have an abortion, and listened to arguments on *Frontiero v. Richardson*, which would insure equal benefits for military personnel. Before announcing its decision on *Frontiero*, the Court agreed to consider together the Cohen and LaFleur pregnancy cases.[8]

Justices' memos on the impending pregnancy cases suggest a range of dispositions toward equal rights for pregnant workers. Justice Lewis Powell, who resisted the teachers' equal protection arguments, did not want to "bracket" women with "minorities, aliens, and indigents." Justice Harry

Blackmun, more receptive to equal protection, had doubts. "It is easy to say that any regulation which relates to pregnancy is automatically sex discrimination," Blackmun wrote. "I am not at all certain that this is necessarily so." Still, Blackmun began to consider the argument that mandatory leave violated equal protection rights, and found his way to an equal protection rationale. "We certainly determine leave for any temporary disability," he wrote. "Is pregnancy really different?" His colleagues disagreed. In *Cleveland Board of Education v. LaFleur* (1974) the justices chose 7–2 to steer clear of an equal protection ruling. The majority opinion, written by Justice Potter Stewart, often at the Court's center, resolved the case in the teachers' favor on due process grounds. The school boards had violated the teachers' due process rights by unreasonable regulation, the Court stated. The *LaFleur* decision aggrieved feminists because it did not mention sex discrimination nor did it recognize the pregnancy cases as equal protection cases. "A Court that had confidently announced the right to abortion only a year earlier," wrote *New York Times* reporter Linda Greenhouse, "now appeared tongue-tied in the presence of pregnant school-teachers."[9]

The next year, the Supreme Court heard a related case. A Utah law made pregnant women ineligible for unemployment benefits from the end of the second trimester (twelve weeks before the expected childbirth) until six weeks after childbirth. Mary Ann Turner, who had been fired for reasons unconnected to her pregnancy, sued the state for the deprivation of benefits; the decision in *Turner v. Department of Security of Utah* (1975) invalidated the part of the law that excluded pregnant workers, again on a due process basis.[10]

The Supreme Court had thus far stepped cautiously. The Court had decided in favor of worker-plaintiffs in pregnancy cases but had staved off the feminists' equal protection goals. To feminist lawyers, the distinction between due process and equal protection analysis of pregnancy issues was salient. In a due process decision, judges decide what is reasonable (Is a school board's regulation reasonable?). Such a decision is never secure; with a less stringent regulation, for instance, the court might reach a different conclusion. Equal protection, a higher standard, shifts the mode of analysis to some type of comparison between pregnant employees and other types of employees. Only equal protection, feminist lawyers believed, would push the feminist agenda forward.[11] A second batch of pregnancy cases held the potential to fulfill feminist goals. The new cases, yet more contentious, involved recompense for the disabilities caused by pregnancy. Supreme Court decisions in these cases satisfied feminists even less.

In 1972, Carolyn Aiello, a state employee in California, was hospitalized for an ectopic pregnancy. With three coplaintiffs, employees similarly afflicted by pregnancy-linked disabilities, Aiello sued the state system of disability benefits for public employees. The plan paid medical disability and hospital benefits to its workers out of a fund established by deductions of 1 percent of all workers' wages; each of the four women plaintiffs had sought disability benefits when ailments connected to pregnancy made them unable to work. But the benefit plan excluded pregnancy (also excluded from benefits: persons confined to institutions for dipsomania, drug addiction, or sexual psychopathy). Wendy W. Williams, the young lawyer for the employees, had an exceptional track record in equal rights. As a law clerk to California's chief justice, only a few years earlier, Williams had drafted the egalitarian decision in *Sail'er Inn v. Kirby* (1971). She now argued that pregnancy discrimination was sex discrimination and that under the California program, women were denied equal protection: "California's disability program discriminated on the basis of sex because it provided total coverage for men and only partial coverage for women." The state law also violated the EEOC guidelines on pregnancy of 1972, Williams charged. California argued that to include pregnancy would be "extraordinarily expensive" and would make the benefit program "impossible to maintain." In May 1973, in *Aiello v. Hansen*, a federal district court agreed 2–1 with the plaintiffs that the California regulation violated the equal protection clause (Hansen was the director of the state Department of Human Resources).[12]

Williams had first intended to press the pregnancy case of one of the plaintiffs in state court, not in federal court. She had ended up in federal court when several cases merged and when another lawyer left. Now, as she had mounted a constitutional challenge to a state law, the case of the pregnant employees was on an express train to the Supreme Court. A few facets of the lawsuit changed en route. Lloyd Geduldig replaced Sigurd Hansen as director of the state's Department of Human Resources; this changed the name of the case. California had agreed to pay the costs of ectopic pregnancies, including that of Carolyn Aiello, who was no longer a party to the case but whose name remained on it.[13]

In *Geduldig v. Aiello* (1974) the Supreme Court agreed with the state of California. In a 6–3 vote, the Court reversed the district court and rejected the workers' claim. In this instance, the Supreme Court finally mentioned the equal protection clause only to find that it did not apply. According to the majority opinion, again by Potter Stewart, the California plan did *not* discriminate by sex or violate the equal protection clause. Rather, it treated "non-pregnant persons," male and female, alike. "There is no risk from which men are protected and women are not." This conclusion—"that discrimination on the basis of pregnancy was not sex discrimination" stunned

Wendy Williams. "Justice Stewart managed at one stroke to assert that pregnancy is unrelated to gender—is sex-neutral—and to imply that pregnancy's unique features make it readily distinguishable from other disabilities and hence properly excludable from the comprehensive disability program" without coherent explanation, Williams wrote. Equal protection remained out of reach. The dissenters (Justices Marshall, Brennan, and Douglas) agreed with Williams's equal protection argument.[14]

Another blow to feminists followed in *General Electric Company v. Gilbert* (1976). The case involved not a state fund but a similar insurance plan run by a private company, General Electric. The GE plan paid part of a worker's wages for up to three weeks of absence due to any disability with only one exception: disability caused by pregnancy. Martha Gilbert, a GE employee, challenged the company's policy. Her lawyer, Ruth Weyand, counsel to the electrical workers union and veteran of the civil rights movement, had challenged Westinghouse as far back as 1950 for excluding pregnancy under its disability program. Weyand brought a class action suit. The GE exclusion violated EEOC's new 1972 policy that covered pregnancy; the exclusion of pregnancy from disability benefits now violated Title VII. GE argued that disability plans cost 170 percent more for females than for males, and that with maternity coverage for thirteen weeks, such plans would cost 330 percent more. GE also feared subterfuge by employees: doctors might be willing to give certificates of disability "to women who wish to malinger." Finally, GE feared yet greater impingements on employers' prerogatives. If women received pregnancy benefits, "men would demand benefits for absence taken for childcare."[15]

Federal district and appellate courts agreed with Martha Gilbert. The Supreme Court did not. Justice William Rehnquist, speaking for the majority, wrote a companion opinion to that of Justice Stewart in *Geduldig*. GE's policy—a penalty on childbirth—was not sex discrimination, wrote Justice Rehnquist, because pregnancy differentiates women from men. Lawmakers were free to include or exclude pregnancy or any other disability. The GE regulation simply distinguished between "pregnant women and nonpregnant persons"; this was not sex discrimination. Rehnquist went further and dealt with the EEOC's 1972 provision on pregnancy. Under Title VII, a neutral rule might have a discriminating effect. In this instance, said Rehnquist, the GE rule (excluding solely pregnancy from benefits) did not discriminate. When women resembled men (as in the case of broken bones) they were treated like men. But pregnancy disability represented an "*additional* risk, unique to women."[16]

The *Geduldig* and *Gilbert* decisions outraged the lawyers for employees. But there was a way around them. As Justice Blackmun had observed in his notes after *Gilbert*, "If we are wrong, [C]ongress can change." Feminist lawyers agreed. Within weeks, Ruth Weyand, who had argued Martha Gilbert's case, and Susan Deller Ross, author of the EEOC guidelines on pregnancy and now a staff lawyer at the ACLU, chaired a new coalition, the "Campaign to End Discrimination against Women Workers," a group of over two hundred organizations—feminists, unions, civil rights advocates, and reproductive rights advocates, including in this case, both prochoice and prolife advocates. The coalition urged Congress to move beyond the Court—to end discrimination against pregnant workers through legislation. Ross and Wendy Williams, the lawyer in *Geduldig* and now a law professor at Georgetown, drafted a bill to "prohibit sex discrimination on the basis of pregnancy" and defended it before a House committee. The Supreme Court, charged Ross, had "virtually nullified the sex discrimination provisions of Title VII." Ruth Bader Ginsburg joined the chorus that challenged legislators to act. The Supreme Court's response to the pregnant worker had been "ostrich-like," she claimed. Were Congress "genuinely committed to eradicating sex-based discrimination," wrote Ginsburg, it could provide "firm legislative direction assuring job security, health insurance coverage, and income maintenance for childbearing women."[17]

The appeal to Congress was shrewd. "The hard-boiled legislator has a soft side when it comes to women workers," reformer Alice Hamilton had observed in 1924. Like counterparts of yesteryear, legislators of the 1970s sought to please their constituents; these now included working mothers. Ruth Bader Ginsburg would again ask Congress to approve an amendment to Title VII years later in similar circumstances—when her colleagues on the Supreme Court issued *Ledbetter v. Goodyear Tire and Rubber* (2007), a decision adversely affecting women workers to which she strongly objected. In 1978, as it would in 2009, Congress bypassed the Supreme Court by changing the law.[18]

THE PREGNANCY DISCRIMINATION ACT (1978)

The Pregnancy Discrimination Act of 1978 (PDA), an amendment to Title VII, stated that pregnant workers "shall be treated the same for all employment-related purposes as other persons not so affected, but similar in their ability or inability to work." Employers of fifteen or more persons—as in Title VII—could not treat pregnancy more or less favorably than other temporary, nonoccupational disabilities; to treat pregnant workers differently than other workers was sex discrimination. "On the basis of sex" in Title VII now included "pregnancy, childbirth, or related medical conditions"; the law affected hiring, promotion, benefits, and medical disability. It passed overwhelmingly, 376 to forty-three in the House and seventy-five to eleven in the Senate. Support for passage among legislators reflected traditional views more than feminist views, historian Melissa McDonald points out. To vote against the bill was to oppose motherhood. The law, proponents in Congress argued, enabled women to support their families. Feminists endorsed this effective rationale.[19]

The PDA reversed *General Electric v. Gilbert*. To treat pregnant workers differently than other workers was to discriminate. But the new law provided no specific benefits to pregnant workers; its impact depended on the benefits that an employer provided for *other* workers. The employer with a medical benefits plan in place would have to include pregnancy in the plan; the employer that provided no benefits for any worker might continue this practice. (Like GE, employers feared massive expense plus predatory benefit-grasping among pregnant workers who in fact planned to remain at home anyway.) Still, the PDA changed the ground rules. It also surged to the center of debate; within months it had generated a new set of federal discrimination cases.

In *Newport News Shipbuilding and Dry Dock v. EEOC* (1983), the Supreme Court provided a new benefit for men. Newport News had always given employees and their spouses comprehensive hospitalization and medical expense coverage save for childbirth, where it provided reduced coverage. With PDA in effect, the company improved childbirth coverage for its female employees but not for male employees' wives. To avoid sex discrimination, the Court said, Newport News would have to give male employees the same benefits as female employees; the company had to raise the childbirth benefits for wives of male employees. Equal rights, the Court made clear, did not simply mean female advantage. The decision of course rested on the Court's certainty that "the sex of the spouse is always the opposite of the sex of the employee."[20] The next PDA case brought new challenges.

After PDA passage, five states (Massachusetts, Connecticut, Montana, California, and Wisconsin) went further than the federal law and enacted maternity leave legislation (mandates on employers to offer unpaid leaves with job security to pregnant workers). The California law of 1978 provided that employers must grant pregnant workers up to four months of unpaid leave with job security. State legislators believed that the law met the equality standards that feminists had endorsed. In 1982, a California bank employee, Lillian Garland, filed a complaint with the state's Fair Employment and Housing Commission that her employer had violated the state law. When

Garland had tried to return to work after a three-month leave for a difficult pregnancy, the bank had said her job was gone and that there was no similar job for her to take; in consequence, she had lost her home and custody of her daughter. Garland claimed her right to resume her old job under state law. The bank argued that the state law, which provided special treatment for women workers, was invalidated by the PDA, which had banned special treatment. With other businesses, it sued to repeal the state law. To the business community, pregnancy rights were the start of a drift toward further worker entitlements. According to sociologist Lise Vogel, "The bank hoped to treat employees returning from leave for pregnancy as badly as it treated other workers returning from leave for temporary disability.[21]

The bank's case against the state, *California Federal Savings and Loan v. Guerra*, split feminists into feuding camps. All agreed that Lillian Garland deserved to return to her job; they disagreed on how the law should insure this outcome. According to NOW and the ACLU, the bank could obey both the state law and the PDA by providing disability leave not only for pregnant women but also for all workers with temporary disabilities. Their argument: pregnancy was analogous to other disabilities, and any form of "special" treatment was undesirable. Other feminists (among them the Southern California ACLU chapter and Betty Friedan) argued that a degree of special treatment was necessary in order to achieve equal results, and that pregnancy was a real sexual difference. According to this position, equal treatment—such as that provided by the PDA—can yield unequal results. Hence, strict equality, with no room for difference held hidden disadvantages.[22]

Since the 1960s, feminist lawyers had used the amicus brief to sway courts toward an equal rights agenda. In the instance of *Guerra*, with feminists divided, feminist lawyers sought equal rights in four amicus briefs with varied approaches to "difference." Those who signed the amicus brief for NOW included important veterans of equal rights litigation, including Wendy W. Williams, who had argued the losing side in *Geduldig*, and Susan Deller Ross, now at Georgetown Law School. NOW saw a clash between the California law and PDA. The state law treated pregnancy as "sui generis," NOW stated. The federal law, however, mandated equal treatment of pregnancy. Indeed, the state "had done exactly what Congress aimed to avoid by passage of the PDA." But NOW rejected the bank's effort to thwart Lillian Garland's claim. Instead, it proposed a remedy to satisfy both laws: "extension of the statute to apply to all workers." Title VII required "the extension of benefits, not their removal," NOW concluded. The state law "must be extended to cover the non-pregnant disabled employee." The ACLU brief, written by Joan Bertin, an ACLU lawyer since 1979, opposed the "sui generis" approach to pregnancy law and agreed with NOW that job protection should be extended to all workers. Rejecting the gender stereotypes reflected in protective legislation, the ACLU brief dismissed the California law as a species of protective law. "[L]egislative distinctions drawn on the basis of sex (and pregnancy) are inherently dangerous even when they purport to convey advantages."[23]

Two coalitions of feminists, in contrast, urged the Court to uphold the California law. The Coalition for Reproductive Equality in the Workplace (CREW), led by Betty Friedan, drew support from the ILGWU, Planned Parenthood, and many California labor unions, women's organizations, and officeholders. CREW's amicus brief, written by Christine Anne Littleton of UCLA, denied any link between the California law and protective legislation of the past. "The statute is *not* protective," declared CREW; it was intended "to remedy the *discriminatory* impact of inadequate leave policies," not to impose discrimination. The law did not "*require* women to take leave," as protective laws had in fact done. Rather, it "obligated employers to assure women who choose to have children that their jobs will not therefore be placed in jeopardy." CREW also defended the state law as a gain for reproductive rights. "Men who work can work and have children," the CREW brief stated. "Women who work must have some leave from work so that they too can work and have children." CREW's defense, Lise Vogel points out, shifted the focus from workplace to family, and from equal employment opportunity to procreative freedom, which it saw as "the heart of the controversy."[24]

Equal Rights Advocates, a feminist law firm in San Francisco, supported by local women's law groups, offered the legal analysis of gender difference proposed by Herma Hill Kay (whose law students at Boalt Hall had shaped the plaintiffs' argument in *Sail'er Inn v. Kirby* in 1971). Kay developed an equal protection argument that included "difference." According to her mode of "episodic analysis," pregnancy imposed real (if temporary) difference in the workplace, a difference that the California law recognized. Her proposal: to compare female workers and male workers who indulged in "reproductive behavior." The difference: Unlike prospective fathers, prospective mothers risked losing their jobs. Kay's mode of comparison challenged Judge Haynsworth's contention that maternity and paternity cannot be compared. "On both legal and philosophical grounds," Kay stated in an article, "the temporary inequality that stems from the condition of pregnancy can and should be considered within a framework of equal opportunity for both sexes." Unlike protective laws, which led to inequality, Kay explained, the type of "difference" law that she supported provided a safe-guard for women "from the loss of employment during pregnancy." The California law, said Equal Rights Advocates, led to equality. California turned to Kay's analysis and to the brief of Equal Rights Advocates for its own argument to the Supreme Court.[25]

The case that began with Lillian Garland's complaint reached the Supreme Court in 1986. Did Title VII, amended by the PDA of 1978, preempt a state law insuring unpaid leave and job retention to workers disabled by pregnancy? To the bank's lawyer, Theodore Olson, in oral argument, "when a state government selects out a class of individuals and determines that those individuals shall have certain benefits, and sets up an enforcement mechanism for that purpose, that is special treatment." Such special treatment resembled protective laws, Olson charged. Pointing to "decades of legislation which had provided special protection to women," he denounced "this stereotype that somehow women needed to have extra special protection in order to be brought up to the level of man." To California's defender, Marian M. Johnston, who relied on the amicus brief of Equal Rights Advocates, the state law was legitimate and egalitarian. Women, like men, could now have children without facing job loss. "All it requires them [the employers] to do is to keep the job available for the woman once she returns to work." Without such a policy, the pregnant employee "will lose her job due to her pregnancy." The bank's analysis, Johnston charged, "would lead to the absurd result that . . . you could treat pregnant employees as harshly as you treat employees with other medical conditions."[26]

In *California Federal Savings and Loan Association v. Guerra* (1987), the Supreme Court upheld the state law 6–3. According to the majority opinion by Justice Thurgood Marshall, the two statutes were not in conflict; special treatment for pregnancy did not contradict the equality mandated by the PDA. To reach this conclusion, Marshall narrowed the Court's mission: "[O]ur sole task is to ascertain the intent of Congress" when it approved the PDA. First, Congress "was aware of state laws similar to California's law but apparently did not consider them inconsistent with the PDA." Second, PDA and the state law shared a common goal, "to achieve equality of employment opportunities." Third, the employer was free to extend "comparable benefits to other disabled employees." Indeed, the opinion urged this development: "[W]e agree with the Court of Appeals' conclusion that Congress intended the Pregnancy Discrimination Act to be 'a floor beneath which pregnancy disability benefits may not drop—not a ceiling above which they may not rise.'" Marshall had carved out a path among feminist stances by accepting "special treatment" as a stepping-stone to "equal treatment." The majority opinion thus preserved the benefit that women workers had gained from the state law and pointed the way toward a law that would give disability rights to all workers—the outcome that California Federal had sought to preclude. With *Guerra*, writes lawyer Martha Minow, the Supreme Court began "to break free of the difference conundrum at least with regard to pregnancy in the workplace." The decision "replaced the unstated norm of the male worker without family duties with a new norm of a worker with family duties."[27]

Justice Antonin Scalia joined the majority because he opposed federal preemption of state law. The three dissenters, Justices Byron White, Powell, and Rehnquist, declared that PDA left "no room for preferential treatment of pregnant women." The dissenters conveyed in their argument an attitude put forth by Justice Sutherland in *Adkins v. Children's Hospital* in 1923. By insisting on equality, their statements suggest, feminists had asked women workers to forfeit benefit.[28] The dissenters defended an important terrain, a last bastion of "able white man" jurisprudence. Justice Marshall, in contrast, understood the hazard of bias and the nature of equality. The case presented an insoluble challenge. The solution he offered, one that catered to two clashing feminist positions, was strategic. The *Guerra* decision provided a halfway step, not utterly dissimilar from the "entering wedge" strategy of yesteryear. It preserved the California law—along with feminist visions of more far-reaching change down the road.

Guerra by no means resolved the special treatment/equal treatment conflict that had erupted among feminists. To lawyer Wendy W. Williams, the decision imposed "asymmetry" on the PDA. "For symmetrists [like herself], it was only half a loaf," she wrote, "a half loaf fraught with difficulties." To lawyer Joan C. Williams, reporting on post-*Guerra* conflicts, the "assimilationist" stance that Wendy Williams assumed had one clear implication: "No maternity leaves." The decision baffled state legislators, who could not gratify one group of constituents without alienating another. Congress faced a similar dilemma. California Democrat Howard Berman, who, as a state legislator, had propelled the state maternity leave law of 1978 to victory, had hoped, when elected to Congress in 1982, to steer a similar measure into federal law but found that he had stepped into a pit of controversy.[29] To move forward called for a paradox: a gender-neutral form of pregnancy policy. Starting in 1985, Representative Patricia Schroeder, Colorado Democrat and co-chair of the Congressional Caucus on Women's Issues, led a drive in Congress for such a policy. In February 1990 Congress made yet another contribution to the pregnancy debate.

TOWARD FAMILY LEAVE

The Family Leave Act of 1990 provided up to twelve weeks of unpaid leave to workers with family emergencies, including birth, adoption, and serious health conditions. President George H. W. Bush vetoed the measure twice, in 1990 and 1992. Such a leave, he stated, should be voluntary on the part of employers—a longtime tactic to delay or undercut regulation of employer prerogatives. Congress tried again, and in 1993, new president Bill Clinton signed the Family and Medical Leave Act (FMLA). The law enabled employees in large workplaces to take up to twelve weeks annually of unpaid leave for their own disabilities or to care for family members, such as new infants, sick children or spouses, or aged parents. With FMLA, Congress deconstructed pregnancy into two components: disability and care for others; each component was stretched to include the nonpregnant. California's pregnancy law, upheld in *Guerra*, had thus served as an "entering wedge" for a broad-based gender-neutral policy that satisfied (or seemed to satisfy) feminist demands. FMLA was also (in its own way) the first federal law to provide maternity leave. It applied to all public sector employees and to private sector employees in firms with fifty or more workers.[30]

Employers objected. By now the business community, which had battled similar leave proposals for several years, had long dropped the affinity for equal rights that it had espoused in the era of single-sex protective laws. According to employers of the 1990s and their advocates, the new family leave law, like its vetoed antecedents, shackled management, slowed productivity, drove up costs, and deprived workers of alternative (if unspecified) gains—or as President Bush stated in his 1990 veto message, "Mandated benefits may limit the ability of employers to provide other benefits of importance to their employees." Senator Bob Dole of Kansas told his colleagues in 1992 that FMLA, though "well-intentioned," would force employers to "cut back on something else, including creating new jobs." Exemption of small business would be only temporary, opponents warned. Like employers who had fought protective laws in decades past, foes of family leave saw it as an ominous precedent. According to a Republican congressman from North Carolina in 1987, "This disturbing trend is nothing short of Europeanization—a polite term for socialism." In some instances, business critics derided the measure as a "yuppie vacation law," a gift to well-off households. "The family leave bill is another example of the crass hypocrisy that afflicts the leisured class on Capitol Hill," charged an editorial in the conservative *Washington Times* in 1991. "Its champions sanctimoniously call it 'pro-family,' but it really places a tax on mothers who work because they must work to support their families. The type of 'family' it would truly benefit would be two law-yers who marry each other."[31]

Other critics assailed the family leave law for not doing enough. Unpaid family leave provided only meager benefits to recipients, far less than the paid maternity leaves that the President's Commission on the Status of Women had recommended in 1963 or those that pregnant workers received in European states. In France in 1991, for instance, pregnant workers en-joyed the option of sixteen to twenty-six weeks of paid leave, at 84 percent of their salaries, with benefits and job protection; parents could share full-time leave until a child was three. Pregnant workers in Sweden received twelve weeks of maternity leave at 80 percent of their pay plus options for parental leave. Comprehensive welfare plans in other European states simi-larly provided extensive benefits. Moreover, family leave in the United States reached only a portion, perhaps 60 percent, of all workers, those in larger workplaces (with fifty or more employees). Those at small firms, intermit-tently employed, or recently hired (in the past year) gained no benefit. Nor did workers who could not afford unpaid leave. Here the critiques of some feminists overlapped with those of conservative critics about a "yuppie" law. FMLA most clearly assisted well-off employees, female or male (workers who were likely to be the spouses of other well-off employees), with the fi-nancial resources to take advantage of it. A woman worker of modest means, especially if single, might well prefer a European-style option of paid mater-nity leave (had such an option existed), even if that option involved "differ-ence," to the unbiased, unfunded, and perhaps unavailable or unusable op-tion of family leave.[32]

With all its limitations, the Family and Medical Leave Act fulfilled femi-nist goals; it pushed policy in a new direction and helped fuse workplace demands with those of families. FMLA changed the substance of employ-ment law to reflect the needs of all workers, not just men. It recast the na-ture of the worker from male-and-always-ready-to-work to a gender-neutral individual with potential disabilities and family responsibilities. It affected family life by extending a benefit—voluntary unpaid leave—to men. Over-all, family leave was transformative; it addressed "difference" in a gender-neutral and egalitarian framework. FMLA did not stand alone in this en-deavor; it was part of a larger, coordinated effort in Congress to provide substantive equality and reconfigure economic citizenship.[33] Still, its pas-sage marked a charged moment in the advance of equal rights and a prece-dent for future achievement. The Supreme Court upheld the power of Con-gress to enact the family leave provisions of FMLA in *Nevada Department of Human Resources v. Hibbs* (2003).[34]

Meanwhile, another pregnancy question had arisen. Did the PDA apply to company policies that barred women from workplaces that could prove toxic to unborn offspring? Here, pregnancy policy veered into a new area: fetal vulnerability. Lawmakers and feminists also returned to a concern of the Progressive Era, the hazardous work environment.

THE TOXIC WORKPLACE

Protective laws had long barred women from workplaces seen as dangerous, such as mines, bars, and the core rooms of foundries (iron, brass, steel). Such laws had kept women out of heavy industry. As single-sex protective laws sank in the 1970s, upset by Title VII, a movement for fetal protection arose. Like protective laws, fetal protection policies kept women, or at least most women (those who were pregnant or capable of becoming pregnant), out of a wide range of industrial jobs. Feminist lawyers found fetal protection anathema, a return to the paternalism that had always handicapped women workers. "Despite the enactment of Title VII, little seems to have changed when the question is whether to limit women's employment opportunities for the good of their potential children," wrote lawyer Mary Becker in the 1980s. Moreover, feminist lawyers charged, fetal protection was an excuse that employers could use to escape the responsibility of insuring workplace safety for all employees.[35]

The policy of the Johnson Controls Company, a manufacturer of automobile batteries, suggests the impact of the fetal protection movement. Lead, an integral component of batteries, had long been recognized as a toxic substance. Before the Civil Rights Act of 1964, the company hired no women in battery manufacturing, only in office positions. In the 1970s, the federal government pressured the company to hire women on the production line. In 1977 Johnson Controls began a voluntary fetal protection policy; it warned women employees of the risk of lead exposure and urged women to avoid jobs that involved such exposure. In 1982 the company replaced the voluntary policy with a mandatory policy that excluded all fertile women ("women who are pregnant or capable of bearing children") from jobs in which lead exposure might be high; OSHA determined that lead exposure presented danger in all jobs in which employee blood levels rose above 30 micrograms of lead per 100 grams of blood. The policy also excluded fertile women from positions that might lead to promotions to jobs that involved lead exposure. The reason for exclusion: exposure to lead posed unacceptable "potential risk" to an unborn child. Women who wanted assembly-line jobs in plants that produced auto batteries needed a doctor's certification that they were sterile or had undergone sterilization procedures. The mandatory policy was needed, the company said, because eight women had become pregnant under the voluntary policy.[36]

The type of fetal protection policy adopted at Johnson Controls, widespread among corporations, had already drawn attention at American Cyanamid, which ran a paint production plant in Willow Island, West Virginia. In late 1977 Cyanamid announced that it would exclude all women workers under fifty who were not sterilized from jobs that exposed them to lead. (Of 560 employees, thirty were women, of whom twenty-three worked in such jobs.) Five women in the lead pigment department had then undergone sterilization in order to keep their jobs. In 1979 Cyanamid closed the lead pigment department. The sterilized workers now had no jobs; they sued the company for sex discrimination. "I thought there was no option for me," said Betty Riggs, a plaintiff, then twenty-six and the mother of one. "That was my only way out, to keep my job, to keep my sanity, to keep my family afloat." The company settled the case in 1983 before it came to trial with a modest payment ($200,000) to the workers who had sued plus costs and attorneys' fees. Meanwhile, in 1979 OSHA fined American Cyanamid for its sterilization requirement and for failing to find alternatives to it. The case that grew out of OSHA's suit and the company's response ended up in 1984 in a federal appeals court, where a three-judge panel upheld the sterilization policy. Judge Robert Bork wrote the opinion. "This is not an anti-woman decision," he told the Senate Judiciary Committee during the 1987 hearings on his (failed) nomination to the Supreme Court. "The company was offering women a choice." Fetal protection policies similar to the one that offered "choice" at American Cyanamid persisted elsewhere. The range of industries affected included chemical, petrochemical, rubber, tires, and plastics, as well as paint and batteries.[37]

The United Auto Workers, which represented the employees at Johnson Controls, had long been active in the women's movement. The UAW's "Women's Department" had campaigned against protective laws since the 1960s; union leaders had been active in the start of NOW and union lawyers were involved in feminist campaigns. In early 1984, the UAW launched a class action suit against Johnson Controls on behalf of seven workers—six women and one man—from company plants in various states. The union charged sex discrimination and violation of the PDA of 1978. Among the workers from the Fullerton, California, plant: Elsie Nasan would have to be sterilized or lose her job. Mary Craig had been sterilized to keep her job. Donald Penney had applied for a transfer from the assembly line in order to lower his blood lead level while trying to conceive a child; his transfer had been denied. Each plaintiff presented another version of grievance and each was adamant, UAW lawyers reported. Ginny Green, age fifty, who had worked on the battery assembly line in Brattleboro, Vermont, had been transferred from that position to a job washing the protective masks of the men who replaced her. She had been unable to prove that she was sterile. "I felt I was good enough to work on the line for eleven years," she told an interviewer. "Why take me off now, just because of that stupid thing."[38]

Was the company's policy a legitimate bona fide occupational qualification? Was the policy "facially neutral" under Title VII, as Johnson Controls claimed, because its purpose was "benign"? Did the company's hope to avoid liability in lawsuits for fetal deformity justify such a policy? Alternatively, did Title VII, amended by the PDA of 1978, forbid such a fetal protection policy? Was the exclusion of women who were or might become pregnant sex discrimination? As the Johnson Controls case began its ascent through the federal courts, it became a dispute among judges as well as between the contesting parties. In January 1988, a federal district court in Wisconsin first tackled the case. District judge Robert F. Warren, a Gerald Ford appointee (1974), decided in favor of Johnson Controls. Judge Warren found the fetus at risk from low levels of maternal exposure to lead. Had the employer rushed to exclude women before cleaning up the workplace or investigating the potential damage to male workers? The answer did not matter. "[T]he court simply cannot overlook this possibility of severe harm only to the fetus," said Judge Warren. "As a concern for society and future generations this court must uphold the fetal protection policy." As the policy was not "facially discriminatory," Judge Warren said, the BFOQ defense was not an issue. Did acceptable alternatives to the exclusion policy exist? The UAW had not shown what they were.[39]

In September 1989, the Seventh Circuit Court of Appeals, in a 7–4 en banc ruling, confirmed the district court's decision. Judge John L. Coffey, a Republican appointee of 1982, wrote the majority opinion in favor of Johnson Controls. Women's infertility could be a BFOQ for certain jobs, the court asserted. Johnson Controls had demonstrated that the policy was a valid business necessity; its concerns about tort liability were legitimate. The plaintiffs had not proved discrimination; the company sought to protect fetuses, not to discriminate. UAW evidence about the effect of lead on men was "speculative and unconvincing." Title VII permitted distinctions between men and women if they were based on "real physical difference" (as opposed to fictitious or stereotypical differences). Finally, the Seventh Circuit saw women employees as potentially negligent. Women earned wages in order to "better their family's station in life," Judge Coffey wrote, and "might somehow rationally discount" risk to the unborn in "the hope and belief" that an infant would be unaffected. For women workers, in short, good pay might trump fetal risk. However, more was as stake. Risks to the unborn were "shared by society," which would have to support the handicapped child who had been damaged by lead exposure in utero. Here the court restated a point from the *Muller* decision of 1908, as well as from the brief for Illinois in *Ritchie v. People* (1895): if women workers made poor choices, society would pay the price. In sum, said the Seventh Circuit, Johnson Controls had sought to improve working conditions and had no alternative to excluding fertile women.[40]

But a trio of dissenters in the Seventh Circuit had questions about Judge Coffey's opinion and picked it apart; the dissenters spoke directly to the Supreme Court justices who would next review the case. Judge Richard Dickson Cudahy observed that of the twelve federal judges who had thus far considered the case, "none had been female." The case demanded "some insight into social reality," not just "disembodied rules." Judge Cudahy compared "the situation of the pregnant woman, unemployed or working for the minimum wage and unprotected by health insurance" to a counterpart on the assembly line, "exposed to an indeterminate lead risk but well-fed, housed and doctored." He then brought to the foreground a vital question: "Whose decision is this to make?" Judge Richard Posner wanted more evidence on all the scientific questions in dispute. "The issue of the legality of fetal protection is as novel and difficult as it is contentious," he wrote. "The record in this case is too sparse. The district judge jumped the gun. . . . By affirming on this scanty basis we may be encouraging incautious employers to adopt fetal protection policies that could endanger the jobs of millions of women for minor gains in fetal safety and health." Judge Frank Easterbrook concluded the assault. The case, he declared, was "the most important sex-discrimination case this court has ever decided." He returned in part to the question about decision making. "No legal or ethical principle compels or allows Johnson to assume that women are less able than men to make intelligent decisions about the welfare of the next generation, that the interests of the next generation always trump the interests of living woman [women] and that the only acceptable level of risk is zero. . . . To insist on zero risk . . . is to exclude women from the industrial jobs that have been a male preserve. . . . Laudable though its objective may be, Johnson may not reach its goal at the expense of women."[41]

The dissenters' critiques battered the Seventh Circuit's majority opinion. By the time the case reached the Supreme Court in 1990, recent developments had begun to tilt the scales more heavily in favor of the UAW. Two important decisions in similar cases, in a California court of appeals (involving another Johnson Controls worker) and in the Sixth Circuit, had rejected the BFOQ defense and invalidated fetal protection policies. Moreover, since the first appeal in the UAW case, amicus briefs had piled up in support of both parties to the case. Businesses and allied interests endorsed Johnson Controls' fetal protection effort. Even more groups sought to buttress the UAW. By 1991 over 110 organizations (supporters of women's rights, labor, and workplace safety) had signed ten amicus briefs that stressed the harmful effects of fetal protection policies on women workers. Assembled by Joan Bertin of the ACLU, author of the ACLU's amicus brief in *Guerra*, the amicus briefs played a major role in the UAW case.[42]

Marsha Berzon, the associate general counsel of the AFL-CIO, who represented the UAW before the Supreme Court, had experience in pregnancy law. She had contributed to the drafting of the PDA and to antifetal protection litigation of the 1980s. Berzon argued that the Johnson Controls fetal protection policy was facial discrimination on the basis of sex and could not be justified as a BFOQ under Title VII. The exclusion of women was not a business necessity, she said; less discriminatory alternatives were available. The UAW challenged the scientific basis of the Johnson Controls policy. Berzon disputed whether levels of exposure to which women workers were subject in fact harmed the unborn and explored the impact of lead toxicity on men. Finally, she argued that the company's alleged concern for the unborn was a pretext for discriminating against women workers. The fetal protection policy kept women from a broad range of jobs and "sanctions re-segregation of the work force," as Berzon declared in oral argument. To remove women from well-paying jobs and health insurance or to deny them access to such jobs would deprive them of adequate income and medical care and thus also injure the unborn. Women workers would end up where they always had been, in jobs dominated by women in which their labor was indispensable, and these jobs too held fetal risks. A loss for the UAW, Berzon claimed, would close twenty million industrial jobs to women because of toxic substances in the workplace. Under Title VII, the only issue was whether or not women could perform on the job; women employees must make their own assessments of risk.[43]

Johnson Controls contended—as it had since the outset—that the company's interest in avoiding harm to third parties (the unborn) justified its fetal protection policies. "The company has a legal duty to avoid injuries to the unborn that result directly from the toxic hazards of its own manufacturing operation," the brief for Johnson Controls stated. BFOQ analysis could include potential tort liability against the company for fetal injuries, the company claimed. But Johnson Controls failed to argue its way around the PDA, which now amended Title VII. An important moment in oral argument came when Justice Sandra Day O'Connor (who had become the Supreme Court's first woman member in 1981), questioning Stanley Jaspan, the company's lawyer, charged: "You are not coming to grips with the effects of the Pregnancy Discrimination Act." A fetal protection policy that might have passed muster before 1978 was no longer viable.[44]

THE *JOHNSON CONTROLS* DECISION (1991)

Harry Blackmun of Minnesota (1908–1999) had been an appellate judge on the Eight Circuit when President Nixon nominated him to the Supreme Court in 1970. Blackmun was Nixon's third choice: the first had been Clement Haynsworth, who in 1973 wrote the Fourth Circuit opinion in *Cohen v. Chesterfield County School Board* ("Pregnancy and maternity are sui generis"). A lifelong Republican, Blackmun was expected to be a conservative voice on the Court, a "strict constructionist." Instead, he became the author of *Roe v. Wade* (1973), which upheld the right to abortion by invoking a constitutional right to privacy. Thereafter, as Justice Blackmun shifted toward more liberal views, new appointments made the Court more conservative. At first wary, Blackmun came to appreciate feminism; this was clear in the opinion he wrote for *Johnson Controls*.

In *UAW v. Johnson Controls* on March 20, 1991, the Supreme Court unanimously held that the company policy violated Title VII. "The bias in Johnson Controls' policy is obvious," wrote Justice Blackmun. "Fertile men, but not fertile women, are given a choice as to whether they wish to risk their reproductive health for a particular job." Unlike women, men did not have to provide proof of sterility to gain employment; the company's policy categorized workers on the basis of their potential for pregnancy, which violated Title VII as well as the PDA of 1978. Even a benevolent motive could not justify a discriminatory policy. The company could not use the BFOQ defense, which involved only a worker's effectiveness on the job: "[W]omen as capable of doing their jobs as their male counterparts should not be forced to choose between having a child and having a job." Even though lead exposure might harm the unborn, Johnson Controls could not prove that lead exposure prevented female employees from performing essential tasks. (The burden of proof now rested on the employer and not on the employees, as the Sixth Circuit had stated in 1989.) Nor could tort liability justify a discriminatory policy under Title VII. But tort liability was unlikely henceforth to bother employers. "Without negligence, it would be difficult for a court to find liability on the part of an employer," Justice Blackmun wrote. If an employer fully informed a woman employee of risk and did not act negligently, "the basis for holding an employer liable seems remote at best." Toward the end of the decision, Justice Blackmun returned to the question of freedom of choice and "who would choose," the issue to which Judge Cudahy alluded in his Sixth Circuit dissent. "Decisions about the welfare of future children must be left to the parents who conceive, bear, and support them rather than to the employers who hire those parents," Justice Blackmun wrote.

> Concern for a woman's existing or potential offspring historically has been the excuse for denying women equal employment opportunities [Here Justice Blackmun cited *Muller v. Oregon*]. Congress in the PDA prohibited discrimination on the basis of a woman's ability to become pregnant. We do no more than hold that the Pregnancy Discrimination Act means what it says.
>
> It is no more appropriate for the courts than it is for individual employers to decide whether a woman's reproductive role is more important to herself and her family than her economic role. Congress has left this choice to the woman as hers to make.[45]

With these statements, Justice Blackmun provided a final terminus to the *Muller v. Oregon* decision of 1908. The *Johnson Controls* litigation also provided a reverse image of the 1908 case—a precise counterweight—in which most of the particulars had been transformed into their opposites.

As in many unanimous decisions, some justices had qualifications. Justices White, Anthony Kennedy, and Rehnquist, in a concurring opinion written by Justice White, voiced their own rationale. They left a path open for a company that chose to exclude fertile women to shape a valid BFOQ defense. Justice Scalia, in a separate concurring opinion, said the Court could take into account the costs to a company. The concurring opinions sought to bolster employer immunity from liability, to which Justice Blackmun referred. Perhaps they did. In *Johnson Controls*, the Supreme Court ended fetal protection policies and insured that millions of jobs remained open to women. It also handed Johnson Controls and other corporations a consolation prize: tort liability for fetal deformity would be "remote at best." Finally, the *Johnson Controls* decision marked definitively the end of single-sex protective laws and the rationale that had once sustained them.[46]

Like the FMLA of 1993 (yet to come), the *Johnson Controls* decision did not accomplish all workplace goals that feminists had promoted. It did not end disputes over workplace pregnancy or over the PDA; federal courts found much more to debate in the decades ahead. Nor did the decision much change labor practices at Johnson Controls; unable to bar women from assembly-line jobs, the company discouraged women from such jobs and steered them toward less hazardous—and less gainful—jobs. Some businesses required women workers to sign waivers in which they assumed responsibility for reproductive health. The type of "choice" that the decision insured, between a more toxic work environment and lower-paid work, was a constrained choice. Finally, the decision did not address health and safety on the job or make a dent in workplace toxicity. Instead, it had liberated women workers to risk health consequences in the workplace. To scholar Cynthia Daniels, assessing the case in 1992, this outcome presents a paradox. "To ignore difference is to risk placing women in a workplace designed for and by men, with all of its hazards and lack of concern for the preservation of life and health," Daniels contends. "On the other hand, to treat women differently in the workplace is to reinforce those assumptions and economic structures which form the foundations of women's inequalities." Neither model, Daniels notes, adequately addresses workplace risk.[47]

The lawyers who shaped the UAW case (Marsha Berzon and her colleagues Carin Ann Clauss and Joan Bertin) recognized the Supreme Court opinion's liabilities. As its critics argued, "the Court had not addressed the underlying health issues," the UAW lawyers wrote. "[T]he opinion does not protect anyone's health, but simply sanctions equal exposure of women and men to working conditions dangerous to their health and the health of any future offspring." But the lawyers defended their accomplishment. "Legal strategies necessarily reflect the limitations of the legal system," they contended.

> That system has a tendency to deal with societal problems in an incremental, subdivided way that can be frustrating to those seeking an immediate, global answer. To work within that system, litigants are constrained to proceed in a measured fashion in structuring their lawsuits and often cannot rely on litigation alone to reach the ultimate goal.

Courts decide only "the legal questions presented by the precise dispute before them," as had been the case in *Johnson Controls*. Health questions had not been "directly at issue." Title VII, the federal law that the Court interpreted, addressed only sexual equality, not health issues, even though many facts concerning the impact of lead on health and reproductive health were central to showing that discrimination occurred. Still, the lawyers saw the equal rights question decided in *Johnson Controls* as "an essential first step to the resolution of the occupational safety and health issues and corporate responsibility questions concerning reproductive health generally." The litigation, "while not the ultimate solution to reproductive health in the workplace, was a necessary building block in reaching that goal."[48]

To the UAW advocates, the *Johnson Controls* decision of 1991 was thus an "entering wedge"—an "essential first step"—to solving the problems about workplace safety and employer responsibility, a step without which no further steps were possible. What steps should come next? "The most effective strategy for reducing reproductive and developmental health risks in the workplace would be a voluntary effort by employers," the UAW lawyers wrote. They also recommended "affirmative steps" from OSHA to lower risk and to curb employer violation of regulations, plus public activism, legislative hearings, and legislation on workplace safety. "The debate now returns to health and safety," wrote political scientist Sally J. Kenney, who analyzed the case in 1992. "[I]t remains to be seen how employers will fashion gender-neutral policies that protect the reproductive health of all employees."[49]

But the "entering wedge" was not always a viable strategy. As it turned out, the *Johnson Controls* decision was more a last step in the history of protective laws than a first step toward health rights in the workplace. Employers did not rush to fashion gender-neutral policies to promote reproductive health. The coalition of women's rights advocates, labor advocates, and health and safety advocates that had formed to challenge fetal protection policies and support the UAW in *Johnson Controls* did not survive to pursue further goals. The victory for women workers in *Johnson Controls* did not pave the way toward more stringent health and safety regulations. The UAW lawyers had a point: the adversarial process had limits. It did not lend itself to solving several problems simultaneously. Just as important, the Supreme Court strove for a balance between equal rights and employer demands. Because the Court sought to hand down a unanimous opinion, one that all of the justices would endorse, the *Johnson Controls* decision was in some ways a split decision. It empowered women workers but it let employers off the hook. It provided "choice," but choice meant risk—and the options for employees were limited. Finally, the decision downplayed the public interest. The "poisoning of the human system," as Felix Frankfurter and Josephine Goldmark had argued in 1916 (when pressing for shorter hours for men), was present, "to a greater or lesser degree, throughout the industrial system." This remained the case in 1991.[50]

· · · · ·

Workplace pregnancy posed the challenge of "difference" in many ways. Could employers dismiss women from state jobs because of pregnancy or impose on them mandatory unpaid leave? Could states or businesses refuse to fund maternity-related costs in medical disability programs? Could pregnant workers take leaves and retain their jobs? Could employers bar women from jobs that involved exposure to substances that might harm unborn children? Courts, legislators, and feminists faced a gauntlet of questions through the 1970s and 1980s. Federal judges often distanced the subject of pregnancy; few had been pregnant workers themselves. Legislators proved less resistant. Step by step, feminist lawyers and a series of worker-plaintiffs expanded the rights of pregnant workers—and of those who might become pregnant. The most enduring steps in shaping pregnancy policy were the PDA of 1978, which barred discrimination against pregnant workers; the FMLA of 1993, which offered up to twelve-week unpaid leaves to employees in larger enterprises for family and medical emergencies; and the *Johnson Controls* decision of 1991, which barred fetal protection regulations as a form of sex discrimination.

All were contested conclusions, full of liabilities. None definitively solved the problems they tackled. The PDA, a law far more demanding than it first seemed, opened the door to continual litigation; federal courts faced ongoing issues linked to workplace pregnancy, especially in the area of benefits. Without state disability laws and employer-funded disability plans, pregnant employees lacked options; women in the lowest-level and most precarious jobs typically escaped the PDA's reach. The FMLA, another substantive step toward gender equality, offered only limited (and unpaid) benefit, unavailable to workers with the fewest resources. The *Johnson Controls* decision left workers of both sexes as well as unborn infants open to harm from toxic substances; remedies for reproductive injuries in the workplace remained elusive. But each step brought the pregnant worker further into the equal rights framework that feminists had envisioned. Collectively, advances in pregnancy law confirmed the value of "equal treatment" as a practical strategy to secure feminist goals. Perhaps the equal treatment approach to pregnancy, as Wendy Williams had argued in the 1980s, had proved "the one best able to reduce structural barriers to full workforce participation of women, produce just results for individuals, and support a more egalitarian social structure."[51] In any case, by the 1990s, equal treatment was the only strategy.

Debate over each shift in pregnancy policy revived the specter of protective laws. Feminist lawyers who objected to California's maternity leave law in the 1980s rejected it as a variant of protective laws ("inherently dangerous even when they purport to convey advantages"). Feminist defenders of the California measure, in contrast, distinguished protective laws, which forced women workers to leave work when pregnant, from the California law, which obliged employers to preserve jobs for pregnant workers on leave. Either way, protective laws of decades past drew condemnation. The *Johnson Controls* case revived the specter of protective laws in another way; feminist pressure groups united to oppose the fetal protection movement as a tactic to exclude women from better-paid jobs, as protective laws had formerly done—although freeing women workers from the hazard of fetal protection policy exposed them to the hazards of the toxic workplace. Justice Blackmun seized the opportunity of the *Johnson Controls* decision to reject the essence of protection and exorcize its last remnant: "Congress has left this choice to the woman as hers to make." The landmark decision restored agency to women workers, spared employers potential lawsuits, and left a gap where the public interest should have been.

Change in pregnancy law thus concluded the long history of single-sex protective laws, a history that began with preparation for *Ritchie v. People* (1895) when lawyers from Florence Kelley's office placed the issue of the unborn and "sexual functions" in the argument for Illinois's eight-hour law. Single-sex laws had enjoyed a long and eventful double life; they had served both as a pathway to labor standards and as a barrier to gender equality. By the early 1990s the laws were rattling bones. They had been moribund since 1968, when a federal court rejected California's protective measures in *Rosenfeld v. Southern Pacific*; by 1971 death was imminent. Two decades later, Justice Blackmun's opinion was protective legislation's last requiem.

As single-sex protective laws faded from view, other workplace issues drew feminist energy. By 1990, 58 percent of women were in the labor force, where they held about 45 percent of all jobs. Two-thirds of married women worked, as did 68 percent of women with children; the working mother had become the norm. Paid maternity leave, endorsed by PCSW in 1963, and universal day care plans, vetoed in 1971, had never materialized. Feminist attention turned to strategies to balance the demands of work and family, to ways to raise wages in vocations women dominated, to the threat of the "glass ceiling" that barred women's advance beyond middle management, and to the new option of affirmative action. Anita Hill's appearance before the Senate Judiciary Committee in the summer of 1991 steered national attention to the growing discussion of sexual harassment in the workplace. Elements of protection, reconceived, reinvented, and reconstructed, now rested on a groundwork of equality. Future steps toward workplace equality would depend in part on the courts, in larger part on legislators, and in largest part on women wage earners, with whose history the rise and fall of single-sex protective laws had been so deeply entwined.

Conclusion

Protection Revisited

"Nothing could be more revolutionary than to close the door to social experimentation," Louis D. Brandeis told the Supreme Court in 1915, when he defended Oregon's minimum wage law for women workers in *Stettler v. Oregon*. "The whole subject of women's entry into industry is an experiment." Brandeis had already mentioned the possibility that the Oregon law might include "economic and social error"; the doubts of critics that it "might not be the best remedy"; and the prospect that it might "lead to some other evils which later legislatures may have to deal with, possibly by repeal of this law."[1] The following year, after Oregon's supreme court had

■ ■ ■

Group of Girls by Lewis W. Hine (1911). Photographer Lewis W. Hine, who created collections of images for the National Child Labor Committee and the National Consumers League, found these young workers in Chicopee, Massachusetts, a factory town. Investigating the textile mills, Hine discerned an unsavory workplace environment. "A young fellow made a very vulgar remark and they all laughed," he wrote in his notes for this photo. "Next day I heard one of the girls use profanity before all the men and boys." Library of Congress.

upheld a ten-hour general law, Felix Frankfurter, the new counsel to the National Consumers' League, promoted the next stage in the progressive experiment: a transition from women-only law to law that would affect men. "[O]nce we cease to look upon the regulation of women in industry as exceptional," Frankfurter explained, "as the law's graciousness to a disabled class, and shift the emphasis from the fact that they are *women* to the fact that it is *industry* which is regulated, the problem is seen from a totally different aspect."[2]

Invocation of the experimental suits the subject. Protective laws for women workers, "the law's graciousness to a disabled class," began as part of a two-step progressive experiment. The narrative of their rise and fall veers closer than most to the accidental, unanticipated, and unpredictable. It is a story of close calls and near misses, false hopes and unintended consequences. The laws had their own volatile chemistry. Once launched, each type of law defied reformers' expectations and followed its own trajectory. Maximum hours laws, at first the most viable of single-sex laws, eventually became the most controversial; minimum wage laws, at first the most precarious, followed a reverse path. The impact of the laws on women workers, always in flux, defied precise measurement. Workers' experiences, according to the Women's Bureau in 1928, rested more on "real forces" such as technological change, and on "other influences," such as changing attitudes. The passage of time inevitably brought surprises; the contexts in which the laws applied changed continually. To mention a few areas of unpredictability, NCL leaders and their lawyers foresaw neither the longevity of single-sex laws nor the shifts in circumstance that would make them suspect decades later. The set of convictions that made single-sex protective laws so appealing to Progressive Era Americans—beliefs about the male breadwinner, the female dependent, and the marginality of women workers—eventually served to undermine the laws and to derail them in the 1960s and 1970s.

Over the course of a century, protective laws for women workers left a double imprint on US history. The laws set precedents that led to the Fair Labor Standards Act of 1938 and to modern labor law; they also sustained classification by sex, a tradition of gendered law that abridged citizenship, impeded equality, and endured until late in the century. Although either facet of the laws can be explored in isolation, the two parts were conjoined and interdependent; the "entering wedge" strategy bound them together. Whether single-sex protective laws were in ascent or decline, each facet of their double imprint is significant.

To what extent did protective laws help women workers? From the outset, single-sex laws held potential for both advantage and injury. The most widespread type of protective law, statutes that required seats, ventilation, and fire escapes, improved working conditions in factories; maximum hours law shortened workdays, although employers might reduce wages; the controversial minimum wage raised pay, as it seemed to do for many workers briefly in the District of Columbia, contrary to the experience of Willie Lyons. Even foes of protective laws conceded that the laws had once (in the past) served positive purposes. "Factory hours were steadily reduced," a critic of the 1940s declared. "Working conditions were improved." But single-sex protective laws always had the capacity to impose damage, and the negatives increased with time, especially in the decades after World War II. Manufacturing changed; the role of women in the workforce changed; the nature of the female labor force changed; and the potential downside, the "debit side," of women-only protective laws rose. Compensatory law (in Justice Brewer's words, legislation "designed to compensate for some of the burdens which rest upon her") might offer benefit, reinforce disparity, or do both in turn or at once. The instability in effect of protective law—the continual shift in its impact—was a key characteristic.[3]

One variable facet of the protective agenda was the interplay between women-only protective laws and "general" wage-and-hours law that affected men. The long history of overtime, its role in shaping gendered law, and its ramifications over time suggests both the unstable nature of protective law and the unpredictability of its consequences.

LOOKING BACK: THE CLASH OVER OVERTIME

Muller v. Oregon in 1908 certified the viability of women-only laws, made them central to the protectionist campaign, and enabled reformers to pursue an "entering wedge" strategy. The *Muller* decision also placed women beyond the "borders of belonging," to use Barbara Young Welke's term; it reinforced inequality or "stunted citizenship"; and it affirmed women's distinctive status in law: "[I]n a class by herself . . . even when like legislation is not necessary for men and could not be sustained."[4]

Within a decade, when Oregon in 1913 enacted a general ten-hour law, the ground rules for protective law shifted. Oregon's new general law, to affect men in industry, provided for up to three hours a day of overtime at time-and-a-half pay for the extra hours. Unprecedented in law, overtime began as an effort to impel compliance, to deter employers from demanding additional hours. Still, the concept was elastic. Overtime might make hours limits less exacting for employers and extra hours more palatable for male employees. "Workmen, of course, prefer twelve hours when they can make more money than they can in eight hours," as economist John R. Commons observed in 1917.[5] Overtime also imposed a potential barrier between male and female employees. If a general law coexisted with a women's maximum hours law, as occurred in Oregon, overtime distinguished the working hours of men. The innovation of overtime in general law sharpened the meaning of women-only maximum hours laws.

"With women, you could talk about maternity, motherhood, the next generation, and so forth," Felix Frankfurter recalled. To defend maximum hours laws for men required a new rationale. The huge brief for Oregon in *Bunting v. Oregon* (1917) underscored the role of men as citizens. But it failed to speak of overtime. The Supreme Court—after some dispute—sustained the Oregon law; the justices disputed whether the 1913 law was a maximum hours law or a wage law in disguise. Dispute recurred when the Court considered the Adamson Act of 1916, a federal emergency measure to preclude a railroad strike; the law provided an eight-hour day for interstate railroad workers with overtime at time and a half. Again, the Court upheld the law. Meanwhile, the Oregon law of 1913 proved a precedent without impact. Other states ignored it. But the overtime provision remained a vital innovation, one that would circle back to intersect with the rest of the protective agenda.[6]

Mention of overtime recurred in the New Deal, when Frances Perkins pulled out of her desk drawer plans to put "a floor under wages and a ceiling over hours." The Walsh-Healey Act of 1936, a federal eight-hour law for public contractors, provided for overtime. So did the Fair Labor Standards Act in 1938. FLSA fulfilled progressive demands and built on protectionist precedent, or, as Josephine Goldmark noted, "its roots lie in the preceding thirty years." The law abolished child labor and provided minimum wage and maximum hours to men and women in many occupations. It also brought overtime back into play. Quietly FLSA removed the three-hour-a-day lid on overtime. FLSA also contained a special requirement: if federal law and state law on labor standards clashed, the "higher standard" (the state standard) would prevail. This provision targeted women: if state law provided a higher minimum wage or shorter hours for women workers, state law trumped federal law. FLSA preserved the gendered law of the Progressive Era.[7]

FLSA both validated the campaign for single-sex protective laws and undermined it. With part of their mission accomplished, women reformers, who had fought so long for wage-and-hour laws, found their impact curtailed. Labor standards now ran on two tracks, and FLSA, which covered mainly men, was the major track. But reformers retained their sphere of influence in the states. After 1938 Women's Bureau leaders defended state laws, which covered some of the women workers that FLSA excluded, and sought—with less success—to extend the reach of state law to women workers excluded from protection entirely. FLSA, in contrast, edged forward. As it did so, overtime, the ignored precedent of 1913, took on new import.[8]

Overtime surged into use in World War II. Defense employers needed overtime to boost productivity, and employees used it to meet rising living costs. The Department of Labor still saw overtime as a deterrent to overwork. "The fact that extra hours are penalized by extra overtime costs has proved sufficient to keep hours at reasonable levels and yet flexible enough to make it possible to work more than forty hours a week when necessary, as it was during the war," Frances Perkins declared in 1946. The Women's Bureau coalition, too, persistently viewed overtime as a barrier to long hours. But it rapidly became something else entirely.[9]

After World War II, use of overtime rose yet further, as industry responded to pent-up consumer demand. Workers covered by FLSA increasingly depended on it. By the postwar years overtime had mutated from a deterrent into an employer prerogative. Among modern labor laws, overtime standards "require the most radical reorganization of work arrangements," economist Ronnie Steinberg notes. "The employer is allowed to work the labor force as many hours per week as he or she wants as long as employees are paid premium pay for hours worked beyond the government-specified workweek." Overtime provided flexibility to employers; it spared them the costs of hiring new workers, of training those workers, and of paying the growing costs attached to them—health insurance, fringe benefits, pension plans. By midcentury, about one-third of a worker's compensation was in benefits. Employers weighed the cost of overtime when they set pay scales; employees counted on overtime pay as a source of income. Overtime thus defied Progressive Era expectations and reversed them. It neither deterred longer work hours nor spread work around. Instead, employers used overtime to lengthen hours and hire fewer new workers. If covered by FLSA, women workers sometimes found that state hours limits precluded overtime; if not covered by FLSA, as was more likely, they lacked access to premium pay. Silently and steadily, overtime reinforced the division of labor into male and female sectors. If jobs required overtime, they were mainly jobs for men. Between 1940 and the end of the 1960s, the millions of employees covered by overtime tripled.[10]

In the 1960s overtime became a central issue in the last stage of argument about protective laws. Concern with overtime arose in the President's Commission on the Status of Women in the early 1960s, where it stymied the Committee on Labor Standards. Could maximum hours laws be extended to men? The committee favored this solution. Overruling the committee, the commission urged extension of FLSA standards that provided overtime. After Title VII, when women workers sued to dislodge maximum hours laws, the issue of overtime arose again. Plaintiff Velma Mengelkoch in 1966 expected overtime to be voluntary under Title VII, but a federal court in 1968 saw the issue more realistically: "It is not a matter of making women earn overtime when they want to, but an obligation to work overtime whether they want to or not on pain of being discharged," the court explained.[11]

By 1970, other facets of protective law that had split the women's movement were fading. "Beneficial" laws that improved working conditions, the vast bulk of protective laws, could be extended to men; state extension of minimum wage laws to men had been in progress since the 1950s; night work and exclusionary laws were dead letters; and laws that imposed weight limits folded in federal court in the late 1960s. Only the clash between mandatory overtime and hours limits energized debate, as it did among women members of UAW Local 3 in 1969 and in congressional hearings of 1970. Maximum hours laws provided women workers "with a shield against compulsory overtime," Myra Wolfgang told the Senate Judiciary Committee. "While all mandatory overtime should be optional for both women and men, it is absolutely mandatory that overtime for women be regulated." Protective laws' foes took another stance. "Real protection would not bar from overtime and premium pay hours a single girl who is trying to save money for college or a widow who is the sole support of two sons," Susan Deller Ross argued. "[T]hose men and women who *do* want overtime should not be penalized because of the desires of those who do not want it."[12]

Might women workers request exemption from maximum hours laws? Might they request exemption from compulsory overtime? Was resolution of this issue feasible? Considering such questions, two academic commentators of 1970, Raymond Munts and David C. Rice, noted "the paucity of information on the possible effects of rooting out protective law." Munts and Rice envisioned a situation in which the Supreme Court would have to decide "whether equality for some women necessarily entails misery for others." They concluded that "the only remaining way to achieve both equality and protection is through laws which require the employee's consent in assigning overtime work." ERA supporter and law professor Leo Kanowitz, testifying before the Senate Judiciary Committee, recommended a similar solution: state laws to insure "voluntary overtime." The laws would bar employers from firing workers, male or female, who refused overtime work, and bring controversy over protective laws to an end. Were such laws possible? As Munts and Rice noted, "Employers have a huge stake in unilateral control of overtime." The achievement of voluntary overtime was, to borrow Pauline Newman's words of 1921, "as easy as getting the moon to play with."[13]

Even as the last arguments over overtime flared, single-sex maximum hours laws failed in federal court. By the end of 1971, appeals courts had weighed in with terminal sentences. Title VII rejected the "romantic paternalism" of protective laws, declared the Fifth Circuit in *Weeks v. Southern Bell*, and bestowed the "power to decide" on women workers themselves. "The premise of Title VII is that women are now to be on equal footing with men," declared the Ninth Circuit in *Rosenfield v. Southern Pacific*. "[I]ndividuals must be judged as individuals."[14] *Reed v. Reed* in 1971 and passage of an ERA in 1972 affirmed that the era of protective laws was over.

In a popular book of 1991, economist Juliet B. Schor picked up the story of overtime and its consequences. Americans of the 1990s worked more hours of overtime than ever before, Schor reported. The disincentive to long hours offered by FLSA in 1938 had "turned into a powerful incentive for workers to work as many hours as they could." Legislation to regulate overtime, Schor suggested, had "contracted both leisure and employment, the two things it was designed to expand."[15] Schor's *Overworked American* provided an updated counterpart to Florence Kelley's plea for "the right to leisure" in 1905. Overtime, an innovation of 1913, was a wild card in the history of protective law. At first a feature that distinguished general law from women-only laws, it became a major labor standard *and* an employer prerogative. Always distinctive among the regulations that protectionists endorsed, overtime embodied the most unpredictable aspect of protective law—an ability to change shape, to reverse paths, and to mutate into something else.

MOVING ON: AFTER PROTECTION

Title VII of the Civil Rights Act of 1964 changed the fate of single-sex protective laws. Barring discrimination in employment on the basis of sex as well as race, Title VII catalyzed the feminist movement of the 1960s. Overdue, unexpected, and enacted without legislative hearings, the sudden addition of sex to employment discrimination law was a leap into uncertainty. That Title VII would affect protective laws was unforeseen by the Women's Bureau in 1964, by the Equal Employment Opportunity Commission in 1965, or by the National Organization for Women in its first year. But by the end of 1966, landmark cases were underway. Women workers began by filing complaints with the EEOC and then by suing employers and/or the states. Judges hesitated only briefly; by 1971 federal courts determined that Title VII trumped state protective laws. The states chimed in; state legislatures revoked single-sex laws and state attorneys general renounced them. Most state protective laws, those that involved factory facilities, working conditions, and the minimum wage, became general law, but "restrictive" laws were doomed. By the mid-1970s, single-sex protective laws (except for the disputed issue of pregnancy regulations) had sunk from sight.

What followed the death of women-only protective laws? What public policies replaced them? FLSA expansion in 1966 and after brought labor standards to women workers who had been bypassed by federal law, including, in 1974, domestic workers. New Deal labor standards, including overtime, the minimum wage, and the many extensions of FLSA, were the legacies of protective laws. Title VII kept growing, too; amendments steadily enhanced its authority. In 1972 Congress enabled the EEOC to bring suit and extended the fields of employment that Title VII covered. Thereafter Congress and the courts reformed employment law. Adverse pregnancy decisions of the 1970s led Congress to pass the Pregnancy Discrimination Act of 1978, an amendment to Title VII; the Supreme Court rejected protective laws definitively in *Johnson Controls* in 1991, and Congress finally achieved the Family and Medical Leave Act in 1993. In 1987 in *Johnson v. Transportation Agency*, the Supreme Court upheld a voluntary affirmative action program. Such a program, instituted by a public employer, in this case a California county, to remedy a statistical imbalance of women in the workforce, did not violate Title VII, said the Court. EEOC guidelines in 1980 recognized sexual harassment as a form of sex discrimination prohibited under Title VII; federal courts soon legitimized this vital addition to equal rights. A trio of cases—*Meritor Savings Bank v. Vinson* (1986), *Ellison v. Brady* (1991), and *Harris v. Forklift Systems* (1993)—showed how sexual harassment shaped a "hostile environment" in the workplace and constituted discrimination. Inconceivable in 1964, when Title VII was enacted, sexual harassment law, the most original and critical step toward workplace equality, set a global precedent. Although the states failed to ratify an ERA in 1982, in sum, a "de facto ERA" had evolved—an amalgam of statutes and court decisions that provided equal rights, in much the manner that Pauli Murray had envisioned in the 1960s. Courts discarded remnants of the "gendered imagination" that had prevailed in the era of single-sex protective laws. "[A] self-fulfilling cycle of discrimination . . . fostered employers' stereotypical views about women's commitment to work and their values as employees," the Supreme Court declared as it upheld a part of FMLA in 2003.[16]

Even as the de facto ERA took hold, obstacles to workplace equality curbed its impact. In the last third of the century a global economy evolved; manufacturing declined, unions shrank, and jobs vanished, often to developing nations with feeble labor standards. "[T]hirty years ago, women did not emerge from inequality at work into full economic citizenship in 'men's jobs,' the stable, well-paid factory or professional-managerial work that had been the backbone of postwar prosperity," historian Bethany Moreton observes in her recent study of Wal-Mart. "Rather, under the stress of deindustrialization, men's jobs came to look more like women's work." Fast food outlets and chain stores, the nation's largest employers, offered nonunion, low-wage jobs; employers turned to workers who were part-time or temporary or independent contractors rather than those who fell under full-time labor standards. A second obstacle: the feminist revolution left an unfinished agenda. Neither Congress nor the courts fulfilled the range of goals for working women that feminists had supported in the 1960s. Hope for a national day care system faded after 1971, when President Nixon vetoed the Child Development Act; national policy never included paid maternity leave, as proposed by the PCSW in 1963, or its post-FMLA equivalent, paid family leave. Employees who envisioned a European-style benefit system were unlikely to see it. Concern arose that the women's movement had been co-opted by a business ethos, that "how do I get up there" pervaded feminist values, and that the least advantaged women employees failed to benefit from workplace gains. Postprotection public policy at the century's end sought to reconcile competing demands of work and family; to redress systematic bias; and to reach women workers who lacked options beyond contingent, low-paid jobs.[17] Two routes were legislation and litigation.

Several legislative initiatives of the 1980s and 1990s included echoes of the long feud over protective laws. Comparable worth, or pay equity, a plan to raise wages in occupations that women dominated, failed to engage Congress but shaped labor negotiations and left imprints in state history, as in Washington and Minnesota. The campaign revived labor feminists' use of the term "comparable skills" in the first version of an equal pay bill in 1945. Proposals for pay equity evolved into demands for "Paycheck Fairness," legislation to amend the 1963 Equal Pay Act, to narrow reasons that employers might cite for pay disparity, and to bar retribution against complainants.[18] The omnibus Economic Equity Act of 1981–96, a bipartisan effort, revised regulations in areas adjacent to workplace issues: pensions, tax law, social security. The multifaceted legislation sought to dismantle gender systems inherited from New Deal law and to provide substantive equality, as enabling legislation for an ERA would have done. At least one ambitious option faltered. In the early 1990s the Clinton administration suggested that legislators consider use of unemployment insurance to fund family leave; that proposal made no headway. Still, the Economic Equity Act contributed to the de facto ERA. The law's piece-by-piece nature reminds historians of the "specific bills for specific ills" campaigns of social feminists, especially the League of Women Voters, as far back as the 1920s.[19]

Lawsuits under Title VII, the workhorse of antidiscrimination law, remained challenging. Such suits rested mainly on the initiative of private individuals. Problems that had arisen earlier persisted: corporate lawyers imposed extensive discovery demands; employers continued biased practices until compelled by courts to discard them. Lawsuits that sought redress for large groups of employees floundered. A long-term class action sex discrimination suit against Sears Roebuck that covered the years 1973–80, a case initiated by NOW and argued by the EEOC, failed in 1988, when the Seventh Circuit found the EEOC's statistical analysis faulty.[20] An even larger class action suit began in 2000 on behalf of up to 1.5 million current or former Wal-Mart workers. Californian Betty Dukes, the lead plaintiff, a six-year Wal-Mart employee, had been denied training needed for advancement. Charging discrimination in pay and promotion, the plaintiffs contended that Wal-Mart culture fostered gender bias. Dismissing the claim about corporate culture, the Supreme Court ruled 5–4 in *Wal-Mart v. Dukes* (2011) that the employees lacked enough in common to meet class action requirements; without "questions of law or fact common to the class," the case could not proceed as a class action. The plaintiffs remobilized, but the decision had raised the bar for class action suits. Justice Ginsburg, among the dissenters, charged that the majority "erred" in its focus on dissimilarities among class members "rather than on what unites them." She also found that Wal-Mart decision makers at the store level were "steeped in a corporate culture that perpetuates gender stereotypes" and that "gender bias suffused Wal-Mart's company culture."[21]

Supreme Court preference for the claims of business over those of employees drew most attention in a Title VII case that involved a single plaintiff, a middle manager who worked among male competitors on a "little industrial frontier," as economist Elizabeth Faulkner Baker might have labeled it in 1925. Lilly Ledbetter, employed at an Alabama Goodyear Tire plant, sued her company in 1998 for pay disparities over twenty years that had violated Title VII and the Equal Pay Act of 1963. "Goodyear gave me smaller raises than my male co-managers, over and over," she claimed. Only a chance incident, a coworker's letter, revealed the disparities, years after the fact. The Supreme Court agreed in *Ledbetter v. Goodyear Tire and Rubber Company* (2007) that discrimination had occurred but rejected Lilly Ledbetter's claim 5–4 because she had not filed a complaint within 180 days of the first incident, as provided in Title VII. Dissenting from the bench, a rare event, Justice Ginsberg took issue with Justice Samuel Alito's majority opinion. "Pay disparities, of the kind Ledbetter experienced, have a closer kinship to hostile work environment claims than to the charges of a single episode of discrimination," Justice Ginsburg argued. She appealed to Congress to step in, as she had in the wake of decisions in pregnancy cases of the 1970s. "This is not the first time the court has ordered a cramped interpretation of Title VII, incompatible with the statute's broad remedial purposes," Justice Ginsberg stated. "Once again the ball is in Congress's court. . . . [T]he Legislature may act to correct this Court's parsimonious reading of Title VII."[22]

In 2009 Congress amended Title VII by changing the statutory limitation period under the law; a violation now occurred each time an employee received a paycheck resulting from "a discriminatory compensation decision." The 2009 law insured to workers rights that the 2007 Supreme Court decision had invalidated. Aggrieved employees, as always, under Title VII, would have to take the initiative. The law would "make it easier for women to file a claim without it being kicked out of court because it's filed within a certain time frame," one of Lilly Ledbetter's lawyers told an interviewer, "but they've got to come out and challenge it."[23] Lilly Ledbetter's case reminded Americans that protection of equal rights under Title VII was a work in progress.

• • • • •

Conflict over single-sex protective labor laws pervades women's history in the twentieth century. The stunning success of the National Consumers' League and its indomitable general secretary Florence Kelley initiated a substantial body of state law. Enacted mainly between 1908 and 1917, women-only protective laws provided a springboard to general labor standards and offered tangible benefits: improved factory conditions, shorter hours, and the start of the minimum wage. The laws might also limit income, crush opportunity, and diminish citizenship. Classification by sex, "the law's graciousness to a disabled class," cemented women's secondary role in the workplace and society. The campaign for protection led directly to the establishment in 1920 of the Women's Bureau, a protectionist bulwark that defended the laws for five decades. By the 1920s division over the laws split the women's movement. Social feminists endorsed protective laws for women workers as a step toward "industrial equality." Members of the National Woman's Party, supporting an equal rights amendment, warned of hazards. "If women can be segregated as a class for special legislation," lawyer Gail Laughlin argued in 1922, "the same classification can be used for specific restrictions along any other line which may, at any time, appeal to the caprice or prejudice of our legislators."[24] New Deal victories—when the Supreme Court upheld a minimum wage law for women workers in 1937 and Congress passed FLSA in 1938—vindicated the long campaign for protective laws. Single-sex laws continued in the states, as did division among women activists. The feud between factions persisted through the 1950s and into the early 1960s.

The impact of the civil rights movement and Title VII of the 1964 Civil Rights Act suddenly changed protection's fate. By 1966 lawsuits targeting single-sex protective laws were underway, and within five years the laws sank in court and in the states. Debate over maximum hours laws persisted, but as Esther Peterson argued in 1970, "history is moving in this direction." Lawsuits over the rights of pregnant workers and fetal disability regulation continued in federal court through the 1980s. A final dismissal of protective law came in the *Johnson Controls* decision of 1991. "Concern for a woman's existing or potential offspring historically has been the choice for denying women equal employment opportunities," Justice Blackmun stated. "Congress has left this choice to the woman as hers to make."[25]

Clara Berwick Colby, Florence Kelley's correspondent of the 1880s, had reached a similar conclusion about decision making earlier in the century. Colby moved in 1904 from Iowa to Portland, Oregon, bringing along her suffragist publication, the *Woman's Tribune*. In 1906, when the Oregon Supreme Court upheld the state's ten-hour law for women workers, Clara Colby was at hand in Portland to voice her opinion. "The whole subject is very difficult and it had better be left to woman's own judgment as to what is necessary and desirable," she observed. "The state has no right to lay any disability upon a woman as an individual and if it does as a mother, it should give her a maternity pension which would tend to even up conditions and be better for the family."[26]

Acknowledgments

■ ■ ■

I AM PROFOUNDLY INDEBTED to Alice Kessler-Harris and Cynthia Harrison, who reviewed my manuscript for the Princeton University Press, for their expertise, insights, generosity, and welcome suggestions. I am similarly indebted to Melvin I. Urofsky and Rosalind Rosenberg for their invaluable advice and encouragement over the past decade. I am grateful to many friends and colleagues who read chapters, shared research, provided documents, wrote recommendations, and otherwise offered assistance over the years. Let me thank Liz Abzug, David E. Bernstein, Ellen Chesler, Robert D. Johnston, Lisa Keller, Ellen S. Leventhal, Premilla Nadasen, Richard Pious, Richard Polenberg, Thad Russell, Martha Saxton, Herb Sloan, Lisa Tiersten, Deborah Valenze, Carl Wennerlind, and Susan Zuccotti. I am grateful to the National Endowment for the Humanities for a fellowship to work on protective laws in 1999–2000; to members of the New York Bar Association Legal History Committee for their attention in 2009; and, overwhelmingly, to the members of the History Department at Barnard College, past and present, who have been a reservoir of collegiality and enthusiasm.

My involvement with the Princeton University Press has been a wonderful experience. I am deeply grateful to editor-in-chief Brigitta van Rheinberg for her solicitude and advice, and to Claudia Acevedo, editorial assistant, and Leslie Grundfest, production editor, for their exceptional patience and help. I thank copyeditor Dawn Hall for her hard work; thanks also to senior copywriter Theresa Liu and to Dave Luljak, my superb indexer. My gratitude to the editors of Politics and Society in Twentieth-Century America at Princeton University Press; it is an honor to be part of their series. Finally, I thank my family for enduring many years of protective laws and for much assistance along the way. I am very grateful to Isser Woloch, David Woloch, Alex Woloch, Dana Goldberg, and Karla Oeler. Thank you also to Lewis Woloch and Benjamin Woloch, who have enriched our lives, who have become wonderful readers, and who might like to see their names in print.

Notes

■ ■ ■

CHAPTER 1: ROOTS OF PROTECTION

1. Florence Kelley, *Autobiography of Florence Kelley: Notes on Sixty Years*, ed. Kathryn K. Sklar (Chicago: Charles H. Kerr, 1986), 17, 83; Kelley, "The Factory Laws in Illinois" (1894), in *Social Justice Feminists in the United States and Germany: A Dialogue in Documents, 1885–1933*, ed. Kathryn Kish Sklar, Anja Schüler, and Susan Strasser (Ithaca, NY: Cornell University Press, 1998), 91, 93–94; and Kelley, *Some Ethical Gains through Legislation* (New York: Macmillan, 1905), 141.

2. Daniel T. Rodgers, *Atlantic Crossings: Social Politics in a Progressive Age* (Cambridge, MA: Belknap Press of Harvard University Press, 1998), 235–39; Ulla Wikander, Alice Kessler-Harris, and Jane Lewis, eds., *Protecting Women: Labor Legislation in Europe, the United States, and Australia, 1880–1920* (Urbana: University of Illinois Press, 1995), 7–14. For European women's debate over protective legislation, 1890–1914, see Karen Offen, *European Feminisms 1700–1950: A Political History* (Stanford, CA: Stanford University Press, 2000), 230–42.

3. For Progressive concerns, see Robert H. Wiebe, *The Search for Order, 1877–1920* (New York: Hill and Wang, 1967); Robert M. Crunden, *Ministers of Reform: The Progressives' Achievement in American Civilization, 1889–1920* (New York: Basic Books, 1982); Rodgers, *Atlantic Crossings*; and Michael McGerr, *A Fierce Discontent: The Rise and Fall of the Progressive Movement in America, 1870–1920* (New York: Free Press, 2003).

4. For Progressive Era protective laws, see Elizabeth Faulkner Baker, *Protective Labor Legislation* (New York: Columbia University Press, 1925); Clara M. Beyer, *History of Labor Legislation for Women in Three States*, Bulletin 66, pt. 1, Women's Bureau, US Department of Labor (Washington, DC: Government Printing Office, 1929); and Elizabeth Brandeis, "Labor Legislation and the Constitution," in *History of Labor in the United States*, vol. 3, ed. John R. Commons et al. (New York: Macmillan, 1935), 399–697. Recent discussions include Judith A. Baer, *The Chains of Protection: The Judicial Response to Protective Labor Legislation* (Westport, CT: Greenwood Press, 1978); Eileen Boris, *Home to Work: Motherhood and the Politics of Industrial Homework in the United States* (New York: Cambridge University Press, 1994); Claudia Goldin, *Understanding the Gender Gap: An Economic History of American Women* (New York: Oxford University Press, 1990), chap. 7; Vivien Hart, *Bound by Our Constitution: Women, Workers, and the Minimum Wage* (Princeton, NJ: Princeton University Press, 1994); Alice Kessler-Harris, *Out to Work: A History of Wage-Earning Women in the United States* (New York: Oxford University Press, 1982), chap. 7; Susan Lehrer, *Origins of Protective Labor Legislation for Women, 1905–1925* (Albany: State University of New York Press, 1987); Julie Novkov, *Constituting Workers, Protecting Women: Gender, Law, and Labor in the Progressive Era and New Deal Years* (Ann Arbor: University of Michigan Press, 2001); Kathryn Kish Sklar, *Florence Kelley and the Nation's Work: The Rise of Women's Political Culture, 1830–1900* (New Haven, CT: Yale University Press, 1995); Theda Skocpol, *Protecting Soldiers and Mothers: The Political Origins of Social Policy in the*

United States (Cambridge, MA: Harvard University Press, 1992), chap. 7; Landon R. Y. Storrs, *Civilizing Capitalism: The National Consumers' League, Women's Activism, and Labor Standards in the New Deal Era* (Chapel Hill: University of North Carolina Press, 2000), chaps. 1 and 2; and Nancy Woloch, *Muller v. Oregon: A Brief History with Documents* (Boston: Bedford Books, 1996), introduction. Wikander, Kessler-Harris, and Lewis, *Protecting Women*, provides a comparative perspective. The quotation is from Alice Hamilton, "Protection for Women Workers," *Forum* 72 (August 1924): 160.

5. E. Brandeis, "Labor Legislation," 457, 461, 541.

6. William E. Forbath, *Law and the Shaping of the American Labor Movement* (Cambridge, MA: Harvard University Press, 1991), 43; David R. Roediger and Philip Foner, *Our Own Times: A History of American Labor and the Working Day* (Westport, CT: Greenwood Press, 1989), 159; Kathryn Kish Sklar, "Hull House in the 1890s: A Community of Women Reformers," *Signs* 10 (Summer 1985): 658–77.

7. "Report of the Secretary," in NCL, *Eighth Annual Report* (1907), 33; Baer, *Chains of Protection*, 17; Kessler-Harris, *Out to Work*, 184; Woloch, *Muller*, 6–7.

8. Baker, *Protective Labor Legislation*, 57–59, 71–99, 144; Florence P. Smith, *Chronological Development of Labor Legislation for Women in the United States*, Bulletin of the Women's Bureau No. 66 (Washington, DC: Government Printing Office, 1929), 248–49, 282–85; Woloch, *Muller*, 7.

9. David A. Moss, *Socializing Security: Progressive-Era Economists and the Origins of American Social Policy* (Cambridge. MA: Harvard University Press, 1996). Chapter 6 on "The Gendered Politics of Protection" suggests that AALL economists and National Consumers' League leaders sometimes disagreed. Kathryn Kish Sklar compares the AALL and NCL in "Two Political Cultures in the Progressive Era: The National Consumers' League and the American Association for Labor Legislation," in *U.S. History as Women's History: New Feminist Essays*, ed. Linda K. Kerber, Alice Kessler-Harris, and Kathryn Kish Sklar (Chapel Hill: University of North Carolina Press, 1995), 36–62. Progressive Era social workers, writes Robert Wiebe, "acted first to disassociate themselves from philanthropy and establish themselves as a distinct field within the social sciences" (*The Search for Order*, 120). For women economists, see Nancy Folbre, "The Sphere of Women in Early Twentieth-Century Economics," in *Gender and American Social Science: The Formative Years*, ed. Helene Silverberg (Princeton, NJ: Princeton University Press, 1998), 35–60.

10. For contrasting interpretations of the impact of clubwomen in the campaign for protection, see Skocpol, *Protecting Soldiers and Mothers*, 396–404, and Landon R. Y. Storrs, *Civilizing Capitalism*, 37–38, 285. Ellen Henrotin's activism is discussed in Sklar, *Florence Kelley and the Nation's Work*, 261–62. For GFWC biennial conventions, see Mary I. Wood, *History of the General Federation of Women's Clubs for the Twenty-Two Years of Its Organization* (New York: History Department, General Federation of Women's Clubs, 1912), "Third Biennial," 71, and "Fourth Biennial," 109–10.

11. Lehrer, *Protective Labor Legislation*, chap. 6; Nancy Schrom Dye, *As Equals and as Sisters: Feminism, the Labor Movement, and the Women's Trade Union League of New York* (Columbia: University of Missouri Press, 1980), chap. 7; Annelise Orleck, *Common Sense and a Little Fire: Women and Working-Class Politics in the United States, 1900–1965* (Chapel Hill: University of North Carolina Press, 1995), parts 1 and 2. Quotes are from Margaret Dreier Robins, *Life and Labor* 1 (November 1911): 325,

cited in Lehrer, *Protective Labor Legislation*, 125; Rose Schneiderman, n.d., cited in Orleck, *Common Sense and a Little Fire*, 123 and 124. For NWTUL's transatlantic roots, see Robin Miller Jacoby, *The British and American Women's Trade Union Leagues, 1890–1925: A Case Study of Feminism and Class* (Brooklyn, NY: Carlson, 1994).

12. Maud Nathan, *The Story of an Epoch-Making Movement* (New York: Doubleday, Page, 1906), xiii. William L. O'Neill astutely sums up the NCL's role in *Feminism in America: A History*, 2nd. rev. ed. (New Brunswick, NJ: Transaction, 1989), 95–98, 151–53.

13. Kelley, *Autobiography*, 71–72; Sklar, "Hull House," 658–77; Sklar, *Florence Kelley and the Nation's Work*, part 2; and Kathryn Kish Sklar and Beverly Wilson Palmer, eds., *The Selected Letters of Florence Kelley, 1869–1931* (Urbana: University of Illinois Press, 2009). For the letter of 1894, see FK to Miss Williams, November 18, 1894, in Sklar and Palmer, *Selected Letters*, 79. Sklar discusses her challenging experience as Florence Kelley's biographer in "Coming to Terms with Florence Kelley: The Tale of a Reluctant Biographer," in Sara Alpern et al., eds., *The Challenge of Feminist Biography: Writing the Lives of Modern American Women* (Urbana: University of Illinois Press, 1992), 17–33.

Florence Kelley's three children, age six and under when she won custody in 1892, lived primarily or at least frequently thereafter with a series of family friends and relatives, collectively or individually, until they entered boarding schools. See the many references to "childhood living arrangements" for John, Margaret, and Nicholas Kelley in Sklar and Palmer, *Selected Letters*, 549; see also Sklar, *Florence Kelley*, 178–80, 223, 225, 311, 371.

14. Karen Hunt poses "the woman question" in *Equivocal Feminists: The Social Democratic Federation and the Woman Question, 1884–1911* (Cambridge: Cambridge University Press, 1996), 1. For Florence Kelley's letter to the *Woman's Tribune* editor (Clara Colby), Heidelberg, Germany (ca. April 1885), see Sklar and Palmer, *Selected Letters*, 25–26. For Kelley's speech to the New York Association of Collegiate Alumnae, see Florence Kelley, "The Need of Theoretical Preparation for Philanthropic Work," in Sklar, *Autobiography*, 104, and Sklar, *Florence Kelley*, 129–35.

15. Josephine Goldmark, *Impatient Crusader: Florence Kelley's Life Story* (Urbana: University of Illinois Press, 1953), 57–59; Sklar, *Florence Kelley*, 256–57.

16. Goldmark, *Impatient Crusader*, 51–53; The Consumers' League of the City of New York, *Seventh Annual Report* (1897), 2; Maud Nathan, "Women Who Work and Women Who Spend," *Annals of the American Academy of Political and Social Science* 27 (1906): 646–50. Daniel T. Rodgers describes the pioneer New York City consumers' league as a "genteel boycott society," *Atlantic Crossings*, 14. Irwin Yellowitz discusses the league's tactics of "direct action" by consumers in *Labor and the Progressive Movement in New York State, 1897–1916* (Ithaca, NY: Cornell University Press, 1965), 42–49. For the NYC league, the Consumers' League of the City of New York, also called the New York Consumers' League (NYCL), see Lara Vapnek, *Breadwinners: Working Women and Economic Independence, 1865–1920* (Urbana: University of Illinois Press, 2009), 77–91. According to historian Dennis Irven Harrison, the Consumers' League of Ohio worked closely with the Urban League, NAACP, and other black organizations. See Harrison, "The Consumers' League of Ohio: Women and Reform, 1909–1937," (PhD diss., Case Western Reserve University, 1975), xii, 70.

17. Nathan, "Women Who Work," 646; Leonora O'Reilly speech in Consumers' League of the City of New York, "Report for the Year Ending December, 1907," 50–51; NCL, *Second Annual Report* (1901), 14; Nan Enstad, *Ladies of Labor, Girls of Adventure: Working Women, Popular Culture, and Labor Politics at the Turn of the Twentieth Century* (New York: Columbia University Press, 1999), 4–5. See also Storrs, *Civilizing Capitalism*, 19.

18. NCL, *Second Annual Report* (1901), 14; NCL, *Fifth Annual Report* (1904), 7; NCL, *Third Annual Report* (1902), 24–25; NCL, *Eighth Annual Report* (1907), 16; Goldmark, *Impatient Crusader*, 58–60; Rodgers, *Atlantic Crossings*, 237; and Kathryn Kish Sklar, "Two Political Cultures," 48–49. For Maud Nathan, see Joyce Antler, *The Journey Home: How Jewish Women Shaped Modern America* (New York: Schocken Books, 1997), 54–61, and Ellen Condliffe Lagemann, *A Generation of Women: Education in the Lives of Progressive Reformers* (Cambridge, MA: Harvard University Press, 1979), chap. 2. Jacqueline Kay Dirks compares Nathan and Kelley as leaders in "Righteous Goods: Women's Production, Reform Publicity, and the National Consumers' League, 1891–1919" (PhD diss., Yale University, 1996), 47–58.

19. Wood, *History of GFWC*, "Sixth Biennial, 139, 146–47 and "Seventh Biennial," 164, 173–74; Florence Kelley, "The Sordid Waste of Genius," *Charities* 12 (May 7, 1904): 453–54, cited in Dirks, "Righteous Goods," 72; Skocpol, *Protecting Soldiers and Mothers*, 392–93; Storrs, *Civilizing Capitalism*, 37–38; Dirks, "Righteous Goods," 71.

20. Clement E. Vose, "The National Consumers' League and the Brandeis Brief," *Midwest Journal of Political Science* 1 (November 1957): 268, 270, 272; Skocpol, *Protecting Soldiers and Mothers*, 382–96; Kathryn Kish Sklar, "The Historical Foundations of Women's Power in the Creation of the American Welfare State, 1830–1930," in *Mothers of a New World*, ed. Seth Koven and Sonya Michel (New York: Routledge, 1993), 75.

21. Goldmark, *Impatient Crusader*, 58; Blanche Wiesen Cook, ed., *Crystal Eastman on Women and Revolution* (New York: Oxford University Press, 1978), 159.

22. Frances Perkins, "Reminiscences of Frances Perkins," part 1, 58–59 (1951–55), Columbia University Oral History Research Collection; John Louis Recchiuti, *Civic Engagement: Social Science and Progressive-Era Reform in New York City* (Philadelphia: University of Pennsylvania Press, 2007), 136–39.

23. Kelley, *Some Ethical Gains*, 168, 107–09, 126, 142, 111–12; Woloch, *Muller*, 24.

24. Kelley, *Some Ethical Gains*, 128, 163–68, 144, 135; Woloch, *Muller*, 24–25.

25. Kelley, *Some Ethical Gains*, 142.

26. Elizabeth Beardsley Butler, *Women and the Trades, Pittsburgh, 1907–1908* (New York: Charities Publications Committee, 1909), 372–73. Butler, a Barnard graduate of 1905, had served as an officer of the New Jersey Consumers' League. The Pittsburgh Survey was a sociological research project.

27. Leslie Woodcock Tentler, *Wage-Earning Women: Industrial Work and Family Life in the United States, 1900–1930* (New York: Oxford University Press, 1979), chap. 1. For a study of independence and initiative among Progressive Era working women, see Vapnek, *Breadwinners*.

28. Butler, *Women and the Trades*, 83; Mary White Ovington, *Half a Man: The Status of the Negro in New York* (New York: Longman, Green, 1911), 143; Barbara Mayer Wertheimer, *We Were There: The Story of Working Women in America* (New York: Pantheon, 1977), 227–28; Sarah Haley, "'Like I Was a Man': Chain Gangs, Gender, and the Domestic Carceral Sphere in Jim Crow Georgia," *Signs: Journal of Women in Cul-*

ture and Society 38 (Autumn 2013): 53–77. For the impact of World War I on black women's employment, see [Emma L. Shields] *Negro Women in Industry*, Bulletin of the Women's Bureau No. 20 (Washington: Government Printing Office, 1922), 2-3. As of 1920, according to the WB, black women constituted over 15 percent of women in industry; tobacco, food, and clothing production employed the largest numbers (36 percent, 12 percent, and 11 percent, respectively).

29. Kelley, *Some Ethical Gains*, 133; E. Brandeis, "Labor Legislation," 462; Sklar, "Hull House," 675; Sklar, "Two Political Cultures," 41. Elizabeth Faulkner Baker uses the term "entering wedge" in *Protective Labor Legislation*, 438.

30. Kelley, "Women Factory Inspectors in the United States," in Sklar, Schüler, and Strasser, *Social Justice Feminists*, 142.

31. *Chicago Tribune*, April 23, 1894, 7, quoted in Sklar, *Florence Kelley*, 261–62; George Martin, *Madame Secretary: Frances Perkins* (Boston: Houghton Mifflin, 1976), 98; Benjamin Cohen to Felix Frankfurter, January 8, 1932, FF Papers, box 45, cited in Hart, *Bound by Our Constitution*, 8.

32. Pat Thane, *Foundations of the Welfare State* (London: Longmans, 1982); Hart, *Bound by Our Constitution*, chaps. 2, 3; Wikander, Kessler-Harris, and Lewis, *Protecting Women*, chap. 3; Beatrice Webb, *Women and the Factory Acts* (London: Fabian Society, 1896), 4.

33. Florence Kelley, "The Sordid Waste of Genius," *Charities* 12 (May 7, 1904): 453–54, cited in Dirks, "Righteous Goods," 72. For Kelley and socialism, see Sklar, "Introduction," to Kelley, *Autobiography*, 8, and Dirks, "Righteous Goods," 58. For one NCL activist's preoccupation with investigation more than with legal strategy, see Florence L. Sanville, *The Opening Door* (Philadelphia: Franklin Publishing, 1967).

34. NWTUL, "Why Labor Laws for Women" (pamphlet) (Chicago: National Women's Trade Union League, 1926), cited in Dye, *As Equals and as Sisters*, 152; Sklar, "The Historical Foundations of Women's Power in the Creation of the American Welfare State, 1830–1930," in Koven and Michel, *Mothers of a New World*, 49; Wood, *History of the GFWC*, 110; Skocpol, *Protecting Soldiers and Mothers*, 398.

35. Josephine Goldmark, *Fatigue and Efficiency: A Study in Industry* (New York: Charities Publications Committee, 1912), 254–55, 283.

36. Orleck, *Common Sense and a Little Fire*, 125; Florence Kelley, "The Right to Differ," *The Survey* 49 (December 15, 1922): 375–76. For changing child custody practices that favored mothers, see Michael Grossberg, *Governing the Hearth: Law and the Family in 19th-Century America* (Chapel Hill: University of North Carolina Press, 1985), 248–53, 281–85. Barbara Young Welke discusses the role of female physical vulnerability in lawsuits against railroads and streetcar companies in *Recasting American Liberty: Gender, Race, Law, and the Railroad Revolution, 1865–1920* (New York: Cambridge University Press, 2001), chap. 2.

37. E. Brandeis, "Labor Legislation," 547; Alice Kessler-Harris, *In Pursuit of Equity: Women, Men, and the Quest for Economic Citizenship in 20th-Century America* (New York: Oxford University Press, 2001), 5–6; Annie Marion MacLean, *Wage-Earning Women* (New York: Macmillan, 1910), 177–78; Hart, *Bound by Our Constitution*, 98–100, 131–32. For discussions of the family wage, see Folbre, "The Sphere of Women," 36–40; Alice Kessler-Harris, *A Woman's Wage: Historical Meanings and Social Consequences* (Lexington: University Press of Kentucky, 1990), chap. 1; and Thomas C. Leonard, "Protecting Family and Race: The Progressive Case for Regulating Women's

Work," *American Journal of Economics and Sociology* 64 (July 2005): 757–91. For a definition of social feminism, see William L. O'Neill, *Feminism in America*, xxiv. To O'Neill, social feminists, "while believing in women's rights, generally subordinated them to broad social reforms they thought were more urgent."

38. Florence Kelley, "Married Women in Industry," *Proceedings of the Academy of Political Science* 1 (1910): 90–96. For the European background of the campaign against married women's work, see Offen, *European Feminisms*, 234.

39. Moss, *Socializing Security*, 111–12; Beatrix Hoffman, *The Wages of Sickness: The Politics of Health Insurance in Progressive America* (Chapel Hill: University of North Carolina Press, 2001), chap. 7, especially 140–45.

40. Louisa Dana Harding, "Male Socialism," *Woman's Standard* 21 (April 1, 1908): 2, in Melvin I. Urofsky, ed., *The Public Debate over Controversial Supreme Court Decisions* (Washington, DC: CQ Press, 2006), 108–9.

41. Ardis Cameron, *Radicals of the Worst Sort: Laboring Women in Lawrence, Massachusetts, 1860–1912* (Urbana: University of Illinois Press, 1993), 94.

42. State of New York, *Fourth Report of the Factory Investigating Commission* (Albany: J.B. Lyon Company, Printers, 1915), 2825.

43. John R. Commons, "Eight-Hour Shifts by Federal Legislation," *American Labor Legislation Review* 7 (March 1917): 141.

44. Sophonisba Breckinridge, "Legislative Control of Women's Work," *Journal of Political Economy* 14 (February 1906): 107–8. For Breckinridge's career, see Ellen F. Fitzpatrick, *Endless Crusade: Women Social Scientists and Progressive Reform* (New York: Oxford University Press, 1990), especially chap. 7.

45. S. P. Breckinridge, "The Illinois Ten-Hour Law," *Journal of Political Economy* 18 (June 1910): 467; Fitzpatrick, *Endless Crusade*, 170.

46. "Labor's Dangerous Proposed Amendment to the Constitution of New York," in National Association of Manufacturers, *American Industries* (October 16, 1905), quoted in E. Brandeis, "Labor Legislation," 545.

47. Florence Kelley, "The Factory Laws in Illinois," in Sklar, Schüler, and Strasser, *Social Justice Feminists*, 94.

48. *The Monitor: Official Publication of the Association of M'F'RS and Merchants (of New York State)* 5 (March, 1919): 16; State of New York, *Fourth Report of the New York State Factory Investigating Commission*, (1915), 2718.

49. Rome G. Brown, "Oregon Minimum Wage Cases," *Minnesota Law Review* 1 (June 1917): 486; *Life and Labor* (June 1921), cited in Orleck, *Common Sense and a Little Fire*, 139.

50. Samuel Gompers, "Judicial Vindication of Labor's Claim," *American Federationist* 7, 283, 284, cited in Forbath, *Law*, 130; Gompers, *Seventy Years of Life and Labor* (New York: E. P. Dutton, 1925), 1: 385; Paul Kens, *Judicial Power and Reform Politics: The Anatomy of Lochner v. New York* (Lawrence: University Press of Kansas, 1990), 22–23; Forbath, *Law*, 15; E. Brandeis, "Labor Legislation," 555–57; Julie Greene, *Pure and Simple Politics: The American Federation of Labor and Political Activism, 1881–1917* (Cambridge: Cambridge University Press, 1998), 80–81, 255–56.

51. *American Federationist* 21 (July 1914): 544, cited in Lehrer, *Origins of Protective Labor Legislation*, 152; "Testimony of Thomas P. Ryan," New York State, *Factory Investigating Commission* (1915), 2873; Kelley, "The New Woman's Party," *The Survey* (March 5, 1921): 827–28. AFL attitudes toward women workers are discussed in E. Brandeis, "Labor Legislation," 555–57; Kessler-Harris, *Out to Work*, 151–55, 202–5;

and Alice Kessler-Harris, "Where Are the Organized Women Workers?" *Feminist Studies* 3 (Fall 1975): 92–105. For the AFL and protective policy, see also Ronnie Steinberg Ratner, "The Paradox of Protection: Maximum Hours Legislation in the United States, *International Labour Review* 119 (March/April 1980): 190–91.

52. Forbath, *Law*, 9, 33, 38–39.

53. Lawrence M. Friedman, *A History of American Law* (New York: Simon and Schuster, 1985), 634–35, 640, 642; Melvin I. Urofsky, *Louis D. Brandeis: A Life* (New York: Pantheon Books, 2009), chap. 9; Urofsky, *A Mind of One Piece: Brandeis and American Reform* (New York: Scribner, 1971), 24–26.

54. Arnold M. Paul, *Conservative Crisis and the Rule of Law: Attitudes of Bench and Bar, 1887–1895* (Ithaca, NY: Cornell University Press, 1960), 164–65; Urofsky, *A Mind of One Piece*, 23–24; Brewer's dissent in *Budd v. New York*, 143 U.S. 551.

55. Morton J. Horwitz, *The Transformation of American Law, 1870–1960: The Crisis of Legal Orthodoxy* (New York: Oxford University Press, 1992), 16.

56. Roscoe Pound, "The Scope and Purpose of Sociological Jurisprudence," *Harvard Law Review* 25 (April 1912): 489–516; Felix Frankfurter, *Reminiscences* (New York: Reynal, 1960), 95; Louis D. Brandeis, "The Living Law," *Illinois Law Review* 10 (February 1916): 463, 469–70; *State v. Buchanan* 19 Wash. 602 (1902).

57. For reformers' dialogue with the courts, see Hart, *Bound by Our Constitution*, 5–9, and Joan G. Zimmerman, "The Jurisprudence of Equality: The Women's Minimum Wage, the First Equal Rights Amendment, and *Adkins v. Children's Hospital*, 1905–1923," *Journal of American History* 78 (June 1991): 192–93. Reformers' relationships with their lawyers is discussed in Hart, *Bound by Our Constitution*, 148–49, and Sybil Lipschultz, "Social Feminism and Legal Discourse: 1908–1923," *Yale Journal of Law and Feminism* 2 (Fall 1989): 131–60.

58. For the gendered role of law, see Michael Grossberg, "Institutionalizing Masculinity: The Law as a Masculine Profession," in *Meanings for Manhood: Construction of Masculinity in Victorian America*, ed. Mark C. Carnes and Clyde Griffen (Chicago: University of Chicago Press, 1990), 133–51, and Barbara Young Welke, *Law and the Borders of Belonging in the Long Nineteenth-Century United States* (Cambridge: Cambridge University Press, 2010). For women lawyers in the Progressive Era, see Felice Batlan, "Notes from the Margins: Florence Kelley and the Making of Sociological Jurisprudence," in *Transformations in Legal History: Law, Ideology, and Methods, Essays in Honor of Morton J. Horwitz*, ed. Daniel W. Hamilton and Alfred L. Brophy (Cambridge, MA: Harvard University Press, 2010), 2: 239–53; the quotes are from p. 241.

CHAPTER 2: GENDER, PROTECTION, AND THE COURTS, 1895–1907

1. Charles Fairman, *History of the Supreme Court of the United States: Reconstruction and Reunion, 1864–1888* (New York: Macmillan, 1971), 1364–72. In *In re Bradwell*, 55 Ill. 535 (1869), the Illinois Supreme Court, in a second hearing, affirmed Bradwell's rejection. This chapter is based in part on Nancy Woloch, *Muller v. Oregon: A Brief History with Documents* (Boston: Bedford Books, 1996), 12–18.

2. *Slaughterhouse Cases*, 16 Wall. 36 (1873); *Myra Bradwell v. State of Illinois*, 15 Wall. 130 (1873). For the *Slaughterhouse Cases*, see Ronald M. Labbe and Jonathan Lurie, *The Slaughterhouse Cases: Regulation, Reconstruction, and the Fourteenth*

Amendment (Lawrence: University Press of Kansas, 2003). Myra Bradwell gave up her fight to join the bar in the 1870s; the Illinois bar accepted her in 1892. For the *Bradwell* cases, see Frances E. Olsen, "From False Paternalism to False Equality: Judicial Assaults on Feminist Community, Illinois, 1869–1895," *Michigan Law Review* 84 (June 1986): 1518–41.

3. Labbe and Lurie, *Slaughterhouse Cases*, 14.

4. Garrett Epps, *Democracy Reborn: The Fourteenth Amendment and the Fight for Equal Rights in Post–Civil War America* (New York: Henry Holt, 2008), 262. For the Fourteenth Amendment, see also William E. Nelson, *The Fourteenth Amendment: From Political Principle to Judicial Doctrine* (Cambridge, MA: Harvard University Press, 1988). Nelson points out that the amendment unleashed two contradictory American beliefs: in equality and in legislatures' power to make law (197–98).

5. Melvin I. Urofsky, "State Courts and Protective Legislation during the Progressive Era: A Reevaluation," *Journal of American History* 72 (June 1985): 65–55; *Ritchie v. People*, 155 Ill. 98 (1895).

6. *Slaughterhouse Cases*, 83 U.S. (16 Wall.) 36, 109–10 (1873); Arnold M. Paul, *Conservative Crisis and the Rule of Law: Attitudes of Bench and Bar, 1887–1895* (Ithaca, NY: Cornell University Press, 1960), 6–7.

7. *In re Jacobs*, 98 N.Y. 98 (1885); *Godcharles v. Wigeman*, 113 Pa. St. 431 (1886); *Millet v. People*, 117 Ill. 194 (1886); Paul, *Conservative Crisis*, 16; *Allgeyer v. Louisiana*, 165 U.S. 578 (1897). For the *Jacobs* case, see William E. Forbath, *Law and the Shaping of the American Labor Movement* (Cambridge, MA: Harvard University Press, 1991), 39–43; Eileen Boris, *Home to Work: Motherhood and the Politics of Industrial Homework* (Cambridge: Cambridge University Press, 1994), chap. 1; and Felice Batlan, "A Reevaluation of the New York Court of Appeals: The Home, the Market, and Labor, 1885–1905," *Social Inquiry* 27 (Summer 2002): 513–18.

8. Josephine Goldmark, *Fatigue and Efficiency: A Study in Industry* (New York: Charities Publications Committee, 1912), 244; *Holden v. Hardy*, 169 U.S. 366 (1898); Holmes's dissent in *Lochner v. New York*, 198 U.S. 45 (1905). Claudio J. Katz tracks the impact of disparities in bargaining power on court decisions in "Protective Labor Legislation in the Courts: Substantive Due Process and Fairness in the Progressive Era," *Law and History Review* 31 (May 2013): 275–323.

9. *Slaughterhouse Cases*, 83 U.S. 36, 62 (1873); Urofsky, "State Courts," 67.

10. Howard Gillman, *The Constitution Besieged: The Rise and Demise of Lochner Era Police Powers Jurisprudence* (Durham, NC: Duke University Press, 1993), 7, 15.

11. The quotes are from *Lochner v. New York*, 198 U.S. 45 (1905), and *Wenham v. State*, 91 N.W. Neb. 421 (1902).

12. Clara Beyer, *History of Labor Legislation for Women in Three States*, Bulletin of the Women's Bureau, No. 66 (Washington, DC: Government Printing Office, 1929), 17, 20.

13. *Commonwealth v. Hamilton Manufacturing*, 120 Mass. 383 (1876); Julie Novkov, *Constituting Workers, Protecting Women: Gender, Law, and Labor in the Progressive Era and New Deal Years* (Ann Arbor: University of Michigan Press, 2010), 60–61.

14. *Ritchie v. People* (1895) and its background is discussed in Kathryn Kish Sklar, *Florence Kelley and the Nation's Work: The Rise of Women's Political Culture, 1830–1900* (New Haven, CT: Yale University Press, 1995), chap. 10; Kathryn Kish Sklar, "Hull House in the 1890s: A Community of Women Reformers," *Signs* 10 (Summer 1985): 658–77; Olsen, "From False Paternalism to False Equality," and Earl. R. Becker, *A*

History of Illinois Labor Legislation (Chicago: University of Chicago Press, 1929), 188–90.

15. Sklar, *Florence Kelley*, 255, 263, 391. According to Sklar, 251, the W. C. Ritchie Company employed 217 women, sixty-four men, fifty-eight girls under sixteen, and eleven boys under sixteen.

16. "Brief and Argument on Behalf of Plaintiffs in Error," by Moran, Kraus, and Mayer, *Ritchie v. People*, Supreme Court of Illinois, Southern Grand Division, May term 1894, 20, 45, 48, 52, 61.

17. Nancy S. Erickson, "*Muller v. Oregon* Reconsidered: The Origins of a Sex-Based Doctrine of Freedom of Contract," *Labor History* 30 (Spring 1989): 241; Sklar, *Florence Kelley*, 257; "Brief and Argument of Defendant in Error," *Ritchie v. People*, Supreme Court of Illinois, Southern Grand Division, May term, 1894, 11, 12, 13, 14–18, 44, 46, 47.

18. *Ritchie v. People*, 155 Ill. 98 (1895).

19. Goldmark, *Impatient Crusader*, 144; NCL, *Eighth Annual Report* (1907), 19; NCL, *Tenth Annual Report* (1909), 22; "Comment," *Yale Law Journal* 4 (1895): 200–201, quoted in Gillman, *Constitution Besieged*, 242.

20. *In re Bradwell*, 55 Ill. 535 (1869); *Bradwell v. Illinois*, 83 U.S. (16 Wall.) 130 (1873); Olsen, "From False Paternalism to False Equality," 1522, 1537–38.

21. Erickson, "*Muller v. Oregon* Reconsidered," 241; Sklar, *Florence Kelley*, 259–60; Cynthia Eagle Russett, *Sexual Science: The Victorian Construction of Womanhood* (Cambridge, MA: Harvard University Press, 1989), 143–48; Theda Skocpol, *Protecting Soldiers and Mothers: The Political Origins of Social Policy in the United States* (Cambridge, MA: Harvard University Press, 1992), 368–71; Thomas C. Leonard, "Protecting Family and Race: The Progressive Case for Regulating Women's Work," *American Journal of Economics and Sociology* 64 (July 2005): 757–91.

22. Urofsky, "State Courts," 77; *State v. Holden*, 14 Utah 71 (1896) concerned the mine; *State v. Holden*, 14 Utah 96 (1896) concerned the smelter.

23. *Holden v. Hardy*, 169 U.S. 366 (1898); Katz, "Protective Labor Legislation," 298.

24. *Holden v. Hardy*, 169 U.S. 366 (1898); Gillman, *Constitution Beseiged*, 123–25.

25. Felix Frankfurter, assisted by Josephine Goldmark, *The Case for the Shorter Work Day* (New York: National Consumers' League, 1916), 1–10, covers laws that limited men's work hours. For the Utah exclusionary law of 1896, see Florence P. Smith, *Chronological Development of Labor Legislation for Women in the United States* (Washington, DC: Government Printing Office, 1929), 257, 283.

26. *Commonwealth v. Beatty*, 15 Pa. Supp. 5 (1900). Judith A. Baer discusses turn-of-the-century women's maximum hours cases in *The Chains of Protection: The Judicial Response to Women's Labor Legislation* (Westport, CT: Greenwood Press, 1978), 53–55.

27. *Commonwealth v. Beatty*, 15 Pa. Supp. 5 (1900); Elizabeth Brandeis, "Labor Legislation and the Constitution," in *History of Labor in the United States*, vol. 3, ed. John R. Commons et al. (New York: Macmillan, 1935), 467; Smith, *Chronological Development*, 243–44, 248; Baker, *Protective Labor Legislation*, 61–62.

28. *State v. Buchanan*, 29 Wash. 602 (1902); Erickson, "*Muller v. Oregon* Reconsidered," 245.

29. *Wenham v. State*, 65 Neb. 394 (1902); Baer, *Chains of Protection*, 54–55.

30. *Low v. Rees Printing Co.*, 41 Neb 138; *In re Morgan*, 26 Co. 415 (1899); Urofsky, "State Courts and Protective Legislation," 77, 79; Henry R. Seager, "The Attitude of

American Courts towards Protective Labor Laws," *Political Science Quarterly* 19 (December 1904): 606.

31. Paul Kens, *Judicial Power and Reform Politics: The Anantomy of Lochner v. New York* (Lawrence: University Press of Kansas, 1990), 79; David E. Bernstein, *Lochner Rehabilitated* (Chicago: University of Chicago Press, 2011), 29–31.

32. *Lochner v. New York*, 198 U.S. 45, 57, 59, 61, 64 (1905).

33. Ibid., 65, 75.

34. For background to the *Lochner* case and to passage of the 1895 law, see Sidney G. Tarrow, "Lochner versus New York: A Political Analysis," *Labor History* 5 (Fall 1964): 277–312; Kens, *Judicial Power and Reform Politics*; and Bernstein, *Lochner Rehabilitated*, chap. 2. Bernstein describes the "close call," 33. For conflicting analyses of the significance of the case, see, besides the above, Cass R. Sunstein, "Lochner's Legacy," *Columbia Law Review* 87 (1987): 873–919, and Gillman, *Constitution Besieged*, 1–18, 126–46. For Justice Vann's concurring opinion, see *People v. Lochner*, 69 N.E. 373 (N.Y. 1904); Seager, "Attitude of American Courts," 609; and Batlan, "A Reevaluation," 522.

35. Julius M. Mayer, *Brief for Defendant in Error, February Term, 1905* (Albany, NY: Brandon Printing, Legislative Printer, 1905), 1–18; Philip R. Kurland and Gerhard Casper, eds., *Landmark Briefs and Arguments of the Supreme Court of the United States*, vol. 14 (Arlington, VA: University Publications of America, 1975), 726–30, 674–76, 706–14. Weismann's remark is from the *New York Times*, April 19, 1905, 1, quoted in Paul Kens, "Lochner v. New York," in Melvin I. Urofsky, ed., *The Public Debate over Controversial Supreme Court Decisions* (Washington, DC: CQ Press, 2006), 96.

36. Bernstein, *Lochner Rehabilitated*, 32–33; Kens, *Judicial Power and Reform Politics*, 108–9, 111, 113–14.

37. "Celebration of Victory," *Bakers Rev.* (June 1905), 41, cited in Bernstein, *Lochner Rehabilitated*, 37.

38. *The Outlook* (April 29, 1905): 1018–19, quoted in Kens, "Lochner," in Urofsky, *The Public Debate*, 99.

39. Roscoe Pound, "The Needs of Sociological Jurisprudence," *Green Bag* 19 (1907): 611–12, quoted in Kens, "Lochner," in Urofsky, *Public Debate*, 100.

40. Some sympathize, for instance, with bottom-rung bakery owners, typically immigrants (like Joseph Lochner), in very small shops, who struggled to keep afloat and faced larger competitors that wanted to put them out of business; some sympathize more with workers in the same cellar shops who labored for inordinately long hours, up to one hundred a week, in abysmal conditions, characterized by flour dust, gas fumes, dampness, and extremes of temperature.

41. *People v. Lochner*, 69 N.E. 373 (N.Y. 1904).

42. *People v. Williams*, 189 N.Y. 131 (1907).

CHAPTER 3: A CLASS BY HERSELF: *MULLER V. OREGON* (1908)

1. Josephine Goldmark, *Impatient Crusader: Florence Kelley's Life Story* (Urbana: University of Illinois Press, 1953), 143.

2. Louis D. Brandeis and Josephine Goldmark, *Women in Industry*, introduction by Leon Stein and Philip Taft (New York: Arno Press, 1969), 47, 49; this book reprints

the Brandeis brief and the 1908 decision, first published by the National Consumers' League in 1908. For the decision, see *Muller v. Oregon*, 208 U.S. 412 (1908). Nancy Woloch, *Muller v. Oregon: A Brief History with Documents* (Boston: Bedford Books, 1996) includes an introduction to the case and primary sources; see 21–40.

3. Caroline J. Gleason [Sister Miriam Theresa], *Oregon Legislation for Women in Industry*, Bulletin of the Women's Bureau No. 90 (Washington, DC: US Department of Labor, 1931), 8; Elaine Gaie Zahnd Johnson, "Protective Legislation and Women's Work: Oregon's Ten-Hour Law and the *Muller v. Oregon* Case, 1900–1913" (PhD diss., University of Oregon, 1982), 64–77, 235; Robert D. Johnston, *The Radical Middle Class: Populist Democracy and the Question of Capitalism in Progressive Era Portland, Oregon* (Princeton, NJ: Princeton University Press, 2003), 52.

4. On laundry work, see Brandeis and Goldmark, *Women in Industry*, 104–12; Elizabeth Butler, *Women and the Trades: Pittsburgh, 1907–1908* (New York: Charities Publications Committee, 1909), 161–91; Caroline J. Gleason, *Report of the Industrial Welfare Commissioner in the State of Oregon on the Power Laundries in Portland* (Salem, OR: State Printing Department, 1914); and Arwen Palmer Mohun, *Steam Laundries: Gender, Technology, and Work in the United States and Great Britain, 1880–1940* (Baltimore: Johns Hopkins University Press, 1999). For the 1902 strike, see Johnson, "Protective Legislation," 331. Johnson's dissertation is invaluable for Oregon labor history, the roots of the *Muller* case, and the decision's local impact.

5. *Wenham v. State*, 65 Neb. 394 (1902); *State v. Buchanan*, 29 Wash. 602 (1902).

6. Gleason, *Oregon Legislation*, 7, 17; Johnson, "Protective Legislation," 76, 92, 93, 96, 98, 331, 332.

7. Gleason, *Oregon Legislation*, 17; Johnson, "Protective Legislation," 105–7, 111, 234.

8. Johnson, "Protective Legislation," 156, 331, 332.

9. Ibid., 108, 110, 156, 236, 332, 344. Muller (or Hans Curt Muller, his complete name) was an aspiring immigrant. Born in 1877, in Johanngeorgestadt, Saxony, Muller was the son of a small tradesman, the owner of a bookstore and bookbindery. After serving in the German army, Muller came to the United States in 1903. He ran the concession for linen products at the 1904 Saint Louis World's Fair before moving to Portland in 1905; see Johnston, *Radical Middle Class*, 19.

10. Johnson, "Protective Legislation," 208, 236–37, 239.

11. Johnston, *Radical Middle Class*, 19; Johnson, "Protective Legislation," 236, 239.

12. Ronald K. L. Collins and Jennifer Friesen, "Looking Back on *Muller v. Oregon*," *American Bar Association Journal* 69 (March 1983): 294–96. For lawyer E.S.J. McAllister's career, see Peter Boag, "Sex and Politics in Progressive-Era Portland and Eugene: The 1912 Same-Sex Vice Scandal," *Oregon Historical Quarterly* 100 (Summer 1999): 158–81. McAllister enjoyed a lively practice until convicted of sodomy in 1913. The conviction was overturned, but in 1914 the county bar excluded McAllister, and he retired. For lawyer Fenton, see Johnston, *Radical Middle Class*, 23; Collins and Friesen, "Looking Back on *Muller v. Oregon*," passim. Muller's unpublished speech, "Labor Unions," undated, is in the William D. Fenton papers, Oregon Historical Society, MSS 1507, Belles Letter Essays Folder, 1, 3. Thanks to Robert D. Johnston for sharing his Oregon research.

13. Collins and Friesen, "Looking Back on *Muller v. Oregon*," 295–96. The list of witnesses subpoenaed appears in Appellant's Brief, Supreme Court of the State of Oregon, March term, 1906, p. 4., Oregon State Archives, case 6412, Drawer 67.

14. For Sears's decision, see *Portland Labor Press*, vol. 5, no. 51 (January 26, 1907), 1.

15. Appellant's Brief, 39–40.

16. Respondent's Brief, the Supreme Court of the State of Oregon, March term, 1906, pp. 3–4, 7–9, 15. Oregon State Archives, case 6412, Drawer 67.

17. Appellant's Brief, 1, 7; *State v. Muller* 48 Ore. 252 (1906).

18. National Consumers' League, *Fourth Report* (1903), 6, 16; NCL, *Seventh Report* (1906), 73, 106, 108; NCL, *Tenth Report* (1909), 21–22; *Oregonian*, November 8, 1906, p. 9, column 3; Johnson, "Protective Legislation," 145–46; Goldmark, *Impatient Crusader*, 154–55; Johnston, *Radical Middle Class*, 24–25.

19. Goldmark, *Impatient Crusader*, 57, 59; Kelley, *Ethical Gains*, 155.

20. Paul Kens, *Judicial Power and Reform Politics: The Anatomy of Lochner v. New York* (Lawrence: University Press of Kansas, 1990), 112; FK to Nicholas Kelley, November 7, 1907, in Kathryn Kish Sklar and Beverly Wilson Palmer, eds., *The Selected Letters of Florence Kelley, 1869–1931* (Urbana: University of Illinois Press, 2009), 102; Goldmark, *Impatient Crusader*, 143, 151–56; Catharine Brody, "Mrs. Florence Kelley, Crusader for Quarter of a Century," *Brooklyn Daily Eagle*, January 25, 1925, 101; Felix Frankfurter, *Reminiscences* (New York: Reynal, 1960), 95. For Florence Kelley's intervention in a state appeal, see Clement Vose, "Litigation as a Form of Pressure Group Activity," *Annals of the American Academy of Political and Social Science* 319 (September 1958): 20–31.

21. Melvin I. Urofsky, *Louis D. Brandeis: A Life* (New York: Pantheon, 2009), 201; chapter 9 explores Brandeis's role in the *Muller* case. See also Urofsky, *A Mind of One Piece: Brandeis and American Reform* (New York: Scribner, 1971), 25–42; Thomas C. McCraw, *Prophets of Regulation: Charles Francis Adams, Louis D. Brandeis, James M. Landis, Alfred E. Kahn* (Cambridge, MA: Harvard University Press, 1984), 82–83, 85, 87; Marion E. Doro, "The Brandeis Brief," *Vanderbilt Law Review* 11 (1958): 786; William W. Fisher III, Morton J. Horwitz, and Thomas A. Reed, eds., *American Legal Realism* (New York: Oxford University Press, 1993), xii. For links between sociological jurisprudence and legal realism, see Morton J. Horwitz, *The Transformation of American Law, 1870–1960: The Crisis of Legal Orthodoxy* (New York: Oxford University Press, 1992), 169–70, and G. Edward White, "From Sociological Jurisprudence to Realism: Jurisprudence and Social Change in Early Twentieth-Century America," *Virginia Law Review* 58 (September 1972): 999–1028.

22. Urofsky, *A Mind of One Piece*, 34–35, and *Louis D. Brandeis*, 202–6; Louis D. Brandeis, "The Opportunity in the Law," *American Law Review* 39 (July–August, 1905): 555, 559; Louis D. Brandeis, "The Living Law," *Illinois Law Review* 10 (February 1916): 463, 469, 470.

23. Brandeis, "Living Law," 467; Doro, "Brandeis Brief," 788; Goldmark, *Impatient Crusader*, 155; Barbara Allen Babcock et al., *Sex Discrimination and the Law* (Boston: Little, Brown, 1975), 28–29; Deborah L. Rhode, *Justice and Gender* (Cambridge, MA: Harvard University Press, 1989), 40; Urofsky, *Louis D. Brandeis*, 214.

24. Goldmark, *Impatient Crusader*, 155, 157.

25. Brandeis and Goldmark, *Women in Industry*, 9–10; *State v. Buchanan*, 29 Wash. 610 (1902).

26. Brandeis and Goldmark, *Women in Industry*, 11–17; see also 1–8 for state laws.

27. Ibid., 18–112; see 18, 24.

28. Ibid., 22, 35, 50, 48.

29. Ibid., 57, 58.

30. Ibid., 59, 77, 82, 103; Clementina Black, "Some Current Objections to Factory Legislation for Women," in *The Case for the Factory Acts*, ed. Beatrice Webb (London: Grant Richards, 1901), 209, 211. For Beatrice Webb, her defense of the factory laws, her brand of Fabian Socialism, and her role in British politics, see Deborah Epstein Nord, *The Apprenticeship of Beatrice Webb* (Amherst: University of Massachusetts Press, 1985), 116–17, 150–52, 272.

31. Brandeis and Goldmark, *Women in Industry*, 104–12.

32. Ibid., 113.

33. Clyde Spillenger, "Revenge of the Triple Negative: A Note on the Brandeis Brief in *Muller v. Oregon*," *Constitutional Commentary* 22 (2005): 5–10.

34. "Brief for the State of Oregon," *Landmark Briefs and Arguments of the Supreme Court of the United States*, ed. Philip B. Kurland and Gerhard Casper (Arlington, VA: University Publications of America, 1975), 16: 37–61.

35. Woloch, *Muller v, Oregon*, 31. Critics of the Brandeis brief include Judith A. Baer, *The Chains of Protection* (Westport, CT.: Greenwood Press, 1978), 57–61; Nancy Erickson, "Historical Background of 'Protective' Legislation: Muller v. Oregon," in *Women and the Law*, ed. D. Kelly Weisberg (Cambridge, MA: Schenkman, 1982), 159–60; Babcock et al., *Sex Discrimination*, 29–30; Deborah Rhode, *Gender and Justice: Sex Discrimination and the Law* (Cambridge, MA: Harvard University Press, 1989), 40–42; Joan Hoff, *Law, Gender, and Injustice* (New York: New York University Press, 1991), 196–203; Susan Lehrer, *Origins of Protective Legislation for Women, 1905–1925* (Albany: State University of New York Press, 1984), 54–56; Lise Vogel, *Mothers on the Job* (New Brunswick, NJ: Rutgers University Press, 1993), 16–21.

36. Blanche Crozier, "Constitutional Law—Regulation of Conditions of Employment of Women—A Critique of *Muller v. Oregon*," *Boston University Law Review* 13 (April 1933): 278.

37. Dean Acheson, *Morning and Noon* (Boston: Houghton Mifflin, 1965), 53; David J. Bryden, "Brandeis's Facts," *Constitutional Commentary* 1 (Summer 1984): 194–295; Woloch, *Muller v. Oregon*, 32. For another mention of "What Every Fool Knows," see Melvin I. Urofsky and David W. Levy, eds., *Half Brother, Half Son: Louis D. Brandeis to Felix Frankfurter* (Norman: University of Oklahoma Press, 1991), 139.

38. For the oral argument Brandeis made in *Stettler v. O'Hara* (1917), an Oregon minimum wage case argued in 1914, and commentary on it, see *The Survey* 33 (February 6, 1915), 521; L. D. Brandeis, "The Constitution and the Minimum Wage," in *The Curse of Bigness*, ed. O. K. Fraenkel (New York: Viking, 1934), 52–69; Alexander M. Bickel, *The Judiciary and Responsible Government, 1910–1921* (New York: Macmillan, 1984), 594, 603, 607.

39. "William David Fenton, Lawyer," *Who's Who in America, 1899-1900* (Chicago: A.N. Marquis, 1899), 683; Johnston, *Radical Middle Class*, 305.

40. "Brief for Plaintiff in Error," *Landmark Briefs* 16: 4–35.

41. Woloch, *Muller v. Oregon*, 34–35.

42. FK to Nicholas Kelley, January 20, 1908, in Sklar and Palmer, *Selected Letters of Florence Kelley*, 171.

43. *Wright v. Noell*, 26 Kan. 601 (1876); *Holthaus v. Farria*, 24 Kan. 784 (1881); David J. Brewer, "Woman Suffrage: Its Present Position and Its Future," *Ladies' World* 30 (December 1909): 6, 29; Michael J. Brodhead, *David J. Brewer: The Life of a*

Supreme Court Justice, 1837–1910 (Carbondale: Southern Illinois University Press, 1994), 42, 175.

44. David J. Brewer, "The Nation's Safeguard," *Proceedings of the New York State Bar Association, Sixteenth Annual Meeting, 1893* (New York: Stumpf and Steurer, 1893), 43–47; Arnold M. Paul, *Conservative Crisis and the Rule of Law: Attitudes of Bench and Bar, 1887–1895* (Ithaca, NY: Cornell University Press, 1960), 70–71, 83–84.

45. *Budd v. New York*, 143 U.S. 517, 551 (1892); *Adair v. United States*, 208 U.S. 161 (1908); Brodhead, *David J. Brewer*, 152–54.

46. Brodhead, *David J. Brewer*, 151–53. In 1907, in a divided court, Brodhead points out, Brewer joined the majority to provide an eight-hour day for laborers and mechanics employed by the United States or by contractors engaged in public works for the federal government. See also Alan F. Westin, ed., *An Autobiography of the Supreme Court: Off-the-Bench Commentary by the Justices* (New York: Macmillan, 1963), 122.

47. *Muller v. Oregon*, 208 U.S. 412 (1908); Brandeis and Goldmark, *Women in Industry*, 45; L. D. Brandeis, "Living Law," 470; Philippa Strum, *Louis D. Brandeis: Justice for the People* (Cambridge, MA: Harvard University Press, 1984), 122; and Owen M. Fiss, *Troubled Beginnings of the Modern State, 1888–1910* (New York: Macmillan, 1993), 176. This discussion of the decision is based on Woloch, *Muller v. Oregon*, 37–38.

48. Barbara Young Welke, *Law and the Borders of Belonging in the Long Nineteenth Century United States* (Cambridge: Cambridge University Press, 2010), 69.

49. *New York Times*, February 26, 1908; *Women's Journal*, March 7, 1908, 38, 40, as cited in Erickson, "Historical Background," 167, 169; Woloch, *Muller v. Oregon*, 38.

50. Clara Colby quote from *Woman's Tribune* 23 (August 11, 1906): 62.

51. Sophonisba Breckinridge, "Legislative Control of Women's Work," *Journal of Political Economy* 14 (February 1906): 107–8.

52. Louisa Dana Harding, "Male Socialism," *Woman's Standard* (April 1, 1908): 2, cited in David E. Bernstein, *Rehabilitating Lochner: Defending Individual Rights against Progressive Reform* (Chicago: University of Chicago Press, 2011), 63.

53. Louisa Dana Harding quote from *Woman's Tribune* 25 (May 9, 1908): 19.

54. *Woman's Journal* (March 21, 1908), 48, cited in Erickson, "Historical Background," 171–72.

55. For critiques of the Brewer decision, see, for instance, Baer, *Chains of Protection*, 123; Kessler-Harris, *Out to Work*, 181; Vogel, *Mothers on the Job*, 24; and Frances E. Olsen, "The Family and the Market: A Study of Ideology and Legal Reform," *Harvard Law Review* 96 (May 1983): 1557.

56. Lehrer, *Origins of Protective Legislation*, 206, 227, 236.

57. Alice Kessler-Harris, *In Pursuit of Equity: Women, Men, and the Quest for Economic Citizenship in 20th-Century America* (New York: Oxford University Press, 2001), 5–6, 30–34.

58. Welke, *Law and the Borders of Belonging*, 5–6, 136, 138.

59. David J. Brewer, "The Legitimate Exercise of the Police Power on the Protection of Healthy Women," *Charities and the Commons* 21 (November 7, 1908): 240–41.

60. For critics of Brandeis who consider these questions, see Erickson, "*Muller v. Oregon* Reconsidered," 229, and Bernstein, *Rehabilitating Lochner*, chap. 3.

61. Johnston, *Radical Middle Class*, 20.

62. In 1916 Caroline J. Gleason entered the Novitiate of the Sisters of the Holy Names. After earning a doctorate at the Catholic University of America, Gleason,

now Sister Miriam Theresa, headed the Sociology Department at Marylhurst College near Portland for thirty years. For her life and career, see "Sister Miriam Theresa Dies," Oregon City, Oregon, *Enterprise-Courier* (May 15, 1962); *Congressional Record—Senate* (May 17, 1962), 7978–79; and Janice Dilg, "'For Working Women in Oregon': Caroline Gleason/Sister Miriam Theresa and Oregon's Minimum Wage Law," *Oregon Historical Quarterly* 110 (Spring 2009): 96–129. Gleason's publications include *Report of the Social Survey Committee of the Consumers' League of Oregon* (Portland, OR: OCL, 1913), *Report of the Industrial Welfare Commission of the State of Oregon on Power Laundries in Portland* (Salem, OR: State Printing Department, 1914), and Sister Miriam Theresa, *Oregon Legislation for Women in Industry* (see footnote 3).

63. Gleason [Sister Miriam Theresa], *Oregon Legislation*, 17, 18; Gleason, *Power Laundries*, 51–52; Johnson, "Protective Legislation," 111, 302–3, 299–311.

64. Gleason [Sister Miriam Theresa], *Oregon Legislation*, 18; Johnson, "Protective Legislation," 96, 138–40, 314, 323, 325, 335, 354, 355–56, 358.

65. For changes in Oregon's women's hours laws from 1903 to 1913, see Florence P. Smith, *Chronological Development of Labor Legislation for Women in the United States* (Washington, DC: Government Printing Office, 1929), 236–37. See also Johnson, "Protective Legislation," 131, 138; Gleason, *Power Laundries*, 9.

66. *Women's Journal* 39 (April 25, 1908): 68, cited in Erickson, "Historical Background," 194.

67. Thomas Alpheus Mason, "The Case of the Overworked Laundress," in *Quarrels That Have Shaped the Constitution*, 2nd ed., ed. John A. Garraty (New York: Harper and Row, 1987), 193 (the essay first appeared in 1964); Ruth Bader Ginsburg, "*Muller v. Oregon*: One Hundred Years Later," *Willamette Law Review* 45 (Spring 2009): 370, 379; post by Tony Mauro on "Re-Envisioning *Muller v. Oregon*," in *The BLT: Blog of Legal Times*, December 16, 2008. For Ginsburg's critical view of *Muller* in the 1970s, see her textbook with Kenneth M. Davidson and Herma Hill Kay, eds., *Texts, Cases, and Materials on Sex-Based Discrimination* (Saint Paul, MN: West Publishing, 1974), 10–17.

68. Ginsburg, "*Muller v. Oregon*: One Hundred Years Later," 365.

CHAPTER 4: PROTECTION IN ASCENT, 1908–23

1. Rosey Safran, "The Washington Place Fire," *The Independent* 70 (April 20, 1911): 840–41. For the Triangle fire and its aftermath, see John F. McClymer, *The Triangle Strike and Fire* (Fort Worth, TX: Harcourt Brace College Publishers, 1998), and David Von Drehle, *Triangle: The Fire That Changed America* (New York, Atlantic Monthly Press, 2003).

2. Josephine Goldmark, *Impatient Crusader: Florence Kelley's Life Story* (Urbana: University of Illinois Press, 1953), 139; Clement E. Vose, "The National Consumers' League and the Brandeis Brief," *Midwest Journal of Political Science* 1 (November 1957): 287.

3. Goldmark, *Impatient Crusader*, 158–64; Elizabeth Brandeis, "Labor Legislation and the Constitution," in *History of Labor in the United States*, vol. 3, ed. John R. Commons et al. (New York: Macmillan, 1935), 459, 474.

4. *Ritchie v. Wayman*, 244 Ill. 509 (1910); Earl R. Beckner, *A History of Labor Legislation in Illinois* (Chicago: University of Chicago Press, 1929), 199–206; NCL, *Eleventh Report* (1910), 31; Florence Kelley, "The Work of the National Consumers' League during the Year Ending March 1, 1910," *Annals of the American Academy of Political and Social Science* 36 (Supplement) (September 1910): 18.

5. NCL, *Twelfth Report* (1913), 26. The Illinois case was *People v. Elerding* 254 Ill. 579 (1912).

6. *People Ex Rel. Hoelderlin v. Kane*, 139 NY supp., 350 (1913), NCL Papers, reel 108; Josephine Goldmark, "The New York 54-Hour Labor Law," *The Survey* 29 (December 14, 1912): 332–33.

7. E. Brandeis, "Labor Legislation," 484–91.

8. *Miller v. Wilson*, 236 U.S. 373 (1915); Clara Beyer, *History of Labor Legislation in Three States*, Women's Bureau Bulletin, No. 66 (Washington, DC: Government Printing Office, 1929), 122; Lucy E. Salwer, "Protective Labor Legislation and the California Supreme Court, 1911–1924," *California Supreme Court Historical Society Yearbook* 4 (1998–1999): 1–22.

9. *Bosley v. McLaughlin*, 236 U.S. 385 (1915); for both California cases, see Beyer, *History of Labor Legislation*, 122–26, and Julie Novkov, *Constituting Workers, Protecting Women: Gender, Law, and Labor in the Progressive Era and New Deal Years* (Ann Arbor: University of Michigan Press, 2001), 159–60.

10. *Bosley v. McLaughlin*, 236 U.S. 385 (1915).

11. *Quong Wing v. Kirkendall*, 223 U.S. 59 (1912), 62, 63; David E. Bernstein, "*Lochner*, Parity, and the Chinese Laundry Cases," *William and Mary Law Review* 41 (December 1999): 266–68; and Alice Kessler-Harris, *A Woman's Wage: Historical Meanings and Social Consequences* (Lexington: University of Kentucky Press, 1990), 40–44. For analysis of legal instances in which race and sex intersect, see Kimberlé Crenshaw, "Demarginalizing the Intersection of Race and Sex: A Black Feminist Critique of Antidiscrimination Doctrine, Feminist Theory, and Antiracist Politics," *University of Chicago Legal Forum* (1989): 139–67.

12. Elizabeth F. Baker, *Technology and Women's Work* (New York: Columbia University Press, 1964), 396.

13. For night work laws in the United States, see US Women's Bureau, *Night Work Laws in the United States: Summary of State Legislation Regulating Night Work for Women*, Bulletin No. 7, October 15, 1919 (Washington DC: Government Printing Office, 1920), 2–3; Mary E. McDowell, "Mothers and Night Work," *The Survey* 39 (December 22, 1917): 335–36; and E. Brandeis, "Labor Legislation," 471–74. For the Berne Conference, see Josephine Goldmark, *Fatigue and Efficiency: A Study in Industry* (New York: Charities Publications Committee, 1912), 62–63. For an overview, see Alice Kessler-Harris, "The Paradox of Motherhood: Night Work Restrictions in the United States," in *Protecting Women: Labor Legislation in Europe, the United States, and Australia, 1880–1920*, ed. Ulla Wikander, Alice Kessler-Harris, and Jane Lewis (Urbana: University of Illinois Press, 1995), 337–58.

14. State of New York, *Second Report of the Factory Investigating Commission*, vol. 4 (Albany, NY: J. B. Lyon, Printers, 1913), 1650–51; Goldmark, *Fatigue and Efficiency*, 211; FIC, vol. 1 (Albany, NY: J. B. Lyon, Printers, 1913), 208–12; Elizabeth Beardsley Butler, *Women and the Trades, Pittsburgh, 1907–1908* (New York: Charities Publica-

tions Committee, 1909), 351–52, 382. Butler was a former secretary of the New Jersey Consumers' League.

15. NCL Passaic Study I, 194–95; Goldmark's 1912 view of nightwork is in *Fatigue and Efficiency*, chap. 10. Her testimony on night work to the FIC is in State of New York, *Second Report of the Factory Investigating Commission*, 4, 1649, 1657. For Kelley's remarks on night work, see State of New York, *Preliminary Report of the Factory Investigating Commission, 1912* (Albany: Argus, Printers, 1912), 1603.

16. State of New York, *Second Report of the Factory Investigating Commission, 1913*, vol. 1 (Albany: J. B. Lyon, Printers, 1913), 195–97, 200; the "Ignorant women" quote is from p. 198.

17. Florence Kelley, "Wage-Earning Women in War Time: The Textile Industry," *Journal of Industrial Hygiene* 1 (October 1919): 276–77, in NCL Papers, reel 100; Mary E. McDowell, "Mothers and Night Work," *The Survey* 39 (December 22, 1917): 335–36.

18. For the development of New York State night work laws, see John Thomas McGuire, "Making the Case for Night Work Legislation in Progressive Era New York, 1911–1915," *Journal of the Gilded Age and Progressive Era* 5 (January 2006): 47–70. For Charles Schweinler and his press, see "The Man Who Printed Magazines," *McClure's Magazine* 41 (September 1913): 111–12. Schweinler's lawyer, Alfred E. Ommen, is mentioned in "Test Woman's Right to Work at Night," *New York Times*, February 20, 1914.

19. *People v. Charles Schweinler Press*, 214 N.Y. 395 (1915); Judith A. Baer, *The Chains of Protection* (Westport, CT: Greenwood Press, 1978), 79–85; Louis D. Brandeis and Josephine Goldmark, *The People of the State of New York, Respondent, against Charles Schweinler Press* (New York: National Consumers' League, 1914); David E. Bernstein, *Rehabilitating Lochner: Defending Individual Rights against Progressive Reform* (Chicago: University of Chicago Press, 2011), 63. For Florence Kelley's opinion, see letter to Katherine Philips Edson, July 16, 1916, in *The Selected Letters of Florence Kelley, 1869–1931*, ed. Kathryn Kish Sklar and Beverly Wilson Palmer (Urbana: University of Illinois Press, 2009), 215.

Factory inspectors twice targeted night work by women at the Schweinler Press. First, Marie Orenstein, an inspector for the New York State department of labor, testified at the Court of Special Sessions on October 8, 1913, that Louise Kindig, "a frail girl of twenty-three," had been working after 10:00 p.m. as a "fly-girl" (carrying loose papers from the presses to a nearby truck that hauled them away). The case ended with Schweinler's suspended sentence. See "Night Work Law Tested in New York State," *The Survey* (December 17, 1913), 313. The second case against Schweinler involved the charge of Esther Packard, former inspector for the FIC and more recently on the payroll of the Consumers' League of New York City. Packard claimed in 1914 that the press employed May Cashel at night as a "fly-woman," to collect loose papers. Wife of a dockworker and mother of three (ages fourteen, twelve, and four), Cashel worked from 6:00 p.m. to 4:00 a.m., while her husband cared for the children and ran the household. She testified in the trial court that she had many rest breaks, that she liked her work, that her health was good (the judge agreed), and that her household needed her income ("her husband's wages would not support the family"). *New York Times* articles on the progress of the case include "Test Woman's

Right to Work at Night," February 20, 1914; "Woman Labor Law Upheld by Court," April 28, 1914; "Women May Not Work after 10 p.m.," July 11, 1914; and "[Court] Upholds Labor Law to Protect Women," March 27, 1915.

20. Goldmark, *Fatigue and Efficiency*, 3, 121.

21. Ibid., 133, 164, 169. Taylorism, a theory of industrial efficiency Frederick Winslow Taylor developed in the 1880s, peaked in influence in the 1920s. Taylorism broke town industrial tasks into minute components; labor saw it as a speed-up. An early study is Horace Bookwater Drury, *Scientific Management: A History and Criticism* (New York: Columbia University Press, 1915). See also Melvin I. Urofsky, *Louis D. Brandeis: A Life* (New York: Pantheon Books, 2009), 240–43.

22. Goldmark, *Fatigue and Efficiency*, 254–55, 283.

23. For laws affecting men, see E. Brandeis, "Labor Legislation," 541–59. Mississippi in 1912 had passed a ten-hour law that targeted all employees in "manufacturing and repair"; state courts at first upheld the law and then upset it. The cases are *State v. J. J. Newman Lumber Co.*, 102 Miss. 802 (1912), and 103 Miss. 263 (1913). See also Ronnie Steinberg Ratner, "The Paradox of Protection: Maximum Hours Legislation in the United States," *International Labour Review* 119 (March/April 1980): 190–91.

24. For the roots of overtime in the nineteenth century, see E. Brandeis, "Labor Legislation," 540–42, 548, 550. For roots of overtime in the Progressive Era, see Melvin Dubovsky, *We Shall Be All: History of the Industrial Workers of the World* (Urbana: University of Illinois Press, 1985), 242, 252, 315, and David R. Roediger and Philip Foner, *Our Own Time: A History of American Labor and the Working Day* (New York: Greenwood Press, 1989), 187–88, 196.

25. E. Brandeis, "Labor Legislation," 482, 493–94; Goldmark, *Fatigue and Efficiency*, 175.

26. Jennifer Friesen and Ronald K. L. Collins, "Looking Back on *Muller v. Oregon*," *American Bar Association Journal* 69 (April 1983): 473; Felix Frankfurter, *Reminiscences* (New York, Reynal, 1960), 97.

27. Felix Frankfurter, "Hours of Labor and Realism in Constitutional Law," *Harvard Law Review* 29 (February 1916): 367.

28. Felix Frankfurter, assisted by Josephine Goldmark, *The Case for the Shorter Work Day* (New York: National Consumers' League, 1916), iii, 63–64, 360–61, 404, 417–18, 428, 532.

29. Frankfurter, *Reminiscences*, 103; *Bunting v. Oregon*, 243 U.S. 426, 436, 437, 438, 439 (1917).

30. E. Brandeis, "Labor Legislation," 555–59; see also Elizabeth Brandeis, "Protective Legislation," in *Labor and the New Deal*, ed. Milton Derber and Edwin Young (Madison: University of Wisconsin Press, 1957), 197.

31. [Caroline J. Gleason], *Report of the Social Survey Committeee of the Consumers' League of Oregon* (Portland, OR: Consumers' League of Oregon, 1913), 68–69.

32. [Gleason], *Report of the Social Survey Committee*, 19–23, 152; Janice Dilg, "'For Working Women in Oregon': Caroline Gleason/Sister Miriam Theresa and Oregon's Minimum Wage Law," *Oregon Historical Quarterly* 110 (Spring 2009): 96; Woloch, *Muller v. Oregon: A Brief History with Documents* (Boston: Bedford Books, 1996), 152–56.

33. NCL, "Report of the Secretary," *Eleventh Report, for the Year Ending March 1, 1910*, 21; Emily Josephine Hutchinson, *Women's Wages: A Study of the Wages of Indus-*

trial Women and Measures Suggested to Increase Them (New York: Longman Green, 1918), 75; E. Brandeis, "Labor Legislation," 502–7; Theda Skocpol, *Protecting Soldiers and Mothers: The Political Origins of Social Policy in the United States* (Cambridge, MA: Harvard University Press, 1992), 404–5; Woloch, *Muller v. Oregon*, 47.

34. Edwin V. O'Hara, *Welfare Legislation for Women and Minors* (Portland: Consumers' League of Oregon, 1912); [Gleason], *Report of the Social Survey Committee*, 20–21.

35. Skocpol, *Protecting Soldiers and Mothers*, 407, 409–11; Friesen and Collins, "Looking Back," 473; Hutchinson, *Women's Wages*, 80, 81–82, 83–84; Florence Kelley, "Minimum Wage Laws," *Journal of Political Economy* 20 (December 1912): 1003.

36. *American Labor Legislation Review* 3 (February 1913): 98. For California women workers against the minimum wage, see Rebecca J. Mead, "Let the Women Get Their Wages as Men Do: Trade Union Women and the Legislated Minimum Wage in California," *Pacific Historical Review* 67 (August 1998): 317–47.

37. R. G. Brown, "Oregon Minimum Wage Cases," *Minnesota Law Review* 1 (June 1917): 486; Howard Gillman, *The Constitution Besieged: The Rise and Demise of Lochner Era Police Powers Jurisprudence* (Durham, NC: Duke University Press, 1993), 163.

38. State of New York, *Fourth Report of the Factory Investigating Commission, 1915*, vol. 5 (Albany, NY: J. B. Lyon, Printers, 1915), 2851–68.

39. *Stettler v. O'Hara*, 69 Ore. 519 (1914); *Simpson v. O'Hara*, 70 Ore. 261 (1914); Friesen and Collins, "Looking Back," 474; Johnson, "Protective Legislation," 320.

40. Felix Frankfurter, assisted by Josephine Goldmark, *Oregon Minimum Wage Cases* (New York: National Consumers' League, 1916), 77, 425, 556, 581, 663, 694.

41. Frankfurter and Goldmark, *Oregon Minimum Wage Cases*, 99; David P. Bryden, "Brandeis's Facts," *Constitutional Commentary* 1 (Summer 1984): 305–11.

42. Alexander Bickel, *The Judiciary and Responsible Government* (New York: Macmillan, 1984), 594–95.

43. *Stettler v. O'Hara*, 243 U.S. 629 (1917).

44. Skocpol, *Protecting Soldiers and Mothers*, 415, 417; Bryden, "Brandeis's Facts," 303; Brandeis, "Labor Legislation," 503. In another protectionist victory of 1917, the Supreme Court upheld the Adamson Act of 1916, a congressional law that made the eight-hour day the basic workday for men operating railroad trains and required extra pay for those who worked overtime, see *Wilson v. New*, 243 U.S. 332 (1917).

45. Mary Van Kleeck, "Women and Machines," *Atlantic Monthly* 127 (February 1921): 250–51; US Department of Labor, Women in Industry Service, *First Annual Report of the Director of the Women in Industry Service for the Fiscal Year Ended June 30, 1919* (Washington, DC: Government Printing Office, 1919), 3; "Reports of the Director, 1918–1948," Women's Bureau Papers, reel 1, box 7, report 5. For the start of wartime agencies, see David M. Kennedy, *Over Here: The First World War and American Society* (New York: Oxford University Press, 1980), chap. 5.

46. For Van Kleeck's career, see Guy Alchon, chapter 10 in Helene Silverberg, ed., *Gender and American Social Science: The Formative Years* (Princeton, NJ: Princeton University Press, 1998), 293–325; *First Annual Report of the Director*, 3, 10.

47. Women in Industry Service, *First Annual Report*, 16; "Reports of the Director," Report 5; [Emma L. Shields], *Negro Women in Industry*, Bulletin of the Women's Bureau, No. 20 (Washington: Government Printing Office, 1922), 40.

48. For the start of the Women's Bureau, see *Second Annual Report of the Director of the Women's Bureau for the Fiscal Year Ended June 30, 1920*, p. 3; Judith Sealander, *As Minority Becomes Majority: Federal Reaction to the Phenomenon of Women in the Work Force, 1920–1963* (Westport, CT: Greenwood Press, 1983), chap. 2; Alice Kessler-Harris, *In Pursuit of Equity: Women, Men, and the Quest for Economic Citizenship in 20th-Century America* (New York: Oxford University Press, 2001), 35–42.

49. Florence P. Smith, *Chronological Development of Labor Legislation for Women in the United States*, Bulletin of the Women's Bureau No. 66 (Washington, DC: Government Printing Office, 1929), 205, 233; Dennis Irven Harrison, "The Consumers' League of Ohio Women and Reform, 1909–1937" (PhD diss., Case Western Reserve University, 1975), 72, 77. Alice Kessler-Harris discusses labor unions' stance toward women workers in "Where Are the Organized Women Workers?" *Feminist Studies* 3 (Fall 1975): 92–105.

50. Alice Kessler-Harris, *Out to Work: A History of Wage-Earning Women in the United States* (New York: Oxford University Press, 1982), 193–94. For streetcar conductors, see *Women Street Car Conductors and Ticket Agents*, Bulletin of the Women's Bureau, No. 11 (Washington, DC: Government Printing Office, 1921), and Maureen Weiner Greenwald, *Women, War, and Work: The Impact of World War I on Women Workers in the United States* (Westport, CT: Greenwood Press, 1980), chap. 4.

51. Nancy F. Cott, *The Grounding of Modern Feminism* (New Haven, CT: Yale University Press, 1987), 124. For reorganization of the National Woman's Party, see Christine Lunardini, *From Equal Suffrage to Equal Rights: Alice Paul and the National Woman's Party, 1910–1928* (New York: New York University Press, 1986), chap. 9, and Amy Butler, *Two Paths to Equality: Alice Paul and Ethel M. Smith in the ERA Debate, 1921–1929* (Albany: State University of New York Press, 2002), chap. 3.

52. Joan G. Zimmerman, "The Jurisprudence of Equality: The Women's Minimum Wage, the First Equal Rights Amendment, and *Adkins v. Children's Hospital*, 1905–1923," *Journal of American History* 28 (June 1991): 203.

53. Meg McGavran Murray, "The Work Got Done: An Interview with Clara Mortenson Beyer," in *Face to Face: Fathers, Mothers, Masters, Monsters—Essays for a Nonsexist Future*, ed. Meg McGavran Murray (Westport, CT: Greenwood Press, 1983), 214. For Clara Beyer's minimum wage experience in Washington, DC, see also Vivien Hart, "Feminism and Bureaucracy: The Minimum Wage Experiment in the District of Columbia," *Journal of American Studies* 26 (Spring 1992): 1–22, and "Conversation between Clara Mortenson Beyer and Vivien Hart, Washington, DC, November 14, 1983," Clara M. Beyer Papers, Schlesinger Library, Radcliffe Institute, Havard University.

54. Elizabeth Faulkner Baker, *Protective Labor Legislation* (New York: Columbia University Press, 1925), 84–88; for a discussion of the mimimum wage battle and the *Adkins* case, see Hart, *Bound by Our Constitution*, chap. 6. Unlike earlier cases on protective laws, the *Adkins* and *Lyons* minimum wage cases concerned a federal law (Congress legislates for the District of Columbia) and therefore involved the due process clause of the Fifth Amendment, which applies to the federal government, not the parallel clause of the Fourteenth Amendment, which applies to the states.

55. Baker, *Protective Labor Legislation*, 88; Florence Kelley, "The Right to Differ," *The Survey* 49 (December 15, 1922): 375–76; *Adkins v. Children's Hospital*, 284 Fed. Rep. 613 (1922).

56. James T. Patterson, "Mary W. Dewson and the American Minimum Wage Movement," *Labor History* 5 (Spring 1964): 136–42, and Susan Ware, *Partner and I: Molly Dewson, Feminism, and New Deal Politics* (New Haven, CT: Yale University Press, 1987), 97–99, 287.

57. Felix Frankfurter, with the assistance of Mary W. Dewson, *District of Columbia Minimum Wage Cases, Brief for Appellants*, vol. 2 (New York: Steinberg Press, n.d.), 872, 1023, 1053; Sybil Lipschultz, "Social Feminism and Legal Discourse, 1908–1923," *Yale Journal of Law and Feminism* 2 (Fall 1989): 154; Woloch, *Muller v. Oregon*, 53.

58. Zimmerman, "Jurisprudence of Equality," 209, 221.

59. "Oral Argument of Wade Ellis," *Landmark Briefs and Arguments of the Supreme Court of the United States*, ed. Philip B. Kurland and Gerhard Casper, vol. 21 (Arlington, VA: University Publications of America, 1975), 623, 630, 636–37, 656–57.

60. For Justice Sutherland, see Joel Francis Paschal, *Mr. Justice Sutherland: A Man against the State* (New York: Greenwood Press, 1969), 119–26, 243–44, and Hadley Arkes, *The Return of George Sutherland: Restoring a Jurisprudence of Natural Rights* (Princeton, NJ: Princeton University Press, 1994), 71–82. For Sutherland's remarks to the Senate, see Paschal, *Mr. Justice Sutherland*, 120.

61. *Adkins v. Children's Hospital*, 261 U.S. 525, 550, 553, 554, 557–58 (1923); Friesen and Collins, "Looking Back," 476; Zimmerman, "Jurisprudence of Equality," 213–14, 221; Bryden, "Brandeis's Facts," 312.

62. Zimmerman, "Jurisprudence of Equality," 222–23, 225; Lipschultz,, "Social Feminism," 151; and Vivien Hart, "*Adkins v. Children's Hospital*," in *The Public Debate over Controversial Supreme Court Decisions*, ed. Melvin I. Urofsky (Washington, DC: CQ Press, 2006), 121–31.

63. *Radice v. New York*, 264 U.S. 292 (1924). Baer, *Chains of Protection*, 87–88, 97; Frances E. Olsen, "From False Paternalism to False Equality: Judicial Assaults on Feminist Community, Illinois, 1869–1895," *Michigan Law Review* 84 (June 1986): 1518–41; Paschal, *Mr. Justice Sutherland*, 126; Florence Kelley to Molly Dewson, March 26, 1924, in Sklar and Palmer, *Selected Letters of Florence Kelley*, 334. Frankfurter's note of July 6, 1924, on his conversation with Brandeis is from Melvin I. Urofsky, ed., "The Brandeis-Frankfurter Conversations," *Supreme Court Review* (1985): 299, 330.

64. National Consumers' League, *The Supreme Court and Minimum Wage Legislation*, introduction by Roscoe Pound (New York: New Republic, 1925), 114, 214. See also T. R. Powell, "The Judiciality of Minimum Wage Legislation," *Harvard Law Review* 37 (1925): 545–73.

65. Daniel T. Rodgers, *Atlantic Crossings: Social Politics in a Progressive Age* (Cambridge, MA: Belknap Press of Harvard University Press, 1998), 238. For Margaret Sanger's brief, see Jonah Goldstein, *People of the State of New York ex rel. Margaret H. Sanger, Ethel Byrne and Fannie Mandell [Fania Mindell], Appellants' Brief in Support of Motion for Stay of Proceedings* (New York: Hecla Press, 1917), 11–56. Ellen Chesler describes the case in *Woman of Valor: Margaret Sanger and the Birth Control Movement* (New York: Scribners, 1992), 152–53, 157–60. For the role of social science in law, see Paul L. Rosen, *The Supreme Court and Social Science* (Urbana: University of Illinois Press, 1972), and Rosemary J. Erickson and Rita J. Simon, *The Use of Social Science Data in Supreme Court Decisions* (Urbana: University of Illinois Press, 1998).

CHAPTER 5: DIFFERENT VERSUS EQUAL: THE 1920s

1. "Conversations with Alice Paul: Woman Suffrage and the Equal Rights Amendment," An Interview Conducted by Amelia R. Fry, copyright 1976 by the Regents of the University of California, Regional Oral History Office, the Bancroft Library, 441–42. For an online version, see "Suffragists Oral History Project," the Bancroft Library, Regional Oral History Office.

2. Fry, "Conversations," 411–12.

3. Amelia Fry, "Alice Paul and the ERA," in *Rights of Passage: The Past and Future of the ERA*, ed. Joan Hoff-Wilson (Bloomington: Indiana University Press, 1986), 8–23; Amy Butler, *Two Paths to Equality: Alice Paul and Ethel M. Smith in the ERA Debate, 1921–1929* (Albany: State University of New York Press, 2002), chaps. 2–3; Christine Lunardini, *From Equal Suffrage to Equal Rights: Alice Paul and the National Woman's Party, 1910–1928* (1986), chap. 9; J. D. Zahniser and Amelia R. Fry, *Alice Paul: Claiming Power* (New York: Oxford University Press, 2014).

4. Fry, "Alice Paul and the ERA," 10–11.

5. *Suffragist* 1 (January–February 1921), quoted in Lunardini, *From Equal Suffrage to Equal Rights*, 159; see also 154, 161. Members of the NWP executive committee that met in September 1920 included, besides Florence Kelley and Alice Paul, Lucy Burns, Alva Belmont, Doris Stevens, Dora Lewis, Charlotte Perkins Gilman, Crystal Eastman, Rheta Childs Dorr, and Harriot Stanton Blatch (Lunardini, *From Equal Suffrage to Equal Rights*, 153).

6. Lunardini, *From Equal Suffrage to Equal Rights*, 153; Butler, *Two Paths to Equality*, 60–61; J. Stanley Lemons, *The Woman Citizen: Social Feminism in the 1920s* (Charlottesville: University of Virginia Press, 1973), 189–91; Ethel M. Smith to Florence Kelley, Washington, DC, October 10, 1921, NCL papers, reel 51, cited in Butler, *Two Paths to Equality*, 98. Gail Laughlin's quote in NWP National Council Minutes, April 11, 1922, NWP Papers, reel 114, cited in Nancy Cott, *The Grounding of Modern Feminism* (New Haven, CT: Yale University Press, 1987), 124.

7. Fry, "Alice Paul and the ERA," 12, 17; Florence Kelley, "The New Woman's Party," *The Survey* (March 3, 1921), quoted in Butler, *Two Paths to Equality*, 66.

8. For Shippen Lewis, a Philadelphia lawyer, see "Women Will Ask Equality in Law," *New York Times*, March 21, 1921, cited in Butler, *Two Paths to Equality*, 134. For Paul's relationship with Albert Levitt, and through him, Roscoe Pound and Felix Frankfurter, see Butler, *Two Paths to Equality*, 93–94. Pound and Frankfurter warned Paul that an ERA would imperil women's labor laws.

In 1943 the wording of the proposed ERA was changed to: "Equality of rights under law shall not be denied or abridged by the United States or by any state on account of sex." See Lunardini, *From Equal Suffrage to Equal Rights*, 162, 164, 165. The Washington College of Law, the first law school founded by women, opened its doors in 1896 and welcomed women and men as students. It became part of American University in 1949.

9. Suzanne LaFollette, *Concerning Women* (New York: A. & C. Boni, 1926), 12; Alice Kessler-Harris, *Out to Work: A History of Wage-Earning Women in the United States* (New York: Oxford University Press, 1982), 224.

10. *Eleventh Annual Report of the Director of the Women's Bureau, Fiscal Year Ending*

June 30, 1929 (Washington, DC: Government Printing Office, 1929), 4. For women's organizations, see Lemons, *The Woman Citizen*. For the WJCC's campaigns for the Sheppard-Towner Act and for a child labor amendment, see Jan Doolittle Wilson, *The Women's Joint Congressional Committee and the Politics of Maternalism, 1920–1930* (Urbana: University of Illinois Press, 2007). John Thomas McGuire assesses the WJLC in "A Catalyst for Reform: The Women's Joint Legislative Conference and Its Fight for Labor Legislation in New York State, 1918–1933" (PhD diss., State University of New York, Binghamton, 2000). For documents of the campaign for protective laws, see Sybil Lipschultz, ed., *Social Feminism, Labor Politics, and the Supreme Court of the 1920s* (New York: Routledge, 2002).

11. Josephine Goldmark considers Florence Kelley's first quarter century at the NCL in "Twenty-Five Years of It," *New Republic* 40 (November 12, 1924): 271–72.

12. Wilson, *The Women's Joint Congressional Committee and the Politics of Maternalism*, chap. 8; see 148–58.

13. Lemons, *The Woman Citizen*, 144–45.

14. Gwendolyn Mink, *The Wages of Motherhood: Inequality in the Welfare State, 1917–1942* (Ithaca, NY: Cornell University Press, 1995), 68; Lise Vogel, *Mothers on the Job: Maternity Policy in the U.S. Workplace* (New Brunswick, NJ: Rutgers University Press, 1993), 33–35. Molly Ladd-Taylor discusses the Sheppard-Towner Act in *Mother-Work: Women, Child Welfare, and the State, 1890–1930* (Urbana: University of Illinois Press, 1995), chap. 6. Beatrix Hoffman covers the AALL plan for maternity benefits in *The Wages of Sickness: The Politics of Health Insurance in Progressive America* (Chapel Hill: University of North Carolina Press, 2001), chap. 7. Dorothy Sue Cobble discusses the efforts of NWTUL leaders to propose labor standards with European colleagues at the end of World War I in "A Higher 'Standard of Life' for the World: US Labor Women's Reform Internationalism and the Legacies of 1919," *Journal of American History* 100 (March 2014): 1052–85.

15. Lemons, *The Woman Citizen*, 143–45; Hart, *Bound by Our Constitution*, 109; E. Brandeis, "Protective Legislation," 501. In 1927 California's State Labor Commission sponsored an amendment to the state's eight-hour law to extend its reach to all women employees in the state (except domestic workers, cannery workers, and graduate nurses). Equal rights advocates claimed credit for the bill's defeat. "[T]his law would have reduced the business and professional women to the expedient of bootlegging work," one opponent declared; see Rose Falls Bres, "Shall There Be Special Restrictive Laws for Women?" *Women Lawyers' Journal* 15 (July 1927): 4.

16. Frankfurter telegram to Kelley, April 10, 1923, and Florence Kelley, "Progress of Labor Legislation for Women," *Proceeedings of the National Conference of Social Work* (Chicago, 1923), 114, quoted in Joan G. Zimmerman, "The Jurisprudence of Equality: The Women's Minimum Wage, the First Equal Rights Amendment, and *Adkins v. Children's Hospital*, 1905–1923," *Journal of American History* 28 (June 1991): 222–23; FK to Victor L. Berger, December 19, 1923, in *The Selected Letters of Florence Kelley, 1869–1931*, ed. Kathryn Kish Sklar and Beverly Wilson Palmer (Urbana: University of Illinois Press, 2009), 328; "Minutes of the Thirteenth Meeting of the Board of Directors," October 25, 1923, NCL Files, reel 2; T. R. Powell, "The Judiciality of Minimum Wage Legislation," *Harvard Law Review* 37 (1925): 545–73.

17. Vivien Hart, *Bound by Our Constitution: Women, Workers, and the Minimum*

Wage (Princeton, NJ: Princeton University Press, 1994), 98, 132–33; NCL Papers, Box 2, 1923 Correspondence, cited in Hart, *Bound by Our Constitution*, 132; Florence Kelley, "The Right to Differ," *The Survey* 49 (December 15, 1922): 375–76.

18. William Lasser, *Benjamin V. Cohen: Architect of the New Deal* (New Haven, CT: Yale University Press, 2002), 53–57; Vivien Hart, "*Adkins v. Children's Hospital*," in *The Public Debate over Controversial Supreme Court Decisions*, ed. Melvin I. Urofsky (Washington, DC: CQ Press, 2006), 127–29.

19. Blanche Weisen Cook, *Crystal Eastman on Women and Revolution* (New York: Oxford University Press, 1978), 158.

20. Florence Kelley, *Twenty Questions about the Federal Amendment Proposed by the National Woman's Party* (New York: National Consumers' League, 1922), 3–7. In 1921 Kelley had sent a list of questions about the ERA to an Ohio member of Congress, Simeon Fess, who had agreed to present the amendment. Kelley's argument dissuaded him. In 1922 the NCL published Kelley's assault as a pamphlet.

21. Cott, *The Grounding of Modern Feminism*, 128; Susan D. Becker, *Origins of the Equal Rights Amendment: American Feminism between the Wars* (Westport, CT: Greenwood Press, 1981), 142; William H. Chafe, *The American Woman: Her Changing Social, Economic, and Political Role, 1920–1970* (New York: Oxford University Press, 1972), 123, 127; Ethel M. Smith, "Special Features: The Equal Rights Amendment," *Congressional Digest* 3 (March 1924): 199, cited in Butler, *Two Paths to Equality*, 96.

22. Frieda Miller quote is from Ethel M. Smith, "Working Women Want Equality but Oppose Blanket Law," February 26, 1922, in NCL Papers, reel 51, cited in Butler, *Two Paths to Equality*, 102; Mary Anderson, "Should There Be Labor Laws for Women? Yes," *Good Housekeeping* 53 (September 1925): 166–80. See also Florence Kelley, "Should Women Be Treated Identically with Men by the Law?" *American Review* 1 (May–June 1923): 277. For the LWV, see Elizabeth Israels Perry, *Women in Action: Rebels and Reformers, 1920–1980* (Washington, DC: League of Women Voters, 1995), 19, and Carina C. Washington, *What Has Been Done . . . to Establish Equal Rights* (Washington, DC: League of Women Voters, 1922), 2, 27. Kathryn Kish Sklar describes the social feminist stance in "Why Were Most Politically Active Women Opposed to the ERA in the 1920s?" in *Rights of Passage: The Past and the Future of the ERA*, ed. Joan Hoff Wilson (Bloomington: Indiana University Press, 1986), 25–35.

23. Clara Mortenson Beyer, "What Is Equality?" *Nation* 116 (January 31, 1923), 116. In this instance, Beyer based her point on a statement by Harvard Law School dean Roscoe Pound, who gave advice to both factions of the women's movement. ("[T]here is no surer method of repealing all legal protection for women than to substitute for the laws now in force general statutes covering all persons," Pound wrote.)

24. *Women Lawyers Journal* 12 (October–November 1922): 4, and (December 1922–January 1923): 12; Florence Kelley to Gertrude B. Lane (editor of the *Woman's Home Companion*) August 7, 1922, NCL Files, reel 100.

25. Mary Beard to Alice Paul, August 15 and August 21 [1914], July 10, 1916; Mary Beard to Elsie Hill, July 10, 1921; Mary Beard to Alma Lutz, January 29, 1937, in Nancy F. Cott, ed., *A Woman Making History: Mary Beard through Her Letters* (New Haven, CT: Yale University Press, 1991), 79–80, 100, 161–62. For Mary Beard, see also Ann J. Lane, ed., *Mary Ritter Beard: A Sourcebook* (New York: Schocken Books, 1977),

and Mary K.Trigg, *Feminism as Life's Work: Four Modern American Women through Two World Wars* (New Brunswick, NJ: Rutgers University Press, 2014), passim.

26. For a historian's strategy to transcend the polarities of the 1920s debate, see Wendy Sarvasy, "Beyond the Difference versus Equal Policy Debate," *Signs* 17 (Winter 1992): 329–62. Historian Joan Scott, considering a different/equal debate of the 1980s, posits the impossibility of resolution in "Deconstructing Equality versus Difference: Or, the Uses of Poststructuralist Theory for Feminism," *Feminist Studies* 14 (Spring 1988): 33–50. For "constitutional community," see Reva B. Siegel, "Constitutional Culture, Social Movement Conflict, and Constitutional Change: The Case of the de facto ERA," *California Law Review* 94 (October 2006): 1418–19.

27. "Women's Industrial Conference" (1923), p. 10, Women's Bureau Papers, Reel 1, Box 1; "Do Working Women Want Protection?" *Nation* (January 31, 1923): 115–16.

28. "Women's Industrial Conference," 10; *Eighth Annual Report of the Director of the Women's Bureau, Fiscal Year Ending 1926* (Washington DC: Government Printing Office, 1926), 11–12.

29. Women's Bureau, *Eighth Annual Report,* 12–14; *Summary of the 1928 Report,* viii; Lunardini, *From Equal Suffrage to Equal Rights,* 166.

30. Fry, "Conversations," 476, 477, 479, 480–81.

31. Leila J. Rupp, *World of Women: The Making of An International Women's Movement* (Princeton, NJ: Princeton University Press, 1997), 139–42.

32. Women's Bureau, *Eighth Annual Report* 12, 14; *Summary of the Report, A Reprint of Chapter II . . . .* Bulletin No. 68, Women's Bureau, US Department of Labor (Washington, DC: Government Printing Office, 1928), ix.

33. *The Effects of Hours Legislation on the Employment of Women,* Bulletin No. 65, Women's Bureau, US Department of Labor (Washington, DC: Government Printing Office, 1928), 45; *Summary of the Report,* v–vi, ix, 3.

34. *Effects of Hours Legislation,* 45–47, 144; *Summary of the Report,* 7.

35. *Summary of the Report,* ix, 1, 22.

36. *Effects of Hours Legislation,* 170, 179, 301, 305.

37. Curriculum Vitae of Elizabeth Faulkner Baker, Barnard College Archives; Baker, *Protective Labor Legislation* (New York: Columbia University Press, 1925); Baker, "At the Crossroads in the Legal Protection of Women in Industry," *Annals of the American Academy of Political and Social Science* 143 (May 1929): 265–79.

38. Elizabeth Faulkner Baker, *Protective Labor Legislation,* 308, 331, 336, 349, 352, 425–26.

39. Claudia Goldin, *Understanding the Gender Gap: An Economic History of American Women* (New York: Oxford University Press, 1990), 197–99.

40. Claudia Goldin, "Maximum Hours Legislation and Female Employment in the 1920s: A Reassessment," *Journal of Political Economy* 96 (February 1988): 189–205; Elisabeth Landes, "The Effect of State Maximum Hours Laws on the Employment of Women in 1920," *Journal of Political Economy* 88 (June 1980): 476–94.

41. Rebekah S. Greathouse, "The Effect of Constitutional Equality on Working Women," *Papers and Proceedings of the American Economic Association* 34 (1944): 224.

42. William E. Forbath, *Law and the Shaping of the American Labor Movement* (Cambridge, MA: Harvard University Press, 1991), 57; Brandeis, *Protective Labor Legislation,*

629; International Labour Office, *Factory Inspection: Historical Development and Present Organization in Certain Countries* (Geneva: [A. Kundig], 1923), 229.

43. William R. Brock, *Investigation and Responsibility: Public Responsibility in the United States, 1865–1900* (Cambridge: Cambridge University Press, 1984), chap. 6, "The Bureaus of Labor Statistics"; ILO, *Factory Inspection*, 230–32.

44. E. Stagg Whitin, *Factory Legislation in Maine* (New York: Columbia University Dissertation in Political Science, 1908), 76, 85.

45. Elizabeth Beardsley Butler, *Women and the Trades, Pittsburgh, 1907–1908* (New York: Charities Publications Committee, 1909), 39–41, 351–53, 382.

46. Elaine Gaie Zahnd Johnson, "Protective Legislation and Women's Work: Oregon's Ten-Hour Law and the *Muller v. Oregon* Case, 1900–1913" (PhD diss., University of Oregon, 1982), 312–20; Caroline J. Gleason, *Report of the Social Survey Committee of the Consumers' League of Oregon* (Portland: Oregon Consumers' League, 1913), 28–29, 33, 76.

47. Baker, *Protective Labor Laws*, 308, 314, 316, 325, 348–49. See also Irwin Yellowitz, *Labor and the Progressive Movement in New York State, 1897–1916* (Ithaca, NY: Cornell University Press, 1965), chap. 7.

48. ILO, *Factory Inspection*, 234–47.

49. George M. Price, *Administration of Labor Laws and Factory Inspection in Certain European Countries*, United States Department of Labor Bureau of Labor Statistics Bulletin No. 142 (Washington, DC: Government Printing Office, 1914), 17, 24–25, 126, 200, 202.

50. Emma Hess to Florence Kelley, 11/5/22, NCL Papers, reel 52.

51. Landon Storrs, *Civilizing Capitalism: The National Consumers' League, Women's Activism, and Labor Standards in the New Deal Era* (Chapel Hill: University of North Carolina Press, 2006), 51–54.

52. "Hearings on Labor Bills Develops an Unexpected Opposition of Women to Passage of Proposed Acts," *Monitor* 5 (March 19, 1920): 1–40; these quotes are from 30–31, 36.

53. "Hearings on Labor Bills," 11, 9, 39.

54. *Life and Labor* 10 (March 1920): 84, and (May 1920): 153.

55. US Department of Labor, Women's Bureau, *Women Street Car Conductors and Ticket Agents*, Bulletin No. 11 (Washington, DC: Government Printing Office, 1921), 36–37.

56. *Effects of Hours Legislation*, 140, 136, 144, 179, 182.

57. Anna A. Carlson to Maud Swartz, November 2, 1922; York, Pennsylvania YWCA to Florence Kelley, November 1, 1922; Louise Jacobs to Katherine Philips Edson, October 31, 1922; Ida Lockhart to Florence Kelley, October 30, 1922, all in NCL Papers, reel 52; Rebecca J. Mead, "'Let the Women Get Their Wages as Men Do': Trade Union Women and the Legislative Minimum Wage in California," *Pacific Historical Review* 67 (August 1998): 318–19, 346. For Katherine Edson, see Jaclyn Greenberg, "The Limits of Legislation: Katherine Philips Edson, Practical Politics, and the Minimum Wage Law in California, 1913–1922," *Journal of Policy History* 5 (April 1993): 207–30.

58. Rose Schneiderman, "Women's Role in Labor Legislation," n.d., reel 2, Schneiderman Papers, in Annelise Orleck, *Common Sense and a Little Fire: Women and Working-Class Politics in the United States, 1900–1945* (Chapel Hill: University of

North Carolina Press, 1995), 123. For the NYWTUL in the 1920s, see Nancy Schrom Dye, *As Equals and as Sisters: Feminism, the Labor Movement, and the Women's Trade Union League of New York* (Columbia: University of Missouri Press, 1980), chap. 7, and Orleck, *Common Sense and a Little Fire*, chap. 4.

59. Baker, "At the Crossroads," 279; Florence P. Smith, *Labor Laws for Women in the States and Territories*, US Department of Labor, Women's Bureau, Revision of Bulletin 63 (Washington, DC: Government Printing Office, 1932), 1–11.

60. Sophonisba P. Breckinridge, *Women in the Twentieth Century: A Study of Their Political, Social, and Economic Activities* (New York: McGraw-Hill, 1933), 65; Siegel, "Constitutional Culture, Social Movement Conflict, and Constitutional Change," 1418–19.

CHAPTER 6: TRANSFORMATIONS: THE NEW DEAL THROUGH THE 1950s

1. Susan Ware, *Beyond Suffrage: Women in the New Deal* (Cambridge, MA: Harvard University Press, 1983), 48, 47, 36, 46.

2. Ibid., 10.

3. Ibid., 17.

4. Eleanor Roosevelt, *It's Up to the Women* (New York: Frederick A. Stokes, 1933), 231–32.

5. Susan Ware, *Partner and I: Molly Dewson, Feminism, and New Deal Politics* (New Haven, CT: Yale University Press, 1987), chaps. 11–14; quote from Frances Perkins, "Reminiscences of Frances Perkins" (1951–1955), VII, 16–17, Columbia University Oral History Research Collection.

6. George Martin, *Madame Secretary: Frances Perkins* (Boston: Houghton Mifflin, 1976), 143–44; Frances Perkins, "Reminiscences," I, 443–44; Florence Kelley to Frances Perkins, January 17, 1929, in *The Selected Letters of Florence Kelley, 1869–1931*, ed. Kathryn Kish Sklar and Beverly Wilson Palmer (Urbana: University of Illinois Press, 2009), 443.

7. Judith Sealander, *As Minority Becomes Majority: Federal Reaction to the Phenomenon of Women in the Work Force, 1920–1963* (Westport, CT: Greenwood Press, 1983), 134–36; Martin, *Madame Secretary*, 3; Kirsten Downey, *The Woman behind the New Deal: The Life of Frances Perkins, FDR's Secretary of Labor and His Moral Conscience* (New York: Nan A. Talese/Doubleday, 2009), 276–78; Perkins, "Reminiscences," I, Part 1, 57; Mary Anderson, *Woman at Work: The Autobiography of Mary Anderson, as Told to Mary N. Winslow* (Minneapolis: University of Minnesota Press, 1951), 148.

8. Sealander, *As Minority Becomes Majority*, 136; Anderson, *Woman at Work*, 148, 184, 238–40.

9. Sealander, *As Minority Becomes Majority*, 134, 136, 158–61; Susan Ware, *Holding Their Own: American Women in the 1930s* (Boston: Twayne Publishers, 1982), 41–49; Dorothy Sue Cobble, *The Other Women's Movement: Workplace Justice and Social Rights in Modern America* (Princeton, NJ: Princeton University Press, 2004), 51.

10. Landon R. Y. Storrs, *Civilizing Capitalism: The National Consumers' League, Women's Activism, and Labor Standards in the New Deal Era* (Chapel Hill: University of North Carolina Press, 2000), 248.

11. Jeff Shesol, *Supreme Power: Franklin Roosevelt vs. the Supreme Court* (New York: W. W. Norton, 2010), 219; William Lasser, *Benjamin V. Cohen: Architect of the New Deal* (New Haven, CT: Yale University Press, 2002), 53–61; Vivien Hart, *Bound by Our Constitution: Women, Workers, and the Maximum Wage* (Princeton, NJ: Princeton University Press, 1994), 131–35; Hart, "*Adkins v. Children's Hospital*," in *The Public Debate over Controversial Supreme Court Decisions*, ed. Melvin I. Urofsky (Washington, DC: CQ Press, 2006), 126–31; and "Conversation between Clara Mortenson Beyer and Vivien Hart, November 14, 1983," Schlesinger Library, Radcliffe Institute, Harvard University, p. 15. For Clara Beyer's growing disaffection for protective law, see Vivien Hart, "Minimum-Wage Policy and Constitutional Inequality: The Paradox of the Fair Labor Standards Act of 1938," *Journal of Policy History* 1 (July 1989): 330.

12. Lasser, *Benjamin V. Cohen*, 56; Shesol, *Supreme Power*, 219; Hart, *Bound by Our Constitution*, 138–40.

13. Lasser, *Benjamin V. Cohen*, 61; Storrs, *Civilizing Capitalism*, 178. For the expansion of minimum wage laws from 1932 to 1935, see Willis J. Nordlund, *The Quest for a Living Wage: The History of the Federal Minimum Wage Program* (Westport, CT: Greenwood Press, 1997), 216.

14. *Morehead v. New York ex rel. Tipaldo*, 198 U.S. 587 (1936); Shesol, *Supreme Power*, 219–20, 406.

15. *West Coast Hotel Co. v. Parrish*, 300 U.S. 379 (1937); Shesol, *Supreme Power*, 412; LDB to FF, March 29, 1937, and April 5, 1937, in Melvin I. Urofsky and David W. Levy, eds., *"Half Brother, Half Son": The Letters of Louis D. Brandeis to Felix Frankfurter* (Norman: University of Oklahoma Press, 1991), 594–95. For Elsie Parrish (1899–1980), see Helen J. Knowles, "'Omak's Minimum Pay Law Joan D'Arc': Telling the Local Story of *West Coast Hotel v. Parrish* (1937)," *Journal of Supreme Court History* 37 (November 1912): 283–304.

16. Knowles, "Omak's Minimum Pay Law," 299. The Supreme Court's shift in 1937 is also discussed in William E. Leuchtenberg, *The Supreme Court Reborn: The Constitutional Revolution in the Age of Roosevelt* (New York: Oxford University Press, 1995), and "AHR Forum: The Debate over the Constitutional Revolution of 1937," *American Historical Review* 110 (October 2005): 1046–115.

17. Shesol, *Supreme Power*, 413–15, 524, 586; Felix Frankfurter, "Mr. Justice Roberts," *University of Pennsylvania Law Review* 104 (November 1955): 311–17; Frances Perkins, "Oral History," Book 7, 71–76; Kirsten Downey, *The Woman behind the New Deal*, 264.

18. Shesol, *Supreme Power*, 522; Martin, *Madame Secretary*, 589.

19. Shesol, *Supreme Power*, 519-20; Hart, *Bound by Our Constitution*, 137.

20. Elizabeth Brandeis, "Organized Labor and Protective Labor Legislation," in *Labor and the New Deal*, ed. Milton Derber and Edwin Young (Madison: University of Wisconsin Press, 1957), 219; Hart, *Bound by Our Constitution*, 164.

21. E. Brandeis, "Organized Labor and Protective Labor Legislation," 218; Frances Perkins, *The Roosevelt I Knew* (New York: Viking Press, 1946), 249; Hart, *Bound by Our Constitution*, 160–62. For the NRA and industrial homework, see Eileen Boris, *Home to Work: Motherhood and the Politics of Industrial Homework in the United States* (New York: Cambridge University Press, 1994), chap. 7.

22. Ira Katznelson, *When Affirmative Action Was White: The Untold Story of Racial Inequality in Twentieth-Century America* (New York: W. W. Norton, 2005), 55–60; Hart, *Bound by Our Constitution*, 155–63.

23. Ware, *Beyond Suffrage*, 104; Hart, *Bound by Our Constitution*, 104; Boris, *Home to Work*, 212; Perkins, *The Roosevelt I Knew*, 265–66; Jonathan Grossman, "Fair Labor Standards Act of 1938: Maximum Struggle for a Minimum Wage," *Monthly Labor Review* 101 (June 1978): 29. For the complex fate of industrial homework under FLSA, see Boris, *Home to Work*, chap. 9.

24. *United States v. Darby*, 312 U.S. 100 (1941); Alice Kessler-Harris, "Law and a Living," in *Gender, Class, Race and Reform in the Progressive Era*, ed. Noralee Frankel and Nancy S. Dye (Lexington: University Press of Kentucky, 1991), 105.

25. James T. Patterson, *The New Deal and the States: Federalism in Transition* (Princeton, NJ: Princeton University Press, 1969), 123–25; Clara M. Beyer to Paul Sifton, March 20, 1939, quoted in Patterson, *The New Deal and the States*, 125; "Conversation between Clara Mortenson Beyer and Vivien Hart," 19.

26. Suzanne Mettler, *Dividing Citizens: Gender and Federalism in New Deal Public Policy* (Ithaca, NY: Cornell University Press, 1998), 199–200, 204; Hart, "Minimum-Wage Policy and Constitutional Inequality," 334.

27. Jean Collier Brown, *The Negro Woman Worker*, United States Department of Labor, Women's Bureau Bulletin No. 165 (Washington, DC: Government Printing Office, 1938), 2; Anderson, *Woman at Work*, 239; Storrs, *Civilizing Capitalism*, 220–21, 345, n. 51; Cobble, *The Other Women's Movement*, 198; Lois Scharf, *To Work or to Wed: Female Employment, Feminism, and the Great Depression* (Westport, CT: Greenwood Press, 1983), 203; Hart, "Minimum-Wage Policy and Constitutional Inequality," 336; Vanessa H. May, *Unprotected Labor: Household Workers, Politics, and Middle Class Reform in New York, 1870–1940* (Chapel Hill: University of North Carolina Press, 2011), 78. Mary Dublin, who led the NCL from 1938 to 1941, married economist Leon Keyserling in 1940.

28. *The Woman Worker* 18 (July 1938): 3.

29. *The Woman Worker* 20 (July 1940): 8; Barbara Babcock et al., *Sex Discrimination and the Law: Causes and Remedies* (Boston: Little, Brown, 1975), 272; Alice Kessler-Harris, *In Pursuit of Equity: Women, Men, and the Quest for Economic Citizenship in 20th-Century America* (New York: Oxford University Press, 2001), 115–16; Ronnie Steinberg Ratner, "The Paradox of Protection: Maximum Hours Legislation in the United States," *International Labour Review* 119 (March/April 1980): 192; Cobble, *The Other Women's Movement*, 142, and Cobble, "The Labor Origins of the Next Women's Movement," *New Politics* 10 (Summer 2005): 6–7 (online). For protective laws when FLSA was passed, see Florence P. Smith, *State Labor Laws for Women*, Women's Bureau Bulletin No. 156, Parts I and II, December 31, 1937, and March 31, 1938 (Washington, DC: Government Printing Office, 1938).

30. Kathryn Kish Sklar, *Florence Kelley and the Nation's Work: The Rise of Women's Political Culture, 1830–1900* (New Haven, CT: Yale University Press, 1995), 142; Mildred Gordon, *The Development of Minimum Wage Laws in the United States, 1912–1927*, Bulletin of the Women's Bureau No. 61 (Washington, DC: Government Printing Office, 1928), 32–35; Storrs, *Civilizing Capitalism*, 198–204, 222–26; "Conversation between Clara Mortenson Beyer and Vivien Hart," 35. For early factory inspectors, see Florence Kelley, "Women Factory Inspectors in the United States," in *Social Feminists in the United States and Germany: A Dialogue in Documents, 1885–1933*, ed. Kathryn Kish Sklar, Anja Schüler, and Susan Strasser (Ithaca, NY: Cornell University Press, 1998), 95–104.

31. *When You Hire Women*, Women's Bureau Special Bulletin No. 14 (Washington, DC: Government Printing Office, 1944); Kevin Starr, *Embattled Dreams: California in War and Peace, 1940–1950* (New York: Oxford University Press, 2000), 126.

32. *State Laws for Women with Wartime Modifications*, December 15, 1944, Part V: Explanation and Appraisal, Bulletin of the Women's Bureau, No. 202 (Washington, DC: Government Printing Office, 1946), 34–35, 39, 42, 49; for overtime, see 29–30. For wartime regulations, see also US Department of Labor, Division of Labor Standards, "The Experience of the States with War Relaxations of Labor Laws," December, 1945, NCL Files, reel 54.

33. D'Ann Campbell, *Women at War with America: Private Lives in a Patriotic Era* (Cambridge, MA: Harvard University Press, 1984), 116–17; David R. Roediger and Philip S. Foner, *Our Own Time: A History of American Labor and the Working Day* (Westport, CT: Greenwood Press, 1989), 261.

34. Rebekah S. Greathouse, "The Effect of Constitutional Equality on Working Women," *American Economic Review* 34, no. 1, part 2, Supplement: Papers and Proceedings of the Fifty-Sixth Annual Meeting of the American Economic Association (March 1944): 228–29.

35. Mary Anderson, "The Postwar Role of American Women," *American Economic Review* 34, no. 1, Part 2 Supplement (March 1944): 240; *State Laws for Women with Wartime Modifications*, 25, 26, 39; Sealander, *As Minority Becomes Majority*, 97, 99; Anderson, *Woman at Work*, 252; Alice Kessler-Harris, *A Woman's Wage: Historical Meanings and Social Consequences* (Lexington: University Press of Kentucky, 1990), 92, 95.

36. *State Laws for Women with Wartime Modifications*, 30, 54–58.

37. Studs Terkel, ed., *The Good War: An Oral History* (New York: Ballantine Books, 1984), 119.

38. Anderson, "The Postwar Role of American Women," 239; Frieda Miller, "What Became of Rosie the Riveter," *New York Times Magazine* (May 5, 1946).

39. Kathleen A. Laughlin, *Women's Work and Public Policy: A History of the Women's Bureau, U.S. Department of Labor, 1945–1970* (Boston: Northeastern University Press, 2000), 5–6; Cobble, *The Other Women's Movement*, 58; Frieda S. Miller, Draft of speech to be given November 11, 1944, to the Illinois and Wisconsin WTUL Interstate Conference, Chicago. WB Papers, reel 19; Sealander, *As Minority Becomes Majority*, 76.

40. Cobble, *The Other Women's Movement*, 11–13, 52, 57, 58; Elisabeth Christman, "Shifting Status of Women: Panel Discussion," *Women's Bureau Conference: The American Woman, Her Changing Role, Worker, Homemaker, Citizen*, February 17 (Washington, DC: United States Department of Labor, 1948), 87.

41. Sealander, *Women's Work and Public Policy*, 101–3; Anderson, *Woman at Work*, 254. Equal pay is discussed in Cynthia Harrison, *On Account of Sex: The Politics of Women's Issues, 1945–1968* (Berkeley: University of California Press, 1988), chap. 3, and Kessler-Harris, *A Woman's Wage*, chap. 4.

42. Loughlin, *Women's Work and Public Policy*, 31–33.

43. Storrs, *Civilizing Capitalism*, 242, 248; David A. Moss, *Socializing Security: Progressive-Era Economists and the Origins of American Social Policy* (Cambridge, MA: Harvard University Press, 1996), 246; Frances Perkins to Felix Frankfurter, June 7, 1945, Rare Book and Manuscript Collection, Columbia University, quoted in Downey, *The Woman behind the New Deal*, 349–50.

44. Annelise Orleck, *Common Sense and a Little Fire: Women and Working-Class Politics in the United States, 1900–1965* (Chapel Hill: University of North Carolina Press, 1995), 261–62; Clara Beyer to Molly Dewson, August 24, 1946, quoted in Mettler, *Dividing Citizens*, 208.

45. Blanche Weisen Cook, *Eleanor Roosevelt, Volume One: 1884–1933* (New York: Viking, 1992), 359; Brigid O'Farrell, *She Was One of Us: Eleanor Roosevelt and the American Worker* (Ithaca, NY: IRL Press, 2010), 89–90; Lois Scharf, "ER and Feminsm," in *Without Precedent: The Life and Career of Eleanor Roosevelt*, ed. Joan Hoff-Wilson and Marjorie Lightman (Bloomington: Indiana University Press, 1984), 238, 245–46. O'Farrell refers to a letter from ER to Frances Perkins of February 21, 1944, that includes a letter written the same day to Rose Schniederman; the letter is in the Frances Perkins Papers, reel 4, correspondence, Columbia University.

46. Josephine Goldmark, "50 Years—The National Consumers' League," *The Survey* 85 (December 1949): 674–76.

47. Ronald W. Schatz, *The Electrical Workers: A History of Labor at General Electric and Westinghouse, 1923–1960* (Urbana: University of Illinois Press, 1983); Ronnie Steinberg, *Wages and Hours: Labor and Reform in Twentieth-Century America* (New Brunswick, NJ: Rutgers University Press, 1982), 98–99, 1–4, 106, 116–17; Dorothy S. Brady, "Equal Pay for Women Workers," *Annals of the American Academy of Political and Social Science* 251 (May 1947): 53–54. Use of overtime by men similarly skyrocketed in postwar Britain; see E. G. Whybrew, *Overtime Working in Britain: A Study of Its Origins, Functions, and Methods of Control* (London: Her Majesty's Stationery Office, 1968). For the economic impact of the GI bill in the immediate postwar years, not discussed here, see Suzanne Mettler, *From Soldier to Citizen: Making of the Greatest Generation* (New York: Oxford University Press, 2005), especially chap. 9, and Melissa Murray, "Made with Men in Mind: The GI Bill and Its Reinforcement of Gendered Work after World War II," in *Feminist Legal History: Essays on Women and Law*, ed. Tracy A. Thomas and Tracey Jean Boisseau (New York: New York University Press, 2011), 84–99.

48. Dorothy Sue Cobble, *Dishing It Out: Waitresses and Their Unions in the Twentieth Century* (Urbana: University of Illinois Press, 1991), 166, 168.

49. Barbara Babcock et al., *Sex Discrimination and the Law: Causes and Remedies* (Boston: Little, Brown, 1975), 93–96; Rhode, *Gender and Justice*, 45.

50. Babcock et al., *Sex Discrimination and the Law*, 94; Rhode, *Gender and Justice*, 45.

51. *Goesaert v. Cleary*, 74 F. Supp. 735 (1947).

52. *Goesaert v. Cleary*, 355 U.S. 464 (1948).

53. Susan M. Hartmann, *The Home Front and Beyond: American Women in the 1940s* (Boston: Twayne, 1982), 132–33. *Hoyt v. Florida*, 388 U.S. 57 (1961) upheld a state law that excluded women from jury service unless they volunteered to serve; the decision was overturned in 1975. For *Hoyt*, see Linda K. Kerber, *No Constitutional Right to Be Ladies: Women and the Obligations of Citizenship* (New York: Hill and Wang, 1998), chap. 4.

54. Felix Frankfurter, "Hours of Labor and Realism in Constitutional Law," *Harvard Law Review* 29 (February 1916): 367, 370; Noah Feldman, *Scorpions: The Battles and Triumphs of FDR's Great Supreme Court Justices* (New York and Boston: Hachette Book Group, 2010), 232; Lasser, *Benjamin V. Cohen*, 269–70; Storrs, *Civilizing Capitalism*, 180, 332 n. 7; "Conversation between Clara Mortenson Beyer and Vivien Hart," 8.

55. Mark Tushnet, ed., *I Dissent: Great Opposing Opinions in Landmark Supreme Court Cases* (Boston: Beacon Press, 2008), 127–31.

56. Anne Davidow practiced law in Detroit for sixty years. Larry Davidow's career is mentioned in Christopher H. Johnson, *Maurice Sugar: Law, Labor, and the Left in Detroit, 1912–1950* (Detroit: Wayne State University Press, 1988), 88, 194, 241, and passim. Anne Davidow's husband, Victor Harrison Seeger Jr., whom she married in 1920, was, in Johnson's account, the younger brother of socialist lawyer Maurice Sugar, a rival of Anne's brother, Larry Davidow, in the AUW battles of the 1930s. See also Susan Morse, "Age Hasn't Mellowed Brother-Sister Team," *Boca Raton News*, January 24, 1979, 5C (online).

57. For feminist analogies to civil rights precedents in the 1960s, see Serena Mayerli, *Reasoning from Race: Feminism, Law, and the Civil Rights Revolution* (Cambridge, MA: Harvard University Press, 2011).

58. Mark V. Tushnet, *Making Civil Rights Law: Thurgood Marshall and the Supreme Court, 1936–1961* (New York: Oxford University Press, 1994), 120–23; Melvin I. Urofsky, *Louis D. Brandeis: A Life* (New York: Pantheon, 2009), 639.

59. Emily George, *Martha W. Griffiths* (Washington, DC: University Press of America, 1982), 11; Cobble, *Dishing It Out*, 166, 168, 171.

60. Cobble, *The Other Women's Movement*, 7, 11–13; Dennis A. Deslippe, *"Rights, Not Roses": Unions and the Rise of Working-Class Feminism, 1945–80* (Urbana: University of Illinois Press, 2000), chap. 1.

61. Cobble, *The Other Women's Movement*, 52, 57–58, 89–90.

62. Ibid., 91; Cobble, "Labor Origins of the Next Women's Movement," 4–7; Deslippe, *"Rights, Not Roses,"* 4–5. Dorothy Sue Cobble assesses union women's stance on protective laws in "Recapturing Working-Class Feminism: Union Women in the Postwar Era," in *Not June Cleaver: Women and Gender in Postwar America, 1945–1960*, ed. Joanne Meyerowitz (Philadelphia: Temple University Press, 1994), 59–75.

63. Gladys Dickason, "Gains and Goals of Women Workers," presented at "The American Woman, Her Changing Role: Worker, Homemaker, Citizen," Women's Bureau Conference of February 17, 18, and 19, 1948, Women's Bureau Bulletin No. 224 (Washington, DC: US Department of Labor, 1948), 23–24.

64. Nancy F. Gabin, *Feminism in the Labor Movement: Women and the United Auto Workers, 1935–1975* (Ithaca, NY: Cornell University Press, 1990), chap. 4; Cobble, *The Other Women's Movement*, 91–92; Cobble, "Recapturing Working-Class Feminism," 71; Deslippe, *"Rights, Not Roses,"* 22, 28.

65. Deslippe, *"Rights, Not Roses,"* 31–33, 35–39.

66. Christman, "Shifting Status of Women: Panel Discussion," 87; Deslippe, *"Rights, Not Roses,"* 22–24; Cobble, "The Labor Origins of the Next Women's Movement," 3–4.

67. Eleanor Roosevelt, "Women in Politics," *Good Housekeeping* 110 (April 1940): 45; Anderson, *Woman at Work*, 162; Catherine E. Rymph, *Republican Women: Feminism and Conservatism from Suffrage through the Rise of the New Right* (Chapel Hill: University of North Carolina Press, 2006), 81–82; Hartmann, *The Home Front and Beyond*, 128–31.

68. Hartmann, *The Home Front and Beyond*, 131.

69. Leila J. Rupp and Verta Taylor, *Survival in the Doldrums: The American Women's Movement, 1945 to the 1960s* (New York: Oxford University Press, 1987), 8, 26–27, 32, 37, 47–48; Judith Paterson, *Be Somebody: A Biography of Marguerite Rawalt* (Aus-

tin, TX: Eakin Press, 1986), xiii, 50; Laughlin, *Women's Work and Public Policy*, 35; Deslippe, *"Rights, Not Roses,"* 30. For NWP legal campaigns in the 1930s, see Richard F. Hamm, "Mobilizing Legal Talent for a Cause: The National Woman's Party and the Campaign to Make Jury Service for Women a Federal Right," *Journal of Gender, Social Policy, and the Law* 9 (2001): 97–117.

70. Rupp and Taylor, *Feminism in the Doldrums*, 136, 137, 139, 141–43, 146, 148; Anderson, *Woman at Work*, 171; Landon R. Y. Storrs, "Red Scare Politics and the Suppression of Popular Front Feminism: The Loyalty Investigation of Mary Dublin Keyserling," *Journal of American History* 90 (September 2003): 518–19, 522. Storrs discusses the loyalty charges faced by Frieda Miller, Esther Peterson, and especially Mary Dublin Keyserling in *The Second Red Scare and the Unmaking of the New Deal Left* (Princeton, NJ: Princeton University Press, 2013).

71. Allida M. Black, ed., *Courage in a Dangerous World: The Political Writings of Eleanor Roosevelt* (New York: Columbia University Press, 1999), 290–93; Alice Hamilton, MD, "Why I Am against the Equal Rights Amendment," *Ladies' Home Journal* (July 1945): 23; Barbara Sicherman, ed., *Alice Hamilton: A Life in Letters* (Cambridge, MA: Harvard University Press, 1984), 385.

72. "My Fair Lady—In Industry," a play sponsored by the National Association of Manufacturers at the 62nd Annual Congress of American Industry, New York, NY, December 5, 1957, pp. 7, 10, from "Speeches of Alice K. Leopold, Women's Bureau Papers, reel 19. Leopold's role is discussed in Loughlin, *Women's Work and Public Policy*, chap. 3; Kessler-Harris, *Out to Work*, 204, 306, 308; Rupp and Taylor, *Feminism in the Doldrums*, 147; and Storrs, *The Second Red Scare*, 105.

73. Quotes are from "Speeches of Alice K. Leopold," Women's Bureau Papers, reel 19. Speeches include: "Age of Opportunity," speech delivered before the Pasadena Women's Club and Altrusa Club, Pasadena, California, October 17, 1957; "Are Lawyers Leaders?" speech delivered before the National Association of Women Lawyers' Annual Convention, New York, NY, July 9, 1957; and "Politics Begin at Home," speech before the Cambria Council of Republican Women, Johnstown, Pennsylvania, April 30, 1957.

74. E. Brandeis, "Organized Labor and Protective Legislation," 233; Elizabeth Faulkner Baker, *Technology and Women's Work* (New York: Columbia University Press, 1964), 406–7; Mettler, *Dividing Citizens*, 208–9; Storrs, *Civilizing Capitalism*, 248–49. For protective legislation at the end of the 1950s, see Alice Leopold, "Labor Legislation Affecting the Employment of Women," *The Book of the States, 1960–1961* 13 (Chicago: Council of State Governments, 1961), 471–78.

75. E. Brandeis, "Organized Labor and Protective Legislation," 233; Baker, *Technology and Women's Work*, 410; Leopold, "Labor Legislation," 471–73; and Cobble, *The Other Women's Movement*, 258.

76. Leopold, "Labor Legislation," 471, 474–78.

77. Baker, *Technology and Women's Work*, 423–24.

CHAPTER 7: TRADING PLACES: THE 1960s AND 1970s

1. Interview with Esther Peterson, 1971, quoted in Judith Hole and Ellen Levine, *Rebirth of Feminism* (New York: Quadrangle Books, 1971), 19; Esther Peterson, "Reminiscences of Esther Peterson: Oral History, 1983," 287–88, Columbia

University Oral History Research Collection; Esther Peterson to Martha Griffiths, October 12, 1971, box 2, Esther Peterson Collection, 1960–88, Schlesinger Library, Radcliffe College, Cambridge, MA, cited in Dennis A. Deslippe, *"Rights, Not Roses": Unions and the Rise of Working-Class Feminism, 1945–80* (Urbana: University of Illinois Press, 2000), 140.

2. Patricia G. Zelman, *Women, Work, and National Policy: The Kennedy-Johnson Years* (Ann Arbor: UMI Research Press, 1982), 24–25. For the PCSW, see Cynthia Harrison, *On Account of Sex: The Politics of Women's Issues, 1945–1968* (Berkeley: University of California Press, 1988). For ER's views on protective laws at the time of PCSW, see Brigid O'Farrell, *She Was One of Us: Eleanor Roosevelt and the American Worker* (Ithaca, NY: ILR Press, 2011), 202, and Lois Scharf, "ER and Feminism," in *Without Precedent: The Life and Career of Eleanor Roosevelt*, ed. Joan Hoff-Wilson and Marjorie Lightfoot (Bloomington: Indiana University Press, 1984), 232, 239, 245–49.

3. Zelman, *Women, Work, and National Policy*, 26–28. For Rawalt, see Judith Paterson, *Be Somebody*, and Mary Becker, "The Sixties Shift to Formal Equality and the Courts: An Argument for Pragmatism and Politics," *William and Mary Law Review* 40 (October 1998): 220–21.

4. Margaret Mead and Frances Balgley Kaplan, eds., *American Women: The Report of the President's Commission on the Status of Women and Other Publications of the Commission* (New York: Charles Scribners, 1965), 55–56, 128–35; Harrison, *On Account of Sex*, 151–54; Dorothy Sue Cobble, *The Other Women's Movement: Workplace Justice and Social Rights in Modern America* (Princeton, NJ: Princeton University Press, 2004), 171–72.

5. Susan M. Hartmann, *The Other Feminists: Activists in the Liberal Establishment* (New Haven, CT: Yale University Press, 1998), 62, 72; Glenda Elizabeth Gilmore, *Defying Dixie: The Radical Roots of Civil Rights, 1919–1950* (New York: W. W. Norton, 2008), 264–66, 276, 391, 400–402; Rosalind Rosenberg, "Pauli Murray and the Killing of Jane Crow," in *Forgotten Heroes: Inspiring American Portraits from Our Leading Historians*, ed. Susan Ware (New York: Free Press, 198), 279–87; Pauli Murray, *Song in a Weary Throat* (New York: Harper and Row, 1987), 183. For a way to conceptualize the problem of double bias that Murray encountered, see Kimberlé Crenshaw, "Demarginalizing the Intersection of Race and Sex: A Black Feminist Critique of Antidiscrimination Doctrine, Feminist Theory, and Antiracist Politics," *University of Chicago Legal Forum* 139 (1989): 139–67.

6. Mead and Kaplan, *The American Woman*, 147–57. Pauli Murray defends her "case-by-case approach" (p. 19) in "A Proposal to Reexamine the Applicability of the Fourteenth Amendment to State Laws and Practices Which Discriminate on the Basis of Sex Per Se," December 1962, Box 50, Murray Papers, Schlesinger Library, Radcliffe College. For Murray's legal strategy, see Serena Mayeri, *Reasoning From Race: Feminism, Law, and the Civil Rights Revolution* (Cambridge, MA: Harvard University Press, 2011), 3, 14.

7. Zelman, *Women, Work, and National Policy*, 30–33; Deborah M. Figart, Ellen Mutari, and Marilyn Power, eds., *Living Wages, Equal Wages: Gender and Labor Marketplace Policies in the United States* (New York: Routledge, 2002), 165, 173.

8. Harrison, *On Account of Sex*, 184, 217; Zelman, *Women, Work, and National Policy*, 37.

9. For the Smith amendment and Title VII, see Jo Freeman, "How 'Sex' Got into Title VII: Persistent Opportunism as a Maker of Public Policy," *Law and Inequality* 9 (March 1991): 163–84; Carl M. Brauer, "Women Activists, Southern Conservatives, and the Prohibition of Sex Discrimination in Title VII of the 1964 Civil Rights Act," *Journal of Southern History* 49 (February 1983): 37–56; Michael Evan Gold, "A Tale of Two Amendments: The Reasons Congress Added Sex to Title VII and Their Implications for the Issue of Comparable Worth," *Duquesne Law Review* 19 (Spring 1981): 453–77; and Cynthia Deitch, "Gender, Race, and Class Politics and the Inclusion of Women in Title VII of the 1864 Civil Rights Act," in *Race, Class, and Gender: Common Bonds, Different Voices*, ed. Esther Ngan-Ling Chow, Doris Wilkinson, and Maxine Baca Zinn (Thousand Oaks, CA: Sage Publications, 1996), 288–307. Smith's quote is from Brauer, "Women Activists," 44. The two NWP members who approached Congressman Smith were Butler Franklin, a diplomat's widow, and lawyer Nina Horton Avery, former president of the Virginia branch of the Federation of Business and Professional Women; see Leila J. Rupp and Verta Taylor, *Surival in the Doldrums: The American Women's Rights Movement, 1945 to the 1960s* (New York: Oxford University Press, 1987), 176.

10. Martha Griffiths, letters to Mary Lou Thompson, March 20, 1970; to Caroline Bird, February 6, 1968; and to Myra Wolfgang, February 17, 1964, quoted in Emily George, *Martha W. Griffiths* (Washington, DC: University Press of America, 1982), 149–50, 151–52; Deitch, "Gender, Race, and Class Politics," 297; Freeman, "How 'Sex' Got into Title VII," 184.

11. Zelman, *Women, Work, and National Policy*, 91; Karen J. Maschke, *Litigation, Courts, and Women Workers* (New York: Praeger, 1989), 102; Jo Freeman, "The Legal Basis of the Sexual Caste System," *Valparaiso University Law Review* 5 (1971): 227.

12. Hugh Davis Graham, *The Civil Rights Era: Origins and Development of National Policy, 1960–1972* (New York: Oxford University Press, 1990), 213–15, 519. For the EEOC report, see *EEOC First Annual Report* (Washington, DC: Government Printing Office, 1966), 43, quoted in Graham, *The Civil Rights Era*, 519.

13. Graham, *The Civil Rights Era*, 217; Susan Deller Ross, "Sex Discrimination and 'Protective' Labor Legislation" in *The "Equal Rights" Amendment Hearings, Ninety-First Congress, Second Session, on J.J. Res. 61 ... May 5, 6, and 7, 1970* (Washington, DC: Government Printing Office, 1970), 400–401. For a discussion of EEOC indecision, see Joseph P. Kennedy, "Sex Discrimination: State Protective Laws since Title VII," *Notre Dame Lawyer* 47 (February 1972): 523–24.

14. Graham, *The Civil Rights Era*, 217, 222. State commissions on the status of women are discussed in Debra W. Stewart, *The Women's Movement in Community Politics in the U.S.: The Role of Local Commissions on the Status of Women* (New York: Pergamon Press, 1980).

15. Pauli Murray and Mary Eastwood, "Jane Crow and the Law: Sex Discrimination and Title VII," *George Washington Law Review* 34 (December 1965): 235, 240, 250–51, 252, 253, 256.

16. George, *Martha Griffiths*, 152–53; Murray, *Song in a Weary Throat*, 358.

17. Ross, "Sex Discrimination and 'Protective' Labor Legislation," 402; Graham, *The Civil Rights Era*, 229–32; Zelman, *Women, Work, and National Policy*, chap. 6.

18. Dr. Catherine Stimpson, ed., Barnard College, in conjunction with the Congressional Information Service, Washington, DC, ed., *Women and the "Equal Rights"*

Amendment: Senate Subcomittee Hearings on the Constitutional Amendment, 91st Congress (New York and London: R. R. Bowker, 1972), 376–77.

19. Statement of the International Union, UAW, Public Hearing of the Equal Employment Opportunity Commission (Washington, DC, May 2 and 3, 1967), and Statement by Marguerite Rawalt, Legal Counsel, National Organization for Women, to EEOC at public hearings (May 2, 1967) in Barbara Babcock et al., *Sex Discrimination and the Law: Causes and Remedies* (Boston: Little, Brown, 1975), 264, 266.

20. Statement of Andrew J. Biemiller, Department of Legislation, AFL-CIO, before the EEOC (June 2, 1967) and Statement of Katherine P. Ellickson on Committee on Labor Standards of the National Consumers' League . . . before the EEOC (May 2, 1967) in Babcock et al., *Sex Discrimination and the Law*, 265, 266.

21. Murray and Eastwood, "Jane Crow and the Law," 235; Martha W. Griffiths, "Women and Legislation," in *Voices of the New Feminism*, ed. Mary Lou Thompson (Boston: Beacon Press, 1970), 108; Judith Hole and Ellen Levine, *Rebirth of Feminism* (New York: Quadrangle Books, 1971), 33–34; Alice Kessler-Harris, *In Pursuit of Equity: Women, Men, and the Quest for Economic Citizenship in 20th-Century America* (New York: Oxford University Press, 2000), 263.

22. Kathleen A. Loughlin, *Women's Work and Public Policy: A History of the Women's Bureau, U.S. Department of Labor, 1945–1970* (Boston: Northeastern University Press, 2000), 93–95, 99, 108, 109, 120–22; Zelman, *Women, Work, and Public Policy*, 92; Landon R. Y. Storrs, "Red Scare Politics and the Suppression of Popular Front Feminism: The Investigation of Mary Dublin Keyserling," *Journal of American History* 90 (September 2003): 491–524.

23. Maschke, *Litigation, Courts, and Women Workers*, 88–91; 101–2; Paterson, *Be Somebody*, 169–91; Hartmann, *The Other Feminists*, chap. 3.

24. Graham, *The Civil Rights Era*, 393–95; George, *Martha W. Griffiths*, 156; Zelman, *Women, Work, and National Policy*, 47; Jo Freeman, *A Room at a Time: How Women Entered Party Politics* (Lanham, MD: Rowman and Littlefield, 2000), 209–10; Irwin Unger and Debi Unger, *LBJ: A Life* (New York: John Wiley and Sons, 1999), 432–33.

25. Graham, *The Civil Rights Era*, 393, 396, 398, 404.

26. Daniel Patrick Moynihan, "Memo to the President of 20 August 1969," quoted in Graham, *The Civil Rights Era*, 399–400; Chuck Colson to Ken Cole, January 2, 1970, and Patrick Buchanan to H. R. Haldeman, September 20, 1971, in Bruce Oudes, ed., *Richard Nixon's Secret Files* (New York: Harper and Row, 1989), 85, 320–21. For the Moynihan Report of 1965, see James T. Patterson, *Freedom Is Not Enough: The Moynihan Report and America's Struggle over Black Family Life* (New York: Basic Books, 2010).

27. Maschke, *Litigation, Courts, and Women Workers*, 102.

28. Velma Mendelkoch's first two district court cases in 1968 were *Mengelkoch v. Industrial Welfare Commission*, 284 F. Supp. 950 (C.D. Cal 1968) and 284 F. Supp. 956 (C.D. Cal. 1968). The third district court case, of October 28, 1968, was *Mengelkoch v. Industrial Welfare Commission*, 395 U.S. 83 (89 S.Ct. 60, 21 L.Ed. 2d 215) (1968). The final case was *Mengelkoch v. Industrial Welfare Commission*, 442 F.2d 1119 (Ninth Circuit, 1971). That decision cited *Muller v. Oregon*, 208 U.S. 412, and *Miller v. Wilson*, 236 U.S. 373 (1915). For Mengelkoch's cases, see Babcock et al., *Sex Discrimination and the Law*, 266, 270; Paterson, *Be Somebody*, 169; Gretchen Ritter, *The Constitution*

as *Social Design: Gender and Civic Membership in the American Constitutional Order* (Stanford, CA: Stanford University Press, 2006), 243.

29. Walt Murray, "Woman Fights Overtime Curb," clipping from a Long Beach, California, newspaper (n.d., probably 1966), American Civil Liberties Records, Box 1144: Folder 3, Employment 1966, Princeton University Archives. I am grateful to Rosalind Rosenberg for the clipping. See also *Mengelkoch v. Industrial Commission*, 284 F. Supp. 950, 955 (C.D. Cal 1968.) Leo Kanowitz discusses the issue of voluntary overtime in *Women and the Law: The Unfinished Revolution* (Albuquerque: University of New Mexico Press, 1969), 124–28.

30. Paterson, *Be Somebody*, 169, 171–72, 193; Maschke, *Litigation, Courts, and Women Workers*, 42–43, 50; Ritter, *The Constitution as Social Design*, 244.

31. *Weeks v. Southern Bell Telegraph and Telephone Co.*, 277 F. Supp. 117 (1967).

32. *Weeks v. Southern Bell Telephone and Telegraph Co.*, 408 F. 2d 2228 (Fifth Circuit, 1969); Maschke, *Litigation, Courts, and Women Workers*, 44; Ritter, *The Constitution as Social Design*, 45; Fred Strebeigh, *Equal: Women Reshape American Law* (New York: W. W. Norton, 2009), 378; Gail Collins, *When Everything Changed: The Amazing Journey of American Women from 1960 to the Present* (Boston: Little, Brown, 2009), 88–94.

33. *Rosenfeld v. Southern Pacific Co.*, 293 F. Supp. 1219 (C.D. Cal. 1968); Shirley Burman, "Women and Railroading," *Trains Magazine* (November 16, 2009) (online).

34. *Rosenfeld v. Southern Pacific Co.*, 444 F. 2d 1219 (Ninth Circuit 1971); Ritter, *The Constitution as Social Design*, 245.

35. *Mengelkoch v. Industrial Welfare Commission*, 442 F. 2d 1119, 1123-24 (Ninth Circuit 1971); Ritter, *The Constitution as Social Design*, 246.

36. Betty Friedan, *It Changed My Life; Writing on the Women's Movement* (New York: Random House, 1976), 211; Maschke, *Litigation, Courts, and Women Workers*, 85–86; Graham, *The Civil Rights Era*, 402; Marialice W. Canter, "State Legislation of Special Interest to Women," *The Book of the States, 1972–1973*, 19 (Lexington, KY: Council of State Governments, 1023), 523.

37. Babcock et al., *Sex Discrimination and the Law*, 271–71, 282.

38. *Bowe v. Colgate Palmolive*, 408 F. 2d 228 (Fifth Circuit 1969); *Richards v. Griffith Rubber Mills*, 300 F. Supp. 338 (D. Ore. 1969); *Cheatwood v. Southern Bell*, 303 F. Supp. 754 (N.D. Ala. 1969); Friedan, *It Changed My Life*, 211.

39. Kennedy, "Sex Discrimination," 542.

40. *LeBlanc v. Southern Bell Telephone and Telegraph*, 333 F. Supp. 602 (D.La. 1971); *Richards v. Griffith Rubber Mills*, 300 F. Supp. 338 (D. Ore. 1969); *Ridinger v. General Motors Corporation*, 325 F. Supp. 1089 (S.D. Ohio 1971); Deslippe, *"Rights, Not Roses,"* 140, 244.

41. *Caterpiller Tractor v. Grabiec*, 317 F. Supp. 1304 (S.D. Ill. 1970); *Ritchie v. Wayman*, 91 N.E. 695 (1910); *General Electric Co. v. Young*, 3 FEP Cases 561 (W.D. Ky 1971).

42. *Sail'er Inn, Inc. v. Kirby*, 5 Cal. 3d 1. 20585 P. 2d 329 (1971); *Krause v. Sacramento Inn*, 314 F. Supp. 171 (E.D. Cal. 1970); John D. Johnston and Charles L. Knapp, "Sex Discrimination by Law: A Study in Judicial Perspective," *New York University Law Review* 46 (1971): 686–91; Strebeigh, *Equal*, 87–90.

43. Kennedy, "Sex Discrimination," 546–48. For protection's decline, see also Allan D. Spritzer, "Equal Employment Opportunity versus Protection for Women Workers: A Public Policy Dilemma," *Alabama Law Review* 24 (Summer 1972):

567–606, and Thomas H. Barnard, "The Conflict between State Protective Legislation and Federal Law Prohibiting Sex Discrimination: Is It Resolved?" *Wayne Law Review* 17 (January–February 1971): 25–66.

44. Babcock et al., *Sex Discrimination and the Law*, 271; Judith A. Baer, *Women in American Law* (New York: Holmes and Meier, 1976), 83. For some state and federal cases of the early 1970s that sustained protective laws (until overturned), see Spritzer, "Equal Employment Opportunity versus Protection for Women Workers," 581.

45. *Phillips v. Martin Marietta*, 416 F. 2d 1257 (Fifth Circuit, 1969) and 400 U.S. 342 (1971).

46. *Reed v. Reed*, 401 U.S. 71 (1971); Strebeigh, *Equal*, chap. 2.

47. *Frontiero v. Richardson*, 411 U.S. 677 (1973); *Craig v. Boren*, 429 U.S. 190 (1976). Discussions include Strebeigh, *Equal*, chap. 3.

48. Spritzer, "Equal Employment Opportunity versus Protection for Women Workers," 606.

49. Kennedy, "Sex Discrimination," 525–27; Stimpson, *Women and the "Equal Rights" Amendment*, 377; Babcock et al., *Sex Discrimination and the Law*, 271; Women's Bureau, Employment Standards Administration, US Department of Labor, *Laws on Sex Discrimination in Employment* (1973), 10–11; Marialice Carter, "State Legislation of Special Interest to Women," 586.

50. Barbara A. Brown et al., *Women's Rights and the Law: The Impact of the ERA on State Laws* (New York: Praeger, 1977), 210–12.

51. Brown et al., *Women's Rights and the Law*, 218–20; Women's Bureau, US Department of Labor, *State Labor Laws in Transition: From Protection to Equal Status for Women*, Pamphlet No. 15, prepared by Jane Walstedt (Washington, DC: Government Printing Office, 1976), 12.

52. Brown et al., *Women's Rights and the Law*, 218–20; Mary Jeanne Coyne, "The Equal Rights Amendment—Is It Needed?" *Women Lawyers' Journal* 58 (1972): 4–6 (includes quote from Marguerite Rawalt); Ruth Bader Ginsburg, "The Need for the Equal Rights Amendment," *Women Lawyers' Journal* 60 (1974): 11–12; George, *Martha W. Griffiths*, 179. For the study by two lawyers mentioned by Ginsburg, see Johnston and Knapp, "Sex Discrimination by Law," cited above in note 42.

53. George, *Martha W. Griffiths*, 168–71.

54. "Statement of Mrs. Myra Wolfgang," *Equal Rights 1970: Hearings before the Committee on the Judiciary, Ninety-First Congress, Second Session, S.J. Res 61 and S.J. Res 231*, September 9, 10, 11, and 15, 1970 (Washington, DC: Government Printing Office, 1970), 28–45. See also Stimpson, *Women and the "Equal Rights" Amendment*, 91–92.

55. Dorothy Sue Cobble, "The Labor Origins of the Next Women's Movement," *New Politics* 10 (Summer 2005): n.p. (online). For "labor feminism," see also Cobble, "Recapturing Working-Class Feminism: Union Women in the Postwar Era," in *Not June Cleaver: Women and Gender in Postwar American, 1945–1960*, ed. Joanne Meyerowitz (Philadelphia: Temple University Press, 1994), 57–83.

56. Ross, "Sex Discrimination and 'Protective' Labor Legislation," 409, 393.

57. Ibid., 393, 395, 396, 397, 399, 409.

58. Kanowitz, *Women and the Law*, 124–28; "Testimony of Leo Kanowitz," *Equal Rights 1970: Hearings before the Committee on the Judiciary* (Washington, DC: Government Printing Office, 1970), 170–78; Brown et al., *Women's Rights and the Law*, 224.

59. For Griffiths's steering of ERA through Congress, see George, *Martha W. Griffiths*, 168–71.

60. Graham, *The Civil Rights Era*, 416–18; Zelman, *Women, Work, and National Policy*, 120.

61. Laughlin, *Women's Work and Public Policy*, 120; Deslippe, *"Rights, Not Roses,"* 140; Cobble, *The Other Women's Movement*, 191; Canter, *State Labor Legislation of Special Interest to Women*, 523.

62. Freeman, *Politics of Women's Liberation*, 212: Graham, *The Civil Rights Era*, 406; Susan Levine, *The American Association of University Women and the Challenge of Twentieth-Century Feminism* (Philadelphia: Temple University Press, 1995), 162–63; Storrs, *Civilizing Capitalism*, 249; "Minutes of the Meeting of the Board of Directors," October 1, 1970, NCL Papers, reel 2, pp. 1–2.

63. "Minutes of the Meeting of the Board of Directors," June 25, 1970, NCL Papers, reel 2, p. 2; Deslippe, *"Rights, Not Roses,"* 140. Landon R. Y. Storrs discusses Esther Peterson's career and the impact of a loyalty investigation in *The Second Red Scare and the Unmaking of the New Deal Left* (Princeton, NJ: Princeton University Press, 2013), 229–31.

64. Laughlin, *Women's Work and Public Policy*, 105, 120; Deslippe, *"Rights, Not Roses,"* 139; Cobble, *The Other Women's Movement*, 196; Storrs, *Civilizing Capitalism*, 249; Landon R. Y. Storrs, "Mary Dublin Keyserling," *Notable American Women, a Biographical Dictionary: Completing the Twentieth Century*, ed. Susan Ware (Cambridge, MA: Harvard University Press, 2004), 342; Mary Dublin Keyserling, "Why I Am a Strong Advocate of the ERA," *Barnard Alumnae Bulletin* (January 1981): 12. Landon R. Y. Storrs discusses Keyserling's career in *The Second Red Scare*, chap. 4.

65. Nancy Gabin, *Feminism in the Labor Movement: Women in the United Auto Workers, 1935–1975* (Ithaca, NY: Cornell University Press, 1990), 203.

66. Alice H. Cook, "Women and American Trade Unions," *Annals of the American Academy of Political and Social Sciences* 375 (January 1968): 126–27; Cobble, *The Other Women's Movement*, 185–86, 187, 193; Deslippe, *"Rights, Not Roses,"* 137–39; Stimpson, *The "Equal Rights" Amendment*, 91–102.

67. Hartmann, *The Other Feminists*, 34; Cobble, *The Other Women's Movement*, 191–94; Deslippe, *"Rights, Not Roses,"* 136, 140; Dennis Deslippe, *Protesting Affirmative Action: The Struggle over Equality after the Civil Rights Revolution* (Baltimore: Johns Hopkins University Press, 2012), 37.

68. Hartmann, *The Other Feminists*, 28, 32–33, 34, 38, 39, 49. For the IUE, see also Deslippe, *"Rights, Not Roses,"* chap. 7, and Mary Callahan, "Forty Years I'm Secretary-Treasurer of the Local," in O'Farrell and Kornbluh, *Rocking the Boat*, 132.

69. Callahan, "Forty Years," 131–32; Cobble, *The Other Women's Movement*, 31; Hartmann, *The Other Feminists*, 147. For women in the electrical industry, see Schatz, *The Electrical Worker*, and Ruth Milkman, *Gender at Work: The Dynamics of Job Segregation by Sex during World War II* (Urbana: University of Illinois Press, 1987).

70. For the vetoed Comprehensive Child Development Act, see Robert O. Self, *All in the Family: The Realignment of American Democracy since the 1960s* (New York: Hill and Wang, 2012), 128–31.

71. Vanessa H. May, *Unprotected Labor: Household Workers, Politics, and Middle-Class Reform in New York, 1870–1940* (Chapel Hill: University of North Carolina Press, 2011), 175–79; Cobble, *The Other Women's Movement*, 178, 200. See also Eileen

Boris and Premilla Nadasen, "Domestic Workers Organize!" *Working USA* 11 (December 2008): 413–37, and Eileen Boris and Jennifer Klein, *Caring for America: Home Health Workers in the Shadow of the Welfare State* (New York: Oxford University Press, 2012). Clara Beyer discusses the extension of FLSA to domestic workers in "Interview with Vivien Hart," November 14, 1983, pp. 29–30, Schlesinger Library, Radcliffe Institute, Harvard University.

72. Margaret A. Berger, *Litigation on Behalf of Women: A Report to the Ford Foundation* (New York: Ford Foundation, 1980), 38–43; *Faro v. New York University*, 502 F. 2d 1229, 1231 (Second Circuit, 1974). For Title VII cases in which African American plaintiffs faced double discrimination of race and sex, see Crenshaw, "Demarginalizing the Intersection of Race and Sex," 141–52.

73. Jane J. Mansbridge, *Why We Lost the ERA* (Chicago: University of Chicago Press, 1986); Mary Frances Berry, *Why ERA Failed: Politics, Women's Rights, and the Amending Process of the Constitution* (Bloomington: Indiana University Press, 1986); Joan Hoff-Wilson, ed., *Rights of Passage: The Past and Future of the ERA* (Bloomington: Indiana University Press, 1986). Pauli Murray's quotes are from *Song in a Weary Throat*, 352.

74. Pauli Murray to Marguerite Rawalt, April 14, 1964, Mary O. Eastwood Papers, folder 7, Schlesinger Library, Radcliffe College; Martha W. Griffiths to Myra Wolfgang, February 7, 1964, cited in George, *Martha W. Griffiths*, 151–52. For a discussion of Title VII's impact, see Deitch, "Gender, Race, and Class Politics," 303–4.

75. A relevant discussion is Raymond Muntz and David C. Rice, "Women Workers: Protection or Equality?" *Industrial and Labor Relations Review* 24 (October 1970): 12–13.

76. Elizabeth Faulkner Baker, *Technology and Women's Work* (New York: Columbia University Press, 1964), 431; Murray and Eastwood, "Jane Crow and the Law," 253.

77. Robert Max Jackson, *Destined for Equality: The Inevitable Rise of Women's Status* (Cambridge, MA: Harvard University Press, 1998), 56–57. For judicial opinion, see Mark Tushnet, "The Rights Revolution in the Twentieth Century," in *The Cambridge History of Law in America*, vol. 3, ed. Michael Grossberg and Christopher Tomlins (New York: Cambridge University Press, 2008), 377–402.

78. Freeman, "The Legal Basis of the Sexual Caste System," 231.

CHAPTER 8: LAST LAP: WORK AND PREGNANCY

1. *Cohen v. Chesterfield County School Board*, 474 F. 2d 395 (1973).

2. Susan Deller Ross, "Sex Discrimination and 'Protective' Labor Legislation," in *The "Equal Rights" Amendment Hearings, Ninety-First Congress, Second Session . . .* (Washington, DC: Government Printing Office, 1970), 397; Women's Bureau, US Department of Labor, "State Labor Legislation Affecting the Employment of Women," *The Book of the States, 1964–1965*, vol. 15 (Chicago: Council of State Governments, 1965), 544; Wendy W. Williams, "Equality's Riddle: Pregnancy and the Equal Treatment/Special Treatment Debate," in *Feminist Legal Theory: Foundations*, ed. D. Kelly Weisberg (Philadelphia: Temple University Press, 1993), 132; Melissa Ann McDonald, "Labor Pains: Sex Discrimination and the Implementation of Title

VII, 1964–1980" (PhD diss., University of California, Santa Barbara, 1993), 377–83, 389–94. The six states with pregnancy leave laws in 1970 were Connecticut, Massachusetts, Missouri, New York, Vermont, and Washington. For the AALL maternity benefit proposal of 1916–17, see Beatrix Hoffman, *The Wages of Sickness: The Politics of Health Insurance in Progressive America* (Chapel Hill: University of North Carolina Press, 2001), 140–50.

3. Serena Mayeri, *Reasoning from Race: Feminism, Law, and the Civil Rights Movement* (Cambridge, MA: Harvard University Press, 2011), 66–67.

4. *LaFleur v. Cleveland Board of Education*, 326 F. Supp. 1208 (C.D. Ohio 1971).

5. *LaFleur v. Cleveland Board of Education*, 465 F. 2d 1184 (Sixth Circuit 1972).

6. *Cohen v. Chesterfield County School Board*, 326 F. Supp. 1159 (E.D. Va. 1971).

7. *Cohen v. Chesterfield County School Board*, 474 F. 2d 395 (Fourth Circuit 1973); Serena Mayeri, *Reasoning from Race*, 63–64, 66–68.

8. Mayeri, *Reasoning from Race*, 90–92; Fred Strebeigh, *Equal: Women Reshape American Law* (New York: W. W. Norton, 2009), 93.

9. *Cleveland Board of Education v. LaFleur*, 414 U.S. 632 (1974); Linda Greenhouse, *Becoming Harry Blackmun: Harry Blackmun's Supreme Court Journey* (New York: New York Times Books, 2005), 213–15; Mayeri, *Reasoning from Race*, 91–92.

10. *Turner v. Department of Security of Utah*, 423 U.S. 44 (1975).

11. Williams, "Equality's Riddle," 137.

12. *Aiello v. Hansen*, 359 F. Supp. 792 (N.D. Cal. 1973) (Hansen was director of the State Department of Human Resources); Williams, "Equality's Riddle," 134; Strebeigh, *Equal*, 91–92.

13. Strebeigh, *Equal*, 91–93.

14. *Geduldig v. Aiello*, 427 U.S. 484 (1974); Williams, "Equality's Riddle," 135, 137; Mayeri, *Reasoning from Race*, 93, 95.

15. McDonald, "Labor Pains," 378, 384; Susan M. Hartmann, *The Other Feminists: Activism in the Liberal Establishment* (New Haven, CT: Yale University Press, 1998), 44–46.

16. *General Electric v. Gilbert*, 429 U.S. 125 (1976); Williams, "Equality's Riddle," 139.

17. Strebeigh, *Equal*, 137–38; Ruth Bader Ginsburg, "Some Thoughts on Benign Classification in the Context of Sex," *Connecticut Law Review* 10 (1978): 826–27.

18. Alice Hamilton, "Protection for Women Workers," *The Forum* 72 (August 1924): 160; Jeffrey Toobin, *The Oath: The Obama White House and the Supreme Court* (New York: Doubleday, 2012), 78–81.

19. Lise Vogel, *Mothers on the Job: Maternity Policy in the U.S. Workplace* (New Brunswick, NJ: Rutgers University Press, 1993), 71–73, 103; McDonald, "Labor Pains," 460–62, 464–65; Strebeigh, *Equal*, 139.

20. *Newport News Shipbuilding and Dry Dock v. EEOC*, 462 U.S. 669 (1983).

21. Vogel, *Mothers on the Job*, 73–76.

22. Lise Vogel, "Debating Difference: Feminism, Pregnancy, and the Workplace," *Feminist Studies* 16 (Spring 1990): 9–32.

23. "Brief Amici Curiae of the National Organization For Women . . . in *California Federal Savings and Loan v. Guerra*," 1, 2, 20, 31. The brief is reprinted in Sybil Lipshultz, ed., *Women, the Law, and the Workplace*, vol. 3 (New York: Routledge, 2003), 2–41. See also Vogel, *Mothers on the Job*, 81.

24. "Brief Amici Curiae of Coalition for Reproductive Equality in the Workplace . . . in *California Federal Savings and Loan v. Guerra*," in Lipshultz, *Women, the Law, and the Workplace*, 3: 67, 69, 71–72; Vogel, *Mothers on the Job*, 84–87.

25. Vogel, *Mothers on the Job*, 83, 84, 87; Herma Hill Kay, "Equality and Difference: The Case of Pregnancy," *Berkeley Women's Law Journal* 1 (Fall 1985): 27–28, 38.

26. Oral argument in *California Federal Savings and Loan v. Guerra*, 479 U.S. 222 (1987) at www.oyez.org, The Oyez Project at IIT, Chicago-Kent College of Law.

27. *California Federal Savings and Loan v. Guerra*, 479 U.S. 222 (1987), 281, 288, 291; Vogel, *Mothers on the Job*, 82, 88–89; Martha Minow, *Making All the Difference: Inclusion, Exclusion, and American Law* (Ithaca, NY: Cornell University Press, 1990), 87–88. For a defense of the *Guerra* decision, see also Gretchen Van Ness, "Expanding the Boundaries of Equality: Taking Pregnancy into Account in *California Federal Savings and Loan v. Guerra*," *Boston College Law Review* 28 (1987): 783–811.

28. *California Federal Savings and Loan*, Dissent by Justice White, joined by Justices Rehnquist and Powell; Vogel, *Mothers on the Job*, 90.

29. Wendy W. Williams, "Notes from a First Generation," *University of Chicago Legal Forum* 99 (1989): 1020–103; Joan C. Williams, *Reshaping the Work/Family Debate: Why Men and Class Matter* (Cambridge, MA: Harvard University Press, 2010), 118; Steven K. Wisensale, *Family Leave Policy: The Political Economy of Work and Family in America* (Armonk, NY: M. E. Sharpe, 2001), 134–35.

30. Vogel, *Mothers on the Job*, 107–8.

31. Quotes from President George H. W. Bush, veto message to FMLA, June 29, 1990; Bob Dole on FMLA to the Senate on August 11, 1992; Representative Cass Ballenger of North Carolina, State News Service, November 18, 1987; and the *Washington Times*, editorial, April 11, 1991; all quotes are from "Cry Wolf Project: Exposing Myths about the Economy and Government," at http://crywolfproject.org.

32. Vogel, *Mothers on the Job*, 153–56; Wisensale, *Family Leave Policy*, 151, 155, 222–26.

33. Patricia A. Seith, "Congressional Power to Effect Sex Equality," *Harvard Journal of Law and Gender* 36 (Winter 2013): 59.

34. Lise Vogel, *Woman Questions: Essays for a Materialist Feminism* (New York: Routledge, 1995), 128–34, and Vogel, *Mothers on the Job*, 153–56. Justice Rehnquist wrote the majority opinion in *Nevada Department of Human Resources v. Hibbs*, 538 U.S. 721 (2003), the first Supreme Court decision to recognize that pregnancy discrimination was unconstitutional under the equal protection clause. The opinion suggests that Justice Rehnquist had changed his views since *General Electric v. Gilbert* (1976).

35. Cynthia R. Daniels, *At Woman's Expense: State Power and the Politics of Fetal Rights* (Cambridge, MA: Harvard University Press, 1993), 61–62; Mary Becker, "From *Muller v. Oregon* to Fetal Vulnerability Policies," *University of Chicago Law Review* 53 (Fall 1986): 1220–21. For the fetal protection movement, see also Sara Dubow, *Ourselves Unborn: A History of the Fetus in American America* (New York: Oxford University Press, 2011), chap. 4.

36. Sally J. Kenney, *For Whose Protection? Reproductive Hazards and Exclusionary Policies in the United States and Britain* (Ann Arbor: University of Michigan Press, 1992), 50–51; Daniels, *At Woman's Expense*, 57, 63–64.

37. Daniels, *At Women's Expense*, 63–64; David L. Kirp, "Fetal Hazards, Gender Justice, and the Justices: The Limits of Equality," *William and Mary Law Review*

34 (1992): 105, 128; Kenney, *For Whose Protection?*, 293, 302. For an analysis of the troubles at American Cyanamid, see Kenney, *For Whose Protection?*, chap. 7. The Robert Bork opinion upholding the company is *Oil Chemical and Atomic Workers International Union v. American Cyanamid Company*, 741 F. 2d 444 (D.C. Circuit 1984).

38. Kirp, "Fetal Hazards, Gender Justice, and the Justices," 104–6; Kenney, *For Whose Protection?*, 250–51.

39. *UAW v. Johnson Controls*, 680 F. Supp. 309, 316 (E.D. Wis. 1988); Kenney, *For Whose Protection?*, 254.

40. *UAW v. Johnson Controls*, 886 F. 2d 871, 886, 889, 890, 897–98 (Seventh Circuit 1989).

41. *UAW v. Johnson Controls*, 886 F. 2d 871 (Seventh Circuit 1989). For the quotes from dissents, see 902 (Cudahy); 902, 906, 908 (Posner); and 913, 920, 921 (Easterbrook).

42. Caroline Bettinger-Lopez and Susan P. Sturm, "*International Union, U.A.W. v. Johnson Controls:* History of Litigation Alliances and Mobilization to Challenge Fetal Protection Policies," Columbia Law School, Public Law and Legal Theory Working Paper Group, Paper Number 07-145, pp. 12–15. The two cases that invalidated fetal protection policies were *Johnson Controls v. California Fair Employment and Housing Commission*, 267 Cal. Rpt. 158 (1990) and *Grant v. General Motors*, 908 F. 2d 1303 (Sixth Circuit 1990). In the first case, Queen Elizabeth Foster, a young worker, had been denied a job at Johnson Controls' Fullerton, California, plant because she refused to provide medical proof of infertility. In the second case, Pat L. Grant, who had worked in various jobs in a GE foundry in Ohio, among them a job as an iron pourer, had been demoted to a lower-paid position because of the company's fetal protection policy.

43. "Brief for Petitioners," *UAW v. Johnson Controls*, 1989 U.S. Briefs 1215, 1, 23; oral argument at www.oyez.org.

44. "Brief for Respondent," *UAW v. Johnson Controls*, 1989 U.S. Briefs 1215, 16; oral argument at www.oyez.org; Kenney, *For Whose Protection?*, 254; Bettinger-Lopez and Sturm, "International Union UAW," 14.

45. *UAW v. Johnson Controls*, 499 U.S. 187, 197, 204, 211 (1991). For a summary of the decision, see David O. Stewart, "Unleaded," *American Bar Aassociation Journal* 77 (June 1991): 38–40.

46. Bettinger-Lopez and Sturm, "UAW International," 18; Daniels, *At Women's Expense*, 92. For the concurring opinions, see *UAW v. Johnson Controls* (1991), 211–24, and Joan C. Callahan, "Let's Get the Lead Out: Or Why *Johnson Controls* Is Not an Unequivocal Victory for Women," *Journal of Social Philosophy* 25 (December 1994): 70. "If this is a victory for anyone," Callahan argues, "it is a victory for employers whose workplaces contain reproductive hazards."

47. Daniels, *At Women's Expense*, 98; Kirp, "Fetal Hazards, Gender Justice, and the Justices," 128.

48. Carin Ann Clauss, Marsha Berzon, and Joan Bertin, "Litigating Reproductive and Developmental Health in the Aftermath of *UAW v. Johnson Controls*," *Environmental Health Perspectives* 101, Supp. 2 (July 1993): 205–6. Clauss represented the UAW in the 1989 *Johnson Controls* case and Berzon in the 1991 case; Bertin assembled the amicus briefs in 1991.

49. Clauss, Berzon, and Bertin, "Litigating Reproductive and Developmental Health," 212–13; Kenney, *For Whose Protection?*, 332. Mary Becker analyzes the impact of *Johnson Controls* in "Reproductive Hazards after *Johnson Controls*," *Houston Law Review* 31 (1994–95): 43–97.

50. Bettinger-Lopez and Sturm, "International Union," 18; Kirp, "Fetal Hazards, Gender Justice, and the Justices," 132; Hester Eisenstein, *Feminism Seduced: How Global Elites Use Women's Labor and Ideas to Exploit the World* (Boulder, CO: Paradigm Publishers, 2009), 53–57. See also Felix Frankfurter, assisted by Josephine Goldmark, *The Case for the Shorter Work Day* (New York: National Consumers' League, 1916), iii.

51. Williams, "Equality's Riddle," 142. For post-PDA litigation on issues involving work and pregnancy, see Julie Manning Magid, "Contraception and Contractions: A Divergent Decade Following *Johnson Controls*," *American Business Law Journal* 41 (September 2003): 115–44. See also Clauss, Berson, and Bertin, "Litigating Reproductive and Developmental Health," 216–17; Dina Bakst, "Pregnant and Pushed Out of a Job," *New York Times*, January 30, 2012; and Alyssa Quart, "Why Women Hide Their Pregnancies," *New York Times*, October 7, 2012.

CONCLUSION

1. Louis D. Brandeis, "The Constitution and the Minimum Wage," *The Survey* (February 17, 1915): 521, 524.

2. Felix Frankfurter, "Hours of Labor and Realism in Constitutional Law," *Harvard Law Review* 29 (February 1916): 367.

3. Rebekah S. Greathouse, "The Effect of Constitutional Equality on Working Women," *American Economic Review* 33, no. 1, part 2 (March 1944): 229.

4. Barbara Young Welke, *Law and the Borders of Belonging in the Long Nineteenth Century United States* (Cambridge: Cambridge University Press, 2010), 69, 77.

5. John R. Commons, "Eight-Hour Shifts by Federal Legislation," *American Labor Legislation Review* 7 (March 1917): 141.

6. Felix Frankfurter, *Reminiscences* (New York: Reynal, 1960), 97; *Bunting v. Oregon*, 243 U.S. 426; *Wilson v. New*, 243 U.S. 332.

7. Frances Perkins, *The Roosevelt I Knew* (New York: Viking Press, 1946) 249; Josephine Goldmark, *Impatient Crusader: Florence Kelley's Life Story* (Urbana: University of Illinois Press. 1953), 205.

8. Landon R. Y. Storrs discusses FLSA and its impact in *Civilizing Capitalism: The National Consumers' League, Women's Activism and Labor Standards in the New Deal Era* (Chapel Hill: University of North Carolina Press, 2000), chaps. 7 and 8. See also Suzanne Mettler, *Dividing Citizens: Gender and Federalism in New Deal Public Policy* (Ithaca, NY: Cornell University Press, 1998), 186–87.

9. Perkins, *The Roosevelt I Knew*, 266.

10. Ronnie Steinberg, *Wages and Hours: Labor and Reform in Twentieth-Century America* (New Brunswick, NJ: Rutgers University Press, 1982), 90, 104, 106; Ronnie Steinberg Ratner, "The Paradox of Protection: Maximum Hours Legislation in the United States," *International Labour Review* 119 (March–April 1980): 185–98; Ronald W. Schatz, *The Electrical Workers: A History of Labor at General Electric and Westinghouse, 1923–1960* (Urbana: University of Illinois Press, 1983), 158–60.

11. Cynthia Harrison, *On Account of Sex: The Politics of Women's Issues, 1945–1968* (Berkeley: University of California Press, 1988), 151–54; *Mengelkoch v. Industrial Commission*, 284 F. Supp. 950, 955 (C.D. Cal. 1968).

12. Nancy Gabin, *Feminism in the Labor Movement: Women in the United Auto Workers, 1935–1985* (Ithaca, NY: Cornell University Press, 1990), 193–209; *Equal Rights, 1970: Hearings before the Judiciary Committee* (Washington, DC: Government Printing Office, 1970), 32, 215.

13. Raymond Munts and David C. Rice, "Women Workers: Protection or Equality?" *Industrial and Labor Relations Review* 24 (October 1970): 12–13 (the authors were a social work professor and a law student at the University of Wisconsin); Leo Kanowitz's statement in *Equal Rights 1970: Hearings before the Committee on the Judiciary*, 170–78; Annelise Orleck, *Common Sense and a Little Fire* (Chapel Hill: University of North Carolina Press, 1995), 139.

14. *Weeks v. Southern Bell*, 408 F. 2d 228 (Fifth Circuit 1969); *Rosenfeld v. Southern Pacific*, 444 F. 2d 1219 (1971).

15. Juliet B. Schor, *The Overworked American: The Unexpected Decline of Leisure* (New York: Basic Books, 1991), 31, 141. The subsequent history of overtime law suggests yet further ways in which the law can empower employers. See, for instance, Ross Eisenberg, "It's Time to Update Overtime," *New York Times*, January 11, 2014, about a need to raise the salary threshold for exemption from overtime, and David S. Joachim, "Obama Orders Rule Changes to Expand Overtime Pay," *New York Times*, March 14, 2014, about employer tactics (classification of employees as managerial) to make employees ineligible for overtime pay.

16. Melvin I. Urofsky, *Affirmative Action on Trial: Sex Discrimination in Johnson v. Santa Clara County* (Lawrence: University Press of Kansas, 1997), 166; Catherine MacKinnon, *Sexual Harassment of Working Women: A Case Study of Discrimination* (New Haven, CT: Yale University Press, 1979); Anita Faye Hill and Emma Coleman Jordan, eds., *Race, Gender, and Power in America: The Legacy of the Hill-Thomas Hearings* (New York: Oxford University Press, 1995); *Meritor Savings Bank v. Vinson*, 477 U.S. 57 (1986); *Ellison v. Brady*, 924 F.2d 872 (Ninth Circuit, 1991); *Harris v. Forklift Systems*, 510 U.S. 17 (1993). For the "de facto ERA," see Reva B. Siegel, "Constitutional Culture, Social Movement Conflict, and Constitutional Change: The Case of the De Facto ERA," *California Law Review* 94 (2006): 1323–420. The Supreme Court upheld FMLA in *Nevada Dept. of Human Resources v. Hibbs*, 538 U.S. 721 (2003).

17. Bethany Moreton, *To Serve God and Wal-Mart* (Cambridge, MA: Harvard University Press, 2009), 50. For work/family issues, see Joan C. Williams, *Unbending Gender: Why Family and Work Conflict and What to Do about It* (New York: Oxford University Press, 2000), and *Reshaping the Work-Family Debate: Why Men and Class Matter* (Cambridge, MA: Harvard University Press, 2010). For concern about affinities between feminism and business values, see Hester Eisenstein, *Feminism Seduced: How Global Elites Use Women's Labor and Ideas to Exploit the World* (Boulder, CO: Paradigm Press, 2009), and Nancy Fraser, *Fortunes of Feminism: From State-Managed Capitalism to Neoliberal Crisis* (New York: Verso, 2013). For the transformation of work, see David Weil, *The Fissured Workplace: Why Work Became So Bad For So Many and What Can Be Done to Improve It* (Cambridge, MA: Harvard University Press, 2014).

18. Sara M. Evans and Barbara N. Nelson, *Wage Justice: Comparable Worth and the Practice of Technocratic Reform* (Chicago: University of Chicago Press, 1989); Dorothy

Sue Cobble, *The Other Women's Movement: Workplace Justice and Social Rights in Modern America* (Princeton, NJ: Princeton University Press, 2004), 99, 107, 219–21.

19. For the Economic Equity Act, see Patricia A. Seith, "Congressional Power to Effect Sex Equality," *Harvard Journal of Law and Gender* 36 (2013): 1–70. Responses to the article include Serena Mayeri, "Filling in the (Gender) Gap," and Suzanne Kahn, "Valuing Women's Work in the 1970s: Home and the Boundaries of the Gendered Imagination," online on the journal's website. Mayeri makes the point about "specific bills" (p. 4).

20. *EEOC v. Sears Roebuck & Co.*, 839 F. 2d 302 (Seventh Circuit 1988); Thomas Haskell and Sanford Levinson, "Academic Freedom and Expert Witnessing: Historians and the *Sears* Case," *Texas Law Review* 66 (1988): 1629–59. For the roots of the suit against Sears, see Katherine Turk, "Out of the Revolution, into the Mainstream: Employment Activism in the NOW Sears Campaign and the Growing Pains of Liberal Feminism," *Journal of American History* 97 (September 2010): 399–423.

21. For Wal-Mart, see Moreton, *To Serve God and Wal-Mart*; Barbara Ehrenreich, *Nickeled and Dimed: On (Not) Getting By in America* (New York: Henry Holt, 2001), chap. 3; Nelson Lichtenstein, ed., *Wal-Mart: The Face of Twenty-First Century Capitalism* (New York: New Press, 2006); and Adam Liptak, "Justices Rule for Wal-Mart in Class-Action Bias Suit," *New York Times*, June 20, 2011.

22. *Ledbetter v. Goodyear Tire and Rubber Co.*, 421 F 3d. 1169 (2007). For probusiness bias, see Adam Liptak, "Friend of the Corporation," *New York Times*, May 15, 1913, and "Steady Move to the Right," *New York Times*, June 28, 1913. For Elizabeth Faulkner Baker's conclusions of 1925, see *Protective Labor Laws* (New York: Columbia University Press, 1925), 425–26.

23. Crystal Jarvis, "An Interview with a Newsmaker: Jon C. Goldfarb, Attorney," *Birmingham Business Journal* (March 9, 2009).

24. NWP National Council Minutes, April 11, 1922, NWP Papers, reel 114, cited in Nancy Cott, *The Grounding of Modern Feminism* (New Haven, CT: Yale University Press, 1988), 124.

25. *UAW v. Johnson Controls*, 499 U.S. 187, 211 (1991).

26. *Woman's Tribune* 23 (August 11, 1906): 62.

Index

■ ■ ■

Note: Page numbers in italic type refer to photographs.

CPSIA information can be obtained
at www.ICGtesting.com
Printed in the USA
BVOW03s0357110417
480898BV00002B/27/P

9 780691 176161